ELEVENTH EDITION

Principles and Types of Speech Communication

BRUCE E. GRONBECK
The University of Iowa

RAYMIE E. McKERROW
University of Maine

DOUGLAS EHNINGER

ALAN H. MONROE

HarperCollins*Publishers*

Cover and part opener illustrations by Mark Penberthy

Acknowledgments appear on page 519, which is an extension of this copyright page.

NATIONAL COLLEGE
OF IRELAND
LIBRARY

Library of Congress Cataloging-in-Publication Data

Principles and types of speech communication/Bruce E. Gronbeck . . .
   [et al.].—11th ed.
      p.   cm.
   Includes bibliographies and index.
   ISBN 0-673-38591-4
   1. Public speaking.   I. Gronbeck, Bruce E.
PN4121.P72   1990   89-35375
808.5′1—dc20   CIP

   3 4 5 6 – RRC – 94 93 92 91

Preface

Principles and Types of Speech Communication has been a mainstay in the basic speech course, an acknowledged leader in communication studies, for over half a century. Longevity comes to textbooks that look both backward and forward—backward to their grounding in timeless principles of speech composition, and forward to new ideas that keep them ahead of the field.

The living authors of *Principles and Types of Speech Communication*, 11th edition, have built upon the solid foundation laid by Alan H. Monroe (1903–75), former Professor of Communication at Purdue University, and Douglas Ehninger (1913–79), former Professor of Speech at the University of Florida and then at The University of Iowa. Professor Monroe made his mark in communication studies largely through the publication in 1935 of this pedagogically innovative textbook, with its justly famous "Monroe's Motivated Sequence" and exploration of the factors of attention and types of imagery. Professor Ehninger supplemented Monroe's social-scientific bent with his strong commitment to the history and philosophy of rhetoric.

Ehninger and Monroe intertwined research and concepts from the whole of communication studies into *Principles and Types of Speech Communication.* Monroe grounded the book in the new psychologies of the 1920s and 1930s, and then kept evolving its social-scientific foundations as the center of psychological research moved from the developmental perspective of those earlier years to the cognitive (belief-attitude-value) perspective of the 1950s and 1960s. In this edition, we have continued that psychological evolution, introducing the language of one of the newer cognitive psychologies, schemata theory. Ehninger broadened Monroe's foundation with his abiding interest in contemporary rhetorical theory, introducing into the book its stress on occasion, an interest in situational theory, the material on kinds of claims, and especially the strong chapter on argumentation. Each early author, thus, brought expertise that made *Principles and Types of Speech Communication* a durable instructional instrument.

We are not only indebted to these giants in the field, however; to succeed through the years, a book must keep up with the flow of new research and the latest thinking about teaching students how to talk publicly. *Principles and Types of Speech Communication*, 11th edition, seeks to remain the flagship of communication studies through forward-looking ventures into new features. Eight features stand out:

1. *Focus on both speechmaking in society and student presentations in classrooms.* This book has an obligation to compel the students of communication studies to reflect seriously upon the Communications Revolution and its implications for responsible citizens. Throughout, we ask you to think about political, economic, religious, and social messages in your environment—to analyze them, to understand their strategic bases, and to learn to construct them. Yet, we realize that you are a student seeking to survive and grow in your own environment, the college or university campus; thus, you will find many of our examples and illustrations drawn from campus life both in and out of class. This book asks you to assess your skills where you are, but also to look ahead to a complete life of involvement in your social, work, and political communities.

2. *New emphasis on critical thinking and critical listening skills.* This textbook always has been grounded in analysis: analysis of audiences, of the self, of one's purposes, of the occasions on which one speaks. Our surveys clarify, however, that today's student needs more than that. Speech classrooms are expected increasingly to teach the principles of critical thinking and critical listening—consumer-oriented techniques for examining messages, for assessing their characteristics, and for evaluating their claims in terms of logical and psychological criteria. Such defensive studies of critical thinking are central to *Principles and Types of Speech Communication,* 11th edition, especially the chapters on listening (2) and argumentation/critical thinking (17) and various segments of the *Speaker's Resource Book.*

3. *New stress on up-to-date research in "Communication Research Dateline" segments.* This textbook has prided itself on the firmness of its intellectual base: traditional rhetorical principles and contemporary communication research. The "Communication Research Dateline" boxes that appear in almost every chapter recognize the importance and usefulness of current research, reviewing studies and then pointing out their practical implications for communicators. Among the research traditions examined are those of advertising, survey research, nonverbal communication, psychology, intercultural communication, argumentation, and television studies. Not only will you find ideas you can use as a speaker, but "Communication Research Dateline" items will introduce you to the work of academic communication professionals.

4. *New sensitivity to the ethical issues facing speakers.* You are surrounded by major ethical dilemmas in public communication: the Iran-Contra hearings and trials, confidential information about citizens that is gathered without their knowledge, negative political advertising, promotional hype for local news programs, credibility gaps in the White House, corporate whistleblowing. Some of those ethical issues have a bearing on discussions in your own public-speaking classrooms. *Principles and Types of Speech Communication,* 11th edition, has been designed to push those issues to the foreground of your thinking through discussions

of personal integrity and plagiarism, a *Speaker's Resource Book* section on communication ethics, a section on sexist language in Chapter 12, and a concern throughout for your credibility as a speaker. You must face up to such issues as you prepare to speak; in addressing them, you will learn much about yourself and your role in society.

5. *Expanded* Speaker's Resource Book. The *Speaker's Resource Book*, new to the 10th edition, has been an unqualified success among teachers and students. Teachers appreciated the extra topics provided, and students gained access to readings on specific topics they needed more information about. Among the noteworthy additions to the *SRB* this edition are segments on radio and television speaking and a discussion of the differences between men's and women's communication habits that is sure to spark interesting discussions.

6. *Four-color presentation.* In this book's smaller sibling, *Principles of Speech Communication*, we found that a four-color presentation helped students engage the subject matter more completely and more easily. We therefore have brought color into this edition of the "big book." Four-color presentations will help you understand emphases, spot special features, translate diagrams and figures into meaningful concepts, and come to grips with the "real world" of communication as presented in four-color photographs. Your world is in color and so is this book.

7. *New chapter-end summaries and critical thinking exercises.* As the leading full-sized textbook in the field of communication studies, *Principles and Types of Speech Communication*, 11th edition, uses a full communication vocabulary; it teaches you how to talk precisely about public speaking. Because of that stress on vocabulary, we have added to the end of each chapter both a summary and a list of terms for easy review. As well, new exercises stressing analysis and critical thinking are included in the chapter-end materials.

8. *Expanded services.* Scott, Foresman/Little, Brown knows that its college-level line of textbooks will thrive if the company offers a full range of services to the classroom teacher and college student. Over the years, *Principles and Types of Speech Communication* has been a leader in such services, and this edition is no exception. Available with this edition to teachers of public speaking are an instructor's manual (now presented in a loose-leaf notebook for easy use); test banks (in the instructor's manual and on computer diskette); *Milestones in Communication*, a compilation of articles from *Time* magazine illustrating the power of communication in twentieth-century society; three videotapes of student speeches; 35mm slide transparencies; and acetate transparencies of materials useful for in-class projection and discussion. The company's commitment to communication studies is visible in these expanded services to the classroom.

These features make *Principles and Types of Speech Communication*, 11th edition, a decisive innovator in the field. In addition, every chapter has been revised to include, as appropriate, new sections on such topics as computerized library searches, gender-neutral language, the meaning of "occasion" in speech communication, new theories of persuasion, ceremony and ritual in the community, the relationships between traditional organizational patterns and Monroe's motivated sequence, new ways to organize motivational appeals, and others already mentioned.

Overall, we think this edition of the most popular public-speaking textbook of the twentieth century has combined traditional and innovative features to keep it on the forefront of communication studies. Both teachers and students can use this book, confident that they are studying public speaking with a book that teaches both speech technique and ways of thinking about and assessing public communication in society.

In all of this work, we have been assisted by a number of communication studies scholars and fellow educators. Among those who evaluated our coverage of material are R. Dahlin, Palomar College; Harold Kinzer, Utah State University; Aileen Sundstrom, Henry Ford Community College (who also reviewed the manuscript); Rita Hubbard, Christopher Newport College; William R. Rambin, Northeast Louisiana University; Patrice Bailey, Florida International University; Barbara Cichy, Bismarck State College; Wayne Hensley, Virginia Polytechnic Institute; Charlotte Forsberg, Black Hills State College; Thomas Baglan, Arkansas State University; Janice Schuetz, University of New Mexico (who also reviewed the manuscript); and Bonnie Clark, St. Petersburg Junior College.

We also are indebted to the following people who critiqued the previous edition and read drafts of new materials for this one: Clark McMillion, University of Missouri-St. Louis; David Payne, University of South Florida; Ronald Matlon, Towson State University; Linda Welden, Appalachian State University; Ethel Glenn, University of North Carolina-Greensboro; Donald Williams, University of Florida; Susan A. Hellweg, San Diego State University; and Cynthia Galivan, Hudson Valley Community College.

A special thank-you is owed Professor Kathleen German of Miami University of Ohio, who has transformed the *Instructor's Guide* that accompanies *Principles and Types of Speech Communication* into the most innovative manual in the field. As well, Christopher, Jakob, and Ingrid Gronbeck, collegians all, continue to contribute their talents for library research; their willing assistance is greatly appreciated.

We also wish to thank Scott, Foresman/Little, Brown for the resources and talents it invested in this project. The master plan for the edition took shape under Communication Editor and long-time friend Barbara Muller and then was executed under the careful scrutiny of Developmental Editor Louise Howe, by now used to untangling and blending our prose. The actual word-by-word manuscript preparation was handled by Project Editor Deb DeBord, who made us consistent and polished our diction. By the end, too, a new Acquisitions Editor, Vikki Barrett, and Editorial Vice-President, Scott Hardy, were in place, and both were most helpful in suggesting new features and ways of serving the basic course market. Speaking of marketing, we are most pleased that Brett Spalding, Meredith Hellestrae, and an army of enthusiastic sales representatives carried this book into the field—to you.

You are the bottom line. We thank you for taking the time to pick up and read this book. We hope you keep in front of you at all times a commitment to excellence in public communication, both to improve your own fortunes and to make your world a better place to live. If you can do that, *Principles and Types of Speech Communication*, 11th edition, will have accomplished its goals.

Bruce E. Gronbeck
Raymie E. McKerrow

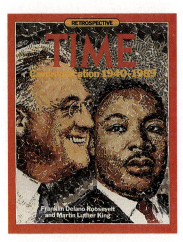

Accompanying this copy of *Principles and Types of Speech Communication*, 11th edition, free of charge, is a copy of *Milestones in Communication*. Published in conjunction with the Speech Communication Association, this special edition of *Time* magazine offers a historical look at *Time*'s coverage of major events illustrating the power of communication in twentieth-century society.

Contents

PART TWO
Preparation 69

CHAPTER THIRTEEN
Using Visual Aids in a Speech 300

CHAPTER FOURTEEN
Using Your Voice and Body to Communicate 318

PART FOUR
Types 343

Sample Speeches for Study and Analysis

PART ONE

Process

"*What other power [than eloquence] could have been strong enough either to gather scattered humanity into one place, or to lead it out of its brutish existence in the wilderness up to our present condition of civilization as [people] and as citizens, or, after the establishment of social communities, to give shape to laws, tribunals, and civic rights?*"

Cicero
De oratore *I.33*

CHAPTER ONE

The Process of Public Speaking

Ours has been called the Age of Communication. That phrase brings to mind a vision of what communications scholar Marshall McLuhan called the **Global Village**,[1] myriad societies of every degree of sophistication linked by communication. The Age of Communication is upon us in large part because of revolutions in communication technologies. With Marconi's development of the wireless radio in the late nineteenth century came the possibility of near-limitless communication between peoples; the cathode ray tube added pictures; the computer chip increased the speed and complexity of messages; and the satellite provided 'round-the-world, instantaneous connections between people of every culture.

Earth became a global village thanks to technological advances. Often overlooked in that phrase, however, is the noun "village." McLuhan emphasized not only the technology of communication, but also the degree to which high-tech communication allows people to be involved in others' affairs. In McLuhan's view, the United States and Israel could act toward each other like backyard neighbors—and so could any two countries with uplink and downlink communication satellite capabilities. Backyard neighbors have a degree of intimacy and mutual knowledge of each other. They watch each other's children grow up and chat about the weather and high price of fresh vegetables. They communicate both formally and informally. It is this sense of villagelike relationships between peoples that impressed Marshall McLuhan when he thought about the Age of Communication.

The point is this: even though the Age of Communication came upon us thanks to technological developments, its primary impact has been upon the way people talk with one another. It has altered radically to whom you can talk and about what, when, why, where, and how. Today your neighborhood extends from Main Street U.S.A. to Red Square U.S.S.R. It has become more important than ever for you to be able to talk publicly with others and to analyze the messages of public speakers from around the globe. The Age of Communication has brought not only new technologies but increased responsibilities.

Private Persons and Public Talk

The Age of Communication has unavoidable impacts upon you. It has brought you into a class on public communication, and, unless you manage to live a hermit's life, it will demand that you communicate publicly, often orally, with a great variety of audiences in diverse situations—at work, in clubs and associations, and during political events and church gatherings. Further, thanks to radio, television, and film, you will be exposed throughout your life to a host of speakers: local mayoral candidates debating the pros and cons of urban redevelopment, Sunday morning televangelists showering you with multimedia salvation, talk shows helping you with your investment and health-care choices, C-SPAN broadcasting the U.S. Congress at work, presidential candidates seeking a new America with themselves at the helm, and world leaders signing treaties in dignified ceremony. With all of the talk you have to prepare and to listen to, you must learn both to produce your own speeches and to analyze critically those of others in order to survive.

The Roles of Speechmaking in Society

Both speaking and listening skills are important because **public communication** for centuries has been the glue that holds societies together. A sense of sharing, the "with-ness" part of the Latin root *cum-munis* (to work publicly with) of the English word "communication," bonds people together. Without public communication, societies could not organize into work and living groups, mark the passage of individuals from childhood to adulthood to retirement, debate and make decisions about important issues, and change the society in necessary ways. Because oral communication flows directly between individuals, it is the preferred form of communication in times of solemnity and crisis. When there is an occasion to celebrate or a crisis to face, leaders inevitably give speeches, because speech unites societies.

More specifically, public speeches perform four important functions for a society:

1. *Speeches are used for self-definition.* Especially on such occasions as Memorial Day, the Fourth of July, Labor Day, dedications of monuments, and centennial celebrations, communities (cultures or subcultures) define themselves, indicating "what they stand for," what it means to be a mem-

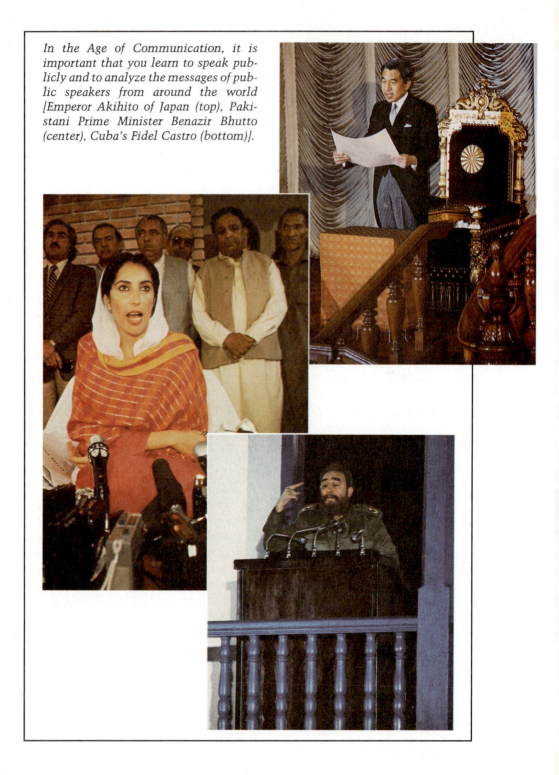

In the Age of Communication, it is important that you learn to speak publicly and to analyze the messages of public speakers from around the world [Emperor Akihito of Japan (top), Pakistani Prime Minister Benazir Bhutto (center), Cuba's Fidel Castro (bottom)].

ber of the community. Just as churchgoers recite creeds and credos aloud, so societies regularly review their defining tenets through speech.

2. *Speeches are used to spread information through a community.* The president announces the latest plans and legislative proposals through public talk; the Surgeon General holds a press conference to update AIDS research findings; the mayor uses a radio interview to spread the word about next week's "Pioneer Days" in town. Much information, of course, is distributed by pamphlets and letters, but spoken information is so much more personalized that informative talk is important.

3. *Speeches are used to debate questions of fact, value, and policy in communities.* Human beings always have fought through their differences with each other. As civilization advanced, verbal controversy replaced physical combat, and the art of public debate was born. From government to the workplace, arguing one's way through to a decision is an important function of oral communication.

4. *Speeches are used to bring about individual and group change.* Persuasion has always been a part of public talk; the earliest books about public speaking dealt exclusively with persuasion as the most important kind of talk. Societies must adapt to changes in their environments, values, and practices; if change is to occur, most people must be persuaded to accept it.

Speechmaking, therefore, performs these four broad social functions in communities. Whether one is talking about "community" broadly (as in a whole society) or narrowly (as in a community of friends), collectivities simply could not exist and function without speechmaking in its various forms.

The Need for Speech Training in the Age of Communication

It ought to be clear that you need public speaking skills to live productively in the Age of Communication. Unless you have the speaking talents necessary to engage in committee discussions, presentations to clients, and the like, you may be in trouble on the job.[2] Your speechmaking skills also affect your ability to change people's minds at neighborhood or corridor meetings; at city or student councils; at political conventions and public hearings; and in the innumerable associations, clubs, and pressure groups that lobby the government. The power of public talk is as important in government as it is in the world of work.

You will become a fully developed, thinking, and forceful human being to the degree that you have learned and practiced speechmaking and other oral communication skills. Ultimately, you speak not only to serve others but also to achieve your own goals on the job and in the public forum. You might even have fun doing it; human beings talk with others both to survive and to play a little.

Communication and Your Career

*I*n most chapters of this text, you will find a *Communication Research Dateline* highlighting a particular aspect of research on the public-speaking process. This first one centers on research dealing with communication and your career.

Since the early 1970s, members of the Speech Communication Association, the national professional organization for speech communication teachers and scholars, have been interested in the relationship of speech training to postcollege employment. In 1972, the SCA published its first book on the subject, *Career Communication: Direc-* *tions for the Seventies.* That book discussed the applications of speech training for students interested in particular careers—counseling, the ministry, police work, telephone company positions, retail sales, direct sales, teaching, and management (focusing on the Sears, Roebuck program). Fifteen years later, following several other general and specific books on job hunting, a broader and more useful book appeared: Al Weitzel's *Careers for Speech Communication Graduates* (1987). In it, Professor Weitzel brings research findings to bear on the great variety of tracks in speech communication education; on

Before you plunge into the activities that will improve your speaking skills, however, it is helpful to visualize the whole process, to think about the various elements that make up communication in general and public speaking in particular. The rest of this chapter will be an examination of those elements and of the competencies they demand.

Public Speaking: A Transactional Model of Communication

A **model** is a representation of a thing or a process. It identifies the key elements and indicates how each affects the operations of all the other elements. A communication system can be reduced to such a model—in fact, to many models, depending upon which aspects of communication are of

the image that communication majors and the outside world have of speech students; on some career options (in particular, the skills needed for careers in training and development, public relations, law, teaching, sales or marketing, and other positions); on some techniques for maximizing employability (including working at internships, joining professional organizations, improving your communication skills, and the like); and on simple steps to find appropriate employment.

A point worth underscoring that comes from this career-related research is that, after completing your communication training, you can profitably pursue either (1) "communication" careers (the ministry, education, politics, advertising, sales, broadcasting, filmmaking, writing, editing, and so on) or (2) "noncommunication" careers (careers that emphasize other special skills, such as accounting, scientific research, insurance, computer science, engineering, nursing, and the like). That is, oral (and written) communication skills, as some

of the sources cited in reference note 2 in this chapter indicate, are useful to virtually *any* entry-level position in American education, business, government work, service industries, or other occupations. No matter what you will do after graduation, think of communication skills training as training for your life work.

FOR FURTHER READING
Bolles, Richard Nelson. *What Color Is Your Parachute? A Practical Manual for Job-Hunters & Career Changers.* Berkeley, CA: Ten Speed Press (published annually); Kennicott, Patrick Curtis, and L. David Schuelke, eds. *Career Communication: Directions for the Seventies.* New York: Speech Communication Association, 1972; Weitzel, Al R. *Careers for Speech Communication Graduates.* Salem, WI: Sheffield Publishing Co., 1987; Weitzel, Al R., and Paul Gaske. "An Appraisal of Communication Career-Related Research." *Communication Education* 33 (April 1984): 181–94.

primary interest. (In the *Speaker's Resource Book* that follows this text's regular chapters, you will find descriptions of several models of communication.)

Speeches are one form of the general human activity called "communication." It is not easy to define a "speech," for there are many types. Some, such as presidential inaugural addresses, are highly formalized; others, such as a few remarks from your seat in a marketing class, may be very informal. Some speeches are read to an audience; watch the next press conference on television. Others are given in an impromptu, off-the-cuff manner, as when you describe the television special you watched last night to some friends. After-dinner speeches tend to be light, while funeral sermons often are dignified and serious.

Despite such differences in formality, presentation, and tone, however, all speeches share some features. All speeches are (1) continuous, purposive oral *messages* (2) delivered by a primary communicator (the *speaker*) (3) through

THE SPEECH COMMUNICATION TRANSACTION

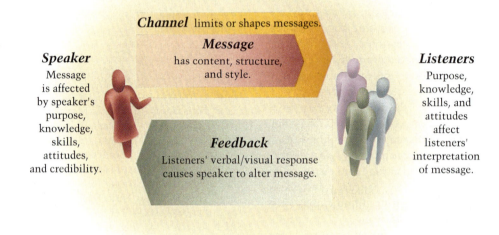

various *channels* (4) to others (the *listeners*) who can *feed back* reactive messages to the speaker (5) in a particular communication *situation*. Given the exchange of ideas going on, speeches are *transactions*. Consider briefly what it means to assert that proposition.

All speeches entail a complex interaction among the five primary elements: message, speaker, listeners, channels, and situation. They work together in a **transactional model** because:

• Both speakers and listeners have mutual rights and responsibilities to make communication work.
• Both speakers and listeners generally are aware of each other's needs and purposes, and so, consciously adapt their messages—speeches and feedback—to the others' presumed conditions and situations.
• Both speakers and listeners are bonded together in a common culture, whose **communication rules** influence the ways they behave in each other's presence.

Thus, I prepare a speech to "give" you, and you, in turn, "give" me your attention and reactions (feedback). From among all of the things I could say about a subject, I actually select only a few, tailoring (adapting) them to your interests, wants, and desires, as well as to limitations of time and space. I draw the comments I make—the values I appeal to, the conventional wisdom I mention—from a pool of values and cultural tenets I share with my listeners. As I assert my right to speak to other members of this culture, so you also assert your right to listen or not, your right to react as you see fit. Hence, the transactional aspects of public speaking integrate the various elements, making them interdependent. That interdependence is achieved through innumerable formal and informal communication rules. With this general understanding of the transactional heart of speechmaking, we now can examine the individual elements.

The Message

In all speech transactions, the speaker's **message** is made up of three variables: content, structure, and style.

Content.   Messages have content; that is, they are *about* something. What is less obvious, however, is the variety of content that goes into speech messages. There are, of course, ideas—the "stuff" being talked about. These ideas often are called the **referential content**. Usually there is **relational content** as well; encoded into speeches are clues to the specific relationships between speaker and audience. Does a speaker mention specific people in the audience by name; refer to warm, common experiences he or she has had with them; and talk frankly? Such a speaker and audience probably have a relationship of similar status, of equality. Does the speaker say "*I* think" or "*I* believe" a lot, tell the audience what to do, and refer specifically to his or her superior knowledge or extensive experiences? Such a speaker and audience probably have a superior-inferior relationship, one of unequal status. Both referential and relational content are important aspects of speech messages. You must learn to control both.

Structure.   A message is necessarily structured or organized in a certain way, simply because we say some things first; others second; and still others third, fourth, and so on. Even if we seem to ramble, listeners will look for a coherent pattern in the message. It is important, then, to provide a pattern as a guide for the audience. That structure may be as simple as numbering points ("First I will discuss . . ., next I will . . ., and finally, I will . . .") or as complex as a full outline with points and subpoints.

Style.   The third variable in every spoken message is style. Just as you must select and arrange the ideas you wish to convey to an audience, so must you select words, arrange them in sentences, and decide how to reveal your self-image to that group of listeners. Selecting and arranging words, as well as revealing yourself to be a certain sort of person, are matters of style. Given the innumerable words from which to choose, the great varieties of sentence structures, and even the many kinds of self-images available to the speaker, many styles are possible. Styles can be "personal" or "impersonal," "literal" or "ironic," "plain" or "elevated," even "philosophical" or "poetic"; such labels refer to particular combinations of vocabulary, syntax (sentence structure), and images of the speaker. "Style," therefore, really has nothing to do with "elegance" or "stylishness"; rather, it includes those aspects of language use that convey impressions of speakers, details of the world, and emotional overtones.[3]

The Speaker

The speaker brings four key elements to every speech transaction: (1) a communicative purpose; (2) knowledge of subject and communication skills; (3) attitudes toward self, listeners, and subject; and (4) a degree of credibility.

Speaker's Purpose.   Every speaker has a purpose. We all have heard rambling talks, of course, but generally you speak in a sustained fashion to achieve a goal. That goal can be as simple as the wish to appear sociable or as complex as the desire to alter someone's ideas without appearing to be rude. You may wish to entertain, call attention to a problem, refute an assertion, ward off a threat, or establish or maintain your status or power.

A speaker brings four key elements to every speech transaction: a communicative purpose; knowledge of the subject and communication skills; attitudes toward self, the listeners, and the subject; and a certain degree of credibility.

Speaker's Knowledge.   Your knowledge of the subject and mastery of communication skills affect the character of your message and your effectiveness. If you have only surface knowledge of a topic, listeners feel cheated; you had better say something important, new, relevant, interesting. Also, to succeed you need to acquire and refine a series of fundamental speaking skills. The communication skills addressed in this book include a wide variety of abilities—setting communicative goals, finding and assembling relevant information, organizing messages in coherent and powerful ways, illustrating them visually, and delivering them with clarity and punch. You already possess many such skills; after all, you have been talking most of your life.

Speaker's Attitudes.   Your attitudes toward your self, listeners, and subject significantly affect what you say and how you say it. All of us have mental pictures of ourselves as persons—self-concepts, or images of the kind of individuals we are and of how others perceive us.[4]

Your **self-image** influences the way you speak in particular situations. If you have little confidence in your abilities or are unsure of your information, you tend to speak hesitantly. Your voice becomes weak, your body stiffens, and you watch the floor rather than your audience. If you are overly confident, you tend to move in the other direction—becoming overbearing and overly familiar, disregarding listeners' needs, and riding roughshod over others' feelings. Ideally, you will find the middle way, with enough self-confidence to believe in yourself and yet enough sensitivity to treat your listeners like human beings.

Part of your treatment of them comes from your perception of your *status*, or relationship, to them—as parent or child, instructor or student, supervisor or employee, subordinate or equal. These **role positions**, in turn, affect your power relationships with and modes of address to audiences. If you perceive your listeners as intellectually inferior, you tend to use a simple vocabulary, clear structure, and concrete ideas. If they seem politically inferior, you might talk condescendingly, or, if you view them as your superiors, you are likely to talk in a deferential manner. You adjust your speaking style to your attitudes toward your listeners.

Your response to the social context in which you speak influences an audience's judgment of appropriateness and *competency*. You learn to communicate appropriately and competently by learning to follow the communication rules that govern society.[5] You have spent a lifetime learning some of those rules; in this book, you will examine many of the explicit ones governing public speaking.

Finally, your speaking behavior is influenced by *how you feel about the subject* you are discussing. Do you really believe what you are saying? Is the subject interesting to you, or did you pick it just to have something to say? Is your subject relevant to anyone else? Your answers to these questions are reflected in the ways in which you use your voice and body, in the intensity of your language, even in your selection of ideas. People can tell whether you are engaged with your subject. A disquieting thought, perhaps, but true, is that as a speaker you verbally and nonverbally convey how you feel about your self, your listeners, and your subject matter.

Speaker's Credibility. In every speaking situation, the speaker's success in winning agreement, inspiring confidence, or promoting ideas is significantly affected by the listeners' estimate of his or her credibility. The term *credibility*—and its relative, image, or **ethos** (Greek for "character")—refers to the degree to which an audience finds you trustworthy, competent, sincere, attractive, and dynamic. Research has repeatedly demonstrated that a speaker who can raise an audience's estimate of these qualities will significantly heighten the impact of the speech. The following generalizations about credibility and communication have been verified by research:

1. References to yourself and your own experience—provided they are not boasting or excessive—tend to increase your perceived trustworthiness and competence; references to others (authorities) tend to increase your perceived trustworthiness and dynamism.
2. Using highly credible authorities increases your perceived fairness.
3. If you can demonstrate that you and your audience share common beliefs, attitudes, and values, your credibility will increase.
4. Well-organized speeches are more credible than poorly organized ones.
5. The more sincere you appear to be, the better are your chances of changing your listeners' attitudes.[6]

As these generalizations suggest, your ability to project yourself as a competent, trustworthy, sincere, attractive, fair, and dynamic speaker may well determine the fate of your message. The message and the messenger are usually inseparable in people's minds.

The Listeners

In all forms of speech, the listeners—like the speaker—have goals or purposes in mind. Moreover, the way a message is received and responded to varies according to the listeners' (1) purpose; (2) knowledge of and interest in the subject; (3) level of listening skills; and (4) attitude toward self, speaker, and ideas presented.

Listeners' Purpose. Listeners always have one or more purposes they want to fulfill. Listeners, no less than speakers, enter into the speech transaction in search of rewards. They may wish to be entertained, informed, advised, or guided. These purposes form their expectations, which control to whom, how, and why they listen.

Listeners' Knowledge of the Subject. In speech transactions, the listeners' knowledge of and interest in the subject significantly affect how they receive and respond to the message. Speakers often are told to address listeners "where they are," which is determined by two factors: their knowledge of the topic and their personal interest in it. A knowledgeable audience is bored by an elementary speech, whereas one with little knowledge is confused by a technical description. Disinterested listeners may even go so far as to walk out on a speaker who has not made the topic relevant to their interests.

Listeners' Command of Listening Skills. Listeners vary in their abilities to process oral messages. Some people were raised in homes in which complex oral exchanges occurred, and others were not. Some people have acquired the ability to follow long chains of reasoning, while some struggle to "see the point" in such messages. Most younger children cannot yet concentrate on difficult speeches, while most college students have been taught to do so. All of this means that as a speaker you must attempt to gauge an audience's listening skills. Because so many audiences are heterogeneous, you often must visually survey the listeners, looking for signs of understanding or puzzlement, acceptance or rejection. Those signs, or cues, are termed **feedback**—reactions "fed back" to speakers during or after their talks. Reading feedback is often your only way of assessing a listener's skill of comprehension.

Listeners' Attitudes. In every speech encounter, the listeners' attitudes toward themselves, the speaker, and the subject significantly affect how they interpret and respond to the message. Just as your communicative behavior is influenced by your attitude toward self, subject, and listener, so do these same factors affect your listeners' responses. Listeners with low self-esteem tend to be swayed more easily than those whose self-image is stronger. Listeners whose opinions seem to be confirmed by the views of the speaker are also susceptible to great influence. Moreover, as a rule, people seek out speakers whose positions they already agree with, and they retain longer and more vividly ideas of which they strongly approve.[7]

The Channels

All speech communication is affected by the channels through which the message is transmitted. The transaction between speakers and listeners occurs through several channels. The **verbal channel** carries the words, the culture's agreed-upon symbols for ideas. The **visual channel** transmits the gestures, facial expressions, bodily movements, and posture of the speaker; these tend to clarify, reinforce, or add emotional reactions to the words. At times the visual channel may be supplemented with a **pictorial channel**—so-called "visual aids," such as diagrams, charts, graphs, pictures, objects, and the like. The **aural channel**—also termed the **paralinguistic medium**—carries the tone of voice, variations in pitch and loudness, and other vocal modulations produced by the speaker's stream of sounds. Like the visual channel, the aural channel heightens some meanings and adds others. Because these four channels are seen and heard by listeners simultaneously, the "message" is really a combination of several messages flowing through all of these pathways. You must learn to shape the messages flowing through all four channels.

The Communicative Situation

All speech communication is affected by the physical setting and social context in which it occurs.

Physical Setting.   The physical setting of the speech influences listeners' expectancies, as well as their readiness to respond. People waiting in the quiet solemnity of a cathedral for the service to begin have quite different expectations than do theatergoers gathered to witness the opening of a new Broadway musical. Listeners at an open-air political rally anticipate a different sort of message from those gathered in a college classroom to hear a lecture on political theory.

The furniture and decor of the physical space also make a difference. Comfortable chairs and soft-hued drapes tend to put discussion groups at ease and promote a more productive exchange. The executive who talks to an employee from behind a large desk in the middle of an impressively furnished office gains a natural advantage, not only because of a superior job but also because of the physical setting.

Social Context.   Even more important than physical setting in determining how a message will be received is the social context in which it is presented. A **social context** is a particular combination of people, purposes, and places interacting communicatively. *People* are distinguished from each other by such factors as age, occupation, power, degree of intimacy, and knowledge. These factors in part determine how one "properly" communicates with others. You are expected to speak deferentially to your elders, your boss, an influential political leader, a stranger whose reactions you cannot immediately predict, and a sage. The degree to which people are seen as superior to, equal with, or inferior to each other in status helps determine each one's communicative style. Certain *purposes,* or goals, are appropriately communicated in different contexts as well. Thus, a memorial service is not a time for attacking a political opponent—a "meet the candidates" night is. Some *places* are more conducive to certain kinds of communicative exchanges than others. Public officials are often more easily influenced in their offices than in public forums, where they tend to be more defensive; sensitive parents scold their children in private, never in front of their friends.

Another way of saying all this is to observe that societies are governed by customs and traditions—communication rules. A communication rule is a guide to communicative behavior; it specifies what can be said to whom and in what circumstances. Although communication rules are guides to communicating, they can, of course, be broken. Occasionally rule breaking is inconsequential; sometimes it determines success or failure; always it involves a certain amount of risk.[8]

In summary, because speeches almost always represent transactions whose appropriateness is determined by cultural rules or expectations, throughout this book you will find explicit pieces of advice—do's and don'ts—that are generally followed. It is not really "wrong," for example, to skip a summary at the end of your speech, but most audiences expect that summary. If you omit it, they might even question your **communicative competence**, your ability to construct a speech in accordance with their expectations. These sorts of expectations do not have to be followed slavishly, for conditions and even speaker talents vary from situation to situation; however, you should follow the rules of communication most of the time, because you want listeners to evaluate your ideas, not your communication skills.

Skills and Competencies Needed for Successful Speechmaking

Because public speaking is an interactive process through which people transact various kinds of business, you must acquire certain skills (psychomotor abilities) and competencies (mental abilities to identify, assess, and plan responses to communication problems). Five basic qualities merit your attention: (1) integrity, (2) knowledge, (3) sensitivity to listener needs and to speaking situations, (4) oral skills, and (5) self-confidence and control.

Integrity

Your reputation for reliability, truthfulness, and concern for others is your single most powerful means of exerting rhetorical influence over others. Integrity is important, especially in an age of electronic advertising and mass mailings—when every pressure group, cause, and special interest can worm its way into the public mind, often with conflicting analyses and recommendations for action. Listeners who have no personal experience with a particular subject seek information and advice from speakers they trust. You must earn their trust if you want to succeed.[9]

Knowledge

Expertise is also essential. No one wants to listen to an empty-headed prattler; speakers should know what they are talking about. So, even though you know a lot about a topic through personal experience, take time to do some extra reading, talk with local experts, and find out what aspects of the topic your potential listeners are interested in.

Rhetorical Sensitivity

Sometimes we talk publicly simply to be talking—for purely *expressive* reasons. Usually, however, we speak for *instrumental reasons*—to pass on ideas or to influence the way others think or act. The most successful speakers are other directed, concerned with meeting their listeners' needs and solving their problems through public talk. These speakers are rhetorically sensitive to others.

Rhetorical sensitivity refers to speakers' attitudes toward the process of speech composition.[10] More particularly, rhetorical sensitivity is the degree to which speakers (a) recognize that all people are different and complex and, hence, must be considered individually; (b) avoid rigid communication by adapting their messages and themselves to particular audiences; (c) consciously seek and react to audience feedback; (d) understand the limitations of talk (sometimes even remaining silent rather than trying to express the unexpressible); and (e) work at finding the right set of arguments and linguistic expressions to make particular ideas clear and attractive to particular audiences.

Being rhetorically sensitive does not mean saying only what you think the audience wants to hear. Rather, it is a matter of careful self-assessment, audience analysis, and decision making. What are your purposes? To what degree will they be understandable and acceptable to others? To what degree can you adapt your purposes to audience preferences while maintaining your own integrity and self-respect? These questions are faced by rhetorically sensitive speakers, and they demand that you be sensitive to listener needs, the demands of speaking situations, and the requirements of self-respect. Rhetorical sensitivity, then, is not so much a skill as a competency—a way of thinking and acting in the world of communication.

Oral Skills

Fluency, poise, control of voice, and coordinated movements of your body mark you as a skilled speaker. These skills do not come naturally—they are developed through practice. Such practice is not a matter of acquiring and rehearsing a bag of tricks. Rather, your practice both inside and outside your classroom should aim at making you an animated, natural, and conversational speaker. Many successful public speakers—discounting the high ceremonial situations of politics and religion—seem to be merely *conversing* with their audiences. That should be your goal: to practice being natural, to practice conversing with others in public.

Self-confidence and Self-control

The competent speaker has self-confidence and self-control. Gaining these qualities usually entails overcoming a series of fears.[11] Audiences are more likely to accept ideas from self-confident than from self-doubting persons. In Chapter 3 we will talk a good deal more about self-assurance and control. Before that, however, we will continue our general orientation to speech-making by looking at it from the other end—from the view of listeners.

Chapter Summary

We live in the Age of Communication, dominated by electronic media, yet pushed, by our intimacy with so many others in the Global Village, to improve our oral communication skills. Speaking skills are important to our society because we collectively use speeches for *self-definition; information giving; debate about questions of fact, value, and policy;* and *individual and social change.* A useful model of public speaking incorporates five elements and their variable aspects: *the message* (content, structure, and style); *the speaker* (speaker's purpose, knowledge, attitudes, and credibility); *the listeners* (listeners' purpose, knowledge of subject, command of listening skills, and attitudes); *the channels* (verbal, visual, pictorial, and aural); and *the communicative situation* (physical setting and social context). Finally, because public speaking is a complex *transaction*, you need certain skills and competencies to be successful: *integrity, knowledge, rhetorical sensitivity, oral skills*, and *self-confidence and self-control.*

Reference Notes

1. Marshall McLuhan and Quentin Fiore, *War and Peace in the Global Village* (New York: Bantam Books, 1968).

2. Carol H. Pazandak, "Followup Survey of 1973 Graduates, College of Liberal Arts" (Minneapolis: University of Minnesota, 1977) (multilith); Jack Landgrebe and Howard Baumgartel, "Results of the Graduation Requirement Questionnaire for College of Liberal Arts and Science Alumni" (Lawrence: College of Liberal Arts and Science, University of Kansas) (typescript); "Instruction in Communication at Colorado State University" (Fort Collins: College of Engineering, Colorado State University, July 1979) (multilith); and Edward Foster et al., "A Market Study for the College of Business Administration, University of Minnesota, Twin Cities" (Minneapolis: University of Minnesota, November 1978) (multilith). These studies all indicate that graduates in the working world find communication skills to be essential for both hiring and promotion. See also the *Communication Research Dateline* in this chapter.

3. For a more complete discussion of communication style, see Chapter 12, as well as John F. Wilson and Carroll C. Arnold, *Public Speaking as a Liberal Art*, 5th ed. (Boston: Allyn and Bacon, Inc., 1983), 227–29.

4. For a discussion of interrelationships between self-concept and communication, see Gordon I. Zimmerman, James L. Owen, and David R. Siebert, *Speech Communication: A Contemporary Introduction*, 2nd ed. (St. Paul: West Publishing Co., 1977), esp. 32–43; and Gail E. Myers and Michele Tolela Myers, *The Dynamics of Human Communication: A Laboratory Approach*, 3rd ed. (New York: McGraw-Hill Book Co., 1980), Chapter 3, "Self-Concept: Who Am I?" 47–72.

5. The importance of appropriateness and competency as standards of judgments is argued for in Bruce E. Gronbeck, "Ronald Reagan's Enactment of the Presidency in His 1981 Inaugural Address," in *Form, Genre, and the Study of Political Discourse*, ed. Herbert W. Simons and Aram A. Aghazarian (Columbia, SC: University of South Carolina Press, 1986), 226–45.

6. These and other generalizations relative to source credibility are most usefully summarized in Stephen W. Littlejohn, "A Bibliography of Studies Related to Variables of Source Credibility," *Bibliographic Annual in Speech Communication: 1971*, ed. Ned A. Shearer (New York: Speech Communication Association), 1–40; cf. Ronald L. Applebaum et al., *Fundamental Concepts in Human Communication* (San Francisco: Canfield Press, 1973), 255–72.

7. See the personality analysis of receivers in Michael Burgoon, *Approaching Speech Communication* (New York: Holt, Rinehart & Winston, Inc., 1974), 64–69.

8. Much research on physical setting and social context is summarized in Mark L. Knapp, *Essentials of Nonverbal Communication* (New York: Holt, Rinehart & Winston, Inc., 1980), Chapter 4, "The Effects of Territory and Personal Space," pp. 75–96. The determinative aspects

of social expectations in human communication generally are discussed in such books as John J. Gumperz and Dell Hymes, eds., *Directions in Sociolinguistics: The Ethnography of Communication* (New York: Holt, Rinehart & Winston, Inc., 1972); and Peter Collett, ed., *Social Rules and Social Behavior* (Totowa, NJ: Rowman and Littlefield, 1977). More specifically, the current state of knowledge about "rules" and their importance in communication is documented in Susan B. Shimanoff, *Communication Rules: Theory and Research*, Sage Library of Social Research, 97 (Beverly Hills: Sage Publications, 1980).

9. A fuller discussion of the role that personal integrity plays in successful public communication is found in Otis M. Walter, *Speaking to Inform and Persuade* (New York: The Macmillan Co., 1966), Chapter 8, "The Ethos of the Speaker."

10. See Roderick P. Hart and Don M. Burks, "Rhetorical Sensitivity and Social Interaction," *Speech [Communication] Monographs* 39 (1972): 75–91; and Roderick P. Hart, Robert E. Carlson, and William F. Eadie, "Attitudes Toward Communication and the Assessment of Rhetorical Sensitivity," *Communication Monographs* 47 (1980): 1–22.

11. "What Are Americans Afraid Of?" *The Bruskin Report* 13, #53; "Surveys Reveal Students' Concern Over Jobs, Public-Speaking Anxiety," *Pitt News*, May 1978.

Key Terms

Global Village	*ethos*
public communication	*feedback*
model	*verbal channel*
transactional model	*visual channel*
communication rules	*pictorial channel*
message	*aural channel*
referential content	*paralinguistic medium*
relational content	*social context*
self-image	*communicative competence*
role positions	*rhetorical sensitivity*

Problems and Probes

1. In a notebook set aside for the purpose, start a Personal Speech Journal. The contents will be seen by only you and your instructor, who may call for the journal at intervals during the term. In your first entry, write about yourself in relation to the six basic qualities needed for successful speechmaking. Consider your integrity. (If you have not engaged in an exercise like this before, it should be a fascinating source of enlightenment for you.) In what areas do you feel you have most knowledge? In what areas would you wish to research to gain more knowledge? Look around your classroom at your classmates who will be your

listeners this term. What do you know about their needs? What do you know about the speaking situation you are about to face? What do you still need to learn? What oral skills do you already possess and what others do you wish to gain? Finally, consider your own self-confidence and control in light of the task before you.

2. Identify and describe three speech transactions in which you participated during the past week. In at least two of these encounters, you should have been the speaker initiating the interaction. Formulate answers to the following questions:

a. In which of the three situations—person-to-person, small group, or public communication—did each of these three transactions take place?

b. What channel or channels did you use?

c. What was your communicative purpose in each case?

d. To what extent do you feel you accomplished your communicative purpose in each transaction? Why?

e. What was the extent of your message-preparation in each of the three instances? If preparation was more mandatory and/or more extensive for one situation than for others, explain why this was so.

f. Show how, in one of these transactions, the physical setting probably influenced what happened. In another, explain how the social context tended to affect the outcome.

Communication Activities

1. To the extent that the physical facilities of the classroom permit, your instructor will arrange for members of the class to seat themselves in a large circle or in smaller groups around two or three separate tables. Informality should be the keynote in this particular activity. After the instructor has completed a brief self-introduction, each class member will provide a self-introduction based generally on the following pattern:

My name is _____.

My major (or my major interest) is _____.

I am enrolled in this college/university because _____.

In addition to a grade credit, what I hope to get from this course in speech communication is _____.

2. Working in pairs, present pertinent biographical information about yourself to another member of the class. This person, in turn, will prepare a short speech introducing you to the group. You, of course, will do likewise for the student with whom you are paired. When these speeches have been completed, draw up a composite picture of the audience to whom you will be speaking during the remainder of the term.

3. Prepare a two-to-three-minute presentation on the topic "a speech I shall always remember." In specifying why you consider a particular address notable, focus on one or more of the factors in the speech communication process discussed in this chapter.

CHAPTER TWO

Public Speaking and Critical Listening

*L*istening is an activity that we all too often take for granted. After all, we have been listening to others since birth—with this amount of practice, why should we bother to study it in a serious manner? Since listening takes up much of our daily life—estimates run as high as 45 percent of our communication time spent in attending to what others say—we should be proficient at it by now.[1] While that might make sense, your experience with your own listening behavior, and with that of others, strongly suggests that excessive practice does not always result in proficiency.

The importance of effective listening cannot be overestimated. In general, listening to others is the means by which we understand ourselves better, learn what others expect of us, and obtain the information and ideas necessary to make informed decisions. Listening is central to the process of presenting ideas orally. For example, effective listening skills are essential in the workplace. Corporations have long recognized that poor listening, which occurs often in meetings and in communication between superiors and subordinates, harms productivity and morale. In response, some companies have instituted training sessions to improve skills at all corporate levels. The Sperry Corporation, for example, has used listening as its advertising theme, "We understand how important it is to listen," and has developed a comprehensive employee training program.[2] In your experience as a student, you may have faced the consequences of not listening to instructions for performing a chemistry experiment, to an oral presentation of the next day's assignment, or to an orally presented schedule for the next exam. Asking classmates what is going on becomes, for some students, a habitual response to their own inattentiveness.

This chapter will discuss listening behavior in general, as it functions within the classroom and in other contexts. Barriers to effective listening behavior, and ways to counteract them, will be presented. Finally, your responsibilities as a speaker, specific to the context of improving the chances of being listened to by audience members, will be discussed.

Types of Effective Listening Behavior

At the most general level, two discrete types of listening behavior can be identified: empathic and critical. Prior to discussing each type, three common attributes need to be identified. First, all listening aims at **comprehension.** If you do not understand what you are hearing, there is little that you can do with the information presented. If your ultimate goal is to act or to give advice on the basis of the spoken words, comprehending is the initial prerequisite—whether you are huddling in the midst of a field hockey game, attending a corporate board meeting, listening to a friend explain a problem, or receiving the next assignment in class. You often are a poor listener because your complex mind can comprehend many more words per minute than speakers can produce clearly. A listener can mentally handle more than 400 spoken words per minute, yet the average speaker produces between 125 and 175 words per minute; thus, the listener needs only about 20 to 25 seconds of every minute to comprehend what the speaker is saying. The resulting time lag—the spare moments when close attention is not needed—provides a tempting route to nonlistening. "Dropping out" to think about other things may be fine, but only if one can remember to "drop in" again on the message. Therein lies the difficulty in effective listening.

The second attribute of all listening activity is that it is a *transactional process.* Whether in the speech classroom or in a meeting, listening is the conduit through which speakers reach their audiences. The conduit works both ways, as the audience in a face-to-face situation sends messages back to the speaker. Listeners can provide three types of feedback: **direct feedback** in the form of verbal or written comments; **indirect feedback,** as in nods, laughs, frowns, and other nonverbal signs that a person is or is not understanding or accepting a message; and **delayed feedback,** such as when classroom speakers are graded by their peers and/or the instructor on their performance. Thus, listening is not a one-way street—"I talk; you listen"—but rather is a dynamic, transactional process in which both speaker and listener participate to create meaning. This leads to the third attribute: listening is an *interpretive* act.[3] Both speakers and listeners modify each other's thoughts and actions—one by making a speech and the other by interpreting it. The "meaning of the message" is not something unique to the speaker, nor is it wholly "inside" the receiver. Rather, meanings are created by the interaction of both. Given the manifold possibilities in any interpretation of oral talk, the refrain "I told them—they just didn't listen" may not be as true as its speaker believes.

THE TYPES OF FEEDBACK

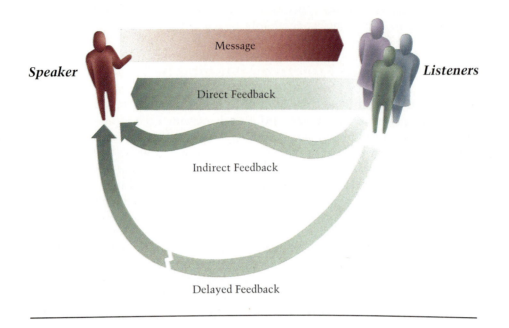

Empathic Listening

Empathy involves putting oneself in the place of another—seeing an event from his or her perspective, and coming as close as possible to understanding his or her feelings or attitudes.[4] The most common context for empathic listening is in *therapeutic* settings. In **therapeutic listening,** the auditor (as single listener) acts as a sounding board for the speaker as that person talks through a problem, works out a difficult situation, or expresses deep emotional stress or confusion. Therapeutic listening is not confined to professional people, such as teachers, lawyers, or psychiatrists. As a student living with roommates in a dormitory or apartment, you already may have found yourself in a situation calling for a "sympathetic ear." Although therapeutic listening most often occurs in interpersonal situations, and generally in more private settings, the same need may exist in a public-speaking situation. Examples include a sports star who apologizes for unprofessional behavior, a televangelist who confesses on nationwide television to moral failure, or even a classmate who reviews a personal problem and thanks a group of friends for help in solving it.

Equally important occasions for listening with empathy occur in times of joy, as when someone wants to tell others about a new love, a new baby, a promotion at work, or an award at school. People seek others both in times of problems and in times of promise. In therapeutic listening, special social bonding between the speaker and listener occurs; the speaker-audience relationship itself can become the focus of attention and a cause for celebration.

Critical Listening

Whereas empathic listeners attend to a person as a result of what is said, **critical listeners** attend directly to the message—to what is being communicated. It may be easier to understand the dimensions of critical listening by considering what it is *not*. First, the opposite of critical listening is **passive listening.** As you read these words, there might be music on in the background; as you study, you might require one kind of sound to drown out all others so you can concentrate. Occasionally you "tune in" to the music, but only to absorb it, not to think about it. While this example suggests a positive role for passive listening, not all instances of passivity are helpful. As you listen to a lecture, your attention to the primary message is passive if you do not think about or analyze the ideas being offered. You have not engaged your whole being, or even a substantial part of it, in the act of attending to and interpreting what is being said. If what is said has important implications for your beliefs or actions (such as having to take a test on the material in the near future), your passivity could have negative consequences.

Second, critical listening is *not* negative listening; the goal is not necessarily to attack what is being said. Rather, it is listening in order to retain the *option* of critique by knowing what is said and how you wish to respond to it. Thus, critical listening demands that auditors become fully engaged with the message not simply in order to understand it, but to interpret it, to judge its strengths and weaknesses, and to assign its worth. You practice listening critically when you evaluate commercials for their sexist or ethnic content, political campaign speeches for their vacuous or false claims, a performance for its artistic merit, or oral arguments for or against a plan of action in the community or at work. When listening critically, you decide to accept or reject a claim; to act or delay action on a project; or to offer praise or blame with respect to an idea's consequences, a person's actions, or an event's significance.

There are two predominant types of critical listening: appreciative and discriminative listening. The primary purpose of **appreciative listening** is to judge the aesthetic value of what is heard, whether a speech, a dramatic play, a musical, or a jazz ensemble performance. One might, for example, listen to Martin Luther King, Jr.'s, "I Have a Dream" speech or John F. Kennedy's Inaugural Address with the principal goal of appreciating their illustration of the art of public speaking: hearing King's resonant voice or recognizing the force of metaphor as an argument for change, or listening to Kennedy's superb verbal style. These are sufficient reasons for understanding why their presentations have become exemplars in the lexicon of public oratory.

Another reason for appreciative listening is to assess a public event, such as an inauguration, the dedication of a new building or statue, or other festive occasions. Even on these occasions, however, appreciation implies active

Listening Behavior

There are several approaches to the study of listening behavior. Some of these focus on theoretical *models* of the processes involved. Goss, for example, takes an "information processing" approach to listening. There are three stages to the model:

1. *Signal processing*—transmitting the message to the listener. This stage becomes problematic only if the speech is unclear or poorly spoken, or the language being used is unfamiliar to listeners.

2. *Literal processing*—taking the words in the message at face value in assessing their probable meaning. It is the first stage of meaning assessment, and it focuses on the denotative meaning of the words used.

3. *Reflective processing*—listening to evaluate. It goes beyond the literal stage to determine what else may be contained in the message (for instance, inferences, motives, and speaker credibility).

In a recent study, Beatty and Payne connected this model of listening to the concept of cognitive complexity, which refers to the levels of complex thinking, or the variety of different thoughts a stimulus produces in the mind. They found that as complexity increases, one

participation. In order to appraise its significance to you and the rest of your community, you need to evaluate the event's worth in terms of certain criteria, and that can only be done if you have engaged yourself fully and attentively during the event. (See Chapter 18.) Thus, appreciative listening aims at making *value* judgments about the speaker, the presentation, and occasionally the event itself.

In **discriminative listening,** the goal is to evaluate the *reasons* being offered through the message—either to believe an idea or to act on the basis of a proposal. The discriminative process involves drawing inferences about both stated and unstated matters—about what speakers are "really" saying, about the cogency of the claims being advanced. By listening carefully to what the speaker is claiming and to the reasons he or she offers for the claim, you will have a basis for determining its reasonableness. "What is really meant" may include an evaluation of tone of voice or a recognition that the "unsaid" is

is better able to recall information presented. In relation to listening, this suggests that as you become capable of bringing more ideas to bear on what is being heard, your ability to listen effectively, as measured by comprehension and recall, increases.

Another approach to listening research has focused on empathic vs. critical listening skills and has examined the interpersonal situation of an employment interview—a setting you may already have had some experience with. For example, a study by McComb and Jablin focused on the degree of empathy displayed by recruiters at a university placement center as they conducted initial interviews with prospective employees. Five specific interviewer behaviors were examined: silence/absence of interruption; probing questions; verbal encouragers; restatements of answers; and clarification questions. Interestingly, the researchers discovered that these behaviors accounted for only 22 percent of the interviewee's perception of the interviewer as empathic, leaving 78 percent unaccounted for.

McComb and Jablin suggest that non-verbal behaviors may account for a large portion of how one perceives the presence of empathy in a listener; furthermore, and as a call for future studies, they observe that there is an apparent gap between what texts on interviewing offer as advice and what actually takes place in an interview situation.

FOR FURTHER READING
Beatty, Michael J., and Steven K. Payne. "Listening Comprehension as a Function of Cognitive Complexity: A Research Note." *Communication Monographs* 51 (1984): 85–89; Goss, Blaine. *Processing Communication.* Belmont, CA: Wadsworth Publishing Co., 1982; Goss, Blaine. "Listening as Information Processing." *Communication Quarterly* 30 (1982): 304–7; Floyd, James J. *Listening: A Practical Approach.* Glenview, IL: Scott, Foresman and Company, 1985; McComb, Karen B., and Fredrick M. Jablin. "Verbal Correlates of Empathic Listening and Employment Interview Outcomes." *Communication Monographs* 51 (1984): 353–71.

more important than the "said" in a given situation. For example, you may have drawn conclusions about how angry your parents were with you based not so much on *what* they said as on *how* they said it. Likewise, a president's attitudes toward a foreign policy controversy, such as the Iran-Contra affair, are evaluated as much by what is left unsaid as by the president's public pronouncements. Can you place your trust in what a speaker is saying, and by accepting the belief or acting on the claim, find that you have not misplaced your adherence?

Discriminative listening involves making choices about the worth of claims; it is the basis for making informed decisions about how you live your life. Whether such decisions concern "Should I study for the exam?" or "Should I present the proposal to my employer?" or "Should I disagree with the professor?" their accuracy potential depends on your prior listening behavior. If you have been only "half there" during class lectures, you will not know

Martin Luther King, Jr., presented his "I Have a Dream" speech at the 1963 March on Washington.

what to study; if you have not been paying attention to your employer's appeal for "new ideas," your speculation about her response to your proposal will produce more anxiety than necessary; if you have not noticed the tone of your professor's statement that "criticism is welcomed," you cannot be sure whether it is.

When you are engaged in the act of listening, whether empathic or critical, the result has significant implications. When you are a member of an audience, you need to decide on a specific listening approach. When listening in a critical mode, appreciative listeners are highly selective; they watch for metaphors, listen to speaking tones, and search out memorable phrases. Discriminative listeners, on the other hand, work hard to catch every piece of information relevant to a proposal, judge the soundness of competing arguments, and consciously select criteria that would justify a decision to accept or reject the proposal. Empathic listeners must decide when to positively reinforce speakers through applause or other signs of approval, thereby serving a therapeutic purpose. As your skill in listening increases, and as you think explicitly about your own purposes *before* attending a speech, you will find your experiences with public presentations becoming more pleasurable and complete. Listening effectively, regardless of your purpose, provides a firm foundation for reaching well-grounded conclusions about what is going on around you. Only through such active listening can you further control the communicative situations in which you interact, whether in social, work, or public settings.

The next sections of this chapter will consider the barriers, or constraints, to effective listening behavior. These apply to both empathic and critical listening, and the emphasis will be on ways to counteract these constraints in public-speaking situations.

Barriers to Effective Listening

As you have learned, listening is a joint responsibility. Both speaker and listener are involved in the transaction, and both must make reasonable efforts to ensure that intended messages are taken in, comprehended, interpreted, and responded to; however, problems arise. Few of us are good listeners; we tend to drop out more often than we drop in. Although estimates of the average listening comprehension rate vary, researchers agree that we do not fully utilize our listening potential.[5] Some studies indicate that we may understand only one fourth of all of the information received aurally.

There are several barriers to effective listening behavior. As a listener, you need to take steps to counteract them; as a speaker, you need to know they exist in order to adjust your message and to diminish their potential negative effects. While there are many such reasons, four are prominent in accounting for poor listening habits: (1) weak extrinsic motivation, (2) personal constraints, (3) environmental constraints, and (4) poor timing of the message.

Weak Extrinsic Motivation

Studies indicate that being told to listen is an ineffective strategy for improving listening skills; being told *why* one should listen and receiving relevant rewards or punishments as incentive increases the *extrinsic motivation* to listen.[6] **Extrinsic motives** are those that arise where some act is a means to some other end. If you are in a class in which the lecturer does not offer any guides as to what to listen for and why, one of two possibilities will occur. Either you will listen closely to everything and take copious notes in the hope that you will be able to sift through and locate essential material, or you will despair of ever knowing what to listen for and tune out. The extrinsic motivation, a decent grade, must be important to you in such situations, or you will simply become a passive listener and hope that studying outside of class will make up the difference. Conversely, the instructor who clearly indicates the essential ideas and tells you which ones are important for next week's exam allows you to focus your attention on key elements in the lecture and to use the remaining material as explanatory support. At the least, you know which information is significant and which is interesting but not relevant to future exams.

The degree of extrinsic motivation in the work place or in social situations also affects listening behavior. If you are in a job in which the perceived rewards for listening carefully are low, your desire to listen actively will be lessened. When incentives to listen are not provided or are not considered important, passive, rather than active, listening is a likely result.

Personal Constraints

The presence or absence of an *internal desire* to listen also affects how well you attend to a message. Listening is not an automatic response to stimuli. You must *want* to listen. While the wailing of a siren generally commands your attention, the sonorous tones of a tired, unenthusiastic speaker will not.

Your *past experiences* also may affect how well you listen. Sometimes the speaker's words trigger a memory or remind you of a present engagement; on these occasions your mind wanders and you focus your attention on personal thoughts, plans, or needs.

Your *attitudes, values,* and *beliefs* also can cause you to give personalized interpretations to spoken messages. When you do not agree with the message, you spend mental time "debating" with the speaker, planning what to say if you have the opportunity. In the meantime, the speaker goes on, unaware that you are missing the full development of her or his ideas. Listeners' mental "debates" can trip them up, as the speaker blithely must respond to uninformed questions with the remark, "As I said in my presentation . . ." Much faulty listening can be attributed to auditors' not giving the speaker the benefit of a complete presentation before drawing conclusions about the accuracy of the claim or the worth of the argument. At times, feelings so color the reception of messages that listeners attribute ideas and motives to the speaker that were not actually present in the speech. This happens most often when listeners disagree with the speaker's ideas, with supporting materials, or with the value premises on which the argument is based.

Sometimes a listener is simply tired or confused about the message, in which case it is easier to become passive. Listening should be an active process; it takes mental energy. Because confusion often arises in oral presentations, it takes energy to sort out ideas. Being passive is much easier than concentrating on the message, but it leads to ineffective listening. It is easier to pretend to listen than to actually do so.[7] Being hungry, fighting a bad cold, or studying all night for a test also can result in listening more passively. Physical needs can take priority over intellectual needs to listen.

Finally, attitudes toward the speaker also color an internal desire to listen effectively. For example, if you have heard that a particular instructor lectures poorly, you will enter the classroom with a negative mind-set. Chances are that your preset notions will be confirmed, not because the instructor is necessarily boring everyone, but because you allowed the person's reputation to interfere with the reality of the communicative situation. Many speakers are not given a fair hearing because the audience accepts conclusions about them or their topics before the speech is presented.

PERSONAL AND ENVIRONMENTAL CONSTRAINTS ON LISTENING

Competing demands on your attention usually allow you to hear and symbolically process only part of a spoken message. Listening with full discrimination rarely occurs.

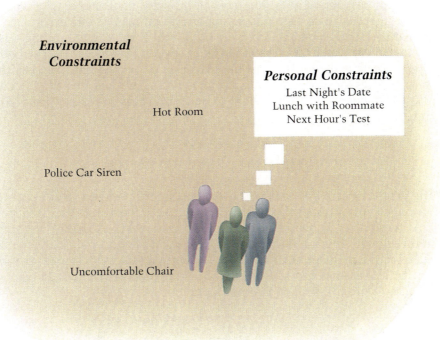

Environmental Constraints

Personal Constraints
Last Night's Date
Lunch with Roommate
Next Hour's Test

Hot Room

Police Car Siren

Uncomfortable Chair

Environmental Constraints

The physical communicative setting also can work against effective listening. Distractions draw attention away from the speech. Seats can be too hard or otherwise uncomfortable; the person next to you might be whispering to someone in the row in front; the room may be too drafty or too hot and stuffy; a police car with its siren going may pass by the open window. Attention to your own physical well-being and comfort or to other external distractions inhibit concentration on the message as the primary stimulus.[8]

Poor Timing

The Greeks understood the importance of the "fitting moment" for speech—the right time to present an idea or to argue for an action. Their term for it was *kairos*; ours is **rhetorical timing.**[9] This concept is as relevant for listeners as it is for speakers. There are good and bad times for attempting to listen to a message, as implied in the preceding discussion of personal and environmental constraints. For example, if you have just paid your taxes, you may not be in the best mood to hear an urgent appeal for money for a social cause, no matter how justified the need.

On a more positive note, you have an intuitive understanding of what it means to speak or to listen at an opportune moment. Your experience is riddled with both good and bad episodes in which appropriate timing was a key ingredient in your success as a listener or speaker. You have learned from experience that listening to an instructor on a "review day" has positive consequences for studying for an exam. You also have learned that listening to instructions when unsure how to perform a task saves you from later embarrassment.

Strategies for Effective Listening

The preceding sections reviewed the components common to all listening behavior, defined empathic and critical listening activity, and discussed problems common to ineffective listening. This section will examine the responsibilities of a listener and the ways in which you can improve your listening behavior as a member of an audience, either in a classroom, social, or work setting. This section also will suggest ways to improve listening skills through an analysis of *self*, *speaker*, and *message*.

Listener Analysis of Self

To become a better listener, you first must identify your listening habits and preferences—your internal desire to listen—and think about them in terms of their productivity. How useful have these habits and preferences been in the past? Have they enabled you to listen as well as you should? If not, should you change your approach? From a positive perspective, think about the times when you were a good listener, when listening well was easy, and when you understood and recalled the most important parts of the message. What types of settings were these? What kinds of things did you do to keep your attention focused on the speaker and the message? Think also about the negative experiences, those times when listening was difficult. Why was it difficult to listen? Was your internal desire to listen insufficient to the task? Were you, for example, uninterested in the topic, bored, or too tired to stay with the speaker for the time required?

You also should think about your listening preferences. Are there people to whom you prefer to listen? Are some classes especially exciting? What

To prepare for a communication transaction, you must determine your purpose in listening. In receiving advice, for instance, consider the personal importance of the message and attend to it accordingly.

features of these people and classes cause you to think and listen eagerly? Do you enjoy situations in which a sympathetic ear is called for? By quickly scanning your habits and preferences, you can begin to identify and to reinforce the positive aspects of your active listening behavior.

After assessing your listening behavior, you can begin to correct habits that have proven ineffective by preparing to listen. Before you enter a communication event, ask yourself the following questions.

What is my purpose in listening? Do I expect to gain information and understanding, to receive advice, or to make a critical decision based on the speaker's presentation? What is the extrinsic motivation—the incentive—for listening? Suppose an employer announces, "Here's what you must do to earn a six-month raise." You probably will pay particular attention to that material, making sure that you understand and can recall it as needed. In this instance, there is sufficient extrinsic motivation to focus on the message. In another case, listening may be influenced by your personal interest in the subject matter or by your commitment to assist a friend, based on the information you receive. Whatever the motive for listening, recognizing why you are listening can better prepare you to analyze the important features of the message. If the message has personal importance, you will be more likely to give it your fullest attention.

Am I impartial about the message being presented? If you are not willing to allow the speaker to complete his or her presentation before you draw conclusions, you may be wasting both the speaker's time and your own. Try setting aside your personal feelings or attitudes about the topic and give the speaker a chance to develop the message to its fullest. This does not mean you should not criticize, only that you will be better prepared to do so by hearing the speaker out. Suspending initial judgment will enable you to listen more carefully to the arguments presented and to offer an appropriate refutation—you will be less vulnerable to the charge "You didn't listen to what I said."

How much do I know about the topic? If you are unfamiliar with a topic but at least curious about it, chances are that you will listen effectively. If you know a good deal about the topic, you can listen to compare your information with that provided by the speaker. How complete are her or his ideas? Are they accurate, up-to-date, and presented fairly? As long as you control the process of comparative analysis by mentally checking off items and returning to the presentation, you have a basis for evaluating the worth of the idea.

What trigger words cause me to stray from the central message? As you hear words that bring up thoughts that are irrelevant to the occasion, resist the temptation to contemplate their significance. For example, a classmate mentions "test" in the context of describing a psychology experiment—the word reminds you that you have a test in the afternoon, and you have not studied all of the material. As difficult as it is to put that issue aside, now is not the time to worry, as you cannot study effectively while the speaker is talking. You also may find your attention wandering as you hear the speaker use unfamiliar words. If a word strikes you as important or interesting, simply jot it down for later consideration. This allows you to redirect your attention to the speech, and to listen further to see if the word is used again in a context that clarifies its meaning or significance.

What do I expect from this speech? Be realistic in setting your personal expectations. If the speaker is a classmate, chances are that she or he is not an authority on the topic but has done sufficient research to offer a fairly complete summary of what experts are saying. If, for example, your classmate is giving a speech about the stock market, you will be disappointed if you hope for hot tips on how to invest your money or for the secret to successful investing. If you expect only to increase your understanding of the market's operation, your reason for listening will more closely match what the speaker can provide.

What do I know about the situation? If you can anticipate the length of the speech, you will do a better job of controlling your listening behavior. Assigned speeches in your class will usually include a time limit; hence, you can prepare to concentrate for five to seven minutes when a classmate presents an informative speech. If you are attending a lecture, you should be prepared for a presentation that will last at least an hour. By practicing your concentration skills in listening to the shorter classroom speeches, you will gradually improve your ability to focus attention on key ideas during longer presentations. Furthermore, does the situation call for an evaluation of the performance's worth, as in appreciative listening, or will you be expected to make decisions on the basis of the presentation, as in discriminative listening? Knowing in advance what is expected of you will prepare you to adopt the appropriate listening strategy.

How favorable is the listening environment? Become aware of the physical constraints that may impede effective listening in particular environments. If you are engaged in therapeutic listening, a loud gathering may be the wrong setting. If your task is to critically appraise a performance or to make decisions on the basis of reasons offered by a speaker, recognize that the physical environment may not be conducive to these ends. If it is possible to listen in relative isolation from others, your chances of being able to concentrate on a message will increase. Thus, if you have an opportunity to record and play back a message, listening alone instead of with a group will help you concentrate and thereby improve your comprehension and retention of the message.[10] If you can sit nearer the speaker, you can reduce the number of potential distractions during the performance. If that is unlikely, recognizing the potential constraints will help you guard against their intrusion into your concentration.

How appropriate is the timing of the message? As is true of the physical environment, you may not be able to affect the timing of the message; however, if you are aware that the timing is not to your liking and that you cannot change it (many students dislike 8:00 classes, for example) you will be better able to make the best of the situation. In the case of an early class, getting sufficient rest may be helpful, or getting up early enough to be thoroughly awake when you get to class may help your concentration. In some cases, such as for an assignment to listen to a televised presidential speech, you may be able to record the speech and review it at a more convenient time, and have the advantage of replaying it to catch things you may have missed. To the extent that timing is favorable, or you can exert some control over it, your experience of the event will be more positive, and your willingness to listen will be enhanced.

Listener Analysis of the Speaker

Speaking does not occur in a vacuum. Both speaker and listener bring personal experiences to the communication environment. In doing so, the listener not only attends to the message the speaker transmits but also considers the speaker's credibility. The following questions can help you evaluate a speaker and his or her effect on your reception of the message.

What do I know or think about this speaker? Whether for good or ill, the speaker's reputation influences your reaction to the message. If a previous experience in listening to the speaker was favorable, you are more likely to respond positively to a new encounter. If you agree with the speaker's position on political issues, you are more highly motivated to listen than if you disagree. If you dislike the speaker, you are likely to allow your views to

Listeners' interest in a communication transaction is tied closely to whether the speaker meets their personal needs. An effective communicator fulfills listeners' expectations, provides information they seek, or satisfies their general desire to listen.

color your perception of the person *and* of the message. Instead of listening carefully to the full presentation, you may succumb to the temptation to argue mentally with the speaker or to dismiss the ideas out of hand. If you take the position that the best defense is a sound knowledge of the opposition, however, you can develop the necessary internal desire to listen carefully in order to build the strongest case for your side.

How believable is the speaker? Answers to this question tend to be based on previous experiences with the speaker or on advance information. If you know that the speaker has misled listeners on a previous occasion, you might expect similar treatment. You can adjust your listening habits to be alert for unsupported conclusions, incomplete statements of fact, or inaccurate assertions. When you listen this way, be especially careful to connect the "errors" to the main points being presented. Otherwise, you will have a motley collection of pieces of the puzzle but no general sense of what goes where. If you suspect the speaker is presenting false information, you must be able to show how this weakens the claim. Simply pointing out the inaccuracy of the information is not sufficient to weaken the claims itself, unless you are certain the audience has already made the connection.

Is the speaker responsive to your needs? If the speaker has done her or his job well, there will be elements in the speech that meet your expectations, provide the information you seek, or satisfy your general desire to listen. A speaker's lack of responsiveness will lessen your attentiveness. For example, if the current President of the United States were to visit your campus, would you expect him to discuss current national issues? If, instead, he spent his entire speech extolling the achievements of his administration, would your personal needs be met? Would you expect him to be aware of, and comment on, events of local interest? If he did not, would your personal expectations be satisfied? In a more informal setting, in which you have the chance to respond, a speaker who monopolizes talk invites lessened listening behavior. A speaker in such a situation who does not ask probing questions to ascertain your interests will not invite your close attention to what is being said.[11] Your interest in listening is tied closely to whether the speaker is meeting your personal needs.

What is the speaker's attitude toward this presentation? Listeners use their ears and eyes to grasp meaning. They assess whether a message is worthy of attention in part by the attitudes the speaker projects through both verbal and nonverbal cues. A speaker who appears flippant or insincere creates an obstacle to productive listening. A speaker who appears condescending invites a defensive listening posture. Even a speaker who is sincere and genuinely interested in the audience may have distracting habits or mannerisms. Can you recall a speaker who paced back and forth while speaking with no real purpose associated with the physical movement, who played with a pencil or paper clip while talking, or who spoke so slowly and in such measured tones that you could not follow the train of thought? When such distractions occur, try to interact with the ideas being presented. Repeat the central points to yourself as a means of ignoring the distractions, or try taking notes on main points to focus more precisely on the ideas as they are developed.

Listener Analysis of the Message

The message is the speaker's product, the *raison d'etre* (reason for being) for the speech occasion. The message provides information, gives advice, or urges decision making or action. As such, the message is the principal focus of your attention. As a receiver, you can focus your energy on the message by structuring your listening behavior in terms of the following questions.

What are the main ideas of the speech? Try to discover the speaker's purpose and list the ideas he or she presents on behalf of that purpose. Usually these can be found by determining the speech's *central idea* or *claim* and identifying the main ideas used as explanation or support. The main ideas serve as the building blocks on which the speaker constructs the speech. The next time you listen to a TV or radio commercial, direct your attention to the statements supporting the thesis. Assuming that the commercial is asking you to purchase a product, what types of statements support this request? Listen the same way to a speech: once you have identified the thesis, what are the major ideas that justify your acceptance of the claim? By focusing attention in this way, the details in the speech will fit with the rest of the message: you need to listen for specifics in light of the overall structure of the speech.

How are the principal ideas arranged? The answer to this question will help you identify and later recall the main ideas. If you become aware early on that the main ideas are arranged in a chronological or spatial pattern, or that the assessment of cause is followed by a listing of effects, you can track the speech's progress from one point to the next. This takes the guesswork out of determining where the speaker will go next in the development of the speech and makes it easier to outline it in your own notes.

What types of supporting materials are used to develop the principal ideas? Consider such things as the timeliness of the data, the quality of the sources, and the specific content of the speech as it unfolds. Supporting materials clarify, amplify, and strengthen the main ideas of a speech. Once you have identified the main ideas and the pattern of their development, listen carefully to the support material to evaluate the significance or worth of the speaker's central idea or claim. If the content of the speech does not make sense to you, the data seem old, or the sources are suspect, you may have reasons to reject the speaker's ideas. Discerning these faults does not mean the idea is necessarily wrong, but it does suggest that this particular speaker's reasons do not justify its acceptance.

Notetaking in the Classroom: Practicing Critical Listening Skills

The strategies discussed in this chapter relate to your current situation as a student in a speech class, as well as to other contexts in which you will be expected to listen. A useful approach to improving your critical listening skills in the classroom is to concentrate on notetaking. Studies indicate that taking notes enhances comprehension and recall following a presentation. Your experience in taking notes over many years of classroom listening may have perfected a method that works for you. On the other hand, when you are faced with unfamiliar material, you may be very tempted to write everything down, or at least as much detail as possible. When you review your notes later, you hope that they will make sense. If you concentrate too hard on taking notes, you may discover that they are relatively meaningless because you did not listen to the message. You "heard" what was said, but you did not take the time to "think about" the content. Studies indicate that *interchanging* notetaking with listening is better than either attempting to listen and take notes concurrently or taking no notes at all.[12] By alternating listening and note taking, you can control when you write, as well as when you listen. You also have a better chance to put down in abbreviated form what you understand about the presentation, and will find the notes are more useful in later review for an exam. In brief, engage your mind in active listening before you engage your hand in writing notes.

Taking notes enhances comprehension and recall following a presentation. By alternating notetaking and listening, you can gain time to think about the information during the presentation. Later, your notes will be more meaningful than if you had not taken the time to listen critically.

Second, as you take notes or simply listen to a speaker, follow this pattern: review, relate, and anticipate. *Review* what the speaker has said, both during and immediately after the presentation. Take the time to summarize the main points of the message and any factual material that appears essential to recall later. The task of reviewing will be easier if you also *relate* the message to what you already know. Consider how consistent the message is with your own knowledge, and consider how you might use additional information in the future. Finally, *anticipate* what the speaker might say next. Given an awareness of the pattern of development, what is the logical direction of the speech? Use the anticipation stage as a way of continuing to focus on the message. Whether the speaker obliges you and does the "logical" thing is less important than the fact that you are interacting with the speaker's logic as you perceive it and are thus in a position to follow the ideas to their conclusion. Reviewing, relating, and anticipating are useful activities during the time differential between your rate of comprehension and the speaker's rate of speaking to keep your attention focused on the message.

There are several other ways you can enhance your classroom experience by actively seeking to improve listening habits. For example, your speech course can be the laboratory in which you sharpen your listening skills. You can practice critiquing other students' speeches and take part in postspeech discussions as a means of checking your understanding of main points and support material. Do not hesitate to provide direct feedback to your classmates by pointing out what was good, what worked, what did not seem to work as well, what came across very clearly, and what remained cloudy. Good, constructive criticism can be either positive or negative but is always supportive. Oral commentary not only provides a beginning speaker with much-needed reaction from peers; it forces you, as a listener, to attend closely to the message. In this way, both you and the speaker gain; the speaker acquires a sense of the reactions being generated by the message and its style of presentation; you gain further proficiency in the art of listening well. You also can listen critically to discussions, lectures, oral presentations, and student-teacher exchanges in other classes, identifying effective and ineffective communicative techniques in a variety of different settings. By listening carefully to speakers outside of class and noting how well their audiences listen, you can develop your own understanding of what works and why.

Speaker Responsibilities

As you have already seen, effective listening depends upon the speaker's fulfilling certain responsibilities. The following material highlights strategies that you, as a speaker, can use to facilitate listener comprehension. These can be discussed in terms of speaker-related strategies and message-related strategies.

Speaker-Related Strategies

Several of the primary variables that affect listening are related to speaker characteristics.

1. *Rate of delivery.* Speaking between 120 and 250 words a minute on the average is an acceptable rate for listener comprehension. While listeners can comprehend much faster rates of speech, this speed allows time to process the message; to engage in reviewing, relating, and anticipating activity while the message is being presented; and to take notes during the "down time" in active listening.

2. *General fluency of speech.* The easier a speech is to hear, the more effective listening behavior becomes. If listeners must strain to hear the speaker or to comprehend words spoken in a thick accent, their listening focus will be on these factors instead of on the message. Speaking clearly and more slowly if you have a strong accent and avoiding frequent pauses or false starts will enhance listeners' perceptions of your general fluency and facilitate active listening behavior.

3. *Visibility.* Position yourself so that you can be seen by all listeners. This will enable them to focus more easily on the message. If there are columns or other obstructions in an auditorium, and the seating arrangement has not taken this into account, you may suggest that people move into unobstructed viewing areas.

4. *Credibility.* As noted earlier in this chapter, your credibility as a speaker influences an audience's perception of you and your message. If you have had a negative experience with the audience in the past, you should realize that, although your credibility may be low, it is not necessarily fixed at that level. By presenting a well-prepared, cogently argued speech with sincerity and conviction, you can go a long way toward improving the audience's estimate of your competence as a speaker.

5. *Speaker likability.* If the audience is already positively disposed toward you as a person, you have a better chance of being heard favorably. If not, the advice concerning credibility applies here as well. Even if your listeners do not like you as a person, you can strive to present a speech in such a way that they must respect you as a competent, well-meaning individual with an idea to offer. In this way, you can direct listener attention to your message, rather than to your personal relationship with the audience.

6. *Similarity in values.* Critical listening depends in part on your listeners' perceptions of the degree of similarity between their values and your own. If the values are generally in accord, listener activity can be expected to be fairly high. If the values are in discord, you can expect some listeners to tune you out simply because they disagree with the value premises underlying your argument.[13] You will learn more about strategies for dealing with discrepant values in Chapter 16.

Message-Related Strategies

As suggested, controlling the message can enhance your chances of being listened to in a critical manner. The following attributes of message design will improve your chances of being heard.

1. *Clear language.* The clearer your message, the less confused your listeners will be. In turn, they will have less reason to drop out and neglect to return. If you use many words that are unfamiliar to the audience or open to a variety of interpretations in the context of the message, you are not helping yourself gain a favorable hearing. When you present concepts that are difficult to comprehend, restate them in different ways so your listeners can understand the material.

2. *Active voice.* In stylistic terms, use active rather than passive voice to give greater emphasis to your ideas. Active voice emphasizes the "doer of the deed," whereas passive voice reverses the emphasis to the recipient of the action. Instead of saying "It was decided by the board of directors

to postpone action," say "The board of directors decided to postpone action." A consistent passive voice may create equally passive listeners, as it makes the speaker appear less involved in the actions being described.

3. *Organized message.* In preparing your speech, adopt a pattern of organization and use it consistently to develop your main ideas. Anticipate points at which your listeners may have difficulty following the speech, and build in internal summaries or transitions to guide them to the next idea.

4. *Capturing and holding attention.* Although some listeners will come to the presentation with a high motivation to listen actively, others may not. Even those who are motivated will vary their listening behavior during your speech. Thus, you need to give the audience members reasons for wanting to listen to your speech. This is largely a matter of gaining and retaining their attention and recognizing that its intensity will ebb and flow during the speech. Speakers must constantly watch for lapses of attention and take steps to secure it.[14] Attention and strategies for gaining it are discussed in Chapter 3.

In addition to these strategies, any action you can take as a speaker to diminish the negative impact of the barriers to effective listening will enhance your message. If possible, control factors in the physical environment, such as noise and temperature, to reduce distractions. Time your presentation to meet the needs and expectations of the audience insofar as possible. Interpret audience feedback during the presentation to help you modify any ideas that appear to be causing confusion or uncertainty. If the listeners perceive that you are making a sincere effort to communicate your thoughts, they will tend to be receptive and will make the effort necessary to be more effective listeners. Your response to feedback is one measure of your desire to communicate effectively. If you look for nonverbal cues from the audience and notice signs of confusion, quickly reassess the way you are presenting the information. You can exert more control over audience comprehension and listening behavior by rephrasing unclear points, by summarizing to clarify and reemphasize your main ideas, and by presenting a cogent summary of the speech's significance—its value to the listeners in terms of their own interests. If time permits, you also can improve audience comprehension by asking for questions; your answers can clear up any confusion or misunderstanding that still remains.

Chapter Summary

A common feature of all listening behavior is the listener's desire to *comprehend* a message. In addition, listening is a *transactional* enterprise—it is a two-way street, a joint responsibility of speaker and listener to maximize the transmission of ideas. A third common feature is that listening is *interpretive;* meaning is not the sole property of either speaker or listener but is created by both participants in the act of communication. Listening is *empathic* when the objective is to put yourself in another person's place, to assume her or his feelings as your own. *Critical* listening is neither *passive* nor *negative.* Rather, it is active attendance to what is said, with a view to evaluating the worth of a performance or an idea. *Appreciative* listening attaches a value to a speech or an event; *discriminative* listening evaluates a speaker's *reasons* to determine whether they are worthy of adoption. In any type of listening, both parties must be sensitive to the points of possible breakdown; *weak extrinsic motivation, personal* and *environmental constraints*, and *poor timing* can impede effective listening behavior. Through the analysis of *self, speaker*, and *message,* you as a listener can exert greater control over your own behavior and improve your comprehension and recall of the message. Through conscious attention to your responsibilities as a speaker you can help diminish the potential causes of poor listening, enhance your credibility, and increase the chances that your message will be received favorably.

Reference Notes

1. See studies reviewed by Andrew Wolvin and Carolyn Coakley, *Listening* (Dubuque, IA: W. C. Brown Co., 1982), Chapter 1; and Kittie W. Watson and Larry L. Barker, "Listening Behavior: Definition and Measurement," in Robert N. Bostrom, ed., *Communication Yearbook 8* (Beverly Hills: Sage Publications, 1984), 178–94.

2. Gary T. Hunt and Louis P. Cusella, "A Field Study of Listening Needs in Organizations," *Communication Education* 32 (1983): 393–401.

3. John R. Stewart, "Interpretive Listening: An Alternative to Empathy," *Communication Education* 32 (1983): 379–92.

4. Ronald C. Arnett and Gordon Nakagawa, "The Assumptive Roots of Empathic Listening: A Critique," *Communication Education* 32 (1983): 368–78; Karen B. McComb and Fredric M. Jablin, "Verbal Correlates of Empathic Listening and Employment Interview Outcomes," *Communication Monographs* 51 (1984): 353–71.

5. For a discussion of these issues, see Carl Weaver, *Human Listening* (Indianapolis: Bobbs-Merrill Publishers, 1972), Chapter 1; Lyman K. Steil, Larry L. Barker, and Kittie W. Watson, *Effective Listening: Key to Your Success* (Reading, MA: Addison-Wesley Publishing Co., 1983).

6. Michael J. Beatty, R. R. Behnke, and D. L. Froelich, "Effects of Achievement Incentive and Presentation Rate on Listening Comprehension," *Quarterly Journal of Speech* 66 (1980): 193–200; Larry R. Smeltzer and Kittie W. Watson, "Listening: An Empirical Comparison of Discussion Length and Level of Incentive," *Central States Speech Journal* 35 (1984): 166–70; Charles R. Petrie, Jr., and Susan D. Carrell, "The Relationship of Motivation, Listening Capability, Initial Information, and Verbal Organizational Ability to Lecture Comprehension and Retention," *Communication Monographs* 43 (1976): 187–94.

7. Arthur R. Miller, "Are You a Lousy Listener?" in George L. Grice and M. Anway Jones, eds., *Business and Professional Communication: Selected Readings* (Dubuque, IA: Kendall/Hunt Publishing Co., 1986), 77–80.

8. For a discussion of personal and environmental constraints (also called internal and external perceptual fields), see Wayne C. Minnick, *The Art of Persuasion* (Boston: Houghton Mifflin Co., 1957), 38–41.

9. Bruce E. Gronbeck, "Rhetorical Timing in Public Communication," *Central States Speech Journal* 25 (1974): 84–94.

10. Michael J. Beatty and Steven K. Payne, "Effects of Social Facilitation on Listening Comprehension," *Communication Quarterly* 32 (1984): 37–40.

11. McComb and Jablin; John A Daly, James C. McCroskey, and Virginia P. Richmond, "Judgments of Quality, Listening, and Understanding Based upon Vocal Activity," *Southern Speech Communication Journal* 41 (1976): 189–97.

12. Watson and Barker.

13. Watson and Barker.

14. Watson and Barker.

Key Terms

comprehension	*critical listening*
direct feedback	*passive listening*
indirect feedback	*appreciative listening*
delayed feedback	*discriminative listening*
empathy	*extrinsic motives*
therapeutic listening	*rhetorical timing*

Problems and Probes

1. How effectively do you listen to others? In this exercise, you are asked to assess your attentiveness as a listener across a variety of situations. On a scale of 1 to 10 (with 10 being high), rate the effectiveness of your listening behavior in the following situations:

_____ a. In a class in which the subject is of interest to you.

_____ b. In a class in which the subject is not of personal interest to you.

_____ c. In a social conversation setting—for example, having coffee with friends or relaxing with co-workers.

_____ d. In a work-related situation in which a supervisor is giving instructions.

_____ e. In a conversation with a close friend.

_____ f. At a lecture you are attending due to personal interest.

_____ g. At a lecture you are required to attend; you can expect to be tested on the material presented.

First, think about your responses—if there are differences in listening "quality" across these settings (and it would be surprising if there weren't) what accounts for them? Second, ask five close friends—people who have observed you in situations similar to those above—to rate your behavior in each situation according to their perception of you as a listener. Collate the responses—are there significant variances between your assessment and the perceptions of others? What might account for them? (See Steil, Barker, and Watson, *Effective Listening,* for an alternate "self-report" of listening skills.)

2. The Greek concept of *kairos* was introduced in a discussion of *rhetorical timing.* As you go through a "typical" day interacting with friends and listening to peers or professors present material in classroom settings, keep an informal diary of the relationship between appropriate timing and your own listening behavior. Which times were most appropriate for listening? Which were not? What accounts for those times in which listening was a positive experience, and for those in which it was a struggle to listen effectively (and one you may have lost)? What can you do as a listener to exert more control over the appropriateness of timing in listening to others? Use the notes in your informal diary as a basis for contributing to a small group discussion of timing as it relates to listening.

Communication Activities

1. You have been asked to give a brief speech to a group of prospective high-school teachers. Your assigned topic is "Ways of Faking Attention as a Listener in a Classroom." Develop a three-to-four-minute speech in which you describe specific mannerisms that students use to appear attentive when, in fact, they are "faking it."

2. You have been asked to present a brief oral statement to a philosophy class on the significance of the following passage from the philosopher Epictetus: "Nature has given to man one tongue, but two ears that we may hear from others twice as much as we speak" (circa 300 B.C.). Using information from this chapter and other sources on listening (see the Reference Notes for this chapter), develop a four-to-five-minute speech explaining why this statement appears to have lasting value as part of conventional wisdom about communication relationships.

3. Working in small groups in the classroom, participate in an exercise to test listening and comprehension skills. Each person in turn will explain a technical term to the others in the group (you might select one from another subject you are studying, such as "existentialism," "black hole," or "oxymoron"). Start with one group member presenting his or her term: the others will listen to the speaker's brief explanation without taking notes, then write on a notecard what they think they heard. After all explanations have been heard, each speaker should collect the cards on his or her presentation and compare the written "understandings" with the original explanation. If there are discrepancies, discuss with group members what might have helped them listen more effectively.

4. For any round of speeches in your class, the professor can ask that each student listen to the speech being presented and write down the speaker's main points and purpose as the listener understands them. Following each speech, class members can compare their lists with what the speaker thought he or she was presenting. For this exercise, focus on what the speaker might have done to enable class members to listen more effectively, in order to reduce any discrepancies that arose between presentation and reception of the message.

CHAPTER THREE

Getting Started: Planning and Preparing Speeches

*T*he first two chapters have provided a foundation for understanding the *process* of oral communication. Now we will turn our attention to the *practice* of speech, beginning with planning. Planning ahead saves time and keeps you from wandering aimlessly through the library or waiting for inspiration at your desk. We will examine the seven steps of speech planning and preparation and then will discuss the actual presentation—the delivery—of your first speeches. We will also discuss three problems beginning speakers face— finding a method of presentation, getting and holding listeners' attention, and gaining self-confidence.

The Essential Steps in Speech Preparation

There is no magic formula for getting ready to talk publicly. The task can be frustrating; however, if you generally follow a series of steps, either in the order presented here or in another that works for you, you will be ahead of the game and in firm control. Those steps—selecting and narrowing the subject; determining the general and specific purposes; determining the central idea or claim; analyzing the audience and the occasion; gathering the speech material; making an outline; and practicing aloud—will all be examined in this chapter, in various degrees of completeness, for some will have complete chapters of their own. This chapter, however, will prepare you to give your first classroom speeches.

Selecting and Narrowing the Subject

The most difficult task for many speakers, especially in a situation as artificial as a speech classroom, is to choose a subject. The following are three
important considerations in selecting a subject:

- What do you know something about?
- What are you interested in talking about?
- What topics can you relate to the audience's situation and interests?

You might begin by listing those topics you have knowledge about, circling
the ones you are willing to talk about in front of others, and thinking about
ways you can relate them to your listeners. Before committing yourself to a
firm choice, though, check your possible subjects in the next two steps; be
sure your choice fits the purposes your instructor intended and that you can
phrase it as a strong central idea or claim.

Once you have selected a workable topic, narrow it so that you can cover
it in the time allowed. How much can you say about a particular subject in
five minutes? You certainly could not tell your listeners everything there
is to know about next month's charity marathon, but you could discuss
(a) differences in strategy among 5K, 10K, half-marathon, and full marathon
races, (b) simple conditioning techniques to help students prepare for a 5K
race, (c) what happens to runners physiologically and psychologically during
a race, or (d) how students can sign up sponsors for races in your school's
town. The narrower your subject, the more fully you will be able to explain
or support the essential points. Also, a narrower subject covered with more
examples and materials usually is more interesting than a once-over-lightly
talk; include a variety of illustrations, data, testimony, and other supporting
material.

Determining the General and Specific Purposes

Once you have completed the first step—selecting and narrowing your subject—you can focus more precisely on why you want to talk about this
subject. What do you want this speech to accomplish? Answering this question involves consideration of both general and specific purposes.

General Purpose. What is the general state you wish your listeners to be
in when you complete the speech? Are you, for example, simply trying to
tell them something they do not—but should—know? Are you seeking to
alter the way they feel about a social, economic, or political issue? Are you
interested in having them take a specific action as a result of your speech?
Answering one of these questions affirmatively will help focus your **general
purpose.**

Specific Purpose. Given your topic, specifically what do you want the audience to know, feel, value, or do? Within the context of a general purpose, a

THE ESSENTIAL STEPS IN SPEECH PREPARATION

7 Practicing Aloud

6 Arranging Materials into an Outline

5 Gathering the Speech Material

4 Analyzing the Audience and Occasion

3 Determining the Central Idea or Claim

2 Determining the General and Specific Purposes

1 Selecting and Narrowing the Subject

specific purpose focuses attention on the particular *substantive* goal of your presentation. Once this is determined, you will be in a position to describe the exact response you want from your listeners: "I want my audience to understand how to prepare for a 5K race." In this instance, you want to inform your audience (general purpose), but, more specifically, you want them to know what steps to take in getting in condition to race.

Determining the Central Idea or Claim

This step in the initial phase flows directly from the preceding step. Can you state your message in a single sentence? If you are seeking to explain an idea or to inform an audience about a process or event, that sentence is the **central idea.** It is a declarative statement that summarizes your speech: "There are five stages in getting ready for a 5K race." In speeches that aim at persuading an audience to adopt a specific attitude or take a particular action, the **claim** summarizes the intent of your argument: "As one means of achieving or maintaining a healthy body, you should consider running."

By this point in the planning process, your speech should be focused precisely on what you wish to convey to your audience. The central idea, in the context of your general and specific purposes, serves as a constant guide as you move into the next phase of preparation. As you research and outline the substance of your message, the relevance of material you include will be governed by these prior decisions. Think of each speech you develop as an instrument for winning a particular response from your listeners. Selecting and narrowing your topic, determining the general and specific purposes, and setting forth the central idea or claim will allow you to identify that response with care and precision.

Analyzing the Audience and Occasion

Listeners are the targets of all speeches. A good public speech, therefore, not only reflects your desires and interests as a speaker but also is responsive to the interests, preferences, and values of the audience to whom it is presented. As noted in the initial step, your selection of a subject should remain tentative until you have considered the audience members. How would they feel about the topic? To do this successfully, you need to analyze the people who compose the group—their age, gender, social-political-economic status, origin, background, prejudices, and fears. In other words, you need to gain a sense of how they will react to the topic you have chosen. You can help yourself decide on a topic if you are aware of how much the audience already knows about the subject, how interested they are in hearing about it, what they may believe in and value, and what their probable attitudes are toward you and your subject. In a public-speaking class, you can estimate these factors by listening to comments made during class discussions and by asking some class members what they think about your tentative plans. In other circumstances, gathering this information may be more difficult, requiring you to become more creative in assessing your audience. Regardless of how it is done, **audience analysis** is a primary determinant of success in speechmaking.

The audience is not the only factor that will make a difference in your choice of topics. As noted in Chapter 1, you also will need to consider the setting and circumstances in which you will be speaking. Are there specific rules or customs that will be important to know and to follow? How long will you have to speak? Will you precede or follow other speakers? What impact will events before or after your speech have on topic selection? Will the physical circumstances be amenable to your speaking style? If not, can you alter them prior to the speech? For example, will you need to obtain a microphone in order to be heard, or will you need to rearrange the physical setting in order to be seen by all audience members? Analyzing the occasion involves serious issues (the impact of group traditions or customs) and mundane issues (physical setting). Your responses to both sets of issues are important in deciding what to talk about; by having this information in advance, you will be more comfortable about the circumstances and about the expectations the audience will have when it is your time to speak.

Gathering the Speech Material

As you move into this phase of preparation, you will be assembling the materials needed to build your speech. Previous to this point, you have assessed your existing pool of information on the subject and made some tentative decisions about personal experiences and other data that could be incorporated into the speech. In most cases, you will find that this knowledge and experience are insufficient. You will need to gather additional information with which to develop, expand, or reinforce your main ideas. You may gather valuable materials from conversations and interviews, from such printed resources as newspapers and periodicals, or from radio or television programs. Thorough research is essential, because you never know when a listener will know more than you do. Good speeches are packed with examples, illustrations, stories, figures, and quotations that a speaker can discover only through systematic and careful research.

Arranging Materials into an Outline

As you assemble the needed material, you can save time by making a preliminary list of the main ideas that you wish to cover in developing your central idea or claim. This list will help guide your selection of specific supportive materials and will help you check to make sure they fit together into a coherent pattern. Your list also can serve as an initial rough outline of the sequence of ideas to be developed. You should wait until you have assembled all of the material to develop a final outline. By keeping the outline flexible, you can adjust the sequence of information as you continue your research.

We will consider outlining in more detail in a later chapter. For the present, follow two rules: *(1)* arrange your ideas in a clear and systematic order and *(2)* preserve the unity of your speech by making sure that each point is directly related to your specific purpose.

Practicing Aloud

You complete your preparation of a speech by trying it out—practicing it in the way you hope to deliver it to your audience. You probably will find that the best method is to talk through the outline, following your planned sequence of ideas, facts, and illustrations. At first your voice will sound odd to you; then, it will become easier to talk to yourself in an empty room, and you will gain self-confidence. Talk through the material over and over until you are comfortable with the sequence, the phrasing, and the clarity of the ideas. The better you know your speech, the stronger your presentation will be.

When you can go through the speech several times without forgetting any points or hesitating unduly in putting your thoughts into words, your preparation is complete. As you practice speaking from your outline, keep a mental image of your listeners and project your speech as though you were actually talking to them. A good speaker talks *with* people, not *at* them; work for that attitude and tone.

These seven steps—from selecting and narrowing a subject through practicing aloud—take you to the brink of public speech communication with real audiences. Good work on the preparation and practice leads to effective performance.

Speech preparation involves gathering the materials you need to build the speech, arranging them into an outline, and practicing your delivery. Preparation and practice lead to effective performance.

Delivering Your First Speeches

For most beginners, delivering their first speeches is very difficult. Many feel anxious and nervous. You may say to yourself, "I'm too nervous to stand up there." "What do I do with my hands?" "Will people think I'm dumb?" Self-doubts, from actual fright to a lack of self-confidence, creep into every speaker's mind; the trick, of course, is to learn to control them. In this chapter, we will deal with three strategies for self-control: (1) selecting the right method of presentation; (2) focusing not on yourself but on capturing and holding the attention of your listeners, and (3) developing and communicating confidence.

Selecting the Method of Presentation

Which method should you use to present your speech? Your choice should be based on several criteria, including the type of speaking occasion, the seriousness and purpose of your speech, your audience analysis, and your own strengths and weaknesses as a speaker. Attention to these considerations will help you decide whether your method of presentation should be (1) impromptu, (2) memorized, (3) read from a manuscript, or (4) extemporaneous.

The Impromptu Speech. An **impromptu speech** is delivered on the spur of the moment without lengthy preparation. The speaker relies entirely on previous knowledge and skill. The ability to speak impromptu is useful in an emergency, but you should limit your use of this method to situations in which you are unable to anticipate the need to speak. When using this method, try to focus on a single idea, carefully relating all significant details to it. This strategy will help you avoid the rambling, incoherent "remarks" that the impromptu method often produces.

The Memorized Speech. As its name implies, the **memorized speech** is written out word for word and committed to memory. Although a few speakers are able to use this method effectively, it presents certain problems. Usually memorization results in a stilted, inflexible presentation; the speaker may be either excessively formal and oratorical or hurry through the speech—pouring out words with no thought as to their meaning. Using a memorized speech makes it difficult for the speaker to take advantage of audience feedback to adjust ideas as the speech progresses. If you memorize your speech, remember that you tend to use more formal language when writing than you do when speaking. Be sure that your speech does not sound like a written essay.

The Read Speech. Like the memorized speech, the **read speech** is written out, but, in this method, the speaker reads from a manuscript. If extremely careful wording is required—as in the president's message to Congress, in which a slip of the tongue could undermine domestic or foreign policies, or in the presentation of scholarly reports, where exact, concise exposition is required—the read speech is appropriate. The ability to read a speech effectively is valuable in certain situations, but this method should not be used unnecessarily. No matter how experienced you are, when you read your message, you will inevitably sacrifice some of the freshness and spontaneity necessary for effective communication. Again, as with the memorized speech, it is difficult to react to audience feedback. Also, the speech may sound somewhat stilted because you use more formal, written language. If you use this method, "talk through" the speech as you are writing it to ensure an oral style.

The Extemporaneous Speech.   Representing a middle course between the memorized or read speech and the speech that is delivered impromptu, the **extemporaneous speech** requires careful planning and a detailed outline. Working from an outline, practice the speech aloud, expressing the ideas somewhat differently each time you go through it. Use the outline to fix the order of ideas in your mind, and practice various wordings to develop accuracy, conciseness, and flexibility of expression. If the extemporaneous method is used carelessly, the result will resemble an impromptu speech—a fact that sometimes leads to a confusion of these two terms. A proper use of the method, however, will produce a speech that is nearly as polished as a memorized one and certainly more vigorous, flexible, and spontaneous. With few exceptions, the speeches you deliver will probably be extemporaneous. For that reason, most of the advice in this textbook assumes the use of that method.

Capturing and Holding Attention: Nine Factors

Listeners' behaviors vary considerably, thanks to thoughts and sensations in their internal and external environments. Essentially, your listeners need reasons for *wanting* to listen. Yet, even when you have their attention, it tends to ebb and flow. So, you must constantly watch for lapses in attention. James Albert Winans, a twentieth-century pioneer in public speaking instruction, expressed this problem succinctly: "Attention determines response." If you cannot gain and hold attention, you are in deep trouble.

What is attention? For our purposes, it can be thought of as *focus* on one element in a given environment, with the result that other elements fade and, for all practical purposes, cease to exist.[1] Consider, for example, a rock concert. Near the end of his concert, Billy Joel breaks into the verses of "Innocent Man." The crowd goes wild, and you join in the cheering. You love that song. You all become quiet during the middle verses, but, by the end, you cannot help yourself—you are singing all of the choruses at the top of your lungs, near to crying for the sheer sweetness of it all. At the end, the place erupts. Billy Joel obliges by repeating the last verse and chorus. Again the place explodes for three or four minutes. As the screaming finally ebbs, only then do you look around. You have spilled your soft drink on your new jeans, the person sitting to your right is sobbing uncontrollably, and you have to use the bathroom. Now that is paying attention! It is this focusing on one message source, or stimulus, to the greater or lesser exclusion of others that is called "attention."

You are not Billy Joel singing "Innocent Man," however; how can you capture and hold attention? Of course, a *vigorous and varied delivery* will help. Likewise, your reputation and trustworthiness (positive *ethos*) can command respect—and attention. *Lively and picturesque language* gives audiences "word-pictures" and makes it easier for them to stay with you. *Fundamentally, however, you will capture and hold attention through the types of ideas you present.* Some types of ideas or images have greater attention value than others.

Ideas can be presented in a variety of ways that have high attention value. Often called the **factors of attention,** these include the following:

- Activity
- Reality
- Proximity
- Familiarity
- Novelty
- Suspense
- Conflict
- Humor
- The vital

Activity.   Suppose you have two TV sets side by side. One shows a singer performing motionless behind a microphone; the other set carries an MTV music video with motorcycles, dry-ice clouds, and three performers with orange hair running around the stage. Which one will you look at? Likewise, ideas that "move" tend to attract attention. Stories in which something happens or in which there are moments of uncertainty usually have attention value.

In addition, a speech as a whole should "move"—it should march or press forward. Nothing is so boring as a talk that seems to stand still, providing far too much detail on a minor point. Instructions and demonstrations, particularly, demand orderly, systematic progress. Keep moving ahead, and an audience will be more likely to stay with you.

Reality.   The earliest words you learned were names for tangible objects—"Mama," "milk," and "cookie." While the ability to abstract—to generalize—is one of the marks of human intelligence, nonetheless there persists in all of us an interest in concrete reality, the here-and-now of sense data. When you speak, refer to specific events, persons, places, and happenings. A few paragraphs ago, this text might have said: "Consider, for example, a rock concert. Near the end of a concert, the singer breaks into the verses of one of his well-known songs. . . ." As an example, such a depersonalized anecdote

THE FACTORS OF ATTENTION

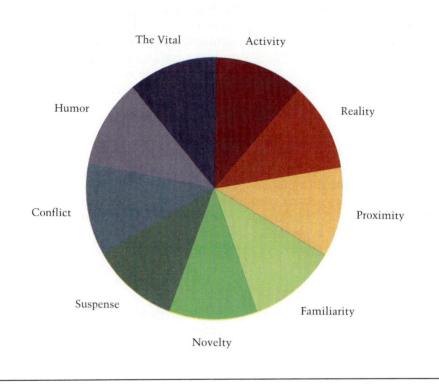

about "a singer" does not have as much human interest and memorability as one about a specific, named performer. Audiences can hang ideas on specific details.

Proximity. A direct reference to something nearby in time or space often orients an audience wondering what you are talking about. For example, when discussing the best methods for test preparation, a reference to next week's midterm can tie the subject directly to listeners' experiences. Consider the following introduction: "Do you realize how much fast food is consumed on this campus? Within four blocks of this classroom are nine restaurants, including a McDonald's, a Wendy's, and a Godfather's Pizza parlor. Two are local submarine houses. Even the student union runs a fast-food counter. A key question you patrons face is: what are your lunch habits doing to your nutrition—to your body and your mind?" Such an introduction brings the topic home.

Familiarity. Especially in the face of new or strange ideas, references to the familiar are attention sustaining. A common device here is the *analogy.* If a speaker explains that the London postal or zip codes are arranged like directions on a compass, with the initial letters indicating directions and the next set of numbers representing degrees or positions, then the speaker is using something familiar to explain something unfamiliar. He or she probably will hold your attention. The familiar is also comfortable. We like to sing songs we know and to hear the old stories about Washington, Lincoln, and Kennedy. We probably have such likes because we share "the familiar" with others, and that sharing brings us closer together. Hence, a comfortable anecdote—if it is not a cliché—is attention holding.

Novelty.   As the old adage has it, when a dog bites a man, it is an accident; when a man bites a dog, it is news. Novel happenings, dramatic advances, or unusual developments attract wide notice. Two special types of novelty are *size* and *contrast.* Insofar as size is concerned, especially large or small objects or amounts attract attention. For example, reference to a $10,000 automobile or to a $90,000 home would not stand out as unusual, but reference to a $30,000 automobile or to a $300,000 home would. In a speech on the high cost of national defense, a speaker caught the attention of his listeners with this sentence: "Considering that it costs more than $5000 to equip an average soldier for combat, it is disquieting to learn that in a year his equipment will be 60 percent obsolete."[2]

Although attention getting in themselves, large and small figures are even more compelling when thrown into contrast with their opposites. Former vice-presidential candidate Geraldine Ferraro, in comparing the earnings of men and women, made this observation:

> I wanted to find out how many women in America earn more than $60,000 a year. I picked that number, frankly, because that is what I, as a member of Congress, earn. I learned that there are only 18,000 women in the entire United States, working full-time, who earn more than $60,000. We represent just one-tenth of one percent of all the women who work full-time in America. By contrast, 885,000 men, 2.1 percent of full-time male workers, are in the $60,000 plus bracket.[3]

In using novel materials, be careful not to inject elements that are so different or unusual that they are entirely unfamiliar. As you have learned, your listeners must at least know what you are talking about. They must be able to relate what you say to things they know and—preferably—have a degree of experience with. Best results are achieved by the proper combination of the new and the old, of the novel and the familiar. Note, too, that novelty may gain attention but will not necessarily hold it.

Suspense.   A large part of the interest in mystery stories arises from uncertainty about their outcome. When giving a speech, you can create uncertainty by pointing out results that have mysterious or unknown causes or by calling attention to forces that threaten uncertain effects. Introduce suspense into the stories you use to illustrate your ideas, especially in lectures or even in demonstrations. Mention valuable information you expect to divulge later in your talk but which requires an understanding of what you are now saying.

Conflict. The opposition of forces compels attention; just look at the ratings for prime-time TV soap operas, which play off extremely strong interpersonal conflicts for their plots. Conflict, like suspense, suggests uncertainty; like activity or movement, it is dynamic. Hence, when President Jimmy Carter wanted to get the American public moving on energy conservation, he talked about energy saving as "the moral equivalent of war." The word "war"—suggesting conflict—gave him a dynamic metaphor. You can carry this further; take time to describe the *details* of the battles. For example, in an informative speech on big-city downtown renovations, you could describe the struggle between the downtown merchants, who want investments in parking lots and attractive visual projects, and the mall owners on the outskirts, who argue that such city-sponsored construction is wasting taxpayers' money and giving the downtown merchants an unfair competitive advantage. Talking merely about urban renewal and public dollars would not have nearly as much attention value as a description of the fight between downtown and outlying investment groups.

Humor. People usually pay attention when they are enjoying themselves. Humor relaxes both the speaker and the listeners. It provides an attention-getting change of pace, and it can establish a link between you and your audience—"the group that laughs together, stays together." When using humor to capture and hold attention, however, observe two guidelines:

1. *Be relevant.* Beware of wandering from the point, of telling a joke just for the sake of telling a joke. If it is not reinforcing an important point, forget it.

2. *Use good taste.* You probably do not want to tell a knee-slapper during a funeral and should refrain from telling off-color stories in a speech, which can offend audience members.

The Vital. People nearly always pay attention to matters that affect their health, reputation, property, or employment. When you hear "Students who take an internship while in college find jobs after school three times as fast as those who do not," you are likely to pay attention. Appealing to the vital, therefore, is a matter of *personalizing* your topic and supporting materials, making them directly and unavoidably relevant, not just to groups, but to specific individuals in your audience.

The vital, humor, conflict, suspense, novelty, familiarity, proximity, reality, and movement—these nine attention getters should be in your arsenal of rhetorical weapons. They give your speech sparkle, vivacity, and force;

they help keep you and your words squarely in the middle of listeners' external and internal environments. They are designed to force an audience to keep coming back for more.

Developing and Communicating Confidence

The third matter you need to think about when speaking in front of a real audience is yourself. You need to consider how you can develop an appropriate amount of self-confidence and then convey that air of dynamism and assuredness to your listeners.

Developing Confidence. You may well feel anxious. You do not wish to fail, and, at times, this fear of failure may overcome your desire to speak. If you have ever been reluctant to raise your hand in class and answer a question, you understand how apprehension can affect your behavior. We can distinguish between two broad classes of communication apprehension, state apprehension and trait apprehension.[4] **State apprehension** refers to the anxiety you feel in a particular situation. You may find it easy to talk with friends but feel very uncomfortable when being interviewed for a job. The phenomenon known as "stage fright" is a common form of state apprehension. In its extreme form, stage fright is experienced physiologically as clammy hands, trembling knees, a dry mouth, and a weak or cracking voice. Psychologically, stage fright sometimes is experienced as a mental block—forgetting what you were going to say. Knowing that you are going to be evaluated by others in a formal setting, whether in a classroom or in a town meeting, can cause some anxious moments.

While some aspects of nervousness are characteristic of the situation, others are a part of your own personality. The second class of apprehension, called **trait apprehension,** refers to your level of anxiety as you face any communication situation. A high level of anxiety may lead people to withdraw from situations in which interpersonal or public communication is required. By attacking your trait fears as they manifest in speaking before others, you will be in a better position to reduce your overall level of anxiety. Although there is no foolproof program for developing self-confidence, the following are some ways to achieve the confidence necessary to complete the speaking task.

1. *Realize that tension and nervousness are normal and even, in part, beneficial to speakers.* Fear is a normal part of living; learn how to control it and make it work for you. Remember that the tension you feel can provide you with energy and alertness. As adrenalin pours into your bloodstream, you experience a physical charge, increasing bodily movement, and psychological acuity. A baseball pitcher who is not "pumped up" before a big game may have a fastball with no zip. A speaker who is not similarly charged will come across as dull and lifeless.

2. *Take comfort in the fact that tension is reduced by the act of speaking.* As you talk and discover that your audience accepts you and some of the things you are saying, your nervousness will tend to dissipate. Physiologically, your body is using up the excess adrenalin it generated; psychologically, your ego is getting positive reinforcement. Shortly after you begin, you realize that your prior preparation is working in your favor and that you have the situation under control. Thus, the very act of talking aloud reduces fear.

3. *Talk about topics that interest you.* Speech anxiety arises in part because of self-centeredness; sometimes you are more concerned with your personal appearance and performance than with your topic. One means of reducing that anxiety is to select topics that are of deep interest to you, topics that will take your mind off of yourself. This makes the situation topic-centered rather than self-centered.

4. *Talk about subjects with which you are familiar.* Confidence born of knowledge increases your perceived credibility and helps control your nervousness. Have you ever wondered why you could talk at length with friends about your favorite hobby, sport, or political interests without feeling anxious, only to find yourself in a nervous state when standing in front of an audience to talk about something you just read in *Newsweek?* Knowing something about the subject may be part of the answer. Subject mastery is closely related to self-mastery.

5. *Analyze both the situation and the audience.* The more you know about the audience and about what is expected of you in a particular situation, the less there is to fear. In the speech classroom, students are usually less nervous during their second speech than during their first. They are more comfortable with the audience and are more aware of the demands of the situation. The same is true in other settings as well; careful analysis of the listeners and their expectations goes a long way toward reducing a natural fear of the unknown.

6. *Speak in public as often as you can.* Sheer repetition of the public-speaking experience will not eliminate your fears, but it will make them more controllable. As you have just seen, speaking a number of times in front of the same group can help reduce anxiety. Repeated experiences with different audiences and situations also will help increase your self-assurance and poise, which, in turn, will lessen your apprehension. As a student, force yourself to speak up in class discussions, join in discussions with friends and others, and contribute in meetings of organizations to which you belong. Find time to talk with people of all ages. Attend public meetings on occasion and make a few comments.

In summary, there are no shortcuts to developing self-confidence about speaking in public. For most of us, gaining self-confidence is partly a matter

Shyness and Public Speaking

*D*o you think of yourself as shy? Does it affect your ability to talk in public? What can be done about it? A leading psychologist, Stanford's Philip G. Zimbardo, defines shyness as "an apprehensiveness about certain social situations due to excessive preoccupation with being critically evaluated, resulting in a variety of behavioral, physical, cognitive, and emotional reactions" (Zimbardo, Glossary, p. xv). Shyness manifests itself in many ways, as the accompanying table indicates. To get at its roots in individuals, Zimbardo and his colleagues developed the Stanford Shyness Survey.

Using such instruments as the Shyness Survey, therapists tailor treatment programs to individual needs. They can help individuals build new social skills, teaching them how to act in situations that are new or strange. They suggest exercises to boost self-esteem if it appears that a person consistently thinks of him- or herself in negative terms. If a shy person's physiological reactions (see the table) are dominant, therapists can teach anxiety management—breathing exercises and other relaxation techniques. Occasionally therapists undertake group and individual sessions devoted to "cognitive reorganization," in which shy individuals learn the bases of their shyness, understand that it need not destroy social relations, and reevaluate the causes to which they attribute it. Therapists also use group sessions as practice arenas by guiding shy people step-by-step through their interactions with others.

of psyching ourselves up, and partly a matter of experience. The sick feeling in the pit of your stomach probably will always be there, at least momentarily, but it need not paralyze you. As you gain experience with each of the essential steps—from selecting a subject to practicing the speech—your self-confidence as a speaker will grow.

Communicating Confidence. If you are now ready to present your first speech, you may be asking, "How shall I deliver my message? Developing self-confidence is one thing, but how can I convey that self-confidence to an

INVENTORY OF SHYNESS REACTIONS

Physiological Reactions	% Shy Students
Increased pulse	54
Blushing	53
Perspiration	49
Butterflies in stomach	48
Heart pounding	48

Thoughts and Feelings	% Shy Students
Self-consciousness	85
Concern about impression management	67
Concern for social evaluation	63
Negative self-evaluation	59
Unpleasantness of situation	56

Overt Behaviors	% Shy Students
Silence	80
No eye contact	51
Avoidance of others	44
Avoidance of action	42
Low speaking voice	40

(Adapted from P. G. Zimbardo, P. A. Pilkonis, and R. M. Norwood, "The Silent Prison of Shyness," The Office of Naval Research Technical Report Z-17, November 1974.)

Continuing research into shyness and ways of overcoming its negative social effects is helping people cope successfully in communication contacts.

FOR FURTHER READING

Zimbardo, Philip G. *Psychology and Life*, 11th ed. Glenview, IL: Scott, Foresman and Company, 1985, 447–50.

audience?" The following guidelines should help you communicate self-confidence.

1. *Be yourself.* Act as you would if you were having an animated conversation with a friend. Avoid an excessively rigid, oratorical, or aggressive posture. At the same time, do not become so comfortable in front of the group that you lean on the wall behind you or sprawl all over the lectern. When you speak, you want your listeners to focus on your ideas, not on the way you are presenting them.

Decision Making

*I*n discussing the rhetorical choices you will make in developing a speech, it is assumed that you are an accomplished decision maker consciously aware of the choices that you make in everyday situations. Is this an accurate assessment? Three studies concerning various facets of making decisions suggest that we are not as accomplished as we might be.

Recent research by Donohew et al. indicates that a person may be only partially aware of the decisions that he or she makes. The terms they use to describe this level of self-awareness include "automatic pilot," "automaticity," and (oddly enough) "mindlessness." *Partial awareness* means that you do not focus consciously on every decision you make. Since you are familiar with the processes involved in walking, you do not think about every move. Similarly, familiar social situations require little conscious attention. Your behavior in class, for example, is part of what might be called a "script"—you know what to expect and how to respond in that setting, and you make conscious decisions only when something unexpected occurs. This is not necessarily a negative trait (otherwise you might not be able to walk and chew gum at the same time); it allows you to focus attention on the really important issues. In this instance, the relative "newness" of selecting a speech topic and narrowing it appropriately requires greater focus and involves you in a larger number of conscious rhetorical moves.

listeners because you think "it's good for them to hear this." It may be, but will they listen? Whatever the topic, it is the speaker's responsibility to make it interesting to the audience. A topic may be of interest to listeners for one or more of the following reasons:

- *It concerns their health, happiness, or security.* For instance, you might talk to a group at a nursing home about changes in Medicare regulations.
- *It offers a solution to a recognized problem.* You might suggest ways your group could raise funds in order to participate in a national conference.
- *It is surrounded by controversy or conflict of opinion.* You might speak on the proposed relocation of a town dump to a site near your campus.

Select a subject appropriate to the occasion. A demonstration speech on body-building might succeed in your speech classroom, but bringing a horse

Other researchers have studied the personality traits involved in making decisions. Plax and Rosenfeld, for example, studied the nature of making "risky" decisions, and concluded that risk takers are "persistent, effective in their communication, confident and outgoing, clever and imaginative, aggressive, efficient and clear thinking, and manipulative and opportunistic in dealing with others." Driver and Mock identified four general approaches to making decisions based on the way people use the amount of data available, on the number of options they analyze, and on their interest in speed and efficiency. The approaches were characterized as: *decisive*, in which a minimum amount of data is analyzed and one option is arrived at; *flexible*, in which data are minimal but seen as serving different ends at different times; *hierarchic*, in which data are carefully arranged in precise order toward an optimum solution; and *integrative*, in which as much data as possible is examined, and as many options as possible are generated to maximize the chance of success.

Whether people tend to use one style consistently or to vary their style as the occasion changes is a subject requiring further study.

These decision styles have implications for the process of selecting speech subjects; beginning with an integrative style, for instance, generates multiple options for review. Shifting to a decisive style reduces those to realistic possibilities. Using a hierarchic style further enables the speaker to select the optimum subject for the particular set of circumstances.

FOR FURTHER READING

Donohew, R. Lewis, Murali Nair, and Seth Finn. "Automaticity, Arousal and Information Exposure," in Robert N. Bostrom, ed., *Communication Yearbook 8.* Beverly Hills, CA: Sage Publications, 1984, 267–84; Driver, M. J., and T. J. Mock. "Human Information Processing, Decision Style Theory, and Accounting Systems." *The Accounting Review* (1975): 490–508; Plax, Timothy, and Lawrence Rosenfeld. "Correlates of Risky Decision-Making." *Journal of Personality Assessment* 40 (1976): 413–18.

to class and demonstrating how to saddle the animal could be out of place. Consider whether the occasion is the right setting for what you want to do. The same speech on body-building might not be appropriate at a dedication of a new senior citizens' center, but a speech reflecting the need for exercise at all ages—and the fact that the new center is equipped for exercise classes— would be fitting.

In sum, remember that even when your topic is assigned, you still need to approach it in ways that play off your strengths. Your speech must reflect the interests that you and your audience share and be appropriate to the speech occasion. If you have difficulty thinking of such a topic—and selecting the topic is often the most taxing and time-consuming part of the process— study the list of subject categories on the endsheets of this textbook. The topics listed there are very general and do not exhaust the possibilities;

however, the list may "trigger" ideas, especially more narrowly focused ones, that you had not thought about when you began the task of selecting a subject for a speech.

Narrowing the Topic

A general subject or topic is of little value until it is narrowed to a manageable size. Narrowing a subject area to a more precise topic involves three primary considerations.

Narrow your topic so that you can discuss it adequately in the time allotted for the speech. If you are responding to an in-class speech assignment that will last five to seven or eight to ten minutes, you cannot begin to do justice to "The Rise and Fall of Baseball as the Premier American Sport." Instead, you might describe three or four changes baseball has made in response to television coverage, or you might explain the development of a specific pitch. Put simply: fit the topic's breadth to the time you have available to speak.

Gauge your topic so that it is neither above nor below the comprehension level of the audience. If, for example, you want to talk about laser technology or the existence of "black holes" to students in your speech class, you should focus attention on basic, elemental principles. If the audience were a group of senior physics majors, the nature of the material presented and its levels of complexity would necessarily change.

Narrow your topic to meet the specific expectations of your audience. Listeners who expect to hear about gun safety and the newest programs of the National Rifle Association may be upset if, instead, you lecture them on the need for stricter gun control laws or solicit their support for legislation banning the sale of "Saturday night specials." The announced purpose of the meeting, the demands of the particular context, and group traditions can affect audience members' expectations of what they are to hear. Violate audience expectations only when you feel it is absolutely essential; however, be prepared for the consequences of your disavowal of tradition.

Narrowing a topic amounts to finding one, two, or three points that you can establish, clarify, or support in the time limit allotted for your presentation. For example, suppose you decide to talk informatively about science fiction to fulfill a speech class assignment. Within that general topic area are numerous subtopics, including:

• The beginnings of science fiction—Shelley's *Frankenstein*
• The differences between science fiction and fantasy
• The nature of "hard science" in science fiction novels
• The major writers of science fiction—such as Heinlein, Clarke, LeGuin, Asimov
• Asimov's Three Laws of Robotics
• The nature of "space opera" as science fiction
• The major periodicals publishing science fiction short stories

- The history of the Hugo Award for science fiction writing
- Recent literary trends in science fiction
- Major science fiction films
- The use of science fiction to present political messages
- The images of women in science fiction
- Art and science fiction

Given this list of subjects, you will need to narrow further to match your knowledge and interests to the interests of the audience, to the occasion, to the time available, and to the level of audience knowledge about the subject. Consider the following possibilities in sifting through these subtopics to select a speech that would meet a five-to-seven-minute time limit:

1. *Subjects I know something about*
   The differences between science fiction and fantasy
   Major writers of science fiction
   Asimov's Three Laws of Robotics
   "Space opera"
   Political messages in science fiction
   The major periodicals in science fiction
   The images of women

2. *Subjects interesting to me*
   All except art and science fiction

3. *Subjects potentially interesting to the audience* (speech class)
   Science fiction versus fantasy
   "Hard science" in science fiction
   The major writers of science fiction
   Asimov's Three Laws of Robotics
   "Space opera"
   Political messages in science fiction
   The images of women
   Science fiction films

4. *Subjects appropriate to the occasion* (informative speech situation in speech class)
   All are appropriate

5. *Subjects I can talk about in the time available* (this may require further narrowing)
   Two or three major differences between science fiction and fantasy
   An introduction to the works of one major writer, or to a writer's major series (for example, Asimov's *Foundation* series)
   The image of women in Anne McCaffrey's *Crystal Singer*
   The political message in LeGuin's *Always Coming Home*

6. *Subjects I can fit to the audience's comprehension level*
   The most difficult would be "hard science" issues, depending on the audience's background in science.

All other subjects should be within the general knowledge level of the audience, even if they have not read science fiction novels.

7. *Subjects that will meet audience expectations in this rhetorical situation* Any of these subjects would meet the audience's general expectations about an informative speech.

The process of narrowing may lead to a subject that is "best" for a particular occasion; as the previous sample process indicates, it also may leave you with several possibilities. If that is the case, you need to decide which subject, narrowed to the time limit, will best fit your interests as well as those of the audience. Which subject can you make the most interesting—which can you involve the audience in as you talk?

In sum, selecting and narrowing involves: (1) analyzing your own experiences and background for topics about which you are knowledgeable and interested, (2) thinking about your audience's interests and abilities, (3) considering the demands of a rhetorical situation, and (4) narrowing the topic area to develop a subtopic you can cover adequately (a) in the time allotted and (b) in accordance with audience and situational expectations. All of this may seem a complicated chore, and at times it will be. Nevertheless, if you approach the issue systematically, you often can sift through the options available, decide on a "prime subject," and move on to the rest of the demands of speech preparation.

Determining the Purposes

Once you know what you want to talk about, the next task is to consider a series of "whys" already implicit in much that has been discussed: Why do *you* wish to discuss this subject? Why might an *audience* want to listen to *you*? Why is this subject appropriate to *this occasion*? These questions can be easily answered by considering the following three points in sequence: think about the general purposes that people have in mind when they speak in public; then consider the specific purposes you wish to accomplish in speaking; and then focus on the central idea or the claim that expresses the principal message you wish to communicate to an audience. In addition, you may find it helpful to phrase a working title for your speech, which will keep your principal aim in front of you as you engage in the remaining tasks of preparation.

General Purposes

The general purposes for speaking reflect the "end states" you wish to create in your audience. Do you wish your listeners to *be informed* as a result of your message, to *be persuaded* that your ideas are worth acceptance, to *be moved to action* on the basis of your appeals, or to *be entertained* by the way you phrase your message? While these "end states" are not mutually exclusive (you may make a moral point through humor, for example), they

THE GENERAL PURPOSES OF SPEECH

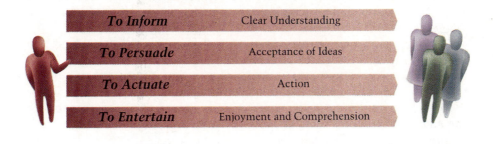

To Inform	Clear Understanding
To Persuade	Acceptance of Ideas
To Actuate	Action
To Entertain	Enjoyment and Comprehension

are sufficiently discrete to form the basis for discussion as general purposes for speaking.

Usually, you talk to others publicly because you possess some knowledge of potential relevance and benefit to them, or because you hope to alter their fundamental beliefs about events in their world, their attitudes toward life, or the actions they have been or ought to be taking. Unless you are a professional comedian, your use of entertainment as a general purpose will involve conveying information or persuading the audience to accept or act on your ideas. Therefore, we will focus primary attention on speeches designed to inform, to persuade, and to actuate. We will consider the types of speeches that accompany each of these general purposes later in the text, with a major emphasis on the processes of informing and persuading. In this section, we will consider the major *goals* of each of these three purposes.

To Inform.   When your object is to help listeners understand an idea or comprehend a concept or process, or when you seek to widen their range of knowledge, the general purpose of your speech is **to inform.** This is a primary goal of your communication professors when they report results of their research at professional meetings and then publish their studies in such journals as *Communication Monographs* and the *Quarterly Journal of Speech.* This also is the goal of elected officials when they explain their actions to their constituents; of college professors teaching chemistry, speech, philosophy, art, or any other subject; and of supervisors explaining new safety measures to plant workers.

To evoke a response of understanding, you must change the level or quality of information your listeners possess. By providing examples, statistics, illustrations, and other materials containing data and ideas, you seek to alter or expand their general or specific knowledge about an idea, policy, process, concept, or event. Just "telling them the facts" may not be sufficient to bring about a change in information quantity or quality. Not only must an informative speech provide raw data not previously known or perceived in a particular way, but its message and supporting materials must be structured and presented in such a way that the audience grasps the import of the whole. For example, an informative speech on how to build a stereo set must include the necessary information and must present it in an orderly sequence of steps. Understanding depends not only on learning *what* to do, but also on *when* to do it and *why.*

In some cases, your listeners may be familiar with the "raw data" you wish to present but still lack understanding. They may, for example, know the mathematical term "set" but not be able to work within the rules of set theory. In such a case, they have not yet integrated their knowledge into a usable whole; in this instance, your job as an informative speaker is to help the audience structure their knowledge into a new, more meaningful unit of information that they can use.

When your purpose is to clarify a concept or process for your listeners— to introduce them to new material, terms, and previously unknown relationships—your objective is to inform. The response you seek from an informative speech is primarily conceptual or cognitive—an adjustment in the audience members' body of knowledge. Several types of speech are considered informative in their general purpose: speeches of definition, demonstrations, oral instructions, reports from committees or task forces, and lectures. In each instance, information transmission and sharing are the primary thrusts of the presentation.

To Persuade or to Actuate. The purpose of a **speech to persuade** or **to actuate** is to influence listeners' state of mind or their actions. Because both use similar strategies, we will examine them together. While it may be argued that all speeches are persuasive to a degree, there are many situations in which outright persuasion is a speaker's primary purpose.[1] For example, promoters and public relations experts try to make you believe in the superiority of certain products, persons, and institutions. Lawyers seek to convince juries of the guilt or innocence of their clients. Social action group leaders exhort tenants to believe in the need for city codes protecting their rights. Politicians debate campaign issues and strive to influence voters' perceptions of who should represent their interests in the state legislature, Congress, or the White House.

Beyond speaking to influence your listeners' beliefs and attitudes, you also may go a step further and try to move them to action. You may want them to contribute money, sign a petition, sign an organ donor card, or participate in a demonstration. The distinguishing feature of an actuative speech is that, instead of stopping with an appeal to listeners' beliefs or attitudes, you ask them to alter their behavior in a specified way.

To influence or alter your listeners' beliefs and actions, you need to present well-ordered arguments supported by facts, figures, examples, and the opinions of experts. You will find it necessary, however, to do more than simply state the facts. Persuasion involves psychological as well as logical processes; you need to use motivational appeals relevant to listeners' needs and desires as part of an overall rationale for change in listener behavior. In order to

Speakers who attempt to alter listeners' behavior must go beyond the mere presentation of facts to appeal to listeners' psychological needs and desires.

change minds and move people to action, you must be sensitive to the rational and motivational aspects of audience psychology—topics that will be discussed at length in later chapters. For the present, keep in mind that facts alone, even if "airtight" as far as the case for change is concerned, are often insufficient to move people to change their behavior. Consider all of the information connecting cigarette, cigar, and pipe smoking to various forms of cancer, as well as the issue of passive smoking. If facts alone were sufficient, people should want to stop. What is the motivational appeal that will lead a listener to take action in such an instance?

To Entertain. To entertain, amuse, or otherwise provide enjoyment for listeners is frequently the general purpose of an after-dinner speech, but other kinds of talks also may have enjoyment as their principal aim. A lecture on travel, for example, contains information but also may entertain an audience through exciting, amusing tales of adventure or misadventure. Club meetings, class reunions, and similar gatherings may provide the opportunity for a "roast" of one or more of the people present. In these situations, the effective use of humor is a key ingredient in being judged "funny" as opposed to "tasteless" by the audience.

Often a speech to entertain is more than a comic monologue. Humor in speeches to entertain generally has a purpose other than or beyond mere enjoyment. Even the humor at a roast is intended to convey affection and genuine appreciation for the talents of the person being subjected to the barbs of friends and colleagues. Think of some of the great humorists: Mark Twain used humor to inform Eastern audiences about life in the Midwest and Will Rogers used his radio talks and commentaries on political realities during the Great Depression to help create a sense of American unity and common effort. More recently, Art Buchwald shows us our foibles and moral dilemmas and Russian-born comic Yakoff Smirnoff uses tales of ordinary life in the Soviet Union to note the contrasts to American values of freedom and democracy.

A speech to entertain is humorous yet serious. Evening entertainments, parodies, satires, and most other forms of public-speaking humor are subtle and often difficult to master. For these reasons, we will discuss them later in this book. For now, the best advice on the use of humor is to avoid trying to "be funny" if you are not, by nature, accustomed to using humor in your everyday encounters with others. Contriving a humorous story that falls flat with your audience leaves you in an uncomfortable position, especially if you use it as the opening line and you have the rest of the speech to present.

As you have learned, to inform, to persuade or actuate, and to entertain are the general "end-states" that guide your reason for speaking. Just as topics are narrowed to subtopics, and often further, your general purpose needs to be narrowed to more specific ones in order to focus audience attention on the content of your presentation.

Specific Purposes

In addition to your general purpose, your speech will have one or more specific purposes representing the actual goals you want to achieve. Although concrete, specific purposes can be extremely wide ranging. You will want to make some specific purposes explicit as part of your speech; for example, you can tell your listeners precisely what you want them to understand or to do as a consequence of listening to your presentation. Some specific purposes may remain private, known only to you; for example, you hope to make a good impression on the audience or receive a high grade on the presentation, although you most likely would not say that as part of the speech.

Specific purposes can be short-term or long-term. If you are speaking to members of a local food cooperative on the virtues of baking their own bread, your short-term purpose might be to get people to try your recipe; your long-term objective might be to induce them to change their food-buying and food-consuming habits.

Theoretically, you can have any number of public and private, short-term and long-term specific purposes when you speak. Practically, however, you will want to reduce your list of goals to a *dominant* one—with all others enhancing the likelihood of success of your primary objective. Given this reduction, the specific purpose is *the response you wish to elicit from the*

THE PRIVATE AND PUBLIC PURPOSES OF SPEECH

> ### *Private Purpose*
> I hope I can make them understand how this system really works, because I'd like to lead the party myself.

> ### *Public Purpose*
> Today I would like to explain how the party caucus system works.

audience. Formulated into a clear, concise statement, the specific purpose delineates exactly what you want the audience to understand, enjoy, feel, believe, or do.

Suppose, for example, that as part of a student teaching assignment, you are asked to explain to a high-school civics class how the Democratic and Republican party caucuses work, in preparation for a class project on participation in the upcoming state elections. You would have several purposes in this presentation: with reference to the subject, you want to demonstrate that caucusing allows for grassroots participation in the electoral process, to review step-by-step the procedures that each party uses during the caucus, and to explain what the rules on voting for a candidate allow and do not allow. From a personal perspective, you want to show that you are knowledgeable and, hence, competent to speak on the issue, as well as to show an observing teacher or supervisor that you are well organized and can present ideas clearly. The first of these specific purposes is a long-term goal, while the other two related to the subject are short-term goals. The personal goals are private rather than public. All of these specific goals can be summarized, however, in a statement of the specific purpose: "To show members of the class how they can participate in the party caucus of their choice during the class project."

Central Ideas or Claims

Once you have settled on the specific purpose for your speech—the one dominant response that you wish from the audience—you are ready to express that goal in terms of concrete subject matter. You are ready to compose a central idea or a claim (sometimes termed a thesis), which will form the controlling thought of your speech. A *central idea* is a statement that captures the essence of the information or concept you are attempting to communicate to an audience. A *claim* is a statement that phrases the belief, attitude, or action you wish the audience to adopt. Central ideas are characteristic of informative speeches, while claims form the core of persuasive and actuative speeches. Speeches to entertain also have a controlling thought— either as a central idea with an orientation toward conveying information or as a claim with an orientation toward making a moral point or exhorting to action through the use of humor or other devices.

Precise phrasing of your central idea is important, because your wording captures the essence of your subject matter and purpose and focuses audience attention on *your* reasons for speaking, rather than on *their* reasons for listening. Assume, for example, that you are giving an informative speech on the use of science fiction to present political messages. Each of the following central ideas suggests a different emphasis for such a speech:

1. Science fiction novels are as much about the present as they are about the future.
2. Ursula LeGuin's novel *Always Coming Home* carries an implicit political message about how we, in the present, should live our lives.
3. The political worlds created in science fiction must be believable; thus, the genre cannot escape making choices that reflect writers' preferences—we learn their politics by reading the fictional works.

Each speech focusing on one of these central ideas will develop uniquely and will require different kinds of material for support or illustration. The first version stresses the idea that science fiction, although ostensibly set in the future, actually tells us something about our everyday lives. The second version focuses on the same theme but develops it through a close analysis of a major writer's work. The third version suggests that authors' political views are reflected in their writing and that one can look at the political choices made in the fictional works to discern writers' views.

Phrasing a claim is an even more crucial preparatory step than casting a central idea, because your wording colors the emotional tone of your message, its line of development, and your relationship with your audience. Note the effect of the following examples.

Varying the audience's perception of your intensity:
1. "Do not eat cured pork because it is *unhealthy.*"
2. "Do not eat cured pork because it is *carcinogenic.*"
3. "Do not eat cured pork because it *will kill you.*"

As you move from version one to version three, feelings are phrased with greater intensity; each successive version expresses your attitude in harsher, more graphic language.

Varying the reasons for taking a certain course of action:
1. "Make use of the Writing Lab because it will help you in your English courses."

2. "Make use of the Writing Lab because you will get higher grades in all courses in which writing is expected."
3. "Make use of the Writing Lab because better writing will lead to better jobs after graduation."

These three examples vary the rationale for the action you wish audience members to take. Presumably, one can act for a variety of rationales; your claim should be phrased in a way that captures what you think will be the most compelling reasons for *this particular audience.* In this instance, each reason may be further developed as part of a speech on using the Writing Lab. Each reason may tap interests or needs of different people in the audience, but generally you may reach all members with a rationale sufficient to get them to act on your advice.

Varying the evaluative criteria for judging something:
1. "The new football stadium is an *eyesore.*" (aesthetic judgment reflecting architectural standards)
2. "The new football stadium is *unsafe.*" (personal safety judgment reflecting engineering standards)
3. "The new football stadium is *the result of wealthy donors giving money to athletics when it should have gone to academic programs.*" (value judgment reflecting priorities for spending)

Each of these claims condemns a new building on campus, but in a different way. The first version reflects artistic values—what is attractive or ugly. The second version implies that structural flaws exist in the building, while the third complains that the money would have been better spent on other needs. Were you to advocate the first version, you would need to demonstrate that (a) aesthetic values are important criteria for judging buildings, such as stadiums, and (b) the physical appearance of the stadium harms the artistic integrity of the campus as a whole. For the second version, you would need to present specific flaws in the design and construction of the stadium. In defending the third version, you would need to document the other problems that exist on campus and offer reasons for their taking precedence over the construction of a new stadium. In each case, the selection of particular criteria will control the main features of the speech's ultimate development.

When all of these features are put together, you have the elements for initiating your speech outline. These points will focus your research efforts, as they will indicate the type and quantity of information needed to accomplish your goals.

Informative Speech

Subject: Science fiction

General Purpose: To inform

Specific Purposes:
• To show how science fiction conveys a political message

Precise phrasing of your central idea or claim is important, because your wording captures the essence of your subject matter and purpose and focuses audience attention on your reasons for speaking.

- To explain LeGuin's use of political themes (dominant purpose, recast into central idea)
- To convey confidence in handling the subject

Central Idea: "LeGuin's novel *Always Coming Home* contains a political message."

Actuative Speech

Subject: Accident insurance for youth sports groups

General Purpose: To actuate

Specific Purposes:
- To have city officials purchase insurance for their recreational programs (dominant purpose, recast into claim)
- To show how such protection can be provided at a reasonable cost
- To be perceived favorably by the audience
- To overcome opposition to spending money on this type of protection

Claim: "The City Council should authorize the purchase of the accident insurance plan I am offering for its youth sports programs [because such protection is essential in the event of a lawsuit; because the policy I am offering is less costly than others available; and because the city cannot rely solely on the accident insurance purchased by the families of youth participants]."[2]

In summarizing this material, carefully think through your general and specific purposes before you begin to construct a public message. A sensitivity to the general purposes will guide your thinking about selecting and structuring your speech materials. Focusing attention on all of your specific purposes will allow you to understand your own aspirations and fears about this particular speech, its potential range of effects on your audience, and the measures by which you can gauge these effects. Considering both sets of purposes also enables you to define central ideas or claims and, thus, capture in your mind—and set before your audience in clear language—the primary thrust of your speech.

Wording the Working Title

To complete your initial thinking about purposes, you often will want to write down a working title. Although it may seem odd or even unnecessary to consider a title during the preliminary stages of speech preparation, there are several concrete advantages of doing so. First, a working title helps you, as speaker, capture the essence of your thoughts and feelings. By phrasing the working title, you highlight the key concept or idea that the speech content will reflect. This can guide you in determining what will be relevant or irrelevant, central or peripheral, significant and insignificant in the development of the speech. Second, speakers often are required to announce titles ahead of time to allow for publicizing the event. Conventions and conferences always require a title well in advance; college professors often develop a working title of a research paper as much as nine months prior to the meeting at which it will be presented. A speaker at a local business meeting may need to provide a title that will be used for advance publicity in the local paper or in the organization's newsletter or meeting announcement.

Four guidelines can help you select and phrase a working title. *A title should be relevant to you, the audience, and the occasion.* If, for example, you are giving a speech on business and political ethics, you might consider a title such as "The Eleventh Commandment," as did the speaker who claimed that the commandment "Thou shalt not Steal" has been supplemented in some business and political circles by another: "Thou shalt not get caught." The title created some curiosity about the speech, as audience members wondered what would be added to the "Ten Commandments" they already knew. Just as important, the title reflected the significance of the subject by connecting it to a set of Commandments whose importance already was accepted.

A title should be provocative. Former Speech Communication Association President Marie H. Nichols, during her presidential year (1969), traveled around the country delivering a speech entitled "The Tyranny of Relevance." This was an attack on those who felt colleges and universities should be concerned primarily with such relevant courses of study as those in social action and the personal exploration of life experiences. She acknowledged that such courses were potentially university-level subjects but argued that single-minded attention to "relevance" may cause students to lose sight of other goals of higher education. Her title captured the spirit of the moment, as the cry for "relevance" was being heard in the late 1960s. The title engaged the attention of audiences and helped listeners retain the central point of her message. As you contemplate the provocative nature of possible titles, also seek to make the title *productive.* If an audience is initially hostile to you or your message, a provocative title may simply distance them further. Thus, do not seek to create irritation or raise questions about your sensitivity to audiences through the selection of a title. To entitle a speech before feminists "The Coddling of Women by the Political Parties" may be provocative, but it can hardly be expected to gain you a fair hearing.

The title should be brief. Imagine the effect of announcing your title as "The Effects upon High-Track, Mean-Track, and Low-Track High-School Juniors of Pretesting for Senior-Year Competency Testings." Besides being unclear, the title is far too long and does not engender curiosity or arouse interest. A better choice might be "Tracking Juniors: A Means to Successful Testing as Seniors?" or "A Pretest in Time Saves Nine—or More." These two may lack some precision, but they are generally engaging for the right audience and decidedly more provocative than the first choice.

A title chosen for advance publicity should be fairly general. If you have to commit to a title well in advance, you will want to preserve flexibility in how the speech will be developed. The title "Science Fiction as Political Statement" is sufficiently precise to give the audience an idea of your general topic area yet allows you to alter the development of the subject as you plan the speech. This also will reduce the chance that you will have to explain any such alterations.

Remember that your working title is just that—something to start to work with. If, as you gather your supporting material, you become excited about a certain aspect of your subject matter that you had not planned to cover, go ahead and explore it. Change your title to reflect your new direction or emphasis. If you have already committed to a title, you may find that your new direction will violate the expectations you have generated. If so, explain this when you present the speech; if you convey your reasons with enthusiasm and sincerity, the audience will, in all likelihood, become more interested in your new direction or purpose.

Selecting Subjects and Purposes: Strategic Choices

Public speaking elicits mental and behavioral responses from listeners. The selection processes discussed previously are designed to help you elicit the *desired* responses. As you review these, it is clear that you have several conscious choices to make in this early stage of speech preparation. By way of summary, let us review some of the factors that will determine the actual decisions you must make.

Private and Ultimate Aims

You must take into account your own interests and abilities as you select subjects and purposes. Few of us can talk convincingly or even sincerely about something in which we have little or no interest; few of us dare move into specialized areas in which audience members are likely to be more expert than we are. Furthermore, at times we must think through carefully how much we are personally willing to risk in front of others. For example, suppose you work for a firm that you are convinced is patently sexist in its promotion policies. The past record clearly suggests that it seldom promotes women to upper-level managerial positions. You find that you are given a chance to talk about promotions at an open meeting of the firm. How far do you go? What do you say? Your *private aim* may be one of getting your frustrations heard, regardless of the consequences. Your *ultimate aim* is to get some women, including yourself, into higher managerial positions. A harangue on the evils of sexism, replete with threats to report the firm to an equal opportunity agency, might satisfy your private aim, but would harden others' resistance to change.[3] After thinking through the situation, you might decide on a less risky course, such as an informative speech with the specific purpose of presenting a review of the numbers of men and women promoted within the firm to upper levels of management over the last ten years. You also could point out the number of women potentially ready for promotion within the company and discuss the "head-hunting" agencies that keep records of women interested in and qualified for managerial positions. Casting your speech as an informative speech would allow you to unite your private and ultimate aims in a message that both satisfies your private convictions and enhances your future upward mobility within the firm. If this option seems to be one of "wimping out," you will need to confront your own conscience, make a deliberate choice, and say what you feel has to be said regardless of the consequences.

Listeners' Authority or Capacity to Act

For a speaker to demand of a group of students that it should "abolish all required courses" would be foolish if the final decision concerning course requirements is in the hands of the faculty. The audience is better advised to take actions within its power to effect change; for example, to conduct a collegewide survey of student attitudes toward required courses and present it to the faculty, to print it in the campus newspaper, or to have students from different majors talk about the impact of the requirements on their own programs of study at a general meeting of the faculty. As a speaker, limit your specific purposes and claims to behaviors that are clearly within the domain of the audience's authority or power. Asking more of the audience than it can hope to accomplish will only cause frustration and may lessen interest in your ultimate aim.

Public speaking elicits certain mental and behavioral responses from listeners. Their attitudes, the nature of the speech occasion, and the time limits imposed on the situation all affect the speaker's task of preparing a message.

Listeners' Pre-existing Attitudes

A group of striking workers who believe they are badly underpaid and unfairly treated by their employer probably would be hostile to suggestions that they return to work under the existing conditions. They might, however, approve plans to submit the issues to arbitration by a disinterested person whose fairness and judgment they respect. If you are speaking to an audience whose attitude is hostile to your message, you might, in a single speech, be able to convince your listeners that there is merit in your side of the issue. You will be hoping for too much if you expect the audience to disavow their current beliefs and embrace yours or to take positive action on the basis of your request. In this instance, your specific purpose must be adjusted to what will be reasonable to obtain from the audience members, given their experiences and present attitudes. Do not ask for a response you cannot reasonably expect from people holding their particular feelings or beliefs. Even though you believe they are wrong, conveying that impression will only harden their resolve to sustain present beliefs and attitudes.

The Nature of the Speech Occasion

To ask for contributions to a political campaign fund might be appropriate at a pre-election rally, but to pursue this specific purpose at a memorial service for a public official would be decidedly out of place. A public processional toward a gravesite by the President of the United States and other foreign leaders is not the time for a reporter to press for answers to questions. An athletic awards ceremony is hardly the occasion for a presentation on the workings of a catalytic converter or a speech on the need to ban handguns. Be sure your specific purpose is adapted to the mood and spirit of the occasion on which you speak.

Time Limits

You may be able to induce a hostile audience to postpone a decision on a proposal without talking very long; however, if your goal is to change their feelings and convictions in order to endorse your proposal, you will need more than a few minutes. Similarly, if your subject is complex, you may be able to inform your listeners, sufficiently for them to understand your proposal, in a fifteen-minute speech. You may, however, need to give additional speeches to convince them that action on the basis of the information you offer is in their best interests. Do not attempt to secure a response that an audience cannot give in the time available.

Chapter Summary

When you have *selected* a topic that meets your needs, as well as those of the audience and occasion, and *narrowed* it to fit the occasion and time available, your speech preparation will be off to a sound start. You will have decided on an *informative, persuasive,* or *actuative* purpose, or you will have elected to *entertain* the audience through the use of humor. With this in mind, you also will have determined the range of *specific purposes* that you can handle in this situation. From this range, you will have determined which specific purpose will be the dominant one and recast it as your *central idea* or *claim* being advanced in the speech. Selecting a *working title* highlights the general thrust of your speech. Finally, you will have considered the five strategic issues—*private* and *ultimate aims, listener's authority or capacity to act, listeners' attitudes,* the nature of the speech *occasion,* and *time limits.* You will have begun to use them in choosing appropriate material to accomplish your speaking objectives. Inevitably, attention to these considerations will improve your self-confidence: you will know precisely what you want to do and why you want to do it. Such knowledge is of immeasurable value in making you more secure as you continue the task of speech preparation.

Reference Notes

1. It can be argued that all speeches are persuasive. *Any* change in a person's stock of knowledge, beliefs, attitudes, or ways of acting represents the kind of adjustment in one's mental and emotional state that can be attributed to persuasion, as long as symbols were used to induce the change. From a psychological perspective, it may be argued that it is impossible to separate

"informative" and "persuasive" messages. We are taking a *rhetorical* perspective, in which the symbols used to evoke a certain kind of response, as well as the strategies used in that process, provide an *orientation* that is overtly one of informing, persuading, actuating, or entertaining an audience. Hence, you will find separate discussions of these later in the textbook. See Gary C. Woodward and Robert E. Denton, Jr., *Persuasion & Influence in American Life* (Prospect Heights, IL: Waveland Pr., Inc., 1988), Chapter One.

2. Your phrasing of the claim may not include the reasons, the "because" clauses, that justify its acceptance at this stage of the preparation process. You may be better able to specify these once you have gone on to the next step, that of analyzing the audience.

3. From a research perspective, there are several theories or psychological models that can be used to explain this "hardening" process. Within *consistency theory*, any message that is inconsistent or "discrepant" with a person's other beliefs will cause that person to react negatively to it. *Dissonance theory* explains the same process by arguing that when two perceptions clash explicitly, a person experiences dissonance or disharmony; because we prefer consonance or harmony among our beliefs, we act to remove the forces of disharmony. These actions can take the form of discrediting the source of the message, or discrediting the "facts" presented. Another theory stresses an individual's *latitudes of acceptance and rejection*. This approach argues that we can tolerate information or latitudes counter to our own position, but there are limits to how far we are willing to go. Appeals to beliefs or attitudes that call for relatively small adjustments in our current position on an issue, which fall within our range of acceptance, are likely to be successful. Appeals that fall outside, or belong to our latitude of rejection, are likely to make us stronger than ever in our original position. On topics where we have very little information or little direct involvement, our latitude of acceptance is very wide, but on other topics where we think we know a lot or have a very strong opinion, our latitude is likely to be very narrow. Part of a speaker's job in analyzing an audience is to determine the range of acceptance and rejection as it relates to the particular speech being prepared. For reviews of these and other theories, see R. P. Abelson et al., eds., *Theories of Cognitive Consistency* (Chicago: Rand McNally & Co., 1968). For practical applications, see Woodward and Denton; and Stephen W. Littlejohn and David M. Jabusch, *Persuasive Transactions* (Glenview, IL: Scott, Foresman and Company, 1987).

Key Terms

speech to inform

speech to persuade

speech to actuate

Problems and Probes

1. This chapter makes clear that, for each speech, the speaker must take occasion into account. Consider your classroom as an occasion—the room, your classmates, and the instructor. How does each of these affect your choice of a

subject? Does the room's location, size, or configuration permit certain types of demonstration speeches but not others? What are your classmates interested in hearing about, either as informative or persuasive topics? Has your instructor indicated that certain topics are not suitable for presentation in class? Develop short answers to each of these questions, and be prepared to discuss them in small groups during class. The class might use this discussion as the basis for preparing an "Issues Survey" that would provide more precise data on interests and attitudes on a wide variety of topics.

2. Attend a speech or lecture on campus with a few classmates. As you listen to the presentation, each member should take notes on the following: *general purpose, specific purpose,* statement of *central idea* or *claim.* In terms of these factors, how well does the speaker meet your needs as an audience member? How is this done, or not done? Take notes in response to this issue, and be prepared to discuss your reactions in class.

3. Attend a campus or community event for which a speaker will be the "entertainment." If the audience expects the presentation to be humorous, does the speaker accomplish this objective? How does the speaker use humor successfully or unsuccessfully? Take notes on your perceptions of the event, and be prepared to discuss why this event did or did not work as an entertaining occasion.

Communication Activities

1. Deliver a brief impromptu speech on a topic that interests you. Your instructor will allow a question and comment period so that audience members can indicate whether the topic interests them, or the degree to which you were able to arouse interest.

2. List five topics that would be inappropriate for class presentation. During class, present a brief impromptu speech in which you indicate why each would be inappropriate if developed as a complete speech. Note the effect of unplanned humor in your speech, or in those of other class members (not all will necessarily be humorous, but some will inevitably cause the audience to relax and enjoy the thought of a speaker actually presenting such inappropriate ideas).

3. Working in small groups, prepare an "Issues Survey." Each group member will come to class prepared with five topics that are of interest in an informative context, and five that are of interest if the speech assignment were to be persuasive (there may be some overlap). Discuss your list of topics within your group, sorting out ideas that overlap with those of others in the group, and develop one list. Assign one person to collate a readable list and bring it to the next class, with copies for everyone in the group. Using a simple three-point scale (1 = very interesting; 2 = interesting; 3 = very uninteresting), each group will respond to the five items in each category. Collate responses on a single copy. The instructor will collect all ballots and prepare a master copy from all of the groups' ideas or reactions. Select an informative or persuasive topic from the list that scores among the lowest (most uninteresting) and develop a speech with the specific purpose of arousing audience interest.

CHAPTER FIVE

Analyzing the Audience and Occasion

*P*ublic speaking is **audience centered.** As earlier chapters have stressed, it is crucial that you interact with the people you address. Selecting and narrowing the topic, establishing your purposes, and framing a central idea or a claim all require consideration of your audience. So do the remaining steps in speech preparation. It is time to look more closely at the audience and occasion. In the words of Donald C. Bryant, the essence of the rhetorical process since ancient Greece has been that of "adjusting ideas to people and people to ideas."[1]

Because it is impractical to consider each listener individually, you must analyze listeners as members of groups. You should look for common situational and psychological denominators to help you target your messages to that collection of people. Identifying the role characteristics and physical attributes of your listeners (**demographic analysis**) will help you determine their psychological components (**psychological profiling**). The theme stressed throughout this chapter is this: *The goal of audience analysis is to discover which facets of listeners' demographic and psychological characteristics are relevant to your speech purposes and ideas.*

Closely related to audience analysis is examination of the situation or occasion. As noted in Chapter 3, members of a culture tend to have rather strong expectations of what will (and will not) be said on certain occasions. For example, a preacher at the funeral of a man who had serious shortcomings when it came to interacting with family members and fellow workers will not dwell on those shortcomings. The preacher probably will say only that he had some "weaknesses like us all," and praise the man's virtues. To violate such audience expectations with a speech condemning the man's vices probably would cause the family and friends of the deceased to rise up in anger, muttering about "respect for the dead." A sense of occasion is always important.

How can we learn about the relationship between occasions and audience expectations? That is a difficult question, because occasions—births, deaths, graduations, memorials, tributes, nominations, and so on—are so varied. If you are to achieve your purposes, however, you must learn to analyze occasions. Consequently, this chapter has a second theme: *An "occasion" includes a time and place set aside for particular events and activities; speakers must learn what people expect on those occasions and meet the expectations as completely as possible.*

After discussing analysis of the audience and the occasion, this chapter concludes with some advice on how to use the results of your analyses in the construction of arguments and ideas for your speeches.

Analyzing the Audience Demographically

A demographic analysis is a study of social and physical traits people hold in common. Because you can directly observe many of these traits, it often is easier to begin with a demographic analysis of your audience, rather than with a psychological profile. When you begin your analysis, you will want to ask the following questions:

- *Age:* Are my listeners primarily young, middle-aged, or older people? Does one age group seem to dominate a mixed audience? Is there a special relationship between age groups—parents and their children, for instance?
- *Gender:* Is my audience predominantly male or female, or is the group equally made up of both genders?
- *Education:* How much do my listeners already know about my subject? Does their educational or experiential background allow them to learn about my subject easily and quickly?
- *Group membership:* Do these people belong to groups that represent special attitudes or identifiable values?
- *Cultural and ethnic background:* Are audience members predominantly from particular cultural groups? Do my listeners share a special heritage?

The importance of demographic analysis for you as a speaker does not lie in simply finding answers to such questions. Rather, *the key is to decide if any of these demographic factors will affect your listeners' ability or willingness to understand and accept what you want to say.* In other words, you must determine which factors are *relevant* to your audience and then shape your message accordingly.

For example, if you are addressing a group of senior citizens at a local seniors club, you obviously must consider age and group membership. You will probably adapt to your listeners by (1) speaking more loudly if some of them are hearing impaired; (2) choosing examples that are likely to be part of their experiential background; (3) considering their spare-time activities and interests; and (4) compensating for your lack of shared experiences through the use of local or common illustrations, examples, and other supporting material.

Demographic analysis can help you select and phrase your key ideas. It aids you in understanding your listeners by pinpointing the factors that may influence their ability to understand your message or accept what you say. Such variables as age or gender can determine how they experience events and what they think. Demographic analysis can help you adapt your message more effectively to your listeners.

Analyzing the Audience Psychologically

It is also useful to divide audience members into psychological groups on the basis of their fundamental beliefs, attitudes, and values. This is especially important if you intend to influence your listeners' thinking. You need to know what ideas they already accept before you can hope to alter their thoughts or actions. Sometimes careful demographic analysis of your listeners can provide clues to how they think. For example, members of the National Rifle Association generally think constitutional rights are important; Daughters of the American Revolution are proud of their family heritage; and most Ph.D.'s believe education is fundamental to the development of human intellectual potential. This section will examine some ways that speakers can use beliefs, attitudes, and values to inform and persuade audiences.

Beliefs

Beliefs are ideas about what is true or false in the "real world." They arise from firsthand experience, evidence read or heard, authorities who have told us what is true, or even blind faith. For example, you might believe that "Calculus is a difficult course" (firsthand experience), that "This university is dedicated to improving the quality of our lives through education" (university promotional literature), that "Learning is a lifelong activity" (something your parents or instructors have told you), or that "Getting an education increases your chances of landing a good job" (something you hope is true).

We hold beliefs for many reasons, and our beliefs can differ in important ways. Beliefs vary in the degree of *certitude* with which we hold them. We hold some beliefs to be externally verifiable—*facts*—while others are per-

THE VARIETIES OF BELIEF

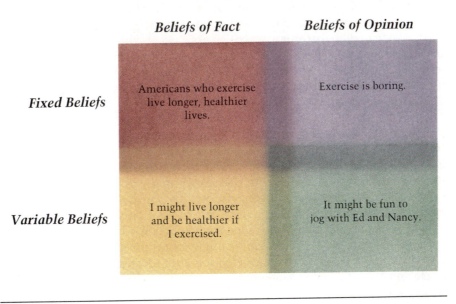

Beliefs of Fact *Beliefs of Opinion*

	Beliefs of Fact	Beliefs of Opinion
Fixed Beliefs	Americans who exercise live longer, healthier lives.	Exercise is boring.
Variable Beliefs	I might live longer and be healthier if I exercised.	It might be fun to jog with Ed and Nancy.

sonal *opinions*. Some beliefs are relatively open to change (*variable*), while others are not (*fixed*). Both facts and opinions can be fixed or variable. Let us examine each of these subclasses.

Facts and Opinions.   We all hold beliefs with varying degrees of certainty. Facts are strong beliefs that you think are open to external verification. When you say, "It's a fact that tomatoes are fruits," "Research has proven that infant blue whales gain an average of 10 pounds per day," or "It's a fact that whenever this country engages in a war, the economy booms," you are stating that you are very sure of those beliefs. Facts are usually held with certainty because you are convinced that you have hard evidence to back them up. In addition, you think that others can verify their accuracy. In sum, a fact is a belief that you hold firmly and think is supported with strong evidence.

Opinions are another matter, however. When you identify an opinion, such as "It's my opinion that our current administration is neglecting the problems of the poor" or "In my opinion, she's right," you are signaling that your belief-statements are personal. You are letting your listeners know that your statements are being offered as your own views of a situation. You are telling them, at least indirectly, that your commitment to the statement is not especially strong and that you may not have sufficient external evidence to support the claim. Thus, an opinion is a personal belief held with less certitude and supported with less compelling external evidence than a fact.[2] Since both facts and opinions are matters of belief, however, the accuracy of their "truth" can be relative. Sometimes the difference between fact and opinion is blurred. In colonial America, for instance, many people "knew for a fact" that regular bathing caused illness, just as their ancestors "knew" that the earth was flat and located at the center of the universe. If an opinion is widely held, it may be taken as fact. It is important to recognize that opinions and facts are psychological concepts that can be believed both individually and collectively.

Fixed and Variable Beliefs.   A second way of viewing beliefs is to determine their degree of certitude. Some beliefs are fixed, while others are variable. **Fixed beliefs** are those that have been reinforced throughout your life, making them central to your thinking. Obviously, many of your early childhood beliefs are fixed, such as "Bad behavior will be punished" and "If you work hard, you will succeed." Other beliefs become not only fixed but anchored as well; especially as you grow older, such beliefs harden in your mind and are highly resistant to change. For example, as people grow older, they tend to vote along political party lines election after election; they tend to purchase and drive the same kind of vehicles; they tend to believe that certain people and occupations are respectable and others are not; and they tend not to change religions or churches. Therefore, the demographic variable of age may indicate fixed beliefs. Fixed beliefs become habituated and can even be called *stereotypes*, because we often generalize our fixed beliefs to larger groups. For example, we might say, "All Republicans are honest," "People who do things like that should be arrested!" or "Never trust a German shepherd."

In contrast, **variable beliefs** are less well anchored in your mind and experiences. You might enter college thinking you are very well suited by temperament and talent to be a chemist; then, after an instructor has praised your abilities in a composition class, you might see yourself as predestined to be a writer; next, you might take a marketing class and find out that you are very good at planning advertising campaigns; and so on, as you experience one class after another until you select a major and degree program. In this case, your beliefs about your talents and the best ways to use them change with your personal experiences. The testimony you have heard from various authority figures has influenced these variable beliefs, and, since they are still not firmly fixed beliefs, they change as you encounter new experiences.

Before you speak, it is important to know which of your audience's beliefs are fixed (difficult to change) and which are variable (more easily altered). In addition, it is important to realize what information your listeners hold as fact and as opinion. Assessing the nature of your audience's beliefs is important for three reasons:

1. *You can reinforce or alter their beliefs using strategies similar to the ways in which people normally accept beliefs.* For example, knowing that audiences often establish beliefs based on the statements of authorities will encourage you to use similar testimony as you seek to influence your listeners' views.

2. *Such assessments should help you outline some of the appeals you can make within your speech.* If audience analysis shows that your listeners consider empirical evidence to be factual, you can use scientific studies or statistical data in your speech. If, on the other hand, they believe in the divine inspiration of certain religious documents, you can cite quotations or illustrations from these sources. Such facts can be used to support your central idea or claim.

3. *These assessments allow you to set realistic expectations as you plan your talk.* Not all audience beliefs are equally amenable to change through speeches. You should not try to accomplish impossible goals in a single speech. You will probably encounter psychological resistance when you try to destroy too many facts and fixed beliefs.

Later in this chapter we will discuss in more detail these questions of selecting belief-centered claims and setting speech goals.

Attitudes

The second aspect of psychological profiling is understanding audience attitudes. **Attitudes** may be defined as tendencies to respond positively or negatively to people, objects, or ideas. Attitudes express individual preferences or feelings, such as "Democracy is better than communism," "Discrimination is wrong," "The Statue of Liberty is a beautiful monument," and "I like my public-speaking class."

Because attitudinal statements express our preferences, predispositions, reactions, and basic judgments, they often control our behavior. We tend to do things we like and avoid things we dislike. As a speaker, you should consider the dominant attitudes of your audience. Especially relevant are the audience's attitudes toward you, your subject, and your speech purpose. One dramatic example of the strength of attitudes occurred when the Coca-Cola Company introduced "new Coke" with disastrous results. Even though extensive blind taste tests showed that people preferred the new flavor, consumers reacted negatively to the product because of their attitudes of loyalty to the classic formula. Their attitudes controlled their purchasing behavior, and the company was forced to "reintroduce" Coca-Cola Classic®.

The Audience's Attitudes Toward the Speaker. The attitudes of an audience toward you as a speaker will be based in part on your reputation. Your behavior during the speech will also influence the audience's attitudes toward

VALUES AND RELATED BELIEFS/ATTITUDES

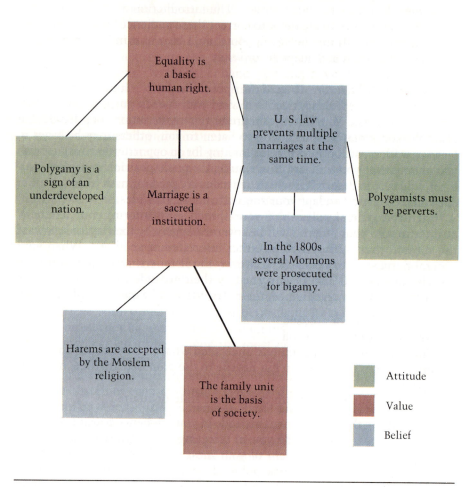

and their audible reactions—laughter, applause, fidgeting, whispering—can all be clues to their attitudes toward you, your subject, and your purpose. The conscientious communicator develops a keen awareness of these signs of audience feedback and adapts the message accordingly.[5]

Values

The third important component of audience psychology is values. **Values** are the basic components for organizing one's view of life. They are habitual ways of looking at the world or responding to problems. Values often are the foundation for beliefs and attitudes that cluster around them.

Attitudes, beliefs, and values are interdependent. That is, they tend to form consistent clusters that reinforce and repeat one another. Values are more basic than attitudes or beliefs because they represent broad categories that can motivate specific attitudes and beliefs. Thus, a person may hold a certain value, such as "Human life is sacred." That value can be expressed in multiple attitudes, perhaps including "Abortion is wrong" and "Mercy killing is immoral." Beliefs also may support this value—for example, "A fetus can survive as a human being," "Most Americans are opposed to abortion rights legislation," and "Religious authority ought to be respected on questions of morality."

Values, then, are an individual's habitualized reasons for holding particular attitudes and beliefs. Even more broadly, however, we can talk about **value orientations** (sometimes called **ideologies**), which are the views of life taken by relatively large groups of people. Over the last three decades, for example, Americans have read about the Establishment, the Silent Majority, the Counterculture, Yippies, Me-ism, Situational Ethics, Freaks, New Politics, the Old Guard, Libbers, Rednecks, the Moral Majority, Yuppies, Neo-Liberals, and Neo-Conservatives. Social and political value orientations come and go, and, while you need not join every trend, you must be conscious of the effects of ideologies on people's valuative tendencies.[6]

Discovering the values that your listeners habitually bring to bear on issues is a critical part of audience analysis. These values organize and often influence the beliefs and attitudes they express. For example, knowing that members of a student senate are strongly motivated by sociological issues (how the social life of the university will be affected) and pragmatic concerns (how much it will cost) will help you if you are trying to persuade them to allocate funds for bringing a Sheena Easton concert to campus. Unless you can discover *common ground*—shared values—among them, you may well be in communicative trouble. A search for common ground is a crucial final step in audience analysis.

Analyzing the Speech Occasion

Sometimes analyzing the occasion is simple: you know you are attending a Foreign Policy Club meeting, you have been there dozens of times, and you know what they expect from you when it is your turn to discuss a world hotspot for ten minutes. At other times, occasions are complex, with many rules governing what can be said, how and when you can talk, and in what manner you must treat other people. First, you need to understand what occasions are and then explore how best to analyze them profitably.

The Idea of an Occasion

To formalize the definition suggested earlier, an **occasion** is a set of activities that occurs in a time and place set aside for those activities to fulfill collective purposes for and by people who have been taught the special meanings of those activities. Let us examine that definition more closely.

Polling Techniques

*T*oday there are at least 2000 firms devoting major portions of their work to public opinion polling, not counting many times that number of businesses and academic organizations conducting surveys; more than $4 billion is spent annually on polling. Population surveys as we know them began in the seventeenth century, and, thanks to telephones and computers, have been refined into precise social sciences.

One of the most innovative political pollsters is Richard Wirthlin, founder of a company known as Decision/Making/Information. Wirthlin quit his job in the economics department at Brigham Young University to become a full-time pollster; he is responsible for an important innovation in audience analysis.

Wirthlin invented the "tracking" or "rolling sample" technique used in presidential elections. To track a candidate, he begins by asking each of 500 randomly selected voters a small set of questions. After five nights of questioning voters, Wirthlin has collected 2500 responses—a large sample for survey research. On the sixth night, he adds another 500 voters but drops the answers from the first night; on the seventh, he adds another 500 people but drops the answers from the second night; and so on, to the week of the election (when he starts adding 1000 voters). This procedure gives him daily polling results, with tabulations reflecting changes in people's minds produced by events, candidates' statements and actions, and so on. The "rolling sample" gives him dynamic access to people as they make decisions throughout the election period.

Political campaigners speak to thousands, even (in the case of presidential candidates) millions of voters. Sampling public opinion, thus, lies at the heart of audience analysis for politicians. For that matter, it is also important to all of us as we watch economic indicators, estimate our chances to live to a ripe old age, handicap our bowling scores, or figure out if our communities are giving enough to United Way. We are, as Alonzo and Starr have called us, "a nation of numbers watchers." You, too, will find audience surveys of great help to you in preparing speeches both in this class and in other settings.

FOR FURTHER READING

Alonzo, William, and Paul Starr. "A Nation of Numbers Watchers." *The Wilson Quarterly* 9 (Summer 1985): 93–123; Levy, Mark R. "Polling and the Presidential Election," in "Polling and the Democratic Consenses." *The Annals of the American Academy of Political and Social Science* (March 1984): 90; Martin, L. John. "Preface," in "Polling and the Democratic Consenses." *The Annals of the American Academy of Political and Social Science* (March 1984): 9.

An "occasion" is a set of activities that occurs in a predetermined time and place to fulfill collective purposes for and by people who have been taught the special meanings of those activities.

. . . in a time and place. Regular occasions, such as religious services, usually occur at special times (often Fridays, Saturdays, or Sundays) in special places (often buildings identified as churches). Special events, such as political conventions, happen at specific times and in halls designed for them. Those times and places can take on special meanings of their own. Sunday morning in the United States is such a special time; few other special occasions besides church are allowed to occur then. The places where justice is handed down—courtrooms—are specially designed to emphasize permanence (made out of marble), spaciousness (high ceilings in oversized rooms), elevation (the bench rises above all other chairs so the judge looks down on everyone else), and impartiality (a black robe to hide the individualized features of the judge).

. . . collective purposes. Most important, perhaps, people design occasions to meet particular group needs: worship (church), justice (courts), passage to adulthood (bar mitzvahs, confirmations, "coming-out" or debutante balls, and commencement ceremonies), remembrance of basic values or heroes (monument dedications and such holidays as Memorial Day), recognition of leadership and power (inaugurals and coronations), and the like. These are all activities that group members tend to do collectively. A one-person ceremony does not mean much. A group ceremony does, however; it recognizes

the importance of the group, its claims upon its membership, and the group's power to confirm status upon people.

. . . special meanings. You do not enter the world knowing how to pray, to cheer, to dedicate, to mourn with others, or to inaugurate. Those are all *social* activities you must learn, either through instruction or through imitation.[7] It is a sign of group membership to know and understand the meaning of the activities that constitute an occasion. Outsiders do not, but insiders do.

Occasions vary a good deal as to their purposes, their complexity, and even their formality. A visit from a particularly beloved (or feared) relative may be an informal yet important "special occasion" in some families; other occasions—such as those mentioned previously—are much more formal. No matter what their formality, however, all occasions are governed by *rules* (do's and don'ts), by *roles* ("parts" different people play), and **judgments of competency** (assessments about how well people play their parts). We usually have rather specific expectations of what will happen during occasions.[8]

Audience Expectations on Speech Occasions

Speech occasions, too, can range from informal (a brief statement of your position in a classroom discussion) to formal (a farewell from your class to your sorority). Whether informal or not, however, a speech occasion shares characteristics with most other occasions:

- The *set of activities* that constitute a speech (standing or sitting in front of an audience, talking in a sustained fashion for (usually) a mutually agreed upon period of time, for a particular purpose) is known to both speaker and audience members. For example, unless someone is an outsider, he or she will know what to expect when you rise to talk to the local Rotary Club about your experiences as a Rotary International Scholarship student in Germany last year.
- The *time and place* of speeches usually are predetermined. You often are told how long to speak and when, and the room in which you are speaking usually is adjusted to accommodate speeches—a raised platform, a lectern, audience members seated in front of you and facing you, audiovisual equipment you may require, and perhaps a microphone in a big room. The whole setting usually says, "This is a place for public speaking and not interpersonal chitchat."
- The *collective purposes* that a talk is to fulfill are likewise known ahead of time when a speech is announced. Both you and your audience usually know the general purpose of your talk—to inform, persuade, actuate, or entertain. Some occasions are so formal that your specific purposes also are understood by listeners, as when you nominate someone for office during the election portion of a business meeting, when you pay tribute to a valued employee upon her retirement, or when you explain zero-

Speech occasions, like other occasions, are characterized by rules, roles, and judgments of competency.

coupon bonds to your Business Majors Club. The knowledge of purposiveness that speaker and audience share is vitally important in bonding them together and in ensuring that communication actually will occur; that knowledge comes from mutual understanding of the occasion.

- Both you and the listeners have been taught *how to speak (and to listen) on particular occasions.* No one came into the world knowing how to give a speech in general, let alone how to construct particular types of speeches—such as after-dinner talks, quarterly sales reports, or speeches supporting a proposed energy conservation policy. That is one of the reasons you are in this class: to learn more about speaking on particular occasions.

A "speech occasion" is every bit as demanding of you as any other social or political event. This means that speech occasions, like other occasions, are characterized by rules, roles, and judgments of competency—in other words, by audience expectations.

The common lore about public speaking is filled with communication rules: do not mumble; trustworthy speakers are more effective than mistrusted ones; extemporized speeches, other things being equal, are preferable to read speeches; in an introduction, orient audience members, give them reasons for listening, forecast the development of your speech, and seize attention; the larger the audience, the larger your gestures must become. As you can tell, these communication rules come from several sources—social scientific study, experience, and things your grandmother or your textbook told you. As noted in Chapter 1, such rules can be violated and you sometimes can get away with doing so in a speech. You might, however, pay a price. If an audience judges you ignorant or flaunting of communication rules, they may write off your message. Ignoring rules can be risky.

The matter of roles is a bit more complicated. There is no good scheme for classifying all of the possible roles speakers play. So far, we have discussed general roles—informer, persuader, entertainer—and suggested other, more specific ones. Thus, on one occasion, you might be an instructor (listeners expect to be taught); an arguer (listeners are looking for rational, reason-governed persuasion); a nominator (listeners must elect someone to office); or a eulogist (listeners are waiting to hear someone praised). Whatever your role, the way you perform it usually should conform to audience expectations. If you violate a role expectation, perhaps by preaching when people are expecting dispassionate information, you could get into trouble. A president of a corporation who prepares a comic monologue in place of his or her serious, annual report on the health of the firm would be in grave difficulties as a result of playing the wrong role.

If you cannot offer information clearly, arguments rationally, or motivational appeals rousingly, your listeners might judge you to be incompetent. A positive judgment of competency is a sign that you have learned well your society's ways of talking publicly; a negative assessment indicates you still have important things to learn about speaking before particular audiences in particular situations. Some standards for judgment are general—for example, the standards for delivery and appropriate language use (see Chapters 12 and 14). Many, however, are attached to specific occasions. By tradition, a presidential inaugural address must begin with, among other things, the phrase "fellow citizens," in recognition that the president, unlike a king, is "one of us." Also by tradition, first-year members of the United States Senate do not speak but are expected to listen; then, in their second session, they can deliver their "maiden speech," awaited by the others interested in the oratorical power of the yearling politician. A senator who spoke too soon would be considered brash, unthinking, and in violation of tradition—incompetent.[9]

Audience expectations, thus, come into play almost every time you speak; those expectations are rooted in large part in the situation in which you are talking, in the occasion. You have to analyze its roles, its expected role requirements, and its general and specific standards for competency if you are to be ready to speak effectively.

Factors to Consider
When Analyzing Occasions

You will have to learn the specific demands of particular occasions each time you speak. We can, however, discuss some of the more general questions raised in most speaking situations, including queries about the nature of the occasion, the prevailing rules, the physical conditions, and the events preceding or following your speech.

The Nature and Purpose of the Occasion. Is yours a voluntary or a captive audience? A **voluntary audience** attends a speechmaking event primarily because of interest in the speaker or subject. A **captive audience** is required to attend, perhaps at the explicit instruction of a boss or under threat of a failing grade in a course. In general, the more captive your audience, the less initial interest members will show and the greater will be their resistance to accepting your information or point of view.

Are your subject and purpose in line with the reason for the meeting, or are you merely seizing the occasion to present some ideas you think important? Are you one in a series of speakers whom the audience has heard over a period of weeks or months? If so, how does your speech subject relate to those previously presented? These are important questions to answer when you are analyzing the nature and purpose of the occasion. In other words, the nature and purpose of the occasion—as well as the interest level you can sense among those attending it—often dictate a series of general decisions you will make in your approach to the speech transaction.

The Prevailing Rules or Customs. Will there be a regular order of business or a fixed program into which your speech must fit? Is it the custom of the group to ask questions of the speaker after the address? Do the listeners expect a formal speaking manner? Will you, as the speaker, be expected to extend complimentary remarks or to express respect for a tradition or concept? Knowing the answers to these questions will help you avoid feeling out of place and will prevent you from arousing antagonism by an inappropriate word or action.

In addition to probing the general customs prevailing in a group, you may need to go a step further by discovering specific rules for formulating your messages. If you are delivering a report on some research you have undertaken, you will be expected to review the research of others before you discuss your own study. A member of the U.S. Senate must always refer to an opponent as "The Honorable Senator from _____" even if he or she is going to disagree violently with that person. The speaker at the Friars' Club of New York is expected to mercilessly but good-naturedly excoriate the person who is the object of that evening's "roast." Part of your task of understanding communication rules, therefore, is to analyze the specific customs and traditions governing particular audiences in particular places.

The Physical Conditions.   Will your speech be given outdoors or in an auditorium? Is the weather likely to be hot or cold? Will the audience be sitting or standing? If sitting, will the members be crowded together or scattered about? In how large a room will the speech be presented? Will an electronic public address system be used? Will facilities be provided for the audiovisual reinforcements you will use, or must you bring your own? Will you be seen and heard easily? Are there likely to be disturbances in the form of noise or interruptions? These and similar environmental factors affect the temper of the listeners, their span of attention, and the style of speaking you will have to use as you adjust to the speech environment.

Events Preceding or Following Your Speech.   At what time of day or night will your speech be given: immediately after a heavy meal or a long program, both of which can induce drowsiness and reduce listener interest? just before the principal address or event of the evening? By whom and in what manner will you be introduced to the audience? What other items are on the program? What are their tone and character? All these things will influence listeners' interest in your speech. In some instances, you will be able to use the other events on the program to increase interest or belief in your own remarks; sometimes they will work against you. In any case, you must always consider the effect that the program as a whole may have on your speech.

Using Audience Analysis in Speech Preparation

Neither demographic nor psychological analysis is an end in itself, nor will merely thinking about the speech occasion produce foolproof speech preparation strategies. Rather, you are carrying out such analyses to discover what might affect the reception of you and your ideas. You are searching for relevant factors that can affect the audience's attitudes toward you, your subject, and your purpose and that, consequently, should guide your rhetorical decisions. What you learn about your listeners and their expectations through systematic investigation can conceivably affect every aspect of your speech—right down to ways you phrase important ideas and deliver your thoughts. This section will concentrate on ways in which the results of your analyses can help you phrase your purposes and select your dominant appeals.

Audience Targeting: Setting Realistic Purposes

Few of us have difficulty determining our general speech purposes—to inform, to entertain, to persuade or actuate. Once this is done, you need to determine realistically what you can expect to accomplish with a particular audience in the time you have available. As you think about **targeting your audience,** five considerations should arise: your specific purpose, the areas of audience interest, the audience's capacity to act, the audience's willingness to act, and the degree of change you can expect.

Your Specific Purpose. Suppose you have a part-time job with your college's Career Planning and Placement Office; you know enough about its operations and have enough personal interest in it to want to speak about career planning and placement to different audiences. What you have discovered about different audiences should help you determine appropriate specific purposes for each. If you were to talk to a group of incoming freshmen, for example, you would know:

- They probably know little or nothing about the functions of a career planning and placement office (for example, they have few beliefs, none of which is fixed).
- They probably are predisposed to look favorably on career planning and placement (given job anxieties among college graduates).
- They probably are, at their particular stage of life and educational development, more concerned with such pragmatic issues as getting an adviser, registering, and learning about basic degree requirements than they are with such longer-range matters as post-degree placement (and may not value your information without motivation).
- They are likely, however, to see you as an authoritative speaker and, hence, are willing to listen to you.

Given these audience considerations, you probably should keep your speech fairly general: feed them basic, not detailed, information about career planning and placement; remind them that the office can relieve many of their later anxieties as graduation nears; show them how thinking about possible careers will help them select majors and particular courses. You might phrase your specific purpose as follows: "To brief incoming freshmen on the range of services offered by the Career Planning and Placement Office." That orientation would include a basic description of each service and a general appeal to use the services to make some curricular decisions.

Were you, instead, to talk about this subject to a group of college seniors, you would address the audience differently. You would discover:

- They already know something about the Career Planning and Placement Office (since they probably have roommates and friends who have used or are preparing to use such services).
- They have strong positive feelings about career planning and placement (because they are hoping to use such services to find jobs when they graduate).
- They tend to value education pragmatically—that is, for how it has prepared them to "earn a decent living."
- They may view you as an unqualified speaker on this subject, especially if you are not a senior or are unemployed.

Speakers must determine what they can expect to accomplish with a particular audience in the time they have available.

Given these factors, you should be much more specific in some areas. You would want to describe the special features of this office's operations rather than simply outline its general duties. Your listeners need to know "how" not "what," because they already know "what." You would reassure them that the office is successful in placing many students but suggest that they allow ample time for résumé development, job searching, and interviewing. Also, you should demonstrate your expertise by talking about career possibilities across a variety of fields (especially if you know what fields are represented in the group you are addressing). You might phrase your specific purpose like this: "To inform graduating seniors about Midstate University's philosophy of career planning and placement, about ways the office can help students find employment, and about specific types of information and assistance the office provides students." Audience analysis, therefore, will focus your specific purposes and determine which are most appropriate to your listeners.

Areas of Audience Interest. You can use both demographic and psychological analyses to help you decide what ideas will interest your listeners. This is critical in narrowing your topic choice and choosing specific ideas to develop. Suppose you know something about computer programming. An audience of industrial managers probably would be very interested in hearing how computers can make their companies more cost effective; a group of hospital administrators might want to learn how to enhance recordkeeping and patient services; the Internal Revenue Service would appreciate an application in tax fraud discovery; and a mixed, "public" audience will be curious about how computers will transform their everyday lives in the twenty-first century.

Sometimes, however, you will want to create a new set of interests in an audience. For example, you might suppose that an audience of doctors will be interested in finding out about the latest drugs for pain relief, given their medical-scientific values. Yet, you may want the audience to understand the psychological effects of such drugs and the related ethical questions of their use by unstable patients. You can create a new set of interests by tying new interests to old ones. For this speech, you might phrase your central idea as follows: "Knowing more about the psychological effects of the latest drugs available for pain relief will make you a more humane as well as a more medically expert physician." Phrasing the central idea in this way explicitly ties the interests you are trying to create to ones the audience already has.

The Audience's Capacity to Act.   As was noted in the section on narrowing speech topics, limit your request to an action that lies within your listeners' range of authority. Do not ask them to accomplish the impossible. To demand of a group of striking workers that they place a tariff on imported goods is unrealistic; however, you can ask them to boycott foods and products benefiting from artificially low tariffs and to visit their local congressional representative at his or her next local office hours.

Sometimes your audience analysis will reveal that different segments of your audience have varying capacities to execute actions. In that case, you will want to address those segments separately in the action step of your speech. In talking with a local school's PTA about instituting an after-school program of foreign language and culture instruction, you will want to target each subgroup with a different call to action:

> *Parents:* "Prepare a petition for the school board, enroll your children in the program, and help find community volunteers to work in it."
> *Administrators:* "Seek funding from the school board for the after-school program."
> *Teachers:* "Volunteer at least one after-school period a week to help with instruction."

As you can see, each call for action is suited to the range of authority and talent possessed by each portion. (We will discuss this further when we look at audience segmentation later in this chapter.)

The Audience's Willingness to Act.   Not only must you be concerned with audience authority, but also with audience will. You must try to figure out how much you can expect an audience to do, given the situation or occasion.

For example, a speech soliciting blood donors has a better chance of success when given at a dorm meeting to discuss service projects than it does in your speech classroom. People attending the dorm meeting *want* to do public service, or they would not have come. People in your classroom are strongly aware that you are "practicing" public address; hence, they are (usually) more distanced from you, more analytical of your appeals, and less caught up in the spirit of advice-following; they are difficult listeners to reach because they hear so many appeals from fellow students during the term. Your assessment of an audience's will or desire may affect the wording of your claim. Addressing a dorm meeting, you might phrase your claim in this fashion: "Running a campuswide blood drive is the best service project our dorm can undertake this semester." Dealing with the same subject in your speech classroom, given the audience's general disinterest in starting big projects, you might phrase the claim differently: "You should give blood as a matter of personal commitment to your fellow human beings in need." The first phrasing recognizes the purpose of the occasion (identifying a dorm project) and acknowledges that the listeners want to do something. The second plays down or ignores the occasion (classroom speech), because that occasion does not encourage listeners to take your advice; instead, the wording personalizes the subject, allowing the speaker to tug on at least a few heartstrings. Willingness to act, thus, is usually related to listeners' expectations in a situation and should be taken into account when you phrase your goals or purposes.

Degrees of Change. Finally, as was suggested earlier, you must be realistic about the expected degree of change in your listeners' attitudes and beliefs. How much information can you present for consideration? If your time is limited or your average listener's attention span is short, you must limit the information you present. Such demographic factors as age and educational development will help you answer these questions. Also, deciding whether your information is new or already known will influence how much material you can cover in a single speech. How intensely can you motivate an audience to react to a topic? If your listeners are strongly opposed to downtown renovation, a single speech, no matter how eloquent, will probably not reverse their opinions. One attempt may only neutralize some of their objections—which is a more realistic goal for a single speech. How much action can you expect after your speech? If your prespeech analysis indicates that your listeners vehemently oppose nuclear power plants in your area, you can probably persuade many of them to work long hours at a variety of activities, such as picketing, lobbying, and telephone marathons; however, if they are only moderately committed to opposing nuclear facilities, you might ask for a small monetary donation and no actual time commitment.

In other words, audience analysis should help you determine how to phrase your specific purpose and central ideas for maximum effectiveness. Understanding your audience should also give you a more realistic expectation of what changes in behavior, attitudes, and commitments can occur in your listeners.

Audience Segmentation: Selecting Dominant Ideas and Appeals

So far, we have been dealing with audience analysis as it helps you target your audience as a group. Keep in mind, however, that no matter how people are crowded together, arranged in rows, or reached electronically, they are still individuals. As was noted when discussing psychological profiling, your beliefs, attitudes, and values, although influenced by your culture and society, are ultimately yours. They are the unique products of your experiences and thoughts.

Ideally, it would be most effective if you could approach each listener individually. Sometimes you can, but such communication is time consuming and inefficient when you are dealing with matters of broad public concern. Imagine for a minute the president of this country talking to each of us individually. It is impossible; however, through a televised public speech, he or she can talk to us in our own home as though it were a personal conversation. It is necessary to find a compromise between thinking of an audience either as a homogeneous mass or as a group of solitary individuals. Advertisers use an approach called audience segmentation. **Audience segmentation** is a matter of dividing a mass audience into subgroups, or "target populations," that hold common attitudes, beliefs, values, or demographic characteristics. A typical college-student audience might be segmented by academic standing (freshmen through seniors), academic majors (art through zoology), classroom performance (*A +* to *F*), and even extracurricular activities (ROTC, SADD, Young Democrats, Pi Kappa Delta).

Accurately Identifying Subgroups/Segments. It is important to carefully identify subgroups within your audience. This will not only allow you to better phrase your appeals, but it will help you avoid irritating your listeners unnecessarily. A speaker who began, "Because all you girls are interested in efficient cooking, today I want to talk about four ways a food processor will save you time in the kitchen" would probably alienate two subgroups in the audience. The females probably would be irritated with the stereotyped allusion to them as "girls," while the males who cook would be offended by having been left out. The appeal would be better phrased "Because everyone who cooks is interested in . . . " This appeal aims at the proper audience segment—the culinary masters. Similarly, unless you are sure there are no Roman Catholics in your audience, you probably will want to avoid blaming the Catholic religious hierarchy for the presence of illegal aliens in the United States. This is not to say, of course, that you never directly confront beliefs, attitudes, and values of subgroups represented in your audience—that you always say what people "want" to hear. Obviously, in some areas of this country, the church has been active in the Sanctuary Movement, some business practices have been responsible for part of the unemployment problem, and government has contributed to environmental pollution. You can find ways to talk about those things, but be sure that you avoid stereotyped references to people and groups; that you avoid blanket condemnation of groups of people; and that, when possible, you work around controversial subjects. You should cite ample and unbiased evidence when you challenge a group's beliefs, attitudes, and sacred values.

Selecting Relevant Psychological Statements. Audience segmentation should also help you select statements of belief, attitudes, and values for inclusion in your speech. If you can accurately identify the relevant subgroups, you can include psychological appeals for each in your speech. This greatly increases the personal appeal and potential effectiveness of your message. Suppose you were to give a speech to a local Community Club about the importance of including women in its membership. Your initial segmenting of the audience tells you that the club is composed of businessmen, medical professionals, educators, social service personnel, lawyers, and bankers. By thinking of the club as segmented into such subgroups, you should be in a position to offer each some reasons to support your proposal. You might outline the appeals this way:

Claim: "The membership of the Community Club should be extended to include women."

1. For doctors and hospital workers: a large percentage of the hospital staff is composed of women in all roles, including physicians, nurses, physical therapists, and administrators. Their expertise and commitment to helping others is the foundation of the club's philosophy.
2. For social service workers: the social-team concept is important. It means working with everyone—including women.
3. For educators: women make up the majority of our elementary and secondary school faculties. By limiting membership, we automatically exclude one of the most important resources for our young people—their classroom teachers.
4. For those from community businesses: women control a large proportion of the financial resources of the community as investors, property owners, and heads of households. They could offer a significant contribution to the success of the club.

This is just a sketch of several basic appeals; each would be expanded in an actual speech. From these examples, however, you can see how each is based on beliefs and attitudes you assume are important to segments of the audience. There is an implicit reference to medical ethics based on serving humankind, to the commitment of social services to help people from all

10. P
    n
11. A
12. C
    d

Public
is to d
groun
listene
graphi
age, g
groun
values
of the
place
the pe
shoul
ual ro
tency
ence t
audiei
the d
segme
select

1. I
Univei

2. 1
of Org
of Hu

3. 1
person
sition:
tion, 4

4. 5
Thom
35 (19

5.

A speaker can use a valuative vocabulary to motivate different segments of an audience to listen to and accept his or her information.

strata of life, to educators' beliefs and attitudes that young people are a national resource, and to business commitments to financial responsibility and success. Thus, audience analysis, in combination with audience segmentation, are valuable tools for selecting your main lines of appeal and argument.

Choosing Among Valuative Appeals. Finally, as you might guess, audience segmentation will help you select a valuative vocabulary for your speeches. Even informative speeches, as we will discuss more fully later, need to contain appeals to audience interests. You can use a **valuative vocabulary** to motivate different segments of the audience to listen to and accept your information. For a class demonstration speech, you might say, "Today I want to teach you three basic techniques of Oriental cooking—cutting meats and vegetables, using spices, and quick-cooking your food in a wok. If you learn these techniques, you'll expand your range of expertise in the kitchen [*personal value*]; you'll save money on your food and energy bills [*economic value*]; you'll prepare more-than-satisfying meals for your friends [*social value*]; and you'll prepare nutritious, healthful meals for everyone [*pragmatic value*]." With that statement, you will have given your audience four different reasons for listening and will have a good chance of appealing to everyone in

CHAPTER SIX

Determining the Basic Appeals

Chapter 5 emphasized the importance of audience analysis, with special attention to discovering the listeners' social characteristics, beliefs, attitudes, values, expectations, and group traditions. Who people are, what experiences they have had, what they believe, and what they think is appropriate to say on various occasions all determine how they will respond to your speeches. Equally important in governing these responses are their *motives*—their basic biological; physical; social; and emotional needs, wants, and desires. In this chapter, we will discuss the appropriate and effective use of motivational appeals. The first section will focus on motivational studies of individual behavior and will lead to a discussion of clusters of motivational appeals. Finally, we will look at some advice on using a knowledge of motives and motivational appeals to increase the impact of your message.

Motivation and Motives: The Analysis of Human Behavior

For our purposes, human behavior can be divided into activity that is the result of biological needs, drives, or stimuli and activity that is the result of social motives, desires, or deliberative intent.[1] The motive to eat when hungry or to sleep when tired is the result of biologically determined needs or drives. External stimuli, such as a hot, stuffy room, can also affect your physiological state. If you attend both noon and 1:00 classes, you may find that it is difficult to remain attentive during the 1:00 lecture as you experience strong hunger pangs. In such a case, the impulse to eat rather than to attend to the lecture affects your concentration. Satisfying a **biological motive,** then, is to give in to the impulse to meet a physiological urge.

Social motives are individual goals, desires, or behaviors that are the result of *deliberative intent.* The desire to achieve success on a speech, to get a good grade on a test, to feel needed or wanted by others, or to influence others are all examples of social motives. They are motives related to your personal experiences in your family, with your peer group, at work, and within the community. Desires, such as wanting to be perceived as a nice person or to be included in activities your peers plan, are also social motives. The origin of the motive can be internal, or *intrinsic,* in terms of your own desire to be liked, to strive for excellence, or to enjoy what you do. Its origin also can be external, or *extrinsic,* in terms of specific incentives that impel you toward certain goals (as in higher pay, approval from a friend or employer, or friendship).

In addition to being intrinsic or extrinsic, motives can be discussed in terms of *permanence* and *change.*[2] While theories differ on the extent to which motives are relatively stable or subject to change, we can assume that both conditions are influential in determining behavior. Motives that result from biological or physiological needs are relatively stable over time. They may be in the background temporarily, especially after a huge meal, but they always return as a human impulse requiring a response. Motives also may undergo dramatic and, at times, permanent shifts in their level of importance or intensity. People can undergo dramatic conversions as the result of life experiences. The desire to influence others may be relatively strong early in life, only to diminish in importance as one nears retirement, having achieved the level of influence once desired and tiring of its thrill. The point is that motives are, in part, *dynamic processes,* capable of being altered by the influence of others, or by one's own internal reassessment of their importance.

The Classification of Motives

Although there are several ways to classify motives, we will discuss them in terms of three primary *clusters:* affiliation, achievement, and power or social influence. **Affiliation** covers motives involving the desire to belong to a group, to be well liked or accepted. It also includes such motives as love, conformity, dependence upon others, sympathy toward others, and loyalty. **Achievement motives** are related to the intrinsic or extrinsic desire for success, adventure, creativity, and personal enjoyment. **Power motives** concern activities in which influence over others is the prime objective.[3] These broad clusters will be examined in greater detail later in this chapter.

McClelland's Motive Types

These clusters can be considered either as discrete entities or as interactive. McClelland, for example, has examined different interactions between the general motives of affiliation, power, and what he terms "inhibition"—the degree of willingness to be active in a social setting.[4] The interactions produce four possible behavior types. In Type 1, the desire for Affiliation is high relative to Power, and Inhibition is low; these individuals are happiest within

MOTIVE CLUSTERS

Affiliation	*Achievement*	*Power*
Companionship	Acquisition/saving	Aggression
Conformity	Success/display	Authority/dominance
Deference/dependence	Prestige	Defense
Sympathy/generosity	Pride	Fear
Loyalty	Adventure/change	Autonomy/independence
Tradition	Perseverance	
Reverence/worship	Creativity	
Sexual attraction	Curiosity	
	Personal enjoyment	

a social desire to belong, to be part of a group, is expressive of an affiliative motive. Although not limited to the following examples, a speaker can consider several appeals to listeners' affiliative desires.

Companionship. We all need others—their presence, touch, and recognition of who we are. Maslow saw belongingness as the most important human desire once physiological and safety needs are fulfilled. Thus, appeals of companionship tend to fill persuasive and actuative speeches of conversion, which seek to expand the membership of social, religious, or political-action groups by convincing audience members to join. Such appeals can be phrased explicitly, as in "We care about you," "Join our group and find fellowship with kindred souls," or "Thousands of people like you have found solutions to their problems by joining." The appeals also can be more indirect; a speaker may list several qualities of a group and appeal to audience approval of these qualities.

Conformity. At times, people's sense of belongingness becomes so strong that they feel psychological pressure to be "one of the crowd." Commercials stressing what "the in-group does," what "the serious jogger wears," and what "all true Americans believe" appeal to consumers to imitate the behavior and to conform to the norm being identified. Extensive social scientific research on the power of social comparison and conformity pressures documents the significance of this appeal.[9]

Deference/Dependence. When we perceive that others have wisdom, experience, or expertise superior to our own, we defer to their knowledge and judgment, often from a desire to be accepted by those individuals. Deference can become habitual, in which case we come to depend upon others to provide necessary information, as they are "in a position to know." The successful use of testimony as a form of supporting material depends on listeners' willingness to defer to the source of the testimonial as an authority figure.

Sympathy/Generosity.   All appeals to giving, to support for others, and to self-sacrifice in the name of the "common good" are based on the assumption that your *social self* (the part of you that is bonded to others or that desires social bonding) will overcome your *private self* (the self-centered part of you). By giving, you join a select group of people who assist others in their time of need.

Loyalty.   Periodically, we all need to celebrate our membership in groups and societies so as to renew our commitments to them and to increase our sense of group and social cohesiveness. Speakers often ask listeners to be loyal to friends, family, organizations, states, geographical regions, or even to their country (a strong appeal that was used by both supporters and opponents of the Vietnam War). Appeals to loyalty are rarely used in speeches attempting to change fundamental beliefs, values, or actions; rather, they are typically appeals to the like-minded—to those who already share the speaker's beliefs and values. Such appeals are typical of what are called *reinforcement speeches.*

Tradition.   This appeal, like loyalty, appeals to the audience's sense of its past—of staying in close association with past values, actions, or events. In addition, it can be related to perseverance (as discussed in the achievement cluster). Whereas perseverance stretches your mind into the future, tradition draws your thoughts back to the people, ideas, and institutions that are central to your definition of who you are, what you stand for, and where you belong. Political speeches that talk about "Democratic traditions" or "Republican principles" appeal to values and beliefs that define for you what to think, what to do, and whom to accept or to reject as a political party member. Appeals to tradition can be used in speeches that argue against policies or actions that will alter the present situation in—to your way of thinking— unfavorable ways: "A vote against the proposed city council is a vote for the traditional values of our community." Tradition also can be used to extend one's principles into new arenas: "This new health insurance plan is simply an extension of our continuing tradition of concern for the welfare of our workers."

Reverence/Worship.   Sometimes we must recognize our own inferiority— to others of superior qualities, to institutions we admire, to nature and the cosmos, and to deities that humble us in their magnitude and timelessness. Beyond deference, a sense of reverence or worship leads to submission, to

Motivational appeals are attempts to make salient and relevant a series of motives within an audience through visualization or attribution. Product advertisers use motivational appeals to influence the buying behavior of carefully segmented audiences.

LEVI'S STREETLIGHTS. THE HOTTEST JEANS ON TWO LEGS. Levi's

dependence upon a person or image. Such reverent submission can take three forms: *hero worship, reverence for institutions,* and *divine worship.* As a speaker, you have relatively little power to *create* a sense of reverence in your listeners, but if you know enough about them ahead of time, you can *refer* to objects, people, or institutions they are likely to revere. Speeches advocating the preservation of a nature sanctuary or of historic landmarks scheduled for demolition can make effective use of this appeal.

Sexual Attraction. A staple of advertising trying to sell you deodorant, hair rinse and spray, beer and liquor, and a multitude of other sundries is the appeal to sexual attraction. "Sex sells" is an unfortunate truism to Madison Avenue marketers and advertisers. Actually, as you look closely at such appeals, you will find that the core of their potency lies not so much in their

allusion to particular actions as in a more general idea of personal physical attractiveness that taps into your desire to imitate or to belong to that select group of people possessing such qualities. In some cases, the appeal extends to your sense of adventure or to your secret fantasies. In most ads these days, the appeal to sexual attraction is approached verbally in indirect ways ("When you want to look your very best, use . . ." or "For the executive who wants to be noticed . . ."). An advertisement also may use a *double entendre* (a phrase with two obvious meanings), as in the hair coloring ad that asks "Does she or doesn't she?" The success of such phrases depends on the audience's identifying the product, rather than the sexual allusion, as the focus of the advertisement.[10] As a speaker, you are well advised to keep such appeals under firm control. You can make appeals responsibly, without using sexist language or images.

The Achievement Cluster

Achievement motives concern an individual's desire to attain goals, to excel in certain behaviors or activities, or to obtain prestige or success. Achievement is the fourth rung on Maslow's ladder of motives; it also can be seen as a motive force that "pulls" a person toward the accomplishment of a particular goal.[11]

Acquisition/Saving. In a time of great individual concern for self, as seen in the growth of investment clubs, Supplemental Retirement Accounts, and the like, an appeal to personal desires to acquire possessions (including money) or to the rewards of saving money is potent. Rewards can be described in materialistic terms ("Earn money easily"), social phrases ("Become one of the select few to own . . . "), spiritual appeals ("Lay up for yourselves treasures in heaven"), or personal terms ("This is your chance of a lifetime—buy now"). Motivational appeals to acquisition target the individual rather than the group, and, hence, tend to be used in actuative speeches calling for personal, individual action. Such appeals must be used in the context of the community's standards for acquiring material possessions.

Success/Display. "The successful executive knows . . . " "To make maximum use of your talents, act today to . . . " These and similar appeals depend upon your interest in making a mark, in further actualizing your talents and abilities. An advertisement that encourages you to read the *Wall Street Journal*, for example, appeals to your desire to improve your ability to control the marketplace or to better position yourself for the next step up the corporate ladder. Such motivational appeals are often found in actuative speeches in which the speaker's goal is to encourage individuals to adopt a particular self-help product or a course of action.

Pride. An appeal to pride is an appeal to one's sense of self-worth. Such appeals can motivate individual or collective achievement. In some cases, they can motivate us to excel beyond our own sense of our abilities. Such appeals tighten our loyalties to others in a group ("Be proud of America"). When coupled with an appeal to adventure ("Be all that you can be in the Army") or to creativity, they may move people to great personal exertion. Hence, actuative speeches calling for extra measures of effort from listeners often contain appeals to pride. A speech that calls on the nation to sacrifice much in the face of economic austerity also may invoke pride as an appeal ("We can and will persevere; although the road ahead will be rough, we can take pride in our toughness").

Prestige. As in the case of appeals to pride, this appeal is to an individual's sense of worth—to one's "place" in a social community or within a particular power structure. Ads for luxury automobiles and fine clothes make use of this appeal, as they imply that the owner of such items has "arrived." For example, the recognition of a group's importance to a political campaign conveys high self-esteem to the individuals involved. They achieve success when others notice and publicly pay tribute to their efforts. An appeal to listeners' desire for prestige should take into account their desire for affiliation. For example, do they value driving an expensive foreign car so as to be seen as members of an elite group, or would they be turned off by such an overt appeal?

Adventure/Change. "Taste the High Country!" cries the beer commercial. "Join the Navy and see the world!" says the local recruiter. The human soul yearns for release; we seek risk as a way of validating human worth. In release and risk, however, are potentials for danger, and not every listener is willing to be put in danger. A speech on the glories of skydiving or hang gliding will appeal automatically to some people's sense of adventure, but not to all. This appeal, thus, cannot be used as the primary thrust of an attempt to change people's minds or actions; it tends to work only when individuals are already well disposed toward change but need a nudge to move them to action.

Perseverance. We all realize that change does not come easily and that one must sometimes be patient, yet persistent, in seeking a better world. Many motivational appeals can be phrased to tap into this facet of people's desire to continue efforts to seek change, even when such change seems impossible. Appeals to the future ("We shall overcome"; "Let the word go forth from this time and place . . . that a new generation . . .") are especially potent. Visualizing what the future will be like, and its ability to grant our hopes and aspirations, can be an effective appeal in persuasive speeches, especially ones that promote new ideas or policies.

Creativity. As Maslow noted, the height of self-actualization is a sense of individualized abilities and talents. Ads that urge you to "Draw Me" so as to get a scholarship to a correspondence school art course and cookbooks that insist you can become a gourmet cook by following step-by-step recipes are appealing to creativity—to your desire to achieve or accomplish something that you can call your own. The appeal is especially strong to those people for whom creativity is a worthy goal in and of itself. For the most part, however, it rarely can stand alone; hence, the ads that ask you to test your drawing skill go further to cite personal enjoyment in the act of creating and to mention the material rewards that can follow (in effect, saying, "You may have hidden talents as an illustrator, and think of the money you can make following our training").

Curiosity. Children take apart alarm clocks to find out where the tick is, and adults crowd sidewalks on cold, windy days to gaze at a celebrity filming a movie. Curiosity is sometimes "idle," yet often is the driving force behind such high achievers as experimenters, inventors, scholars, and explorers; however, appeals to curiosity about the world probably will be ineffective in motivating residents of a rescue mission. In Maslow's terms, such people are too concerned with basic survival and safety issues to respond well to such an appeal. The curiosity appeal is best left to those situations in which the lower level (prepotent) needs have been met, and the audience members can afford the time and risk necessary to have their curiosity satisfied.

Personal Enjoyment.   Like appeals to creativity and curiosity, appeals to personal enjoyment depend upon listeners' tendencies toward self-centeredness. While we often act as members of a group and accept a belief or action because it enhances the group's agenda, we also act on our own. We engage in activities or behaviors because they bring us personal enjoyment, recreation, rest, relief from home and work pressures and constraints, aesthetic enjoyment, or just plain fun. In settings in which listeners view themselves as individuals, however, as in giving a demonstration speech at a craft center, this motivational appeal works well.

The Power Cluster

No other motives attempt to influence or exert control over the environment as much as those involved with power. Although people with power motives seek to manipulate others, not all uses of power are negative. With power comes social responsibility—the duty to use power in socially approved ways to obtain benefits for the group, community, or nation. As the discussion of McClelland's behavior types revealed, the interaction between one's desire for social approval (affiliation) and desire for power can determine how intensely he or she feels a sense of social responsibility.

Aggression.   Because human groups tend to be hierarchical, our biological urge to fight for our own rights and territory is translated into appeals to personal and social *competition*. Ad after ad tells how to "get ahead of the crowd" or to "beat your competition to the punch." This appeal should be used carefully, in those contexts that call for collective action against a common foe. A speaker should also be cognizant of the negative impact of blatant, or misplaced, appeals to aggressive action. When the motive to cooperate seems stronger than the motive to compete, appeals to overt action may separate you from your audience.

Authority/Dominance.   Like its cousin, aggression, the appeal to dominance depends for its potency upon listeners' sense of aggressiveness but moves beyond appeals to "win" to the ability to exercise control over others. The appeal to authority or dominance depends on listeners' willingness to see themselves as more important than they are now; therein lies its motivational effectiveness in tapping into people's desire to control their lives. The appeal can be used in actuative speeches that argue for behavior changes and in persuasive speeches urging listeners to accept a policy change in order to gain more control over their environment.

Defense.   Whereas the urge to fight may be considered a natural expression and, therefore, an appropriate motive to invoke in certain situations, we often attempt to curtail or control it. A socially acceptable way to raise people's fighting spirit in a public context is to appeal to common or mutual defense—to the sense of survival that is near the base of Maslow's hierarchy. This is a motivational appeal so accepted in American culture that it was written into the Declaration of Independence and the U.S. Constitution. It is, in most situations, socially unacceptable to hurt someone or to gain personally at another's expense. On the other hand, it is usually acceptable to protect one's own interests or "to save the lives of our children and our children's children." Such appeals tap our fundamental safety needs. The appeal is linked to power in terms of listeners' ability to control their own environment, to continue to exert authority over their collective needs through the defense of their vital interests. Speeches that deal with foreign policy issues—for example, those urging acceptance of new policies—often contain this appeal. A consistent theme in the rhetoric urging continued aid to the Nicaraguan Contras has dealt with protecting U.S. interests.

Fear.   People have a broad range of fears; Burton's list of fears mentioned earlier in this chapter indicates some with motive force. Fear is a powerful appeal, because succumbing to it or overcoming it has direct consequences for the degree of power we possess over our lives. It can be productive, as when an individual is driven to achievement or manifests courage under extreme duress. Fear also can be destructive, as when fear-based prejudice produces socially unacceptable behavior toward others. The power of fear appeals has made it a common motivational tool in advertising: "Speed Kills." "Ring around the collar!" Recall the principle noted at the outset of this discussion of motivational appeals—if you are not afraid of appearing with ring around the collar, such an appeal is ineffective. In using fear appeals, you should stay within the range of acceptable taste; more practically, you will not want to make your appeals so strong that they actually have the opposite effect (called the **boomerang effect** by social scientists).[12]

Autonomy/Independence.   As often as you will be subjected to appeals to conformity, you also will hear such appeals as "Be your own person; don't follow the crowd." Appeals to "know yourself" and "be yourself" are like the appeals to adventure—both draw their force from our struggles to be independent. The expression of individuality, when perceived as a strong motive, can be a powerful appeal in introducing ideas and actions that require a high degree of risk or that are at odds with one's desire to conform. The appeal works especially well in persuasive speeches in which the speaker asks listeners to commit to a belief or to vote for someone—listeners can agree without others' being aware of the commitment made or the action taken. Conversely, when you ask a listener to stand out from the crowd, particularly to take an unpopular stance in public, the appeal is not impossible, but its success is much tougher to achieve.

A Final Comment.   You may have noticed that some appeals in these three clusters seem to contradict one another. Fear appears to be antithetical to adventure. Sympathy and generosity seem opposite to aggression. Remember, however, that the human being is a bundle of contradictory impulses, balancing urges and making decisions between personal gratification and public good. You, too, are a changeable creature who, at various times, may pursue quite different goals—staying up late one night to finish a term paper (reflecting the general desire to achieve) or going out for a good time with friends the night before a major exam (reflecting the general desire for affiliation). Note also that motives can interact, as discussed earlier.

This discussion of motivational appeals is not designed to present the human psyche as if it were orderly or even consistent. Rather, it is an attempt to give you a basic understanding of the nature of human motivation and of various kinds of appeals that you can use to enhance your communicative effectiveness. Hence, we turn next to questions concerning the rhetorical use of motivational appeals in speech development.

Using Motivational Appeals in Speech Preparation

The material we have discussed thus far raises an extremely important question: *How do you decide which motivational appeals to use in your speech?* That is a very difficult question to answer, of course, because so much depends on the specific group of listeners you face, the occasion, and even your own preferences and motives for speaking. In general, however, three factors in the speaking situation can guide your consideration of motivational appeals in the speech preparation process: the type of speech, the demographic analysis of the audience, and personal predilections.

As has been suggested in the descriptions of various motivational appeals, sometimes the *type of speech* you are delivering helps you select appeals. For example, the appeals to individuality often appear in persuasive and actuative speeches whose goals are to free people from previous group associations. Suppose you are attempting to persuade your classmates to forego a generally accepted B.A. degree in favor of a flexible Bachelor of General Studies (with no major and few requirements, available on some campuses), you could appeal reasonably to creativity ("build your own program"), adventure ("break away from the crowd—do something unique"), curiosity ("explore a subject as deeply as you wish or range across a group of courses out of personal interest"), and even success ("get a feeling of achievement from designing and completing your own program"). In contrast, speeches can tap into motives that have a collective thrust—tradition, companionship, defense, deference, conformity, and loyalty. In these cases, the appeal is less focused on individual listeners and more on the audience as a group.

Conducting a *demographic analysis* of audience members—their age, education, and so on—likewise will help you select potentially powerful motivational appeals. As noted earlier, people who have less need to be concerned about survival or safety needs are in a better position to respond to appeals to creativity, independence, personal enjoyment, and generosity. Young people are notoriously prone to appeals to sexual attraction and to testimony from celebrities. Appeals to endurance or perseverance are potent with older listeners. In general, appeals to loyalty, tradition, and reverence also have potential value with middle-aged and elderly listeners. Appeals to ethnic traditions and sense of belonging to a family or community work well with homogeneous audiences gathered to celebrate a holiday or other occasion with clear ethnic identity (for example, Hispanic Heritage Week and Martin Luther King Day).

You also can consider the relationship between your audience and the general motives of achievement and power. If you can assume that people gathered for a political caucus have fairly high power-oriented motives, appeals to success, independence, and authority may be appropriate (regardless of whether this is a mixed audience or a women's political action group).[13] If you are speaking to a group of top industry executives, you can safely assume they will be receptive to appeals to achievement and power. Thus, appeals that maximize "what's in it for me" (without being blatant) could be more effective than appeals to their sense of civic-mindedness or community spirit.

Maslow's hierarchy of needs and desires also can be helpful in analyzing your audience's receptivity to motives. Suppose you were giving a speech in favor of an urban renewal project to inner city residents. Appeals to higher-level desires (self-esteem, achievement, and self-actualization) may not be especially effective, since you are addressing people primarily concerned with their basic physiological needs for food and shelter and their basic safety needs for security and freedom from harm and harassment. Instead, you might emphasize access to goods and services, improved housing, better streetlighting, controlled traffic, and better opportunities for community-centered law enforcement.

Finally, always look to your *personal predilections*—your own beliefs, attitudes, and values—when seeking motivational appeals. Ask yourself the following questions: "Am I willing to ask people to act out of fear, or do I think my appeals should be grounded on such 'higher' motives as sympathy and generosity?" "Do I actually believe in the importance of loyalty and reverence as they relate to this situation?" Use appeals *you* think are important and relevant as reasons for belief or action.

The speech on pages 142–43 was written by a fourteen-year-old eighth-grade student and presented as part of a citywide oratorical contest in Boston, Massachusetts. While there are technical problems with the speech—it lacks the sophistication in language and thought development that a college student is capable of, for example—it nonetheless contains a powerful message. In reading the speech, think about how the speaker uses motivational appeals—for example, does she make a powerful indirect appeal to achievement by telling a narrative story that illustrates its opposite? How would Maslow's hierarchy of needs and desires relate to this speech—does it support or weaken the notion of a "prepotent hierarchy"? Finally, what does the narrative structure allow that other approaches might not in making the appeals compelling

Targeting Motivational Appeals

*T*o be successful, motivational appeals must be targeted to the appropriate audience. Advertising campaign experiences offer support for the twin benefits of audience analysis and appropriately devised appeals. For example, when Tostitos was launched as a new product, the target was female heads of households who watched daytime television. The commercials' spokesperson talked to mothers about the quality of Tostitos as a snack for their children. When later research indicated that the primary purchasers were eighteen-to-thirty-four-year-old adults, the ads were changed, and their timing was shifted to approximate the viewing habits of the new target audience. Instead of talking to mothers, the spokesperson talked to characters of popular television series the audience might have watched when they were younger ("Leave It to Beaver," "Mr. Ed"). The commercials aired on such evening television shows as "St. Elsewhere" and "Cheers." Sales doubled.

Over time, a company might wish to keep a particular identity relationship with the audience, as in the case of Betty Crocker. Rather than stay with the same "model" of a woman likely to symbolize a consumer of Betty Crocker products, the company has maintained its

and forceful? Beyond its illustration of motivational appeals, what further development would improve the speech and raise it to the caliber of a college-level address?

Combining Motivational Appeals

As the preceding discussion suggests, you can combine motives to appeal to an audience or to target segments of it. Targeting strategies are apparent in the following main headings for a speech by a travel agent urging students to take a summer trip to Europe:

Betty Crocker, 1936

Betty Crocker, 1986

appeal to traditional values yet updated the image to stay in tune with the times. In a case of identity change, William Underwood altered its "devil" trademark for deviled ham—in 1959, the then-ninety-two-year-old symbol was changed from one reflecting an evil image to a "smiling, impish Satan."

These and similar changes by other companies indicate a marked sensitivity to the effectiveness of particular consumer-oriented appeals. Additional examples, such as the changes in product images for Marlboro cigarettes and Budweiser beer, also suggest a continual search for motivational appeals that will enhance product identification and sales.

FOR FURTHER READING

Cohen, Dorothy. *Advertising.* Glenview, IL: Scott, Foresman and Company, 1988.

☐ *Acquisition and savings*
☐ *Independence*
☐ *Companionship*

I. The tour is being offered for the low price of $2000 for three weeks.
II. There will be a minimum of supervision and regimentation.
III. You will be traveling with friends and fellow students.

If you are appealing to self-centered interests—to private fears, monetary gain or acquisition, or pride—recognize that people may not wish to acknowledge that these are the motives for their actions. For example, even

A Much More Meaningful Life

Shanita Horton

My name is Shanita Horton and I am a black, fourteen-year-old young lady living in the city of Boston. I have a lot to say about drugs and crime. Drugs are one of Boston's major problems and also has affected me personally.

I have firsthand experience on the devastating dangers of drugs because someone real close to me has been addicted. She started drinking at the age of seventeen and stayed drunk most of the time, not really caring about herself or anyone else.

By the age of twenty, alcohol no longer gave her the feeling she needed so she began smoking marijuana and heroin. She had a little girl now to take care of which she really could not do that well because she was high most of the time.

So she let the little girl go live with her grandmother. Now she had no one to take care of but herself and things really started to go downhill. Being under-educated and having no job to support her habit, she had begun a life of crime. Her criminal activities resulted in her going to MCI-Framingham.

At the age of twenty-two she had given birth to another little girl. When that little girl was two months old she went to live with her godmother because her own mother was on her way back to Framingham prison. How can one's life continue on such a destructive merry-go-round, never getting better, always worse?

At the age of twenty-four not only was she in jail again but she had given birth to another little boy while she was in there. This little boy was born with webbed hands and feet but he is now six years old and has had surgery on his hands. But there's nothing they can do with his feet. Can you imagine how

---

though people may have contributed to charitable causes in order to obtain tax advantages, this is not a rationale they want to be reminded of publicly. Thus, as a speaker, you need to combine appeals to seemingly self-centered motives with more publicly accepted motives for action.

The following example further illustrates how you might combine motivational appeals in a speech to convince a college athletics board of the need to expand women's competitive sports (the motivational appeals are printed in italics). First, introduce the speech with thanks for the fine intramural program now available to women (appeal to prior *generosity* and *sympathy* for women's activities). Refer to existing facilities and equipment (appeal to current *acquisitions* and *pride* in achievements to date). Second, stress the philosophical values of intercollegiate competition for women (such an appeal to professionals often ridiculed as "jocks" and anti-intellectuals can emphasize *pride, prestige, creativity,* or *adventure* as well as the competition that

embarrassing that will be when he gets older and his friends start talking about where they were born?

Luckily for this little boy, he went to live with his grandmother and older sister. Because of the lady's continued destructive behavior, her oldest daughter, at the age of twelve, decided to commit suicide and end it all. She took a lot of pain killers and passed out. Luckily for the little girl, she did not die and older people in the community gave her extra support.

This lady I'm talking about is now thirty-one years old and things aren't any better. She was released from Framingham prison for the umpteenth time about a year ago. It was on a Thursday that she came home. Saturday, two days later, she was rushed to Boston City Hospital on an overdose of heroin.

Drugs and crime broke this lady's family apart. The only reason I know the story so well is because this lady is my mother.

My mother's life will soon be ending because she is dying of AIDS. But because of the grace of God and because of some other people that believe in me and encourage me to realize my fullest potential, I will have a much more meaningful life than my mother.

So even though I cannot change what has happened in the past, I can always want a much more positive future because I do believe everyone has something positive to contribute to society.

I wrote this speech prior to my mother's recent passing. She died on March 31 and I would like to dedicate this to her memory. Thank you very much.

Shanita Horton, "A Much More Meaningful Life," *Boston Sunday Globe*, 22 May 1988.

comes from *aggressive* play). Mention, but with an older, predominantly male audience, do not overemphasize, the matter of equality between the sexes (allay *fears* and gently move on to the issue of *dominance*). Finally, be prepared to answer the board's questions concerning the number of women interested (indirect appeal to *political power/authority*), neighboring schools that could form part of a league (appeal to *competition*), the estimated cost of the proposed program (ease of *acquisition*), and any other questions that might arise. Overall, you would stress appeals to human achievements, with secondary appeals to political and economic value orientations. If the proposal is rejected arbitrarily, your next speech might emphasize the political and economic values and invoke the legal ramifications of refusal. You might use a more confrontative style if you feel this is an acceptable risk to take in persuading a recalcitrant group. This strategy would call for a different configuration of motives.[14]

The Appropriate Use of Motivational Appeals

Using motivational appeals with tact and sound judgment is important to your eventual success as a speaker. The appropriateness of any motivational appeal generally depends upon your speech purpose, the audience and occasion expectations, and your beliefs and values. Beyond that, there are some additional communication rules that can help you select and use motivational appeals.

1. *Avoid blatant or overly aggressive appeals.* Do not say, for example, "Mr. Harlow Jones, the successful banker, has just contributed handsomely to our cause. Come on, now. Imitate this generous and community-spirited man!" Blatantly negative expressions can have a boomerang effect and make solicitation more difficult in the future. An insulted audience is unlikely to react favorably to any appeal you make, whether for belief or for action. To engender a positive response, use appeals that demonstrate respect for the intelligence and the public sensitivities of your audience. Suggest, for example, that contributors will be associated with others in a worthwhile and successful venture and will have the appreciation of those who will benefit from the contributions.

2. *Organize your appeals effectively.* When should you introduce a powerful appeal—at the beginning or at the end of the speech? While this question cannot be answered with finality, it is one you need to consider. If audience members need to be jolted out of a lethargic or indifferent state, a low-key start may simply prolong their lethargy. A strong opening with a powerful appeal may be the best strategy to use. On the other hand, if they are generally galvanized for action, you might want to build on their intensity more slowly and reserve a powerful appeal for the end of the speech—an appeal that will channel their enthusiasm long after you finish. In a later chapter, we will discuss some ways to organize your speech to fit your purpose, audience, and materials. For now, however, note that it also is possible to select an organizational pattern appropriate to the motivational appeals you select. In fact, we will see in Chapter 8, your motivational appeals can control the entire structure of your speech.

3. *Use appeals judiciously.* There is no general rule of thumb for how many appeals a speech should contain. Two primary considerations are (a) the amount of time you have to develop your argument and (b) the degree of audience approval or hostility already present. If time is short, using fewer appeals will give you a better chance to develop each to its maximum effect. If audience members are already predisposed toward your ideas, fewer direct motivational appeals will be necessary. Conversely, if they are hostile, you will have to combine several appeals in order to reach as many listeners as possible. Another approach is to focus on a primary appeal and develop it as a theme throughout your speech. The advantage of such depth is a strong appeal; the potential disadvantage is that the audience may not be receptive to the selected appeal.

4. *Use appeals ethically.* Even in a free and open society, there are ethical bounds that, when crossed by an overzealous speaker, produce public condemnation or even retribution. Using communication ethics is more than a matter of not lying or not misrepresenting yourself to an audience. It is also the ethical use of motivational appeals. Urging audience members to take a course of action because it will make them rich at the expense of others who have less power or knowledge, for example, is an unethical practice; so is an intense, sustained fear appeal that finds hidden conspiracies to destroy the world under every rock and bush. Think carefully about your own ethical limits and about what kinds of appeals outrage you as a listener. The social penalties for overstepping moral boundaries in your appeals can be relatively severe, and you must decide to what degree you are willing to risk social censure for the position you advocate and the way you advocate it.

Chapter Summary

One can think of motives as *springs*—needs or desires tightly coiled and waiting for the right appeal or verbal depiction to set them off. Those springs, when worked by a skillful speaker, can convert the individuals in an audience into a cohesive group ready to think and act in ways consistent with your purpose. This chapter described motives as either *biological needs* or *social motives*, as either *intrinsic* or *extrinsic*, and as *dynamic*. We also discussed their interactive nature, the four types of behavior they can produce, and their grouping into a *prepotent hierarchy*. The primary *clusters* of motives are those oriented toward *affiliation*, *achievement*, and *power*. General guides—the *type of speech, audience demographics,* and *personal predilections*—help a speaker select motivational appeals. Finally, the chapter discussed using motives in *combination*, avoiding *blatant appeals, organizing* appeals effectively, using an appropriate *number of motives*, developing them in *depth*, and using them in *ethical* ways.

Reference Notes

1. Katharine Blick Hoyenga and Kermit T. Hoyenga, *Motivational Explanations of Behavior: Evolutionary, Physiological, and Cognitive Ideas* (Monterey, CA: Brooks/Cole Publishing Co., 1984), Chapter 1. Psychologists are divided over several issues. For example, some argue that all motives are innate (Maslow's theory assumes motives are instinctual), while others argue that at least some are learned (McClelland's theory). Likewise, psychologists differ on the issue of conscious awareness of motives—are we aware of the drive, and if not, how do we control it? This text will take the position that whether innate or learned, motives are reasons for action and, hence, subject to a speaker's potential influence.

2. Hoyenga and Hoyenga; also see Joseph Veroff, "Contextualism and Human Motives," in Donald R. Brown and Joseph Veroff, eds., *Frontiers of Motivational Psychology: Essays in Honor of John W. Atkinson* (New York: Springer-Verlag, 1986), 132–45.

3. Hoyenga and Hoyenga; Brown and Veroff; Abigail J. Stewart, ed., *Motivation and Society: A Volume in Honor of David C. McClelland* (San Francisco, CA: Jossey-Bass, Inc., Pubs., 1982);

Janet T. Spence, ed., *Achievement and Achievement Motives* (San Francisco, CA: W. H. Freeman & Co., 1983).

4. The typology is adapted from McClelland's discussion. See David C. McClelland, *Power: The Inner Experience* (New York: Irvington Pubs., 1975); David C. McClelland, *Human Motivation* (Glenview, IL: Scott, Foresman and Company, 1985); Hoyenga and Hoyenga, 258–60; Veroff, 140–41. The adaptation depends especially upon Veroff's discussion.

5. Abraham H. Maslow, *Motivation and Personality*, 2nd ed. (New York: Harper & Row Pubs., Inc., 1970). In the 1970 revision, Maslow identifies two additional desires—to *know* and *understand* and an *aesthetic* desire—as higher states. These frequently operate as part of the satisfaction of the self-actualization stage; hence, they are included here.

6. For a fuller discussion of attribution theory as it relates to motivation, see Hoyenga and Hoyenga. For a concise review of attribution theory in relation to communication studies, see Alan L. Sillars, "Attribution and Communication: Are People 'Naive Scientists' or Just Naive?" in Michael E. Roloff and Charles R. Berger, eds., *Social Cognition and Communication* (Beverly Hills, CA: Sage Publishing, 1982), 73–106.

7. Dorothy Cohen, *Advertising* (Glenview, IL: Scott, Foresman and Company, 1988), 210–11.

8. Hoyenga and Hoyenga, Chapter 4. A classic work on affiliation is S. Schachter, *The Psychology of Affiliation: Experimental Studies of the Sources of Gregariousness* (Stanford, CA: Stanford University Press, 1959).

9. For discussions of "conformity" and "social comparison theory," see Mary John Smith, *Persuasion and Human Action: A Review and Critique of Social Influence Theories* (Belmont, CA: Wadsworth, Inc., 1982), esp. Chapters 7 and 11.

10. Cohen, 223.

11. Hoyenga and Hoyenga, Chapter 11; Spence.

12. For a review of research on fear appeals, see Erwin P. Bettinghaus and Michael J. Cody, *Persuasive Communication*, 4th ed. (New York: Holt, Rinehart & Winston, 1987), 158–61; Hoyenga and Hoyenga, 154–67.

13. Research indicates that men and women high in power motives behave similarly—both are interested in positions that allow for influencing others, for having an impact on the course of events. See Abigail J. Stewart and Nia Lane Chester, "Sex Differences in Human Social Motives: Achievement, Affiliation, and Power," in Abigail J. Stewart, ed., *Motivation and Society: A Volume in Honor of David C. McClelland* (San Francisco, CA: Jossey-Bass, Inc., Pubs., 1982) 172–218, esp. 197–203.

14. For an attempt to rank, in terms of rhetorical sophistication, possible strategies for proposers of significant change, see John Waite Bowers and Donovan J. Ochs, *The Rhetoric of Agitation and Control* (Reading, MA: Addison-Wesley Publishing Co., Inc., 1971), Chapter 2.

Key Terms

biological motives	power motives
social motives	McClelland's Motive Types
affiliation motives	Maslow's Hierarchy of Needs
achievement motives	prepotent hierarchy

motivational appeals *motive cluster*

visualization process *boomerang effect*

attribution

Problems and Probes

1. Examine the series of advertisements included in this chapter. What are the major motivational appeals used to entice consumer approval and affect behavior? Are the appeals well suited to your interests as a potential consumer? Note that a motivational appeal may be used both in an illustration and in printed form to reinforce each other and the appeal of the ad as a whole. Be prepared to discuss your evaluations in a small group setting during class and to contribute to a general class discussion on the effectiveness of the various appeals.
2. Bring to class examples of at least five different motivational appeals excerpted from a speech or speeches. What are the appeals, and how are they used in the context of the entire speech. Do they add to or detract from the speaker's persuasive effort? What other appeals, given the situation, might the speaker have used? Combine your examples and analysis in a brief written report.

Communication Activities

1. Present a three-to-four-minute speech in which, through the combined use of three related motivational appeals, you attempt to persuade your audience to accept a particular belief or engage in a specific action. (For example, combine appeals to adventure, companionship, and personal enjoyment to persuade listeners to go on a group tour of Europe, or combine sympathy and pride to elicit contributions to a charity drive being conducted by a campus group.) At the conclusion of your speech, ask a classmate to identify the motivational appeals you used. If other class members disagree with that identification, explore with the class the reasons your appeals did not come through as you intended and what you might have done to strengthen their impact.
2. In a small group class discussion, talk about some principles or guidelines that might differentiate ethical from unethical appeals. In the course of the discussion, answer the following questions: (a) Under what conditions would you consider a motivational appeal to listeners' needs or desires an entirely ethical and legitimate means of persuasion? (b) Under what conditions might the same appeal be considered unethical or inappropriate? (c) Where does the ethical responsibility rest: with the speaker, with the audience, or in adherence to a list of external criteria (any of these, all of these)?
3. Assume you have a friend who is considering dropping out of school. Which motivational appeal would you use to convince your friend to continue his or her education if you wanted to direct those appeals to your friend's desire for affiliation, achievement, or power? Do the same with Maslow's hierarchy of needs and desires. What factors are helpful in distinguishing among these general clusters or levels of motives? Illustrate your appeals with specific examples or statements. Discuss your results with classmates in a small group setting during class.

CHAPTER SEVEN

Developing Ideas: Finding and Using Supporting Materials

Once you have selected a topic, determined your general and specific purposes, framed a central idea or claim, and completed your analysis of the audience and the occasion, you are ready to dig into the core of your speech—the materials that develop and support your ideas. If your purpose is to tell others about summer work, for example, you cannot simply assert the central idea "Summer employment opportunities are all around you." You must make it concrete; that central idea calls for examples of employment opportunities in your own town for students with various interests and backgrounds. You need to present precise, usable information. Similarly, if you wish to argue "Garbage-incinerating power plants are unsafe and should be shut down," you need to define "unsafe," to provide statistical and illustrative materials on the safety question, and to offer a plan for shutting down existing facilities without stacking up garbage all over town.

Thus, while the motivational appeals discussed in Chapter 6 draw your listeners into a speech by tying its ideas and proposals to some of the wellsprings of human action, supporting material actually brings those ideas and proposals to life. If you tell listeners to take a school-sponsored tour of Canada's maritime provinces because of their sense of adventure, for example, you still need to provide illustrations that can energize the appeal with graphic details. If you propose tuition prepayment plans as ways for students to save money (appeal to acquisition and savings), you must supply the statistical analysis that demonstrates the savings you are asserting. Hence, motivational appeals and supporting materials work together, one appealing to the "heart" and the other to the "head" of the listener.

The forms of supporting material discussed in this chapter, therefore, are the media of exchange between your ideas and the audience. Their functions are *to amplify, clarify, or justify the beliefs, attitudes, and values you wish to convey to your listeners.* They are the nutrients that sustain your ideas once they have taken root in the minds of others. First, the chapter will define and illustrate the various forms of supporting materials commonly used by speakers. Then, it will suggest some ways of finding, recording, and using them in both informative and persuasive or actuative speeches. Furthermore, the ways in which supporting materials are used will be discussed in the chapters dealing with various types of speeches (Chapters 15–18).

What to Look For:
Forms of Supporting Material

There are seven forms of supporting material that you can use to develop or justify the ideas in your speech: (1) explanation, (2) analogy or comparison, (3) illustration (detailed example), (4) specific instance (undeveloped example), (5) statistics, (6) testimony, and (7) restatement. Often, two or more of these forms are combined, as when statistics are used to develop an illustration or when the testimony of an authority is used to strengthen or verify an explanation. However they are combined, you should select such materials to help audience members make the judgments they need to make.

Explanation

An **explanation** is a description or expository passage that makes a term, concept, process, or proposal clear or acceptable. Explanations tell what, how, or why and are useful in showing relationships between a whole and its parts. They also may give meaning to difficult-to-envision concepts.

Explanations of What. Some explanations describe more clearly what the speaker is discussing; they make ideas more clear and concrete, giving listeners enough details so they can more easily understand the concepts. For example, Vice-President and Director of the Health Care Policy and Program for Owens-Illinois, Inc., Richard J. Hanley, attempted to help the Texas Medical Association understand what a "second opinion program" for insurance is and how it might affect doctors and patients. He needed a clear explanation, which follows:

> Let me describe how our second opinion program works. If a physician recommends that you have an elective surgical procedure that is on our mandatory second opinion list, you must call a toll-free number for assistance.

> The calls are handled by a staff of patient services coordinators, who are specially trained registered nurses. They can provide names of approved, board

certified second-opinion physicians. Owens-Illinois currently has a panel of more than 2,000 physicians who have been approved to provide second opinions under our program. The list now includes more than a hundred here in Texas.

The patient services coordinators also are available to answer questions to help clarify the decision facing the patient. Whether the second opinion confirms or disagrees with the first, the final decision is up to the patient.

The list of mandatory second opinion procedures was developed with the advice of physicians and our insurance carriers. It is made up of procedures that are frequently recommended for conditions that may be amenable to other forms of treatment.

These surgical procedures include: gallbladder, hernia, bunionectomy, knee, hysterectomy, prostate, cataract removal, nose surgery, varicose vein surgery, D&C, tonsils and adenoids, mastectomy, and back surgery.[1]

Mr. Hanley offered a multifaceted explanation of *what* his second-opinion program is and does. He told *how* the procedure works, mentioned *who* in Texas is a part of the program, indicated *why* second opinions are required (in his reference to "other forms of treatment"), and even listed *what* surgical procedures are covered. His listeners' knowledge of what second-opinion insurance requires was complete, especially if his listeners comprised an audience of health care specialists.

Although explanations are good ways to clarify an idea, they should not be too long or complicated, and they should not have to carry the weight of your proof. For example, Mr. Hanley could be sure that, even after his explanation, some of the physicians needed more proof that second opinions would not undermine the authority of the first physician who offered an opinion and that second opinions would not significantly increase the cost of health care. Explanations clarify but seldom prove anything.

Explanations of How. A second class of explanations tells audiences "how"—how something came to be or how something is done. These explanations are especially appropriate when you are demonstrating a process, such as repairing a rust hole in a car fender or listing the steps in carrying out CPR. P. Dorothy Gilbert introduced a speech on chair-caning by elaborating on the process:

The intricate patterns of cane or reed you see on chair seats make the process seem mysterious and all too artistic for most of us. On the contrary, as I will demonstrate to you today, anyone can learn to cane a chair in order to restore a valuable antique or to save a family heirloom. Chair-caning involves five easy-to-learn steps. First, soak the cane to make it pliable; then, clean out the holes through which the cane will be stretched. Next, weave the cane or reed through the holes in four to seven operations. Fourth, tie off the pieces of cane underneath the chair. Finally, lace a heavier piece of cane over the holes to cover them. Let me describe each step, one at a time.

Explanations of how things work, with demonstrations of portions of a total process, can help increase audience attention and interest.

Explanations of how things work, with sample items clarifying each step of a process or demonstrations of portions of a total process, can help increase audience attention and interest.

Explanations of Why. Explanations that account for a thing's existence or present state are called explanations of why. They appear often in academic lectures, as when a chemistry professor explains why a series of chemical interactions produces a particular result. Such explanations lay the foundation for remedying problems; if we are aware of their causes, we can move toward their solutions. Richard T. Montoya, Assistant Secretary for Territorial and International Affairs, U.S. Department of the Interior, explained why massive foreign aid can dampen the economy of needy countries before he offered a remedy:

> Due to inappropriate programs designed by Congress and past Administrations, the dependency is greater than ever. The result of some 15 years of negotiations between the United States and teams of U.S. lawyers representing Micronesia at U.S. taxpayers' expense, has been a deal for independence of sorts, called

"free association" with the United States. The price tag: a staggering $3 billion payable over 15 years. The money is provided to support Micronesia in the standard to which it has been accustomed—that is, $2,000 per capita annually in U.S. assistance. The need is great because little indigenous self-sustaining economic development has resulted from the previous $2 billion that has been spent. Local private sector development is largely limited to stores selling goods to government employees, while exploitation of the available resources—fisheries and tourism—is left to foreigners, mainly Japanese, in exchange for token payments often confused in local minds with economic development.[2]

Notice that Mr. Montoya chose his language carefully, calling the price tag "staggering," deals with other foreign countries "exploitation," and payments "token." Explanations need not be academically detached or unbiased; they can and ought to include the details that support the case you are trying to build.

The following is some final advice on using explanations of why, how, and what. (1) Keep them as brief as you can. They can become so complex and detailed that you lose the audience. (2) Speak in concrete terms; specific images, examples, amounts, and sizes help an audience "see" what is being explained. (3) Combine explanations with other forms of supporting materials. Mr. Hanley's description of second-opinion surgery plans in a previous section could be coupled with statistics on how widespread the plans are; Mr. Montoya's explanation of why our foreign aid is not working in the Micronesian island countries would be strengthened by coupling it with testimony from nongovernmental authorities.

Analogy or Comparison

In an **analogy** or **comparison,** similarities are pointed out between something that is already known, understood, or believed by the listeners and something that is not. Thus, you might explain the game of cricket to an American audience by comparing it with baseball, or you might tell how a thermostat works by comparing it with a simple thermometer. Analogies may be either figurative or literal.

Figurative Analogies. **Figurative analogies** involve phenomena that, although basically different, exhibit comparable properties or relationships. They function especially well in clarifying ideas or concepts by relating them to ideas or objects already familiar to the audience. Dr. Louis Hadley Evans, minister-at-large for the Presbyterian Church, drew these figurative analogies to distinguish between the terms "deist" and "theist":

To you the world is what: a clock or a car? Is it a huge clock, that God once made, that He wound up at the beginning and left it to run of itself? Then you are a *deist.* Do you believe that it is rather a car that God once made, but that does not run without His hand on the wheel, without His ultimate and personal control? Then you are a *theist.*[3]

In this example, the speaker clarified two terms and an abstract concept (God) by comparing two machines whose operation is familiar to the audience. The notion of independence (clock) vs. dependence (car) helped the audience discriminate between two terms whose meaning may be either unknown or unclear.

Literal Analogies. Although analogies which compare things that are unlike—the world with a clock or a car—may be excellent means for clarifying a point or making it vivid, they generally have limited value in justifying a claim. If your purpose is to prove a point, it is more effective to use comparisons of *like* phenomena, using **literal analogies.** Thus, you might argue that a system of one-way traffic on the downtown streets of City X will relieve congestion and promote safety because that is what such a system did in City Y. Thus, when former Secretary of the Navy James H. Webb argued that seapower allows not only control of the seas but also of the land, he used a literal analogy between World War II and the present:

> The fourth goal of American seapower is to be supreme on the sea in order to be supreme on the land. You might recall the historic race for Tunis in World War Two, where the Germans moved a quarter of a million troops from France, principally by airlift into North Africa, but were unable to control the sea in order to supply and reequip them. The end result was disastrous. On the strategic level, the Germans lost twice: we captured more than 200,000 of their best soldiers when we took Tunis, and we did not have to fight those soldiers when we invaded Normandy two years later. In building our own strategy for the defense of Europe, in today's world, we have not forgotten that control of the sea impacts much more than the war at sea.[4]

By comparing Germany's World War II experiences in Europe with America's activity in Europe today, Secretary Webb was able to build an interesting argument for keeping part of NATO's fighting power, not just in air and ground forces, but also in naval units.

Because it attempts to base a conclusion on a parallel instance, an analogy used as proof must meet a rigorous test: *the instances compared must be closely similar in all essential respects.* For Secretary Webb's argument to be convincing as well as interesting, his audience had to accept the parallel. Are the movements of troops and materiel problems faced by contemporary as well as by past armies? (Probably.) Is the U.S.S.R. a potential enemy that threatens Europe in ways that Germany did half-a-century ago? (Possibly.) In a day of nuclear weapons and intercontinental ballistic missiles, is seapower important in the same way it was during World War II? (We need to think about that more.) Audience members, thus, are faced with the question of whether the similarities on which the argument is based outweigh any differences that could be mentioned. This is the question that needs to be asked—and answered clearly—when you try to use an analogy as justification for a claim.

Illustration

An **illustration** is a detailed example in narrative form. It may be used to picture the results of adopting the proposal you advocate or to describe in detail conditions as they now exist. An illustration has two principal characteristics: (1) it uses narrative form—recounting a happening or telling a story and (2) it contains vividly described details. There are two types of illustrations: hypothetical, describing an imaginary situation, and factual, describing an actual happening.

Hypothetical Illustration.   A **hypothetical illustration,** although an imaginary narrative, is believable if consistent with known facts. An audience will judge the illustration on the presumed likelihood of its actually occurring. Pam Williams, Ball State University, used a hypothetical illustration with an unexpected twist:

> Suzanne and Jack are going on a trip. They've been preparing for weeks, making sure all their shots, papers, and passports are in order. However, as they board the plane to leave, they are warned repeatedly, "Don't drink the water, it's bad for you." Suzanne and Jack aren't going to Mexico. They don't live in New York City or Chicago. Suzanne and Jack live in France and they are coming to the United States.[5]

In creating a hypothetical illustration, you can manipulate facts at will, as long as your construction remains plausible to an audience. In Ms. Williams' illustration, the shock value was in challenging the normal assumption that people warned about water quality are U.S. citizens traveling abroad. This approach creates great attention for her premise that water quality in our own country is deteriorating. Such illustrations can go a long way toward clarifying your ideas or stimulating interest in your central idea or claim. The hypothetical illustration also is useful in explaining how something is done; you can create a person and then picture that individual going through the steps in the process. If you want to engage the audience even more, select the name of an audience member for your imaginary journey. Although the hypothetical illustration may set up the situation for you, it falls short of justifying your premise. In her speech on water quality, Ms. Williams went on to provide concrete evidence of deterioration. Because you can manipulate the details of your illustration, the audience may be understandably reluctant to accept your premise without further support. Be sure to provide that support.

Factual Illustration.   A **factual illustration** is a narrative that describes in detail a situation or incident that has occurred. Because details are brought into the story and because the incident actually happened, factual illustration frequently has high persuasive value.

In a speech calling for the development of more creative industrial leaders, P. L. Smith, President and Chief Executive Officer of the General Foods Corporation, supported his call with the following factual illustration:

> An illustration of the fundamental importance of leadership is present at the Chrysler Co. Lee Iacocca has turned this company around. Few of the environmental factors have changed significantly since Chrysler was on the brink of bankruptcy. They're still facing pretty much the same competition, the same taxes, the same unions, the same regulations.
>
> But what they have now is the vision and the commitment of one man—the leader at the top. And through the force of his personality, he has built a leadership team and influenced the behavior of employees, suppliers, investors, customers and even the government. This has turned around a $13-billion company with 80,000 jobs at stake.
>
> That's an incredible accomplishment! And it was done through leadership.[6]

Mr. Smith used this extended illustration to visualize his claim. He then went on with a series of specific instances to supply additional proof for his claim.

Three considerations should be kept in mind when selecting an illustration, hypothetical or factual. *Is it clearly related to the idea it is intended to support?* If the connection is difficult to show, the illustration will not accomplish its goal. *Is it a fair example?* An audience can be quick to notice unusual circumstances in an illustration; if you have focused on the exceptional case, your illustration will not be convincing. *Is it vivid and impressive in detail?* If this quality is absent, the advantage of using an illustration is lost, so be sure your illustrations are pointed, fair, and vivid.

Specific Instance

A **specific instance** is an *undeveloped* illustration or example. Instead of describing a situation with a detailed narrative, you simply refer to it in passing. Specific instances most often are used to make an idea clear and understandable. The reference should be to an event, person, place, or process that your audience already is familiar with. Jane Scott of the University of Iowa opened a speech on architecture in this way: "You all are familiar with Old Capitol, the beautiful pillared building you pass each day walking from class to class. It's a perfect example of federal period Georgian architecture, the subject of my speech this morning." Her brief reference to a well-known building enabled audience members to orient themselves to her topic.

Specific instances also are useful in justifying a claim. In this case, instances may be piled one upon the other until you have firmly established the impression you wish to create. Note, for example, how James K. Wellington demonstrated the serious nature of his claim that "Creative and imaginative students often are not recognized by their teachers":

We should remember that the following persons were all identified as low achievers or misfits:

- Einstein—4 years old before he could speak; 7 before he could read.
- Isaac Newton—was rated a poor elementary school student.
- Beethoven—music teacher said, "As a composer, he is hopeless."
- Thomas Edison—teacher told him he was too stupid to learn anything.
- F. W. Woolworth—worked in a dry goods store at 21, employers would not let him wait on customers; "didn't have enough sense."
- Walt Disney—fired by a newspaper editor; "no good ideas."
- Winston Churchill—failed 6th grade.[7]

With these accumulated data, there could be little doubt that teachers can err in their judgment of a child's ability.

Statistics

Statistics are numbers that show relationships between or among phenomena; the relationships can emphasize size or magnitude, describe subclasses or parts (segments), or establish trends. By reducing large masses of information into generalized categories, statistics clarify the nature of a situation and substantiate a potentially disputable claim.[8]

Magnitudes.   We often use statistics to describe a situation or to sketch its scope or seriousness. Especially if one statistical description of the size of a problem is piled upon others, the effect upon listeners can be strong. Notice this piling-up technique as it was used by Joseph N. Hankin, President of Westchester Community College, in quantifying some of the failings of secondary education:

> One-fourth of 17-year-olds do not know how many quarts are in a gallon; two-fifths cannot say what percent 30 is of 60; half cannot name one of their senators; 44 percent are unable to combine four short sentences into one longer one. 40 to 50 percent of urban children have "serious reading problems." Nearly 40 percent of 17-year-olds cannot draw inferences from written material; only 20 percent can write a persuasive essay; only a third can solve mathematics problems that require several steps. If you think these results are limited to 17-year-olds, you are mistaken. College students and even adults have been found to produce similar results.[9]

Not all uses of **magnitudes,** of course, need such piling-up of instances. Simple, hard-hitting magnitudes sometimes work even better. For example, Brenda Theriault of the University of Maine, arguing that there is "very little nutritional value in a hamburger, chocolate shake, and fries," simply noted that "of the 1,123 calories in this meal, there are 15 calories of carbohydrates, 35 calories of protein, and 1,073 calories of fat."[10] These were all the numbers the audience needed in order to understand the nutrition in a typical fast-food meal.

Segments. Statistics also can be used to isolate the parts of a problem or to show aspects of it caused by discrete factors. In discussing sources of income for a university, for example, you might **segment** the income by indicating what percentages come from tuition and fees, from state and federal government, from gifts and contributions, from such special fees as tickets, and from miscellaneous sources. Then you would be in a position to talk directly about next year's proposed tuition hike. Some arguments using statistical segments are very simple, as is the following example from Richard K. Long, Director of Corporate Communications with the Dow Chemical Company, when discussing Dow's presence in South Africa:

> Today, South Africa's population of some 33 million is two-thirds black, 10 percent colored (mixed races), and 3 percent Asian. The remaining five million citizens are whites, not quite half of whom are Boer descendants. In effect, 15 percent of the population rules the rest.
>
> Given America's experience with segregation and racism, you probably aren't surprised to find opposition to apartheid.[11]

Sometimes the segmenting process is a little more complicated, especially when dealing with less obvious problems. In a speech before a Public Affairs

A speaker can use statistics to describe a situation or to sketch its scope or seriousness. By reducing large masses of information into generalized categories, statistics clarify the nature of a situation and substantiate a potentially disputable claim.

1. *The person quoted should be qualified, by training and experience, to speak on the field being discussed.*

2. *Whenever possible, the authority's statement should be based upon firsthand knowledge.* An Iowa farmer is not an authority on a South Carolina drought unless he or she has personally observed the conditions.

3. *The judgment expressed should not be unduly influenced by personal interest.* Asking a political opponent to comment on the current president's job performance will likely yield biased opinion.

4. *The listeners should realize that the person quoted actually is an authority.* In Mr. Dedmon's statement, we found out who Jon D. Miller is, but he neglected to tell us the qualifications of Alexander Astin.

When citing testimony, do not use big names simply because they are well known. A TV star's opinion on the nutritional value of a breakfast cereal is less reliable than the opinion of a registered dietician. The best testimony comes from subject-matter experts whose qualifications your listeners recognize.

Restatement

Restatement is the reiteration of an idea in different words. It is distinguishable from *repetition,* in which words remain the same. Although they provide no real proof, restatement and repetition often have persuasive impact. Advertisers realize this and spend millions of dollars annually repeating messages—"Budweiser—The King of Beers," "Pepsi for a New Generation," "McDonald's—We Do It All For You."

If speakers simply repeat the same words, however, they risk monotony. This can be avoided by restricting the use of repetition to a single concept or point. Walter F. Mondale, speaking at the 1980 Democratic National Convention, incorporated repetition of a phrase to heighten the impact of his view of the Democratic party and those who speak on its behalf:

> When we speak of peace, the voice is Ed Muskie's. When we speak of workers, the voices are Lane Kirkland's and Doug Fraser's. When we speak of compassion, the first is Ted Kennedy's. And when we speak of courage, the spirit is Jimmy Carter's. When we in this hall speak for America—it is America that is speaking.[17]

Restatement, for most of us, however, is more effective than repetition. Restating an idea in different words or—better—in different frames of reference can be done easily, and it is effective. Note how Charles A. LeMaistre, President of University of Texas M.D. Anderson Hospital and Tumor Institute, used two restatements of annual deaths from tobacco to drive home his point:

THE FORMS OF SUPPORTING MATERIAL

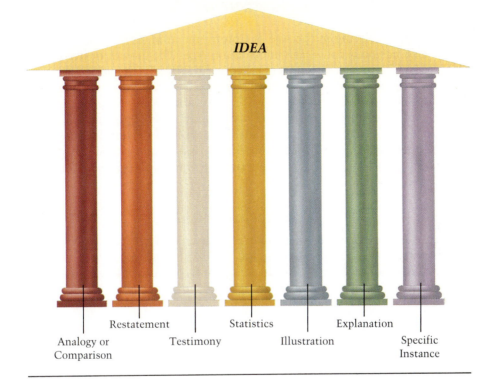

Our focus must be expanded to include an even larger target: the legal manufacture of death-dealing products continues unabated, resulting in almost 500,000
American deaths each year,

  or about one in four of all Americans who die from all causes,

  or almost as many Americans sacrificed in one year as lost their lives in all
wars in this century.

Is the change occurring fast enough? There can be no greater humanitarian
effort than renewed and vigorous prosecution of this issue politically at local,
state, and national levels. There can be no greater or more worthwhile health
crusade than the education of America's young to avoid the use of tobacco.[18]

Notice, too, that Mr. LeMaistre used a repetition of "There can be no greater"
to give his final paragraph a sense of importance and seriousness.

The seven forms of supporting material, singly or in combination, can be
used to clarify or to justify your claims. Express your views, to be sure, but
amplify and develop them further with the aid of restatement, testimony,
statistics, specific instances, detailed illustrations, analogies, and explanations.

Where to Look for Information: Sources of Supporting Material

Not only are we living in the Age of Communication, as noted in Chapter 1; this also has been called the Information Age. The growth of literacy in the world, reductions in the costs of printing, and the advent of electronically stored and retrieved information have all worked together to bury us in data. As a speaker, therefore, you need never lack information—if you can find it. To research speech topics requires that you build a battle plan for gathering relevant information and ideas. Available sources of existing information include publications of all kinds, broadcasts, and computerized data bases. You may wish to generate new information through interviews and letters or questionnaires as well.

Accessing Printed Materials

The most common source of supporting materials is the printed word—newspapers, magazines, pamphlets, and books. Through the careful use of a library—and with the help of reference librarians—you can discover an almost overwhelming amount of materials relevant to your speech subject and purpose.

Newspapers. Newspapers are obviously a useful source of information about events of current interest. Moreover, their feature stories and accounts of unusual happenings provide a storehouse of interesting illustrations and examples. You must be careful, of course, not to accept as true everything printed in a newspaper, for the haste with which news sometimes must be gathered makes complete accuracy difficult. Your school or city library undoubtedly keeps on file copies of one or two highly reliable papers, such as the *New York Times*, *The Observer*, the *Wall Street Journal*, and the *Christian Science Monitor*, and probably also a selection from among the leading newspapers of your state or region. If your library has the *New York Times*, it is likely to have the published index to that paper. By using this resource, you can locate accounts of people and events from 1913 to the present. Yet another useful and well-indexed source of information on current happenings is *Facts on File*, issued weekly since 1940. Also, *NewsBank* provides monthly listings on microfiche of news events from different areas.

Magazines. An average-sized university library subscribes annually to hundreds of magazines and journals. Some—such as *Time*, *Newsweek*, and *U.S. News & World Report*—summarize weekly events. *The Atlantic* and *Harper's* are representative of a group of monthly publications that cover a wide range of subjects of both passing and permanent importance. Such magazines as *The Nation*, *Vital Speeches of the Day*, *Fortune*, *Washington Monthly*, and *The New Republic* contain comment on current political, social, and economic questions. For more specialized areas, there are such magazines as *Popular Science, Scientific American, Sports Illustrated, Field and Stream, Ms., Better Homes and Gardens, Today's Health, National Geographic,* and *American Heritage.*

This list is, of course, merely suggestive of the wide range of materials to be found in periodicals. When you are looking for a specific kind of information, use the *Readers' Guide to Periodical Literature,* which indexes most of the magazines you will want to refer to in preparing a speech. If you need more sophisticated material, consult the *Social Science Index* and the *Humanities Index.* Similar indexes also are available for technical journals, publications from professional societies, and the like. A reference librarian can show you how to use them.

Yearbooks and Encyclopedias.   The most reliable source of comprehensive data is *Statistical Abstracts of the United States,* which covers a wide variety of subjects ranging from weather records and birth rates to steel production and election results. Unusual data on Academy Award winners, world records in various areas, and the "bests" and "worsts" of almost anything can be found in the *World Almanac, The People's Almanac, The Guinness Book of World Records, The Book of Lists,* and *Information Please.* Encyclopedias, such as the *Encyclopaedia Britannica* and *Americana Encyclopedia,* which attempt to cover the entire field of human knowledge, are valuable chiefly as an initial reference source or for background reading. Refer to them for important scientific, geographical, literary, or historical facts; for bibliographies of authoritative books on a subject; and for ideas you will not develop completely in your speech.

Documents and Reports.   Various governmental agencies—state, national, and international—as well as many independent organizations publish reports on special subjects. Among governmental publications, those most frequently consulted are the hearings and recommendations of congressional committees or those of the United States Departments of Health and Human Services and of Commerce. Government documents can easily be explored through the *Congressional Information Service Index.* Reports on issues related to agriculture, business, government, engineering, and scientific experimentation are published by many state universities. Such endowed groups as the Carnegie, Rockefeller, and Ford Foundations and such special interest groups as the Foreign Policy Association, the Brookings Institution, the League of Women Voters, Common Cause, and the United States Chamber of Commerce also publish reports and pamphlets. Although by no means a complete list of all such pamphlets and reports, *The Vertical File Index* does offer you a guide to some of these materials.

Books.   There are few subjects suitable for a speech on which someone has not written a book. As a guide to these books, use the subject-matter headings in the card catalog of your libraries. Generally, you will find authoritative books in your school library and more popularized treatments in your city's public library.

Biographies.   *The Dictionary of National Biography* (deceased Britishers), the *Dictionary of American Biography* (deceased Americans), *Who's Who* (living Britishers), *Who's Who in America, Current Biography*, and more specialized works organized by field contain biographical sketches especially useful in locating facts about famous people and in documenting the qualifications of authorities whose testimony you may quote.

Accessing Nonprint Materials

Useful, up-to-date information also can be found in nonprint resources. The broadcast media and computer memory banks contain today's opinions and facts, not yesterday's set type. Learning to access nonprint resources keeps you abreast of late-breaking information.

Radio and Television Broadcasts.   Lectures, discussions, and the formal public addresses of leaders in government, business, education, and religion are frequently broadcast over radio or television. Many of these talks are later mimeographed or printed by the stations or by the organizations that sponsor them. Usually, as in the case of CBS's *Meet the Press* or National Public Radio's *All Things Considered*, copies can be obtained for a small fee. If no manuscript is available, you may take careful notes or audiotape the program (as long as you make no public use of that tape). When taking notes, listen with particular care in order to get an exact record of the speaker's words and meaning. Just as you must quote items from printed sources accurately and honestly, so are you obligated to respect the remarks someone has made on a radio or television program and to give that person full credit.

Computerized Searches.   Your library may subscribe to one or more computerized data bases. These function much like a printed index. To access a data base, you need to work with a reference librarian in determining what *descriptors* (key words) to enter. An average-sized university library probably has access to upward of two hundred data files, such as ERIC, BIOSIS, PsychInfo, AGRICOLA, Datrex, and MEDLINE.

You also might be able to use one or more of the available public data bases. For example, BRS/After Dark is available by subscription to those with personal computers and a modem (a communication device that links computers through phone lines); CompuServe, The Source, and Dow Jones News/Retrieval are other major consumer-oriented data base services that can be accessed through a modem and computer hookup.

These sources can be valuable time-savers, as they will search for and print lists of articles available in your specific research area. Data bases involve expense, however. Libraries often charge for computer time spent in searching and printing your information, and public data bases charge an initial fee plus per-hour charges for online time. Yet, in an age of information explosion, they can save you a tremendous amount of time and put you in contact with far more material than you could reasonably assemble using only a card catalog and a few reference works.

Generating New Information

At times you will find it necessary or useful to generate information on your own. Two common approaches are to conduct interviews with appropriate persons and to construct and distribute a questionnaire.

Conducting Informational Interviews. The goal of an **informational interview** is clear: to obtain answers to specific questions. In conducting the interview, you hope to elicit answers that can be woven into your speech text. Further, the answers can increase your general understanding of a topic so that you avoid misinforming your audience or drawing incorrect inferences from information obtained through other sources. The interviewee may be a "content expert" or someone who has had personal experience with the issues you wish to discuss. If you are addressing the topic of black holes, who better to help you than a physicist? If you are explaining the construction of a concrete boat, you might contact a local civil engineer for assistance. If, on the other hand, you wish to discuss anorexia nervosa, it may be helpful to interview a person who has suffered through the disorder. Interviews can provide compelling illustrations of human experiences.

There are three general guidelines to observe in planning an informational interview:

1. *Decide on your specific purpose.* What precise information do you hope to obtain during the interview? One caution: if you are interviewing a controversial figure, you may not be best served by engaging in an argument or by assuming a belligerent or self-righteous manner. Even if you disagree with the answers being given, your role is not that of Perry Mason, seeking to win a jury's vote by grilling the witness. This does not mean that your purpose cannot encompass tough questions or questions that seek further clarification of answers that seem "not right." You can raise such questions without provoking an argument.

2. *Structure the interview in advance.* The beginning of an interview clarifies the purpose and sets limits on what will be covered during the session. You also can use this time to establish rapport with the person being interviewed. The middle of the interview comprises the substantive portion: information being sought is provided. Structure your questions in advance so that you have a rough idea of what will be asked when. The interview may not follow your list exactly, but you will have

One common way to generate new information is to conduct an informational interview. The interviewee may be an expert on the content of the speech or someone who has had personal experience with the issue under discussion.

a convenient checkpoint to see whether all the information you need has been presented. Finally, you will find the list useful as you summarize your understanding of the major points. This will help you avoid misinterpreting the meaning given to specific points by the person interviewed. The following format is an example of one you might follow in an informational interview:

I. Opening
    A. Mutual greeting
    B. Discussion of purposes
        1. Reason information is needed
        2. Kind of information wanted
II. Informational Portion
    A. Question #1, with clarifying questions as needed
    B. Question #2, with clarifying questions as needed
    C. [and so on]
III. Closing
    A. Summary of main points
    B. Final courtesies

3. *Remember that interviews are interactive processes.* There is a definite pattern of "turn-taking" in interviews that allows both parties to concentrate on one issue at a time and assists in making the interview work for the benefit of both parties. The interactive pattern requires that both parties be careful listeners, for one person's comments will affect the next comment of the other. You will need to remain flexible and free to deviate from your interview plan as you listen to the answers to your questions. You will have to listen to what is said and almost simultaneously think ahead to the next item on your list of questions. Should you forge ahead or ask intervening questions to clarify or elaborate on a previous response?

Communicative Skills for Successful Interviewers. From this discussion of interviewing and structures for communicating, it should be clear that adept interviewers must have certain communicative skills. *A good interviewer is a good listener.* Unless you take care to understand what someone is saying and to interpret the significance of those comments, you may misunderstand. Because questioning and answering are alternated in an interview, there is plenty of opportunity to clarify remarks and opinions. You can achieve clarification only if you are a good listener (see Chapter 2).

A good interviewer is open. Many of us are extremely wary of interviewers. We are cynical enough to believe that they have *hidden agenda*—unstated motives or purposes—that they are trying to pursue. Too often interviewers have said they "only want a little information" when actually they were selling magazine subscriptions or a religious ideal. If, as an interviewer, you are "caught" being less than honest, your chances for success are vastly diminished. Frankness and openness should govern all aspects of your interview communication.

A good interviewer builds a sense of mutual respect and trust. Feelings of trust and respect are created by revealing your own motivation, by getting the person to talk, and by expressing sympathy and understanding. Sometimes, of course, your assumptions of integrity and good will can be proved wrong. To start with suspicion and distrust, however, is to condemn the relationship without giving it a fair chance.

Sending Letters and Questionnaires. If you need more data than you can find in the library and do not have access to an expert, you can write away for information. This is always risky, as you may not receive the information in time for the presentation. Thus, be sure to write as soon as you have decided on a topic. If you are requesting general information, be as specific about the purpose of the request as you can; this will assist your respondent in forwarding what you are looking for. A letter to the Department of Housing and Urban Development asking "Do you have any information on housing?" is unlikely to be answered satisfactorily, if at all. As you ask for information, explain why you have been unable to locate it on your own. Respondents who think they are being asked to do your work for you will probably be unwilling to help.

On other occasions, you may wish to discover what a group of people knows or thinks about a subject. If, for example, you wanted to give a speech on a proposed halfway house for the mentally ill, you might survey residents in the vicinity. You could send a questionnaire to people chosen randomly from the phone book or to all living within a three-block radius from the proposed home. If you are seeking information on a new college drinking policy, you could survey dormitory residents or members of several classes. With the results, you could construct your own statistical summaries for presentation as part of your speech.

When developing a questionnaire, there are several guidelines to keep in mind:

1. Be sure the form explains the exact purpose of the questionnaire and the procedures to follow in responding to the questions.
2. Keep the form short and to the specific points you wish to have responses on.
3. For ease of summarizing, use closed questions (for example, ask for "yes/no" responses where appropriate and use such categories as "strongly agree/agree/disagree/strongly disagree" if you want ranges of opinion).
4. Phrase questions in clear, neutral language. Do not use loaded terms (for example, "Do you wish to see mentally unbalanced, unpredictable people living next to your children?").
5. Pilot-test the form with a few people to see whether the instructions are clear and to determine if any questions need to be rephrased.
6. If mailing the questionnaire, include a stamped, self-addressed envelope to encourage returns.

Recording Information in Usable Forms

When you find the information you have been looking for, either photocopy it or take notes. Whether you keep your notes on 4-by-6-inch cards or in a notebook, it is helpful to have an accurate, legible record of the materials you wish to consider for your speech. An incomplete source citation makes it difficult to find the information again if you need to recheck it; hurried scribbles, too, are hard to decipher later.

A SAMPLE NOTECARD

Specific Information —

The Discovery of Laser Light

The inventor speaks — General Subject

The laser was born early one beautiful spring morning on a park bench in Washington, D.C. As I sat in Franklin Square, musing and admiring the azaleas, an idea came to me for a practical way to obtain a very pure form of electromagnetic waves from molecules,

Source — *Charles H. Townes, "Harnessing Light," Science 84 (November 1984): 153.*

Many people find that notecards are easier to use than a notebook because they can be shuffled by topic area or type of support. If you use a notebook, however, try recording each item on half a page. Since most of your information will not fill a page, this will save paper; cutting the sheets in half will make it easier to sort your data or to adopt a classification scheme and relate information to particular themes or subpoints of your speech. When preparing notecards, place the subject headings at the top of the card and the complete source citation at the bottom, as in the sample presented above. This way, the card can be classified by general subject (top right heading) and by specific information presented (top left heading).

You need not, of course, always follow these directions exactly. You will find, however, that you will need a classification system so you can put your hands on specific pieces of information as you construct your speeches.

Using Source Material Ethically

Now that we have discussed locating and generating material for your speeches, we come to a major ethical issue, plagiarism. **Plagiarism** has been defined as "the unacknowledged inclusion of someone else's words, ideas, or data as one's own."[19] One of the saddest things an instructor has to do is to cite a student for plagiarism. In speech classes, students occasionally quote material from *Reader's Digest, Newsweek, Time, Senior Scholastic*, or other easy-to-obtain sources, not realizing how many speech teachers habitually scan the library periodicals section. Even if the teacher has not read the article, it soon becomes apparent to most of the class that something is wrong—the wording is not similar to the way the person usually talks, the speech does not have a well-formulated introduction or conclusion, and the organizational pattern is not one normally used by speakers. Often, too, the person who plagiarizes an article reads it aloud badly, another sign that something is wrong.

Plagiarism is not, however, simply undocumented verbatim quotation. It also includes (1) undocumented paraphrases of others' ideas and (2) undocumented use of others' main ideas. For example, if you paraphrase a movie review from *Newsweek* without acknowledging that staff critic David Ansen had those insights, or if you use the motivated sequence as a model for analyzing speeches without giving credit to Alan Monroe for developing it, you are guilty of plagiarism.

Suppose you ran across the following excerpt from Kenneth Clark's *Civilisation: A Personal View:*

> It was the age of great country houses. In 1722 the most splendid of all had just been completed for Marlborough, the general who had been victorious over Voltaire's country: not the sort of idea that would have worried Voltaire in the least, as he thought of all war as a ridiculous waste of human life and effort. When Voltaire saw Blenheim Palace he said, 'What a great heap of stone, without charm or taste,' and I can see what he means. To anyone brought up on Mansart and Perrault, Blenheim must have seemed painfully lacking in order and propriety.... Perhaps this is because the architect, Sir John Vanbrugh, although a man of genius, was really an amateur. Moreover, he was a natural romantic, a castle-builder who didn't care a fig for good taste and decorum.[20]

If you were to use the excerpt in writing a speech, you should do so carefully. The following examples illustrate plagiarism and suggest ways to avoid it:

1. *Verbatim quotation of a passage* (read it aloud word for word)
   To avoid plagiarism: "Kenneth Clark, in his 1969 book *Civilisation: A Personal View*, said the following about the architecture of great country estates in eighteenth-century England: [then quote the paragraph]."

2. *Undocumented use of the main ideas:* "In eighteenth-century England there was a great flurry of building. Country estates were built essentially by amateurs, such as Sir John Vanbrugh, who built the splendid Blenheim Palace for General Marlborough. Voltaire didn't like war and he didn't like Blenheim, which he called a great heap of stone without charm or taste. He preferred the order and variety of houses designed by French architects Mansart and Perrault."
   To avoid plagiarism: "In his book *Civilisation: A Personal View*, Sir Kenneth Clark makes the point that eighteenth-century English country houses were built essentially by amateurs. He uses as an example Sir John Vanbrugh, who designed Blenheim Palace for the Duke of Marlborough. Clark notes that, when Voltaire saw the house, he said, 'What a great heap of stone, without charm or taste.' Clark can understand that

reaction from a Frenchman who was raised on the neoclassical designs of Mansart and Perrault. Clark explains English style arose from what he calls 'natural romanticism.'"

3. *Undocumented paraphrasing:* "The eighteenth century was the age of wonderful country houses. In 1722 the most beautiful one in England was built for Marlborough, the general who had won over France. When Voltaire saw the Marlborough house called Blenheim Palace, he said it was a great heap of stones."
   To avoid plagiarism: Use the same kind of language noted under example 2, giving Clark credit for his impressions.

Plagiarism is easy to avoid if you take reasonable care. Moreover, by citing such authorities as Clark, who are well educated and experienced, you add their credibility to yours. Avoid plagiarism to keep from being expelled from the class or even your school, but avoid it for positive reasons as well: improve your ethos by associating your thinking with that of experts.

Critical Thinking and the Use of Supporting Material

It is one thing to gather and generate supporting materials, but another to use them well. The effective use of supporting material is an exercise in **critical thinking**—assessing the rational requirements for clarifying thoughts and proving something to someone else. As was suggested at the beginning of this chapter, when you must illustrate a central idea or defend a claim, you should ask yourself questions about what the audience members will need before they can understand your idea or accept your claim. Critical thinking about ways to use supporting material involves considering (1) the rational requirements your claim puts on you, (2) the range of supporting material available, (3) the demands a particular audience might make of someone defending such a claim, and (4) the generally perceived power-to-prove of particular forms of support.

Suppose you wish to defend the claim "Universities should build laser technology centers because they can promote state economic growth." Thinking about that claim in terms of the first three factors listed in the previous paragraph, you might come to the following conclusions:

1. *Rational requirements of the claim.* This claim demands that you demonstrate a relationship between university research centers and private-sector economic growth. What sorts of supporting materials might help you with that demonstration? A literal analogy between another state, which has invested in university laser technology centers, and yours would work. Explanations describing the relationship between research and economic development would make sense. Statistics on the number of jobs created by laser technological applications would help, as would testimony from experts.

Skills of the Expert

*T*his chapter has presented what may seem a confusing array of decisions about researching, selecting, and arranging supporting material. How, you wonder, will I ever become an expert? Gaining expertise takes knowledge, experience, and time.

The five-step process by which one becomes an expert has been outlined by Dreyfus and Dreyfus of the University of California at Berkeley:

- *Step 1: Novice.* Learning the rudiments, basic facts, and most basic rules on how to proceed—that is, mastering the type of material contained in this chapter
- *Step 2: Advanced Beginner.* Gaining enough experience to learn which rules to apply in certain situations, beginning to understand more complex rules
- *Step 3: Competence.* Learning to put complex decisions in hierarchies and to consider situational variations by seeing "the big picture." Thus, competent speakers acquire the ability to attack decisions about supporting material step-by-step—deciding quickly what is needed to bolster main claims first and subsidiary claims second, next searching for the perfect final quotation that will epitomize the whole speech, and only then looking for startling statistics with which to open the speech.
- *Step 4: Proficiency.* Working with what the Dreyfuses call "holistic similarity recognition"—recogniz-

2. *Range of available materials.* Can you find all of those materials? Do you have access to studies done of other states? Are statistics on boosts to employment available? Do the experts really believe laser research centers spur local economies? In other words, it is one thing to guess at what would make for good support and another thing to actually find the materials. You may have to settle for thin evidence in some areas simply because the needed data have not been gathered.

3. *Audience demands.* An audience of university administrators would want to know what impact such a laser technology center would have on the campus. How many new faculty members would have to be hired? Are there students who want access to a laser engineering program? What new facilities would be needed, and how much would they cost? Who would pay? In contrast, an audience of legislators might ask different

ing solutions to problems because you recall what worked on a similar previous occasion. After speaking to hundreds of audiences, a political campaigner seldom needs to think through the substance of the speech to a new audience. Rather, that politician has become proficient at recognizing factors in the situation—demographic characteristics of the audience, aspects of his or her positions that would work well with these kinds of listeners, physical cues to appropriate tone, and the like—and adapting to them almost without thinking.

- *Step 5: Expertise.* Acting without thinking. For the expert speaker, public address has been completely internalized and has become a part of the person's basic personality. He or she does not "think" about categories of supporting material, but, rather, ranges through materials and orders them automatically. Proficient speakers represent the top 1 percent; experts are much, much more rare.

What should this mean to you? You will not truly master the art of supporting your ideas or, for that matter, *any* of the arts of public speaking until you have spoken many, many times, in various kinds of situations. As you make your way through those speeches, sometimes effectively and sometimes not, you will acquire increasing sophistication and ease in the process of constructing the substance of your speeches. You should not be discouraged, for most student speakers can become competent, and some will become proficient. There may already be an expert in your class.

FOR FURTHER READING
See Trotter, Robert J. "The Mystery of Mastery." *Psychology Today* (July 1986) for an expanded review of several studies of expertise. For fuller development of the five-step process whereby expertise appears to become something like intuition, see Dreyfus, Hubert L., and Stuart E. Dreyfus. *Mind over Machine.* New York: Free Press, 1986.

questions. Is this another pipedream by heads-in-the-clouds professors? Will our constituencies accept the idea of spending state money to foster private business growth? Are the alumni from this school heavy voters? Is the governor behind this project? Different audiences, thus, expect answers to their own questions in your supporting documents.

4. *Power-to-prove.* Any of the forms of support may be used to clarify, to amplify, or to strengthen; however, some forms tend to accomplish those purposes better than others and are more effective with particular audiences. Explanation, comparison, specific instance, and segment statistics are especially helpful in clarifying an idea. These materials allow the speaker to present information that simplifies an idea for the audience, and they are useful when listeners have little background or knowledge about the topic or when the subject matter is complex. Explanation,

Cable Television—at Your Service!

□ *Claim*

□ *First supporting statement: hypothetical illustration*

□ *Specific instances within the illustration*

□ *Restatement of supporting statement*

□ *Second supporting statement*

□ *Specific instances*

□ *Third supporting statement*

□ *Comparison*

□ *Statistics*

I. Cable television soon will revolutionize your everyday life.

  A. Suppose, on a rainy day a few years from now, you decide to run your errands from your living room.

    1. You turn on your two-way communication unit and begin your round of errands:

      a. On Channel 37, your bank's computer verifies the amount of a recent withdrawal.

      b. On Channel 26, you ask the telephone company to review last month's long-distance charges.

      c. On Channel 94, a supermarket lets you scan products, prices, and home-delivery hours.

      d. On Channel 5, you study a list of proposed changes in the city charter.

        1. You can "call in" for further information.

        2. You can vote from your own home.

      e. Channel 106 gives you access to resource personnel at the public library.

    2. With "cable television at your service," you have accomplished your day's errands with minimum expenditure of time, gas, and parking-meter money.

  B. These possibilities, once thought of only as dreams, are becoming actualities across the United States.

    1. Most cities have public-access channels filled with local talent and ethnic programming.

    2. Ann Arbor, Michigan, and Columbus, Ohio, have been leasing channels to private firms and public utility companies.

  C. Cable television soon will be available to virtually every household in the United States at a reasonable cost.

    1. Because the cost is shared by licensee and householder alike, no one bears an excessive burden.

      a. Commercial users find that leasing a channel costs little more than their computer-accounting systems and print/electronic advertising services.

      b. Studio facilities for the public-access channels are made available at cost in most cable television contracts—normally about $30 per hour.

      c. Current installation charges range from $15 to $50.

      d. Monthly rental fees per household seldom exceed $15 for basic cable service.

□ *Explanation combined with specific instances*

2. The technical characteristics of cable television render it inexpensive.
   a. Some existent telephone lines and equipment can be used.
   b. The conversion box mounts easily on a regular television set.
   c. Studio costs are minimal.
      1. Relatively inexpensive ½" videotape and broadcasting equipment can be used.
      2. Engineering and production personnel need minimal training for cable systems.

□ *Restatement of*

D. Given actual and potential uses, plus the positive cost-benefit ratio, cable television will revolutionize your daily life.

□ *Comparison*

1. Just as the wheel extended our legs and the computer our central nervous system, so will cable television extend our communicative capabilities.

□ *Testimony used as restatement of claim*

2. In the words of Wendy Lee, communication consultant to new cable-television franchises: "We soon will be a nation wired fully for sight and sound. We will rid ourselves of the need for short shopping trips; we will cut the lines in doctors' offices; and we will put the consumer and the constituent into the front offices of his or her corporate suppliers and political servants. The telephone and the motor car will become obsolete."

Chapter Summary

The primary forms of supporting material are *explanations of what, how, and why; analogy or comparison; illustration; specific instance; statistics; testimony;* and *restatement.* These materials can be assembled from *printed materials* (newspapers, magazines, yearbooks and encyclopedias, documents and reports, books, and biographies), *radio and television broadcasts, computerized searches,* and *interviews.* Record the information either on notecards or notebook pages, and use it as supporting materials to *clarify, amplify,* and *strengthen* your presentation. Avoid *plagiarism.* Use supporting materials for both informative and persuasive speeches.

Reference Notes

1. Richard J. Hanley, "Cost Containment of Health Care: The Responsibility of Employers and Doctors," *Vital Speeches of the Day* 50 (November 15, 1984).

2. Richard T. Montoya, "The Foreign Aid Cancer," *Vital Speeches of the Day* 53 (August 1, 1987).

3. Louis Hadley Evans, "Can You Trust God?"

4. James H. Webb, "Seapower: Multilateral Obligations and Multilateral Interests," *Vital Speeches of the Day* 53 (December 1, 1987).

5. Pam Williams, "Don't Drink the Water," *Winning Orations* (1980).

6. P. L. Smith, "Leadership in the Creative Process," *Vital Speeches of the Day* 50 (October 15, 1984).

7. James K. Wellington, "A Look at the Fundamental School Concept," *Vital Speeches of the Day* 46 (February 1980).

8. For a technical yet rewarding introduction to statistical analysis generally, see John Waite Bowers and John A. Courtright, *Communication Research Methods* (Glenview, IL: Scott, Foresman and Company, 1984).

9. Joseph N. Hankin, "Where Were You 12 Years Ago?" *Vital Speeches of the Day* 54 (March 1, 1988).

10. Brenda Theriault, "Fast Foods," speech given at the University of Maine, spring term, 1982.

11. Richard K. Long, "Dow and South Africa?" *Vital Speeches of the Day* 53 (June 15, 1987).

12. Joan D. Aiken, "Working with the Federal Election Commission," *Vital Speeches of the Day* 47 (February 1981).

13. Ronald K. Shelp, "A Crossroads in U.S. Trade Policy," *Vital Speeches of the Day* 53 (August 1, 1987).

14. Carl Hall, "A Heap of Trouble," *Winning Orations.*

15. To protect yourself from the unscrupulous use of statistics, read Darrell Huff, *How to Lie with Statistics* (New York: W. W. Norton & Company, Inc., 1954).

16. Donald N. Dedmon, "Scrutinizing Education in the U.S.," *Vital Speeches of the Day* 50 (November 1, 1984).

17. Walter F. Mondale, "Vice Presidential Acceptance Address," *Vital Speeches of the Day* 46 (August 15, 1980).

18. Charles A. LeMaistre, "Lung Cancer in Perspective," *Vital Speeches of the Day* 54 (July 1, 1987).

19. "Academic Honesty & Dishonesty," Louisiana State University, adapted from LSU's *Code of Student Conduct,* 1981.

20. Kenneth Clark, *Civilisation: A Personal View* (New York: Harper & Row, 1969), 246.

Key Terms

explanation	*factual illustrations*
analogy/comparison	*specific instance*
figurative analogies	*statistics*
literal analogies	*magnitudes*
illustration	*segments*
hypothetical illustration	*trends*

testimony   *plagiarism*

restatement   *critical thinking*

informational interview

Problems and Probes

1. Read one of the speeches in this text. Identify its forms of supporting material. How effective are they in meeting the purpose of the speech? What else might the speaker have done to improve on the use of supporting material?

2. Arrange to meet classmates in the reference room of your college library. Working in groups of four to six, each group member is to locate two of the items in the left-hand column of the following list. First, determine which of the sources listed in the right-hand column contains the material you need. When you locate your items, show your group the source and indicate where it is shelved.

Weekly summary of current national news	*Book Review Digest*
Brief sketch of the accomplishments of Lee Iacocca	*Congressional Record*
	Encyclopedia Americana
Description of a specific traffic accident	*Facts on File*
Text of George Bush's Inaugural Address	local newspaper
Daily summary of stock prices	*New York Times*
Origin of the word "rhetoric"	*Oxford English*
Critical commentary on A. Bloom's *The Closing of the American Mind*	*Dictionary*
	Statistical Abstracts
Current status of national legislation on education reform	*Time*
	Vital Speeches of the Day
	Wall Street Journal
	Who's Who

Communication Activities

1. Present to the class a five-minute central-idea speech, the purpose of which is either to explain or clarify a term, concept, or process. Use at least three different forms of supporting material in developing your idea. To evaluate the effectiveness of your speech, the instructor and other students will consider the following: (a) adequacy of supporting material; (b) appropriateness of supporting material, both as to type and to substance; and (c) insight and skill with which the supporting material is developed.

2. Present to the class a five-minute speech in which you support a specific claim, with the purpose of persuading the audience to accept your ideas. Use at least four different forms of supporting material in developing your justification for the acceptance of your ideas. The class will evaluate your presentation along the lines suggested in activity #1.

CHAPTER EIGHT

Adapting the Speech Structure to Audiences: The Motivated Sequence

*C*hapters 6 and 7 discussed motivational appeals and supporting materials that can be used in developing your speeches. Once you have selected the appropriate appeals and have gathered the information you wish to include in a speech, it is time to consider how to organize that data into a meaningful presentation. As you know from experience, people do not respond readily to a random presentation of information, no matter how accurate it is. Listeners seek to understand the principle of order that underlies your presentation; if they cannot locate one and, hence, cannot follow your line of thought, you run the risk of losing their attention. Your collection of ideas, motivational appeals, and supporting materials need to be shaped into a sensible, coherent whole so that listeners can readily follow your speech to its conclusion.

There are a variety of ways to organize your speech material. Depending upon the nature of the topic, the speaking purpose, and audience needs, some approaches work better than others. Before examining these differences, we will first look at the nature of structure as a general concept and examine in detail an overall perspective on organization known as the motivated sequence. In Chapter 9, we will examine other patterns from a more specific perspective, as they contribute to the internal organization of speeches.

Organization from the Listener's Perspective

From your experience, you know that people learn quickly to sort stimuli into categories of things or events and to predict consequences based on their experiences. In addition, people actively seek coherence in their environment: they try to impose order on their environment if they fail to perceive a natural structure. For example, young children learn to seek relationships among items in their environment. They learn early that one set of furniture comprises a bedroom; another set, a kitchen; and so on. They also learn that animate and inanimate objects are treated differently. By early elementary school, children can determine what is *foreground* in a picture, and what is *background*, or supporting detail. This process of differentiation lends coherence to their perception of the picture. On the basis of your early training, you now apply the same principles automatically to make sense of the various stimuli reaching you. The act of listening to a speech also calls forth the same processes: as the speaker talks, you attempt to determine what is essential (foreground) and what is support (background) in the message.

The importance we attach to structure is further emphasized by the process we use to "fill in" missing elements in a message. If someone says to you, "One, two, three, four," you almost automatically continue with "five, six, seven, eight." Cartoonists can draw a few features of a well-known person, and most readers will be able to identify the individual. If you were presented with a picture of an "unclosed" circle, you would likely still perceive it as a circle, because it parallels complete ones you have seen.[1]

People impose order or coherence in many ways on the stimuli reaching them, or as they communicate their experiences to others. Sometimes people make sense out of events by arranging them chronologically, as when describing the high points of their lives. Occasionally they discuss something they are looking at by moving from left to right or top to bottom. When they want to understand what events led to what consequences, they try to relate causes to effects. At times, the subject under consideration divides easily into parts, as in the case of the three branches of American government or the number of colleges in a university. On other occasions, a person may impose a division, as in the case of inside vs. outside, expensive vs. inexpensive or high vs. low in order to discuss each facet in an intelligible manner. All of these ways of organizing ideas will be further discussed in Chapter 9.

In addition to seeking coherence or structure, there is another important means by which individuals come to grips with the environment and their own thoughts and actions. As noted in Chapter 6, people are influenced by the motives that impel them to act, whether the need or desire is intrinsic or extrinsic. As listeners, we wish to understand how information or proposals relate to us, to our motives for belief and action; we seek, in large part, to place ourselves in our surroundings and to integrate new ideas and proposals into that place.

Our reaction to motives can either be focused on the "problems" that affect our personal lives—that make our lives less comfortable or desirable than they might otherwise be—or on the specific motives which impel us to act. Early in this century, American philosopher John Dewey used a *problem-oriented* focus in devising his "psycho-logic" approach to the resolution of problems. In presenting a pattern for thought, which he called *reflective thinking*, Dewey applied the so-called "scientific method" to individual and group problem solving—to the remedy of "ills" that people deal with in their ordinary lives. In Dewey's view, individuals tend to follow a systematic procedure for solving problems. First, people become aware of a specific lack or disorientation—something is "not quite right" in their immediate environment. Second, they examine this deficiency to determine its scope, causes, and implications. Third, they search for new orientations or operations that would remedy the deficiency, to solve the problem. Fourth, they compare and evaluate possible solutions. Finally, they select a solution—the course of action that seems most likely to put their mind at rest and to handle the real-world dimensions of the problem.[2]

In addition to a problem-oriented focus, individuals also can be inner-directed, or *motivation centered*. Salespersons and advertisers began recognizing this principle in the 1920s. They realized that a person buys an automobile not simply to solve the problem of getting from one point to another, but also to create or reinforce a certain self-image. Similarly, we buy a particular style of clothing to identify with others who wear that style; for example, we make a conscious decision to wear the "Granola look" or the "preppie look." In other words, our personal motivations, hopes, fears, and desires often control the ways we act and the goods we consume.

Alan Monroe (1903–75), the original author of this textbook, knew Dewey's work well. Monroe also had the benefit of personal experience training sales personnel in the 1920s. As he thought about Dewey's psycho-logic and the various sales techniques he had taught people to use, Monroe discovered that he could unite both procedures—one based on the personalized scientific method and the other rooted in an understanding of human motivation—to form a highly *functional* overall organizational pattern that is especially responsive to listeners' goals during a presentation. Since 1935, when the first edition of this textbook was published, that structure has been called **Monroe's Motivated Sequence.** The rest of this chapter will be devoted to this holistic structure for organizing speeches.

Five Basic Steps of the Motivated Sequence

The motivated sequence is functionally similar to Dewey's problem-solving or reflective-thinking procedures. The concept also derives its name from its relationship to human motives; the natural progression of the basic steps is responsive to a listener's desire for coherence and order. Thus, in terms of the preceding discussion, the motivated sequence is both problem oriented and motivation centered.

There are five basic steps in the motivated sequence. As a starting place, you must get people to *attend* to a problem or to feel strongly enough about the deficiency you want them to help correct to be willing to hear more. Then, you can address more specific needs or desires, in relation to individuals' personal sense of *need*. When wants or needs have been aroused, you can attempt to *satisfy* them by showing what can be done to solve the prob-

THE MOTIVATED SEQUENCE

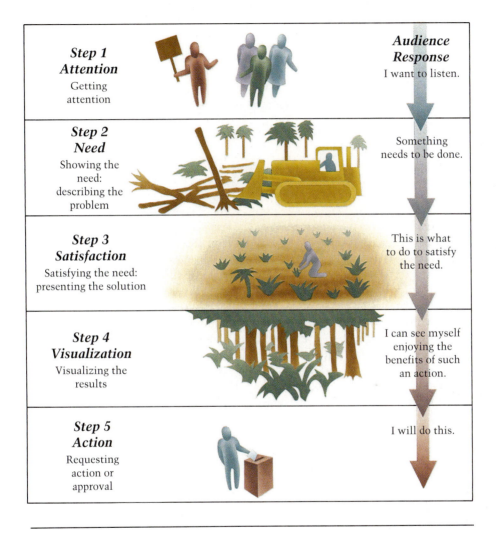

Step 1 ***Attention*** Getting attention		**Audience Response** I want to listen.
Step 2 ***Need*** Showing the need: describing the problem		Something needs to be done.
Step 3 ***Satisfaction*** Satisfying the need: presenting the solution		This is what to do to satisfy the need.
Step 4 ***Visualization*** Visualizing the results		I can see myself enjoying the benefits of such an action.
Step 5 ***Action*** Requesting action or approval		I will do this.

lem or to relieve the impact of the problem on their lives. Simply describing a course of action may be insufficient; hence, you can move to *visualizing* what the environment or situation would be if the action were carried out (or conversely what it would be like if the action were not taken). With these tasks completed, you can appeal to the audience members to *act*—to put into practice the proposed solution to the problem.

Thus, the motivated sequence is composed of five basic steps in the presentation of verbal materials:

Monroe's Original Rationale

*P*rinciples and Types of *Speech* was first published in 1935; in the more than fifty years that have passed, new concepts have been introduced, while original concepts have been revised and updated. Throughout, listeners and their reaction to messages have remained a central theme. In the ten editions preceding this one, the motivated sequence has been an integral part of this listener-oriented approach. The following passages are excerpted from Alan H. Monroe's Preface to the first edition. They clearly support the role the motivated sequence continues to play in speech development.

"The names of the conventional divisions (introduction, body, conclusion) have been discarded in favor of a 'motivated sequence' of five steps, each of which is named to correspond with the function of that step in securing a particular reaction from the audience. These steps are named *attention, need, satisfaction, visualization,* and *action.* Thus, the student is made to realize by the very names of the divisions themselves that he [sic] must first gain attention, then create a feeling of need, satisfy that need, make his audience visualize the satisfaction, and finally impel his listeners to act. It is obvious, of course, that not all five of these steps are needed in every speech. . . .

"This approach to the problem of speech construction is not an untried theory. It has been used for nine years in actual classwork. The ease with which

1. **Attention:** the creation of interest and desire
2. **Need:** the development of the problem, through analyzing deficiencies and relating them to individual needs and desires
3. **Satisfaction:** the proposal of a plan of action that will correct the deficiencies and thereby fulfill individual needs and desires
4. **Visualization:** the verbal depiction of the environment as it will look with the deficiency corrected and the plan implemented
5. **Action:** the final call for personal commitment and specific acts

As you think through the order of these steps, recall Maslow's concept of a hierarchy of needs and desires that build naturally upon one another. In a similar fashion, many speeches proceed from one step to the next; omitting the attention step, for instance, may result in listeners' not hearing the

students grasp the idea and the improvement in the functional effectiveness of their speeches has been marked since this method was adopted. Much less often are their speeches mere exhibitions of skill in 'literary' composition, and more often do students adapt their remarks to the actual audience addressed.

"The history of this particular departure from customary practice deserves brief comment. Books on the psychology of business had long used the functional terms, attention, interest, desire, and action, to describe the process of selling merchandise. Professor G. R. Collins applied this sequence to the public sales talk. In 1926, Dr. P. H. Scott and I conceived the idea of applying this method to all speeches which sought to influence belief or action. In 1929, Mr. J. A. McGee, then on our staff, published a book containing a statement of this approach [John A. McGee, *Persuasive Speaking* (Scribner, 1929)—a 300-page textbook that sold for $1.60.].

"Mr. McGee, however, limited his discussion to persuasive speeches; his conception of the various steps as sharply defined structural units, all five of which must always be used, prevented him from applying the method to many types of speeches where action is not desired. On the other hand, I consider the steps as having a cumulative function, the speaker using only as many of them as the purpose of his speech requires. In this way I have applied the functional approach not only to persuasive speeches but to all types of speeches. Here again the actual use of this approach in my advanced classes on 'Forms of Address' has proved its practical value in demonstrative and informational speeches as well in those which seek to persuade."

From then until now, the *functional* characteristic of the motivated sequence has stood the test of time. Irrespective of the changes that have been made over the years in particular applications, the dominant principles underlying its use remain as Monroe first used them in the classroom and then articulated them in the first edition of this textbook.

FOR FURTHER READING

Monroe, Alan H. *Principles and Types of Speech*. Chicago, IL: Scott, Foresman and Company, 1935, vii–viii, x.

remainder of your ideas. While the sequential patterning of the steps is not a hard and fast rule, adhering to its general order increases the likelihood of success. As a holistic organizational tool, the motivated sequence can be used to structure many different sorts of speeches, on many different topics. As your purpose shifts from informational to persuasive or actuative, the specific form each step takes likewise shifts.

As an overall pattern of development, the most obvious use of the motivated sequence is in persuasive or actuative situations. For example, it helps structure the major points of a speech urging classmates to join a blood donors' group being formed on campus: (*attention*) "If you had needed an emergency transfusion for a rare blood type in Washington County on December 23, 1989, you might not have received it." (*need*) "Blood drives seldom collect sufficient quantities of blood to meet emergency needs in an area such as this one." (*satisfaction*) "A blood donors' association guarantees a predictable, steady supply of needed blood to the medical community." (*visualization*) "Without a steady supply of blood, our community will face needless deaths; with it, emergencies like yours can be met with prompt treatment." (*action*) "You can help by filling out the blood donors' cards I am handing out."

You also can use the motivated sequence to convey information: (*attention*) "Does the prospect of getting AIDS frighten you?" (*need*) "If we are to be less frightened by this insidious disease, we all need to be better informed about the ways we can be infected and about the myths about how it can be acquired." (*satisfaction*) "AIDS can be acquired through specific sexual practices by both males and females and through sharing needles used for drug intake; it cannot be acquired from kissing, from toilet seats, or from sitting across from a person with AIDS." (*visualization*) "With this information, I hope to have allayed irrational fears by being very specific about when you are and when you are not at risk." (*action*) "This information can be useful as you consider the meaning of 'safe sex,' as well as when you encounter victims of the disease."

Sample Speech

The motivated sequence also can be used to talk about larger, more pervasive aspects of social problems. The following speech was prepared by David G. Le Vasseur of the University of Maryland and presented in the 1988 contest sponsored by the Interstate Oratorical Association. As you read the speech, note how Mr. Le Vasseur (1) calls attention to his subject by drawing on the novel *Ivanhoe*, which serves as an analogy explaining how our adversarial court system works today; (2) points out with statistics, examples, analogies, and testimony the crucial need to improve cooperation between opposing lawyers; (3) demonstrates that two changes in our legal proceedings would be means of satisfying that need; (4) visualizes the results of carrying out the proposed solution with an analogy to Great Britain (positive visualization) and a reference to the TV program "LA Law" (negative visualization); and (5) concludes with references to *Ivanhoe* and a call for action.

Justice and the Balance
David G. Le Vasseur

Attention Step

At the conclusion of his adventures, Ivanhoe fights an evil knight in that ancient ritual of trial by combat. Ivanhoe, of course, wins this, and justice is served. Two summers ago when I took a job as a law clerk in a firm, I was under the impression that this ancient practice of trial by combat had ended centuries ago. But has it? /1

Today, in our country, we have what is known as an adversarial system of justice. According to legal historian Stuart Nagel, our current adversary system is the direct descendant of trial by combat started in 11th-century England. Nagel characterizes the adversary system as two sides which "combat" one another, each trying desperately to win its case. /2

But when I worked within our legal system, I did not get that same sense of justice as Sir Walter Scott produced in his novel, *Ivanhoe*. Instead, I saw a legal system that has become too adversarial—a system more concerned with winning the combat than with justice. And this problem is actually getting worse. For example, federal judges have always been able to penalize lawyers for overly adversarial behavior that inhibits justice. Yet, a May, 1987, article in the *Wall Street Journal* points out that in the 50 years prior to 1983, federal judges had to use these sanctions only 50 times, but since 1983, these same sanctions have been used over 500 times. And a current Fordham Law School study reports that these 500 sanctions still touch on only a small fraction of the actual violations. /3

Obviously, our courts and their adversaries are going too far, and if justice for all is to prevail, then we must curtail the adversarial nature of our legal system by first confronting two of the crimes which result in an overly adversarial system, and then by mandating specific judicial reforms, we can perhaps balance the scales of justice once again. /4

Need Step

The first of these crimes, abusive fact finding, occurs before you even get into a courtroom. In our legal system, the process of fact finding is called discovery. During this process, each side in a case gets to ask the opposing side questions. For example, if you are my opponent in a case, I'd send you a set of questions which you, by law, must answer. This sounds fair, doesn't it? The problem is, if I don't ask you the right questions, you don't have to tell me all the facts— no matter how important they are to the case. And today, lawyers are at liberty, and are in fact trained, to construe discovery so that the right question never gets asked. /5

A Chicago lawyer admitted in the Spring, 1982, *Vanderbilt Law Review* that: In the Adversar[ial] system, it's one group's job to get information and the other's not to give it . . . because discovery is a game to see how much you can hide. /6

Former Supreme Court Justice Powell said in Herbert v. Lando that, "The widespread abuse of discovery has become a prime cause of delay and expense in civil litigation," and this position was supported by the Winter, 1987, *Arizona State Law Review*, which points out that they could and should win, simply because it costs too much to play the discover game. /7

This abuse of legal fact finding is distressing, but at least it occurs outside our inner sanctum of justice, the American courtroom. Unfortunately, this inner sanctum is precisely where our second crime is committed: our overly adversarial system promotes highly biased testimony. In medieval trials by combat, the accused and accuser were allowed to hire people to fight their battles for them, and a class of expert warriors evolved. Today, in our legal system, a similar class has evolved—a class of expert witnesses. According to the July 5, 1987, *New York Times*, 12 years ago our country had approximately 160 people who reportedly made their livings as professional or expert witnesses. Last year, there were nearly 4,000 professional witnesses practicing in our country. /8

The crimes associated with expert witness testimony became real to me when I worked as a law clerk. The firm I worked for is what is called a plaintiffs' firm. We sent all of our injured clients to a particular doctor who very consistently issued medical reports which said something to the effect of, "This woman will never be able to work again." But, on the opposing side you had your defense firms, and they always had their doctors, too, who in the same cases would examine the same clients and issue medical reports which said, "This woman should have reported back to work months ago." /9

An honest difference of opinion? Perhaps, but today lawyers can even shop for such differences. TASA, a corporation based in Fort Washington, Pennsylvania, advertises in legal journals that it will find you an expert witness to support any claim you have in any case. /10

TASA's claim may seem outlandish, but it is really not at all surprising. According to the same July 5 *New York Times* article, a recent study conducted by the U.S. Department of Justice concluded that expert witnesses express opinions in court that they would not make in any other context subject to peer review. /11

Satisfaction Step
Somewhere in this whole legal mess there is the truth, but in a system that has grown too adversarial, we may never find it. Let's say this time you are on the jury. Do you have all the facts? And which of these expert witnesses are you supposed to believe? You'll probably never know, because in our legal system those questions are no longer important. All that matters now is who's going to win and who is going to lose this legal combat. Now let's say from this mess, it's your turn to balance those scales of justice. I don't know how you do that. We need a legal system that is less adversarial—one that looks for truth from the beginning. Specifically, at least two changes are called for in our court rules on both the state and federal levels. First, fact finding must be based on finding facts—not on asking the right questions. According to Supreme Court Justice Powell, in his opinion of the 1980 amendments to the Federal Rules of Civil Procedure, each side in a case should create a file which contains everything they know that is not privileged. This file will be submitted to the judge. Both parties will have access to it, and the judge will have the power to enact stiff penalties if any facts are withheld. /12

Second, as advocated in the Winter, 1987, issue of the *Arizona State Law Review*, our approach to expert testimony must change. If both sides agree that an expert such as a doctor is necessary, they must mutually agree upon one expert and then split the cost. /13

Visualization Step
These changes may seem monumental, but the only monumental barrier is our own attitude, for these same changes have already been implemented in

other adversary systems such as Great Britain, where attorneys on both sides of a case have begun to work together; they already share files, and they already share witnesses. Of course, we live in a generation of "L.A. Law" and in a tradition which finds some of its finest oratory in the dramatic courtroom setting. But the answer may lie in this room. As students involved in competitive speech, chances are some of you are contemplating legal careers. If so, don't settle for our adversary system as is, because losing a case isn't a crime—losing sight of the truth is. If you're not contemplating a legal career, remember that we are all responsible for a legal system that is too adversarial. Litigation in our country is growing at a rate three times that of the population, so chances are we will all see each other in court. According to the August 21, 1987, *Wall Street Journal*, there has been a dramatic increase in clients suing their lawyers for either not winning cases, or simply for not winning big enough victories. Remember, before you choose to litigate, what's at stake. Don't pressure your lawyer to win at all costs. Push for what is fair, and what is just. /14

Action Step

For centuries we have been fighting for justice through trial by combat, but that fight should not be against each other—rather, the evil to be conquered is injustice, injustice perpetuated by faulty rules of discovery and through highly biased testimony. /15

Ivanhoe had Sir Walter Scott to assure his victory. We only have each other. We need to make a start. We really do.[3] /16

Structure and Development of the Steps in the Motivated Sequence

Now that the motivated sequence has been illustrated in its entirety, we need to examine more closely the individual steps, noting in particular their internal structuring, the methods for developing them, and the kinds of materials that can be used effectively in each.

The Attention Step

As a speaker, your first task is to gain attention. The attributes of attention and the major devices for obtaining it were covered in Chapter 3. As you plan this step in your speech, review these devices and determine which ones might best stimulate audience interest in your topic. If the audience is lethargic or tired, you need to begin with something more innovative than "Today I'd like to . . ." Thus, the nine factors of attention discussed in Chapter 3 (activity, reality, proximity, familiarity, novelty, suspense, conflict, humor, and the vital) take on special relevance in the opening moments of your presentation.

Your manner of delivery also affects the attentiveness of your audience; the vigor and variety of your gestures and bodily movements and the flexibility and animation of your voice are important determinants of audience

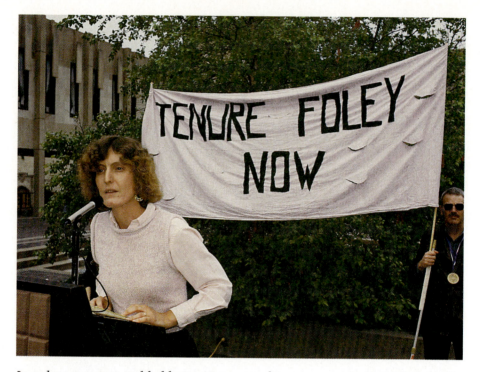

In order to capture and hold attention, a speaker must present ideas that tap listeners' interests and personal motivation.

enthusiasm and interest in your subject. Your credibility, or ethos, as it is judged by your listeners, also assists you in securing their attention. If they already have high regard for you, they are more likely to be attentive as you begin your presentation. The color and impressiveness of your language and style also affect the audience's willingness to attend to your message. A lackadaisical delivery, coupled with a colorless and uninteresting style, is counterproductive. Fundamentally, however, you capture and hold attention through the *types of ideas* you present to your listeners. Your ideas must tap their sense of interest and personal motivation before they will feel compelled to listen.

Although gaining attention is an initial step in bringing your ideas to an audience, remember that *keeping* attention also is vitally important. Keep the same attention devices in mind as you develop the remaining steps in the motivated sequence; in particular, they can be used to heighten attention during the need and visualization steps. A lively, enthusiastic delivery and style also improve your chances of success, as does your satisfaction of the audience's initial assessment of you as a responsible, ethical individual through careful, complete presentation of ideas.

The Need Step

Assuming that the audience is attentive to your message at this point, you have an obligation to lay out the reasons for being concerned about the issue under discussion: Why is the information vital to the well-being of the audience? Why is the problem an urgent one? To accomplish this objective, the need step should include the following:

1. *Statement.* Offer a clear, concise statement of the need. This can be in the form of a central idea or a claim, depending upon your speech purpose. The statement of the need orients the listeners to your specific message. Presumably, what you go on to say will be related to this statement.

2. *Illustration.* Present one or more illustrations or specific instances to give listeners an initial idea of the problem's nature and scope—its degree of importance or significance.

3. *Ramification.* Use the supporting materials discussed in Chapter 7 to clarify your statement of need or to justify the urgency of the problem you wish to have resolved. Additional examples, statistical data, testimony, and other forms of support can supplement the illustrative examples or specific instances you use.

4. *Pointing.* Impress upon the audience members the issue's seriousness, scope, and significance to them. Provide a convincing account of how the issue directly affects their health, happiness, security, or other interests.

In the need step, your primary goal is to *relate your subject to the vital concerns and interests of your audience.* While each of these four tactics may not be essential in every speech, their consideration is a vital part of your preparation. In some contexts, such as explaining the reasons for supporting a call for a nuclear-free Europe to an audience already convinced of its merits, there may not be as much reason to fully develop this section of the speech. If the audience is opposed to or unfamiliar with the idea, it is necessary to flesh out each of these tactics, with particular emphasis on the last one: How does support for a nuclear-free Europe affect each individual in the audience?

The Satisfaction Step

The purpose of this step is to enable your listeners to understand the information you are presenting or to obtain their assent to the belief or action you are proposing. The structure of this step depends somewhat upon whether your purpose is primarily informative, entertaining, or persuasive/actuative. We will discuss the satisfaction step for each of these purposes in turn.

The Satisfaction Step in a Speech to Inform. When your primary goal is to give listeners a clear understanding of a topic or an issue, this step is met when the need for information has been satisfied by the complete presentation of that information. Therefore, the satisfaction step can comprise the bulk of your speech. The development of this step customarily includes:

1. *Initial summary.* Briefly state in advance the main ideas you will cover.

2. *Detailed information.* Discuss in order the facts and explanations pertaining to each of the main ideas.

3. *Final summary.* Restate the main ideas you have presented, together with any important conclusions that can be drawn from them.

The Satisfaction Step in a Speech to Entertain.   When your purpose is to entertain—to present a useful thought or sentiment in a light-hearted, humorous manner—the satisfaction step can constitute the major part of your speech. Your goal is to satisfy the audience that the speech is, in fact, entertaining and that it has conveyed an idea or sentiment worth their time and attention. In developing the satisfaction step in a speech to entertain, follow these guidelines:

1. *Initial statement of theme.* Briefly indicate the sentiment or idea that you will discuss.

2. *Humorous elaboration.* Develop the theme with particular attention to hypothetical and factual illustrations and specific instances that will convey a light-hearted, yet meaningful, message to the audience.

3. *Final summary.* Restate your main theme by connecting your illustrations to the point you wish to make.

The Satisfaction Step in a Speech to Persuade or to Actuate.   In these instances, the satisfaction step is developed as a major subdivision of the speech. The following elements are usually included:

1. *Statement.* Briefly state the attitude, belief, or action you wish the audience to adopt.

2. *Explanation.* Make sure your statement is understood by the audience. Diagrams or charts may be useful in explaining a complex proposal or plan.

3. *Theoretical demonstration.* Show how this belief or action logically meets the problem illustrated in the need step.

4. *Workability.* If appropriate, present examples showing that this solution has worked effectively in the past or that this belief has been supported by experience. Use fact, figures, and expert testimony to support your claim as to the workability of your proposal or idea.

5. *Meeting objections.* Forestall opposition by answering possible objections that might be raised.

and probable. The audience must accept them as real possibilities, not simply as mere chance developments that might accrue from their response to your ideas. In addition, you must make every effort to put your listeners into the picture—to let them see themselves actually living in the future environment you so carefully craft. Use vivid imagery; create mental images that allow the audience members to see, hear, feel, taste, or smell the advantages or disadvantages you describe. The more real you make the projected situation, the greater are your chances of getting a significant, positive response from your audience. The following sample shows how a speaker urging you to plan your college curriculum carefully might develop a visualization step using the contrast method:

> Suppose you enter the university, as nearly 40 percent of our students do, as an "undecided"—either with few interests and even less sense of your educational goals or with many interests that are ill defined or poorly focused. How will you select courses? You might approach the problem in one of two ways: either you "go with the flow," or you seek early advice and plan systematically to ensure graduation after four years.
>
> If you use the first approach, you begin by taking only courses that meet specific requirements (for example, English, speech, math, and science courses). In your second year, you start experimenting with some electives—courses that will not meet specific requirements. You find yourself listening to and accepting your friends' recommendations—"Take Speech 124 because it's easy," "Take Photography 102 because it's cool," or "Take Art 103 because you get to draw what you want." Now comes your junior year. You're nowhere near a major and you're getting close to the three-quarter mark in your education. Your advisor, your parents, and your friends all nag you. You even get down on yourself. In your senior year, you sample some social work courses, finally discovering something you really like. Only then do you realize it will take three or four more semesters—if you're lucky—to complete a B.S.W. degree.
>
> In contrast, suppose you're one of the other half of the "undecided"—those who seek career and personal advisement early. You enroll for the no-credit "Careers and Vocational Choices" seminar in your first semester. While meeting your liberal arts requirements, you take classes in several different departments to test your interests. During your sophomore year, you work with three or four areas of possible interest; you take more advanced courses in these areas to ascertain your interest and ability. Near the end of your sophomore year, you talk with people in Career Planning and meet frequently with your advisor. By your junior year, you get departmental advisors in two majors, find out you don't like one subject as much as you thought, and consult only the second advisor after midyear. You go on to complete the major, taking a summer course between your junior and senior year to catch up because you are a little behind, and obtain your degree "on time."
>
> Carefully planning, experimenting with possible interests, reasoning thoughtfully about your reaction to different areas of study, and rigorously analyzing your own talents are actions that separate the completers from the complainers four years later, so . . . [*move into the action step at this point*]

APPLYING THE MOTIVATED SEQUENCE TO THE GENERAL PURPOSES OF SPEECH

GENERAL PURPOSES

	TO *INFORM* *Understanding, Clarity*	*TO* *ENTERTAIN* *Enjoyment*	*TO* *PERSUADE* *Belief* (*Internal*)	*TO* *ACTUATE* *Specific Action* (*Observable*)
1 Attention Step	Draw attention to the subject.	Draw attention to the theme.	Draw attention to the need.	Draw attention to the need.
2 Need Step	Show why listeners need a knowledge of the subject; point out what problems this information will help them solve.	Show why the theme is worthy of consideration.	Present evidence to prove the existence of a situation that requires a decision upon which listeners must take a position.	Present evidence to prove the existence of a situation that requires action.
3 Satisfaction Step	Present information to give listeners a satisfactory knowledge of the subject to help them solve these problems; begin and end this presentation with a summary of the main points (normal end of the speech).	Elaborate on the theme through numerous illustrations to elicit a pleasurable reaction from listeners.	Get listeners to believe your position is the right one by using evidence and motivational appeals.	Propose the specific action required to meet this situation; get listeners to believe in it by presenting evidence and motivational appeals (as in the speech to persuade).
4 Visualization Step	Sometimes: briefly suggest pleasure to be gained from this knowledge.	Sometimes: briefly suggest what is to be gained through humorous examination of the theme.	Briefly stimulate a favorable response by projecting this belief into imaginary operation (normal end of the speech).	Picture the results of such action or of the failure to act; use vivid description (as in the speech to persuade).
5 Action Step	Sometimes: urge further study of the subject.	Sometimes: implore listeners to consider the lighter side of life.	Sometimes: arouse determination to retain this belief (as a guide to future action).	Urge listeners to take the specific action proposed.

The Action Step

As the table above indicates, only the speech to actuate *always* requires an action step. With other speech purposes, such as to inform or to entertain, you may use something resembling an action step: urging further study of the topic dealt with in an informative speech, using humor to engage the audience's interest in further exploration of a subject, or seeking to strengthen a belief or attitude in meeting a persuasive purpose.

The action step should be relatively brief. Two adages apply: "Stand up, speak up, shut up" and "Tell 'em what you're going to tell 'em, tell 'em, and then tell 'em what you told 'em." Insofar as the action step is concerned, clinch your major ideas, finish your speech briskly, and sit down.

Applying the Motivated Sequence

The preceding material gives a general description of the stages of the motivated sequence and their role in the development of a speech. To further your understanding of this overall structure, regardless of purpose, this section will illustrate how the motivated sequence can be used. The abbreviated outlines contain only enough detail to clarify the nature of each step as it contributes to the progression of the speech. Later chapters will offer more explicit advice on outlining, as well as on integrating specific supporting material and motivational appeals into the structure of the speech.

Using the Motivated Sequence in a Speech to Inform

In general, an informative speech concentrates on the first three steps of the motivated sequence. As always, you need to elicit your listeners' initial attention and sustain it throughout the speech. You also need to motivate them by pointing out why they need to know what you are about to tell them. Finally, you must satisfy this need by supplying information. In most informative situations, this completes your use of the motivated sequence; you have accomplished the purpose and met your listeners' expectations for a finished performance. An action step can be used, however, at the end of the speech in response to a "so what?" question in each listener's mind: "What do you want me to do with this information?" Four steps of the motivated sequence are applied in the following outline of an informative speech about a little-known sleep disorder.

Sleep Apnea

Attention Step
I.   Do you snore, or do you know someone who does?
II. If you snore, do you find yourself falling asleep at odd times during the day, even though you are not tired?

Need Step
I.   For most of us, snoring is simply a laughing matter.
II. For one in ten snorers it may not be: he or she suffers from sleep apnea—a disease that causes a person to stop breathing for short periods of time.

Satisfaction Step

I. Snoring, when severe enough to cause apnea, produces negative effects on one's health.
   A. Apneic snorers suffer from short moments of oxygen deprivation accompanied by higher than normal levels of carbon monoxide, which affect the heart, the brain, and other vital organs.
   B. Apneic snorers develop hypertension (chronic high blood pressure) at a much faster rate than nonsnorers.
   C. Apneic snorers have a much higher incidence of depression and headaches than nonsnorers.
   D. Apneic snorers experience social problems, such as job instability, marital difficulties, inability to concentrate, irritability, and even aggressive behavior at a higher rate than nonsnorers.

II. You can assess the possibility of sleep apnea through a number of methods.
   A. Monitor your own snoring with a tape recorder; listen for pauses that last between ten seconds and one or two minutes.
   B. Have a sleep partner monitor your snoring pattern; time actual breathing lapses characteristic of snoring behavior.
   C. Daytime sleepiness is a major clue to the existence of apnea.

Action Step

I. The next time your rest is interrupted by someone's snoring, remember that, for that person, it may not be a laughing matter.[4]

Using the Motivated Sequence in a Speech to Entertain

As was noted, the speech to entertain may exist for humor in its own right, but more often it uses an occasion for humor to make a serious point. In instances in which you expect the audience only to sit back and enjoy the presentation (for example, at a comic revue), the attention step is the only one required. When you want to both entertain your audience and make a serious point, additional steps are appropriate. In the following outline, all of the steps of the motivated sequence are appropriate to the "moral" the speaker draws from the discussion of optimism vs. pessimism and the concluding appeal for acting as an optimist.

A Case for Optimism

Attention Step

I. Perhaps you've heard the expression "The optimist sees the doughnut, the pessimist, the hole."

Need Step

I. To the pessimist, the optimist is a fool: the person who looks at an oyster and expects to find pearls is engaging in wishful thinking.

II. To the optimist, the pessimist is sour on life: the person who looks at an oyster and expects to get ptomaine poisoning is missing out on the richer possibilities life can offer.

Satisfaction Step
I. The pessimist responds to every event with an expectation of the worst that could happen.
II. The optimist, on the other hand, looks for the bright side.
   A. The day after a robbery, a friend asked a store owner about the loss. After acknowledging that he had indeed suffered a loss, the store owner quipped, "But I was lucky; I marked everything down 20 percent the day before—had I not done that, I would have lost even more."
   B. The optimist is one who cleans her glasses before she eats grapefruit.

Visualization Step
I. When you look on the bright side, you find things to be happy about.

Action Step
I. Be an optimist: "Keep your eye on the doughnut and not on the hole."[5]

Using the Motivated Sequence in a Speech to Persuade

The following speech outline, urging an end to the colorization of classic films, is not a "complete" speech outline, but it provides more detail to show how supporting material is integrated into the various stages and how the overall speech is developed.

Oppose Colorization

Specific Purpose: To convince listeners that colorization of classic black-and-white movies should not be allowed

Attention Step
I. If you like classic movies as I do, imagine my surprise in turning on the television to watch *The Maltese Falcon* and discovering that it had been "colorized"—a process that imposes "natural colors" onto films that were originally shot in black and white.
II. The issue of colorization has divided the Hollywood community and has even generated congressional interest.

Need Step
I. Ted Turner was behind the original impetus to colorize movies for replay on television.
   A. Turner acquired the MGM film library, which included over 3600 films.
   B. Turner Broadcasting has committed $18 million toward the colorization of 100 classic films, from among those it acquired in the MGM purchase.

II. There are several objections to the colorization of classic films.
  A. The most common objection concerns the violation of the original integrity of the film.
    1. For example, John Huston, the director of *The Maltese Falcon*, held a press conference to denounce the colorization of his original work.
    2. A contemporary director, Martin Scorsese, has pointed out that colorization of his 1980 movie, *Raging Bull*, would destroy the artistic integrity of the film.
    3. Nicholas Meyer, director of *Star Trek II*, commented, "It is a mind boggling disservice to the artistry of black-and-white films. They [the original producers/directors] photographed these films using the values of black-and-white photography."
  B. Several arts groups have spoken out against the colorization of classic films.
    1. The Director's Guild of America
    2. The Screen Actors' Guild
    3. The Writer's Guild of America
    4. The American Society of Cinematographers
  C. Federal groups and officials also have protested the process.
    1. The National Council on the Arts and the American Film Institute have expressed their opposition to the process.
    2. Representative Richard Gephardt sponsored a Film Integrity Act to provide legal protection for old films.
  D. There is no current law opposing colorization of classic films.
    1. The principle that an artist's work is harmed by colorization has not been supported by law.
    2. In contrast, the principle does have support in both England and France.

Satisfaction Step

I. How should we protect an artist's original work?
  A. I propose that we support legislation similar to that enacted in England and France.
  B. The legislation proposed by Gephardt will accomplish the goal of protection from colorization.

Visualization Step

I. The enactment of legislation will bring a halt to the colorization of black-and-white films.
  A. When you turn on the TV to watch Laurel and Hardy's *Helpmates* or *Miracle on 34th Street*, you can be sure that it is the original version.
  B. Ending colorization will halt a practice that many view as an immoral intrusion on an artist's original work—after all, the new "color" version is a technician's idea of what colors would have looked like, not a producer's or director's.

Action Step

I. What do I want from you?
  A. I hope you agree that colorization harms the artistic integrity of an original work.
  B. I also hope that I have convinced you that colorization is not an idea "whose time has come."[6]

Using the Motivated Sequence in a Speech to Actuate

All five steps of the motivated sequence are used in a speech to actuate; the audience is asked to go beyond a change in belief state, or an awareness of new information, to actually behave in certain ways. The following outline illustrates how the previous speech can be altered from one with a persuasive orientation to one with an actuative intent. Because the initial steps would remain the same, only the changes in the action step are shown.

Action Step

I. What do I want from you?
  A. For starters, you can boycott those films already colorized; do not watch Turner's colorized films on television and do not rent colorized versions of classic movies.
  B. Second, you can assist me by talking to your friends and convincing them to join the boycott.
  C. Finally, you can take action by writing your congressional representative or senator and urge legislative action to end colorization.

Chapter Summary

This chapter began with an overview of the human need to seek coherence in that which is seen or heard, to make sense out of new experiences as they relate to already known events or ideas. Further, it was noted that people tend to follow a *problem-oriented* approach in seeking changes in their environment and that they also may be *motivation centered* in following their own inclinations and interests. The *motivated sequence* was introduced as a time-tested, flexible organizational pattern for structuring a complete speech. In addition to creating a coherent overall approach to speech development, it provides an orderly approach to problem solving from the listeners' perspective and, thus, embraces their personal motives in listening. The five steps—*attention, need, satisfaction, visualization,* and *action*—were defined and applied in sample speech outlines for each of the major speech purposes. We will return to the motivated sequence at later points in the book.

Reference Notes

1. This "principle of closure" is one of the Gestalt principles of perception (the term "gestalt" refers to "wholeness" and has been used to refer as well to the Gestalt psychologists who researched this issue). For a brief review of Gestalt principles of perception, see John R. Anderson, *Cognitive Psychology and Its Implications* (New York: W. H. Freeman & Co., 1980), 53–56.

2. John Dewey, *How We Think* (Boston, MA: D. C. Heath Co., 1910), 72.

3. David G. Le Vasseur, "Justice and the Balance," *Winning Orations* (1988): 50–52.

4. Information cited in Steve Kaplan, "Snoring," *World and I* 2 (July 1987): 298–303.

5. Based in part on information from *Friendly Speeches* (Cleveland, OH: National Reference Library).

6. Material based on Debra Wishik, "Colorization: Not a Black and White Issue," *World and I* 2 (July 1987): 236–41.

Key Terms

Monroe's Motivated Sequence

attention

need

satisfaction

visualization

action

positive method

negative method

contrast method

Problems and Probes

1. Choose a social controversy as a topic for a speech; specify two audiences, one opposing the issue and the other supporting it (for example, a speech on the need for additional day care facilities presented to a liberal audience and a conservative audience). Using the motivated sequence as a pattern, specify how you would develop each step so it is appropriate to each audience. Write a concluding paragraph that explains the differences between the speeches, as they were adapted to the differing positions of the audiences.

2. The motivated sequence has its own internal logic aimed at satisfying audience questions: attention precedes need, need precedes satisfaction, and so on. Working in small groups, discuss the utility of this perspective as a means of responding to audience expectations. On what occasions might you consider eliminating a step or reversing the order of steps? Would any other pattern have equal or greater utility? At the end of the discussion, be prepared to report your conclusions to the rest of the class.

3. Develop brief outlines for an informative and a persuasive speech using the samples in this chapter as guides. What are the major differences between the outlines—which steps are included or left out of the analysis? What do you do differently in each step in orienting your speech toward presenting information or persuading an audience? Following the outlines, write your response to these questions. Hand in your outlines and response for evaluation by the instructor.

Communication Activities

1. Select a topic for an informative, a persuasive, or an entertaining speech. Develop a specific purpose and a brief outline of the speech, following the appropriate steps in the motivated sequence. Assume that the audience will be your classmates. Working in small groups, each member presents his or her abbreviated "speech"; critique each presentation in terms of its appropriate use of the motivated sequence.

2. Select a topic for a speech that could be either persuasive or actuative. Develop a specific purpose and a brief outline, following the appropriate steps in the motivated sequence. When you come to the action step, develop two approaches—one meeting the needs of a persuasive speech, the other an actuative speech. Working in small groups, briefly review the purpose and the elements contained in the persuasive outline, then indicate how you would alter the speech to make it actuative. Does your specific purpose change as you shift from one speech type to another? Critique one another's approaches to this assignment.

CHAPTER NINE

The Motivated Sequence and Patterns of Internal Organization

*T*he preceding chapter introduced a holistic or overall way of organizing speeches. As noted, the motivated sequence is responsive to the thought processes that listeners often follow when receiving new information or when deciding how to solve a problem. In this chapter, we will consider the relationship between this approach and the patterns of internal organization that fit within various steps of the motivated sequence and that give additional coherence to the development of your message.

Developing Patterns of Internal Organization Within the Steps of the Motivated Sequence

As you recall, the initial step in the motivated sequence is that of **attention**. Normally, this step does not require the use of a specific pattern of organization to accomplish its objective. As we will see in Chapter 10, there are several devices that can be used to introduce the subject of your speech. While these devices can use a time sequence, as in a hypothetical or true story used to open the speech, the overall step does not require a particular pattern.

In contrast, the need and satisfaction steps, more often than not, require the use of a more precise, content-oriented pattern of organization. In both steps, there often is more than one main point. Assume, for example, that you have three main points to develop; an organizational pattern must show the relationship among the points to demonstrate the internal coherence of these steps.

The visualization step may require the use of a specific pattern of organization if you are to be successful in depicting what will or will not happen in the future. There is an implicit time sequence involved, as well as one of influence: "If we do not act today, the situation in the next few weeks will be immeasurably worse."

The final step of the motivated sequence, the action step, should not require a precise organizational pattern. As noted, this step should be relatively brief and to the point: the goal is to leave the audience with a clear message regarding their response to the speech. Devices useful in completing a speech will be discussed in Chapter 10.

Five general criteria should be met in organizing the main points of a speech, regardless of the pattern of organization you use. As previously noted, these criteria relate primarily to the organization of materials in the need and satisfaction steps.

1. *The organization of main points must be easy for the audience to grasp and remember.* Listeners find it much easier to track your ideas if they see how the main points relate to one another. If the structure is clear, the listeners should be able to *anticipate* your next point, because they can discern a particular pattern of organization; they should be able to see how the need and satisfaction steps fit together and how the visualization step (if appropriate) follows naturally. Otherwise, your initial success in eliciting attention diminishes as the audience strives to understand where you are going in the speech or simply gives up the attempt.

2. *The pattern must allow full, balanced coverage of the material it organizes.* The pattern selected to organize main points or subpoints must complement the material. In many cases, this happens naturally, as in describing a recent event (the materials fall into a time sequence) or when explaining how one event will influence another (the materials fall into a cause-effect sequence). If the material and organizational pattern fit together, the audience will find the material easier to grasp.

3. *The pattern should be appropriate to the occasion.* As was noted in Chapter 1, there are some occasions in which speakers are expected to observe group traditions. Political fund-raising speeches, for example, tend to follow a particular format; audiences have come to expect that certain topics or themes will be addressed in a particular order.[1] Choose a form of organization that best meets the demands of the occasion.

4. *The pattern should be adapted to the audience's needs and level of knowledge.* Whereas the motivated sequence bases its approach on listeners' fundamental thought processes, patterns of internal organization

must depend upon other aspects of audience awareness of an issue or a problem. If listeners are not well informed, it may be necessary to speak from a historical perspective, arranging your main points chronologically. In situations in which the audience is well aware of the fundamental issues and the reasons they are important, a full-blown historical analysis would not be necessary. Instead, an analysis of the problem's causes and effects might be better suited to the situation. In this instance, you can follow the satisfaction step by showing how each effect is minimized by the proposed solution.

5. *The speech must move forward steadily toward a complete and satisfying termination.* As you structure the substantive portion of your speech, give the audience a sense of forward motion—of moving through a series of main points with a clear idea of where your ideas are heading and how you are going to arrive at a termination point. Repeated backtracking to pick up lost points will only confuse your audience, and you will lose the sense of momentum your internal patterning (of the need and satisfaction steps in particular) intended to convey. Presenting facts in a random, thoughtless manner does not allow you to clarify a point or to amass data that justify your position.

These are the major criteria that any substantive portion of a speech must satisfy in conveying a coherent, planned message to an audience. Failing to meet any one of these criteria weakens the impact of your entire speech, regardless of how well you plan and execute the other steps in the motivated sequence.

Patterns of Internal Organization

There are several ways in which the main points of your speech can be organized so that their relationship to one another, and their function in each step of the motivated sequence, are clear to an audience. The four most useful options are *chronological patterns, spatial patterns, causal patterns,* and *topical patterns.*

Chronological Patterns

The defining characteristic of **chronological patterns** is their adherence to the order in which events occur. They are useful for orienting listeners who know little about the background of a topic, or for showing listeners that they should hold certain attitudes toward a situation. In the first case, the sequence is called temporal, in the second, narrative.

Temporal Sequence. To use a **temporal sequence,** you begin at a certain period or date and move forward (or backward) systematically to provide background information on a topic listeners know little about. For example,

Organizing information into a temporal sequence enables a speaker to describe systematically the evolution of a process or the history of a program.

you might describe the methods for refining petroleum by tracing the development of the cracking process from the earliest attempts to the present time. You might describe the manufacture of an automobile by following the assembly-line process from beginning to end. Your goals are to create an interest in an area you think your audience should know more about and to present basic information clearly. When speaking about the history of space flights, you might use the following sequence:

Space Flights

Central Idea: "A historical review of space flights demonstrates the evolution of technology."

Attention Step
[Gain audience attention]

Need Step
[Why audience should be interested in subject]

Satisfaction Step
   I.   Pre–NASA planning and development
   II. The origin of NASA and early space flights
   III. From explorations to payload flights
   IV. Future trends in space flights

Visualization Step
[Optional: Show how this information will be useful to listeners—what they can use it for]

Action Step
[Optional: Indicate what you want listeners to retain as information from this presentation]

In this example, the dates separating the main points are not precise, and the periods may overlap (for example, there is no precise date distinguishing exploration and payload interests on NASA's part). Nevertheless, the overall progression of the ideas is one of forward movement.

Narrative Sequence.   If you want to do more than merely offer background information, however, you are better advised to use a chronological pattern that makes a point. *Narratives* are stories that allow you to draw some conclusions about a series of events. For example, Aesop's fables are narratives with a moral about human motivation and action; the series of events surrounding a crime usually are reviewed chronologically by lawyers to point toward the innocence or guilt of a defendant. In **narrative sequences,** therefore, speakers review events or actions to advocate a claim or to clarify the events that have brought about the present situation.[2] If, for example, you want your audience to understand why the failed Equal Rights Amendment drive is such a complex issue, you could use a narrative form to accomplish that purpose.

The Complexities of the ERA Drive

Central Idea: "The Equal Rights Amendment has had a long and complex history."

Attention Step
[Use devices discussed in Chapter 10 to gain initial interest in subject]

Need Step
[Indicate why this issue is still one of vital concern to the audience—even though several years have passed since it was a "hot" political issue]

Satisfaction Step
  I. The Equal Rights Amendment was first introduced into Congress in 1922, only three years after women received the right to vote.
     A. It failed to pass either house for many years.
     B. In 1947, the Senate passed it, although the House did not.
  II. Twenty-seven years later, the Senate passed the ERA, but the House failed to approve it.
     A. It had a chance to pass in 1970, but two riders (excluding women from the draft and allowing prayer in the schools) met with opposition; again it died in the Senate.

    B.   The House finally passed it in 1971.

    C.   The Senate then approved the measure in March 1972.

III. The ratification process began within hours of Senate action.

    A.   Thirty states ratified the ERA within a year.

    B.   Between 1973 and 1975, only four more states ratified the amendment.

IV. Countermeasures soon were taken.

    A.   The movement to rescind also began in 1973, with Nebraska and Tennessee rescinding their support in 1973–74.

    B.   Eight states failed to approve the ERA between 1973 and 1975.

    C.   The momentum gradually diminished, and, for all practical purposes, the drive came to a halt during this period.

V. Moves to revive the ERA in the early '80s were not successful.

    A.   Congress did extend the timetable for keeping the amendment alive.

    B.   Supporters were not able to obtain ratification by the deadline.

    C.   Today ERA is officially dead, although there will be renewed efforts to revive and pass the amendment.

Visualization Step

[Optional: Show how this information will be useful to listeners—what they gain from knowing about the failed ERA drive]

Action Step

[Optional: Indicate what you want listeners to remember from this presentation]

Spatial Patterns

Generally, **spatial patterns** arrange ideas or subtopics in terms of their physical proximity or relationship to each other. Some of these patterns, called **geographical patterns,** organize materials according to well-defined regions or areas so as to visualize physical movement and development. A common presentation of this type is the evening weather forecast: a meteorologist first discusses today's high pressure dome over your area, then the low pressure area lying to the west, and finally the Arctic air mass coming in from northern Canada. The idea of "geography" need not be applied narrowly; the concept can also apply to physical spaces, such as floors in a hospital or library. Speeches arranged in this way also lend themselves to the use of visual aids, whether carefully drawn on poster board or roughly sketched on a chalkboard. The following outline assumes a map is available to help orient listeners:

Alaska's Southeast

Central Idea: "Alaska's Southeast is a large area with both a major city and many small communities."

Attention Step

[Use devices discussed in Chapter 10 to elicit initial interest]

Need Step
[Point out why the audience will find this information useful or important to know]

Satisfaction Step
  I. The area known as Alaska's Southeast is a long, fingerlike area known as the Panhandle, running between Canada's western border and the Pacific Ocean.
 II. The major city, Juneau, lies roughly in the center of the Panhandle.
III. Yakutat Bay and the tiny community of Yakutat lie on the northern edge.
 IV. The communities of Metlakatla and Ketchikan are in the southern tip of the Panhandle.

Visualization Step
[Optional: Indicate how this information will be useful, what listeners will gain from this knowledge]

Action Step
[Optional: Indicate what listeners are to take from this speech that is of major importance]

Other organizational patterns have some of the qualities of a spatial pattern, but without the sense of geographical movement or development. For example, a speaker may want to deal with comparative *magnitude,* or *size.* A discussion of the rail system in China, for example, could focus on the great distances involved in traveling throughout its twenty-six provinces. If you wanted to talk about the comparative advantages of using a small-town vs. a metropolitan bank, or of seeking medical treatment at a small rural medical clinic in contrast to a large university medical center, you would use a spatial pattern but without the physical sense provided by mental or actual "maps." Also, a spatial pattern, as is true of a chronological pattern, often can be combined successfully with other patterns. A speech devoted to the effects of nuclear fallout, for example, could be organized spatially by talking about the effects in the inner city, outlying suburbs, and rural communities.

Whether combined with other patterns or used singly, the spatial pattern has the virtue of visualization. It allows you to provide conceptual clarity and to give listeners a sense of movement through space as your speech unfolds.

Causal Patterns

As their name implies, **causal patterns** of organization move either (1) from an analysis of present causes to a consideration of future effects or (2) from a description of present conditions to an analysis of the causes that appear to have produced them. For example, the cause-effect arrangement can be used in a speech on tenant rights by first pointing out that the community's landlord-tenant codes are outdated, then predicting that, as a result of this

Geographical patterns organize information according to well-defined areas in order to illustrate physical movement and development.

situation, landlords will be able to take undue advantage of tenants. Reasoning in the reverse direction (if the prediction already has come true), you could argue that the effect (tenants are being taken advantage of) is the result of outdated landlord-tenant codes. Compare the following outlines:

Acid Rain (Option 1)

Claim: "Acid rain [cause] is a rising problem because it threatens our health and economy [effects]."

Attention Step
[Draw attention to the importance of the issue]

Need Step
  I. Manufacturing plants across the United States emit harmful acid-forming sulfur dioxide and nitrogen oxides into the air.
 II. The effect of these emissions is damage to important ecological structures.
     A. Lakes and forests are threatened.
     B. The productivity of vital crops is reduced.

   C. Acid particles in the air and drinking water supplies cause 5 to 8 percent of all deaths in some parts of the United States.

Satisfaction Step
[Develop your position on this issue further—get audience support for your position]

Visualization Step
[Indicate what will be the long-run consequences of failure to accept the problem as an important one]

Action Step
[Appeal to listeners' self-interest to gain their continued attention to this issue as a vital issue to remain concerned and informed about]

Acid Rain (Option 2)

Claim: "Acid rain [effect] is primarily the result of modern technologies [causes]."

Need Step
  I. If we are going to control acid rain, we must learn about and deal with its causes.
 II. Human activities cause acid rain.
    A. One primary cause is energy production: acids are given off by power plants.
    B. A second main cause is motorized transportation, especially trucks and auto emissions.

PATTERNS OF INTERNAL ORGANIZATION

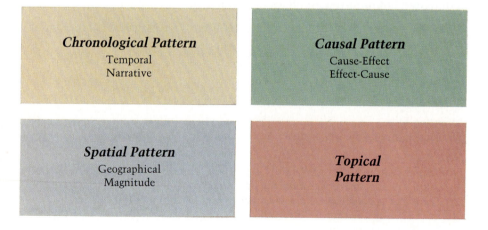

Chronological Pattern
Temporal
Narrative

Causal Pattern
Cause-Effect
Effect-Cause

Spatial Pattern
Geographical
Magnitude

Topical Pattern

The subject to be discussed may suggest an appropriate organizational pattern. Topical patterns are useful in situations calling for an enumeration of items or parts.

Note a characteristic common to both outlines: each starts with the aspect of the situation *better known* to audience members, and then develops the *lesser-known* facets of the problem. As a guiding principle, use a cause-effect sequence when listeners are generally well acquainted with the cause; use an effect-cause sequence when the effect is better known.

Topical Patterns

In many instances, the subject matter of the speech itself suggests an appropriate pattern—one that follows the natural or customary divisions of the topic. For example, financial reports have been standardized into discussions of assets and liabilities; subjects dealing with the federal government may naturally divide into branches—executive, legislative, and judicial; a report on a communication experiment is usually divided into a review of the relevant literature, a discussion of the hypothesis to be tested in light of prior studies, the methods used in the experiment, the results, and a discussion of the significance of the findings. Demonstrating your awareness of the basic patterns in which things have come to be recognized improves your credibility with the audience. Giving a report on a communication experiment that jumbles the above "steps," for example, would result in confusion and suggest to the audience that you were not well prepared.

Principles of Gestalt Psychology

*A*lthough the assumptions of Gestalt psychology have less influence in the study of cognition and perception today, the basic principles of perceptual organization identified by the early Gestaltists remain influential. The early Gestalt psychologists were interested in finding out why things appear the way they do. Five principles remain current in the literature on perception and cognition:

1. *Proximity* suggests that elements close together seem to organize into units of perception; you see pairs made up of a ball and a block, not pairs of blocks and pairs of balls.

2. *Similarity* suggests that objects that appear to be the same are more naturally grouped together; you see

three columns rather than four rows of items.

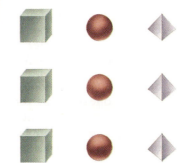

3. *Good continuation* identifies properties that appear to be logical extensions of others—you see the curved line as one figure and the jagged line as another, even though they intersect.

convey your ideas in a clear, coherent manner. Whatever pattern you choose, be sure to use it consistently in organizing both the main points and subpoints. That is, do not mix spatial and causal patterns in arranging main heads, and do not mix patterns while arranging subpoints under a single main head.

There are other methods that can be used to arrange the subpoints of a speech. The following five approaches are useful ways of organizing infor-

themes that should be developed and the particular order in which they should be discussed. If the audience already is familiar with the background, or accepts the causes for the current dilemma, you will waste time organizing a speech in a chronological pattern or using a causal pattern to justify the existence of certain effects. Thus, you need to be sensitive to the demands of the occasion and to the status of the audience's knowledge and position on the issues.

The following outline integrates the motivated sequence and some of the patterns we have discussed in this chapter.

Glasnost—The New Soviet Reform Movement

Central Idea: "The new reforms underway in the Soviet Union are providing major changes, but change is not without its limits."

Attention Step
I. The terms "glasnost" and "perestroika" have entered the American vocabulary, largely due to the efforts of Mikhail Gorbachev, leader of the Soviet Union.
  A. The term "glasnost" does not have an exact equivalent in English, but usually is translated as "openness."
  B. "Perestroika" refers to "restructuring" or to "renewal" of the society.
II. If you have heard these terms but have wondered exactly what they meant, you are not alone.
  A. Soviet experts in this country are trying to predict how Soviet society will change, and how long the changes will last.
  B. Soviet citizens themselves are concerned about the changes.

Need Step
I. Understanding the meaning of these terms will be helpful in at least two ways.
  A. The examples will help you learn what change means, and what it does not.
  B. The discussion will prepare you to digest other evaluations of Soviet change—you will be a better critic of what you hear and read.
II. In this speech, I will talk about three main issues.
  A. First, I will contextualize change in the Soviet Union through a brief glance at two prior periods of change.
  B. Second, I will sketch some of the changes brought about by glasnost and perestroika.
  C. Third, I will indicate the limits that tradition and politics impose on change.

Satisfaction Step
I. To better understand the reforms, you need to recognize that this is not the first "revolution."
  A. Lenin, the architect of the Russian Revolution in 1917, initiated "peredyshka," or a "breathing spell," during which a free market economy and private ownership were allowed.

B. Khrushchev, who many remember primarily for his "I will bury you" speech at the United Nations, freed millions of political prisoners during his years in power.

II. Gorbachev's reform ideas, expressed through both terms, provide for a radical shift in the nature of Soviet society.

A. Glasnost has brought about a new freedom of expression of all facets of Soviet life.

1. The return of the exiled Sakharov from Gorky is an indication of a new attitude toward dissidence.

2. Release of political prisoners, even though some have been forced to emigrate, is another positive sign.

3. Allowing previously banned books to be published or distributed is a sign of change.

a. Orwell's *1984*

b. Pasternak's *Doctor Zhivago*

4. Allowing dissidents in Armenia to express their concerns is a new policy.

5. As a symbol of openness, the Soviet World Affairs Weekly, *New Times*, labels its "Letters to the Editor" page *Glasnost*.

B. Perestroika, although moving at a slower pace, also promises major economic and social changes.

1. The antialcohol program will have significant impact on worker productivity and family happiness.

2. The increase in the minimum wage, from $317 to $336 per month, will help many workers, especially women.

3. Proposed restructuring of prices will affect workers' ability to purchase consumable goods.

4. Control over decisions will gradually be decentralized in certain sectors of the economy.

III. These changes will not come without limits.

A. There have been acts that we would term repressive.

1. While a political exile has been returned, over 175 have been arrested for their exercise of religious beliefs.

2. The editor of a dissident journal, ironically called *Glasnost*, was jailed for a week, and his printing equipment was destroyed.

3. While some books have been published, others have remained on the "banned" list (such as most of Solzhenitsyn's works).

4. While Gorbachev has replaced almost 40 percent of the Central Committee, 90 of the 157 regional secretaries, and 72 of the 101 members of the Council of Ministries, he has not appointed women to prominent places of power (although they represent almost 30 percent of the membership in the Communist party).

B. As Gorbachev has said, "We are going to work within the boundaries of the socialism we have chosen. . . . We are going to move in a calculated, measured way. . . ."

Visualization Step (Optional)

I. With the brief introduction to the reforms under way in the Soviet Union, you should be better equipped to understand what is taking place, and what may not yet occur.

A. You have heard, through illustrations, what glasnost and perestroika mean, or will mean to the citizens of the Soviet Union.

B. Given an understanding of the limits of freedom, you will have a better sense of why there is still "a long way to go" before Soviet freedom of expression and individual economic opportunity match that which we take for granted in our own imperfect society.

Action Step (Optional)

I. If you take nothing else away from this presentation, I hope you at least have an appreciation of the benefits and limits of the spirit of glasnost and perestroika that is animating Soviet politics in the last half of the '80s.[3]

Chapter Summary

The task of building a conceptually clear structure for your major ideas is crucial. Listeners need to "see" and comprehend a pattern to the unfolding of your ideas if they are to make sense out of your attempt to convey them. As long as the pattern you select makes sense in terms of the topic, your purpose, and the expectations of the audience and occasion, your message should be received as a logically coherent approach to structuring your ideas. To assist in this process, this chapter has suggested five criteria that should be reviewed when organizing each step of the motivated sequence, in particular the need and satisfaction steps. The main points, as well as subpoints, of these steps can be organized according to *chronological, spatial, causal,* and *topical* patterns. In addition, subpoints can be arranged according to *parts of a whole, lists of qualities or functions, series of causes or results, items of logical proof,* and *illustrative examples.*

Reference Notes

1. See, for example, the case studies of the presidential inaugural address in Herbert W. Simons and Aram A. Aghazarian, eds., *Form, Genre, and the Study of Political Discourse* (Columbia, SC: University of South Carolina Press, 1986): Karyln Kohrs Campbell and Kathleen Hall Jamieson, "Inaugurating the Presidency," 203–25; Bruce E. Gronbeck, "Ronald Reagan's Enactment of the Presidency in His 1981 Inaugural Address," 226–45; Roderick P. Hart, "Of Genre, Computers, and the Reagan Inaugural," 278–300. Also see Roderick P. Hart, *The Sound of Leadership* (Chicago, IL: University of Chicago Press, 1987).

2. For further discussion of narratives and their use in persuasive speeches, see Bruce E. Gronbeck, *The Articulate Person: A Guide to Everyday Public Speaking*, 2nd ed. (Glenview, IL: Scott, Foresman and Company, 1983).

3. Information based on several sources: The direct quotation of Gorbachev is from "Talking to Gorbachev," *Newsweek* (May 30, 1988): 24–33; "All Roads Lead to Moscow," *Time* (May 30, 1988), 24–26; "Heroines of Soviet Labor," *Time* (June 6, 1988), 28–37; Robert L. Pfaltzgraff, "Gorbachev and the 'New Millenium,'" *World and I* 2 (June 1987): 16–21; Jerry F. Hough, "Glasnost: A Fundamental Reform," *World and I* 2 (June 1987): 22–27.

Key Terms

chronological patterns　　　　　*geographical patterns*

temporal sequence　　　　　*causal patterns*

narrative sequence　　　　　*topical patterns*

spatial patterns

Problems and Probes

1. Read one of the speeches in this text and examine its organization. Identify the need and satisfaction steps in the development of the speech. What are the major points within each step and how are they arranged? What are the sub-points supporting each main point and how are they arranged? Write a brief paper summarizing the results of your analysis.

2. Read three or four recent presidential inaugural speeches, or speeches related to warfare by Roosevelt (WWII), Truman (Korean Conflict), Nixon or Johnson (Vietnam). Note the organization of each. How do the addresses differ in terms of their structure? In what ways are they similar? Write a brief paper in which you consider the possible constraints imposed by the situation on the arrangement of points. Specifically, address one of these questions: How does situation affect an inaugural address? How do different wartime situations affect speech-making by presidents? Conclude your analysis by commenting on the clarity and appropriateness of each address as a "good fit" between context and organization.

3. Working in small groups in class, suggest how the main points can be organized in each of the following topics; assume the end product is to be a short in-class speech.

Why many small businesses fail

Developments in laser technology

Digging for sapphires, gold, or opals

Eat wisely and live long

How the world looks to a dog or a salamander

Racquetball for the beginner

Appreciating impressionist art

Computer literacy

Share your results with the rest of the class. How much organizational similarity is there among groups?

Communication Activities

1. Assume that you are preparing a speech on the merits of fraternities and sororities on campus (your position is that they are generally a positive influence on campus life) for each of the following audiences: (1) Student Senate, composed of representatives from dormitories, fraternities, sororities, off-cam-

pus students, and nontraditional students; (2) Faculty Senate, composed of representatives from the sciences, social sciences, arts and humanities; (3) Administration, composed of student services staff as well as the president and vice-presidents. Prepare a speech that is organized to meet the needs of each audience. In class, meet in small groups and discuss each approach with your classmates. How are the speeches different? How are they the same?

2. Prepare a five-to-seven-minute speech on a subject of your choice for presentation in class. Before you present the speech, critically appraise the organization you have used and write a brief paper defending the approach you took in organizing the main points and subpoints. Immediately after presenting the speech, and taking into account comments from the class, write a brief addendum on the experience of presenting the speech: Did it work the way you anticipated? Would you change your approach in any specific area of the speech? Hand in the analysis to your instructor.

CHAPTER TEN

Beginning and Ending the Speech

*E*very speech, whether long or short, needs a beginning and an end. You begin your speech by orienting your listeners to your speaking purposes. After you have set out your central idea or claim and developed it appropriately, you stop and review what you have said in order to leave your listeners in an appropriate frame of mind.

Unless you *plan* the beginning (**introduction**) and ending (**conclusion**), you could be in trouble, hemming and hawing in front of people who wish you knew what you were trying to say. Taking time to plan introductions and conclusions is an investment; it will pay off handsomely, for strategically sound beginnings and endings prepare audiences and clinch your points.

Think of introductions and conclusions as linked directly to the motivated sequence steps discussed in Chapter 8. Introductions fulfill the attention step; good ones increase interest and tell audiences why they ought to listen to you. Conclusions are tied to either the visualization or the action step; they focus your ideas, illustrate how listeners will profit from your advice, and motivate them to do something about your claims. Thus, in this chapter, we will discuss more specifically the functions of introductions and conclusions, review several methods for actually beginning and ending your talks, and consider factors that determine your choice of method.

Beginning the Speech: The Functions of Introductions

As you think about preparing an introduction to your speech, you need to analyze your audience:

1. Are audience members likely to be *interested*, or must I work especially hard to gain their attention?
2. Are audience members aware of my *qualifications*, or must I establish my expertise?
3. Are there some special *demands of the occasion* that I should recognize, or am I free to go in directions I wish? If I do wish to depart from customary expectations, should I justify my departures?
4. Need I work to create *goodwill*, or are audience members likely to be on my side on this question?
5. Will audience members be able to follow this speech easily, or should I *forecast* the major themes early on?

Let us examine each of these considerations in more detail.

You always must work to gain and hold attention, in some cases more than in others. If, say, your purpose is to convince your classmates that they ought to get involved in student government, they are likely to respond, "Oh, no, not another speech on my civic duty!" In that situation, you may find it useful to review the factors of attention from Chapter 3 to find ways to relate your topic to their personal interests and needs. At other times, your topic may be so timely or compelling that you need not use valuable time justifying your speech's existence.

Second, as a student, you may have some credibility because you are studying certain subjects, yet audiences may consider you something less than expert on such matters as politics, ethics and morality, or construction projects. It usually is advisable to slip in your qualifications in a straightforward (not boastful) way; an audience should be told, for example, about your ten years' experience in the family ice cream store, your four-hour interview with a local nuclear scientist, your semester in Germany, or whatever other experiences are relevant to your topic and expertise. Do not overdo it, but make sure that your command of the topic is clear.

A third function of an introduction is to speak directly to the audience's expectations of what should be happening. When leading a Bible study in your home, you know generally what those present expect from you, so you need not talk about the demands of the occasion with that group. A commencement speaker, however, may note how important the transition is between school and the rest of the life-world, and why certain topics are relevant to that occasion. When there are important expectations (as there often are on special occasions of the type mentioned in Chapter 18), it is advisable to recognize them in your introduction. This lets audience members know you share with them an appreciation for the situation.

Fourth, when delivering a short speech in a class, you probably need not spend time on creating goodwill; however, most audiences appreciate references to how much you value their willingness to listen to you. Especially when an audience is likely to object to what you are going to say, taking time to recognize your differences and to ask for a fair hearing is an important strategy. Aim for warm personal relations with your listeners even when you are going to disagree with their opinions.

Finally, forecasts are useful in almost all speeches. Forecasts allow a listener to see where you are going and to follow along as you get there. With forecasts, you construct a framework that orients the audience and defines your viewpoints.

Not all introductions must gain attention, state your qualifications, satisfy the demands of audience and occasion, create goodwill, and clarify the scope of your speech. Sometimes these things are obvious. Rather, use this list of five functions of an introduction as a general guide, to analyze the audience and to suggest to yourself what your introduction ought to be doing for you.

Types of Speech Introductions

With the functions in mind, you are ready to select specific introductory techniques. The following are eight ways of beginning a speech:

1. Refer to the subject or problem.
2. Refer to the occasion.
3. Extend a personal greeting or make a personal allusion.
4. Ask a rhetorical question.
5. Make a startling statement of fact or opinion.
6. Use an apt quotation.
7. Relate a humorous anecdote relevant to your topic.
8. Cite a real or hypothetical illustration.

Reference to the Subject or Problem

Referring directly to the subject or problem is a very useful introductory strategy when the audience already has a vital interest in hearing your message. Many business conferences invite a speaker with a particular topic or theme in mind; the speaker need not go into detail setting up the importance of the subject. Instead, he or she can begin by stating the subject and moving directly to the first major point of the address. Professor Russell J. Love used this approach when discussing rights of people with severe communication problems:

> My talk tonight is concerned with the rights of the handicapped—particularly those people with severe communication disabilities. I will be presenting what I call a bill of rights for the severely communicatively disabled.[1]

Although such brevity and forthrightness may strike exactly the right note on some occasions, you should not begin all speeches this way. To a skeptical audience, a direct announcement may sound immodest, tactless, or even challenging; to an apathetic audience, it may sound dull. Thus, use such direct references to your topic only when the audience is in tune with you and ready to listen.

Referring directly to the subject or problem is a very useful introductory strategy when the audience already has a vital interest in hearing the message.

Reference to the Occasion

Occasions such as commencement addresses, acceptances of awards, holidays, and keynote addresses at conferences virtually dictate a reference to the reason that brought speaker and listeners together. Explicit reference to the significance of the occasion helps bond a speaker and audience, bringing their thoughts and feelings together. Father William J. Byron, President of The Catholic University of America, for example, accepting the Joseph S. Hogan Award from the Alumni Association of Saint Joseph's University, tied the occasion, the audience, and his own experiences at Saint Joseph's University together through discussion of the occasion:

> It was four decades ago when I first sat in Father Hogan's philosophy class here at St. Joe's. That class met in Room 8, if I remember correctly, in the Barbelin

Building under the great Gothic tower, a Philadelphia landmark. Father Hogan was himself something of a Philadelphia monument. He could reduce metaphysical principles to earthbound simile and memorable metaphor, while opening young minds to transcendent realities and a new awareness of the good, the true, and the beautiful. It is a high honor for me to return to campus today to receive the Hogan Award and to remember with affection the great classroom teacher this award memorializes.[2]

If the time, place, or reason for coming together are important to you and your audience, references to the occasion belong in your introduction.

Personal Reference or Greeting

Another effective way to establish common ground with an audience is to discuss your relationship to the topic or the audience itself in your introduction. This is what Senator Edward Kennedy did when talking about the growing cost of medical care at the American Hospital Association convention in 1987:

> It's a special pleasure for me to be here today. No cause is closer to my heart than quality health care for every American. And there is no group that cares more about that cause than the administrators and trustees of America's community hospitals.
>
> We share a common sense of commitment.[3]

In four short sentences, Senator Kennedy (1) mentioned his own pleasure, (2) expressed his commitment to quality health care, (3) identified his audience's interests as identical with his, and (4) expressed common commitments. In these four sentences, Kennedy used personal references to himself and his audience to get them on the same wavelength.

A personal greeting is especially useful when the audience knows and respects you. Conversely, personal greetings from strangers often set up defense mechanisms in listeners; many of them remember overly familiar magazine and vacuum cleaner sales personnel who greet them with big smiles on the front porch. If the audience does not know you well, avoid making your introduction too personal. Also, even if you have not had much time to prepare, do not blame others for the circumstances. You certainly can indicate that circumstances did not permit you to do a thorough job, but tell them you are being as clear and complete as possible and then go forward, doing the best you can without theatrics.

Rhetorical Question

A rhetorical question is one that is asked without expecting an immediate, direct verbal response. Although you do not want the audience members to answer you audibly, you do hope that they will consider the question and answer it silently. If used sparingly, rhetorical questions can focus audience attention on your subject and involve listeners in your view of that subject.

Asking a group of college sophomores "How would you feel if, at age ninety-five, your social security suddenly ran out?" probably would not be an effective rhetorical question; it is not something that easily draws them in, given their circumstances. On the other hand, asking them "How would you feel if the administration changed core requirements in midstream, suddenly requiring you to complete four additional math and science courses before you graduate?" would be rooted in their present situation and, thus, would be more effective. You then could divide the question and use it to forecast your speech: "What are the new core requirements recently proposed? What will their impact be on college sophomores? What can we do to alter this proposal before it's too late?" Well used in situations in which they are relevant to the audience's circumstances, rhetorical questions unite the topical thinking of speaker and audience.

Clifton R. Wharton, Jr., then Chancellor of the State University of New York and Chairman of the Rockefeller Foundation, used a rhetorical question to focus his 1986 plenary address at the emotionally charged annual conference of the National Urban League:

> From our country's earliest colonial days, education has been the keystone to progress. Yet increasingly large numbers of American Blacks appear to be indifferent, apathetic, or cynical toward schooling and higher learning. Today, the question I'd like to ask is: Are we as Blacks experiencing a crisis of faith in education as the privileged pathway to the future?[4]

This simple introductory device drew in the audience and, simultaneously, made Dr. Wharton's position perfectly clear.

Startling Statement

On certain occasions, you can open a speech with what some writers have referred to as the "shock technique," making a startling statement of fact or opinion. This approach is especially useful when listeners are distracted or apathetic. The following shows how a speech on weight control might be introduced:

> There's a disease sweeping our country. None of us is immune. There are no miracle drugs to combat it, although Americans spend millions of dollars each year trying to deal with the illness. The disease can affect all ages, all economic classes, all ethnic groups. It can cause permanent bodily damage, shorten life span, and even may cause death. Some of you already may be affected; most of you will in some way be touched by this disease. The disease is obesity; the cure, you. Today, I will examine some of the causes of obesity and suggest some preventive measures.

Do not overdo this technique. Few things disgust an audience as much as an overplayed, silly startling statement; false drama, melodramatic stories, and bad shock techniques (for instance, screaming your first two sentences and then saying, "Now that I have your attention . . .") should be avoided. Do *not* bring a Saturday night special into your classroom as part of your speech on gun control. Terrorizing people is more than ethically dubious— it is inhumane. Aim for suspense rather than shock with your startling statements and actions.

Pertinent Quotation

A quotation that conveys the theme of your presentation can provide a good beginning. To be effective, the quotation should be simple and succinct; the audience should not have to ponder inscrutable meanings in order to understand its relationship to your central idea or claim. Warren Manshel of the Dreyfus Corporation, former Ambassador to Denmark, opened a speech on foreign policy in this manner:

> "The Constitution is an invitation to struggle for the privilege of directing foreign policy." That is Edward Corwin's famous description of the Constitution, and the history of executive-congressional interplay in the area of foreign policy is replete with examples to prove his point. Last summer, normal life stopped as the entire nation watched the spectacle of Colonel North defending the Executive against an enraged Congress. A reminder of Watergate days, the spectacle of Senators and Congressmen engaging in televised dispute with members of the National Security Council is evidence of the extent to which U. S. policy abroad has been made hostage to the competition between the President and Congress for dominance in foreign policy. Surely such a situation was not envisioned by the framers of the Constitution: an invitation to struggle is not a declaration of war. Corwin's phrase implies a good deal more civility than either the Congress or the President have lately manifested.
>
> The current stalemate offers proof that something is wrong with our foreign policy process.[5] [From here, he moved into his claim.]

Notice the role of the quotation. It provides the initial thought, which in turn leads to references to recent political struggles. It then is used to critique those struggles ("such a situation was not envisioned by the framers of the Constitution"), making it even serve as initial evidence for Mr. Manshel's claim. He has made good use of a pertinent quotation to open this talk.

Humorous Anecdote

You can begin a speech by telling a funny story or relating a humorous experience. When doing so, observe three communication rules:

1. *Be sure the story is at least amusing, if not absolutely funny.* If it is not, or if you tell it badly, you will embarrass yourself and your audience.

2. *Be sure the anecdote is relevant to your speech.* If its subject matter or punch line is not directly related to you, your topic, or at least your next

couple of sentences, the story will seem to the audience to be a mere gimmick.

3. *Be sure it is in good taste.* In a public gathering, an off-color or doubtful story violates accepted standards of social behavior and can undermine an audience's respect for you. This means that you should generally avoid sexual, racial, antireligious, ageist, and sexist humor.

All three of these standards were observed by David T. Kearns, Chief Executive Officer of Xerox Corporation, when speaking at the Graduate School of Business of the University of Chicago:

> There's a story about a Frenchman, a Japanese and an American who face a firing squad. Each gets one last request. The Frenchman asks to hear The Marseillaise. The Japanese asks to give a lecture on the art of management. The American says, "Shoot me first—I can't stand one more lecture on Japanese management."
> You'll be glad to hear that I'm not going to talk about Japanese management today.
> In fact, if we keep on the right road, we may wind up listening to the Japanese give lectures on American management.[6]

With that, Mr. Kearns was ready to talk about the importance of higher educational institutions in training managers of American companies. While his humor did depend on ethnic references, it was not demeaning of others, and so, was socially acceptable. It also led directly to his claim.

Real or Hypothetical Illustration

One or more real-life incidents, a story taken from literature, or a series of hypothetical illustrations also can launch a good speech. As is the case with humor, any illustration you use should not only be interesting to the audience but also should be connected to your central idea or claim. Deanna Sellnow, a student at North Dakota State University, used this technique to introduce a speech on private credit reporting bureaus:

> John Pontier, of Boise, Idaho, was turned down for insurance because a reporting agency informed the company that he and his wife were addicted to narcotics, and his Taco Bell franchise had been closed down by the health board when dog food had been found mixed in with the tacos. There was only one small problem. The information was made up. His wife was a practicing Mormon who didn't touch a drink, much less drugs, and the restaurant had never been cited for a health violation.[7]

A series of short examples can be equally effective. When cartoonist Garry Trudeau wished to begin a commencement speech at Vassar on skepticism by commenting on the compression of time in modern life, he piled up four

BEGINNING AND ENDING A SPEECH

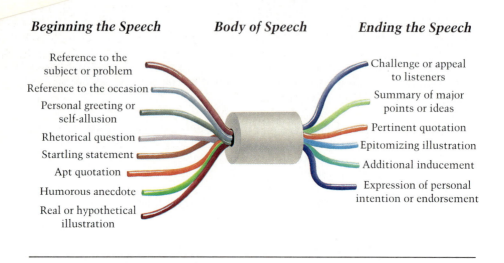

| *Beginning the Speech* | *Body of Speech* | *Ending the Speech* |

Beginning the Speech

Reference to the subject or problem

Reference to the occasion

Personal greeting or self-allusion

Rhetorical question

Startling statement

Apt quotation

Humorous anecdote

Real or hypothetical illustration

Ending the Speech

Challenge or appeal to listeners

Summary of major points or ideas

Pertinent quotation

Epitomizing illustration

Additional inducement

Expression of personal intention or endorsement

quick examples with analogies, stirring in enough humor to engage his audience warmly. The complete text of Mr. Trudeau's speech is reprinted in Chapter 18. Note that the examples, plus their analogies, set the tone for the remainder of the speech.

Combination of Introductory Techniques

Because an introduction has multiple goals—to raise interest, to cite qualifications, to meet the demands of the situation, to increase goodwill, and to forecast the rest of the speech—you often may wish to combine two or more of these introductory strategies. You can and should do so, as long as you remember to keep everything relevant to your purpose and to shape the material so it leads directly into your first point. Suppose you are about to address the Faculty Senate on a proposal to eliminate your school's physical education requirement. You might assemble the following introductory statements:

- "I am pleased that you are allowing me to speak to you today on the physical education requirement. As far as I know, this is the first time a student has been asked to address the Faculty Senate. Your invitation demonstrates your commitment to shared responsibility for academic requirements." [*reference to occasion*]
- "As a recreation major, I'm especially pleased to be talking with you so that I can explain how it is that someone majoring in a physical education discipline is nonetheless opposed to mandatory physical education at this school." [*personal reference*]

- "When the Romans preached 'A sound mind in a sound body,' they did not seek a gymnasium filled through coercion, but through attractive programs and courses." [*quotation*]
- "Must students go through this school forced into physical activities they do not choose for themselves, or can we find ways to draw them into exercise and sport?" [*rhetorical question*]
- "I am going to demonstrate to you today that we can fill the gym with students through smart programming and a curriculum of classes and nonclass experiences. First I will discuss the results of a student body survey we conducted last semester, then I will present a plan for meeting the student body's exercise and competitive needs, and finally I will tell you why it is an educational improvement over compulsory physical education." [*claim plus forecast*]

The eight introductory strategies can work for you, singly or in combination, getting your speeches off to productive starts. You also might consider using these techniques at various points in your speech, whenever interest seems to be flagging. Personal references often can bring an abstract point home by showing listeners the effect of a particular problem in real life. Rhetorical questions, if not overused, make good transitions between points. Quotations and illustrations serve as testimony when you need to provide evidence for a certain point. Humorous anecdotes can relax an audience, especially if you have been presenting difficult or serious material. References to the occasion can help maintain a speaker-audience bond, and startling statements can wake up the "snoozers."

Ending the Speech:
The Functions of Conclusions

Now that you have started the speech and have moved through its claims or central idea and evidence, how do you close? The worst thing you can do is just quit; that confuses your listeners, who expect at least some kind of warning, and steals your chance to clinch the points you are trying to make. Do not just quit; conclude. Leave your audience aware of the finality of your last sentence; provide a sense of completion or rounding-off. As you think about how to do that, ask yourself the following questions:

1. Is a *summary* called for?
2. Does the content lead naturally to a *"so what?"* question?
3. What *mood* do I want the audience to be in as I conclude?
4. How should I *signal* that the speech is ending?

Let us consider these points separately.

You may have developed a complex argument against, say, the B-2 ("stealth") bomber, one that contains some technical materials on defensive and offensive military strategies and overviews of world hotspots. If your argument is complex, you must offer a solid summary to synthesize and unify your speech. Always ask yourself how much your listeners reasonably can be expected to remember and how far you can ask them to go in following your reasoning. Then compensate for complexity with a crystal-clear concluding review.

The "so what?" question provides another area where most of us need to work. You may love coin collecting with all of your heart, but if you have not explained what others can gain from numismatics in terms they understand, you could just as well have been talking to a wall. The significance of your claim must be adapted to *the listeners'* values, desires, and interests.

Third, you probably do not think of mood when preparing to talk publicly, yet it is important. Just as different kinds of music put you in different frames of mind, so do parts of speeches, especially conclusions. Do you want to leave audience members angry, as do many speakers at protest rallies? Do you want to leave them bound together with sympathy and love, as Jesse Jackson did during the 1988 Democratic convention when he used a refrain of "I understand, I really understand" while talking about growing up in hardship? Do you wish to leave them inspired to give time in community service projects? Do you want them finally concerned enough to go to the Registrar after class? Think hard about creating a memorable, lasting mood appropriate to your purpose and topic.

Fourth, while you do not think about it often, you rely on ending signals when you listen to speeches. You rely on them to prepare you for disengagement; at those signals, you usually listen more carefully, waiting for final appeals and pieces of advice. (Sometimes, of course, when you hear "In summary" you say to yourself, "Thank goodness!") You should learn to use the usual (and not so usual) conclusionary signals: "In summary, . . ."; "As I conclude this talk, let me reiterate . . ."; "The poet Robert Frost summarizes what I've been saying . . ." Find signals that work for you, and then actually finish your speech. Few things annoy an audience as much as thinking a speech is over, only to have the speaker go on and on.

Types of Speech Conclusions

Speakers frequently use one or more of the following techniques for bringing their talks to an appropriate end:

1. Issue a challenge or an appeal to the listeners.
2. Summarize major points or ideas.
3. Provide an appropriate quotation.
4. Epitomize the point with an illustration.
5. Offer an additional inducement for accepting or acting upon the proposal advocated.
6. Express their own intention or endorsement.

A speaker can conclude by openly appealing for support or by reminding listeners of their responsibilities in furthering a cause they believe in.

Challenge or Appeal to Listeners

When using this technique, the speaker openly appeals for support or action or reminds the listeners of their responsibilities in furthering a cause they believe in. Such an appeal must be compelling and contain a suggestion of the principal ideas or arguments presented in the speech. Allen A. Schumer, Senior Vice-President for Operations of Miller Brewing Company, urged his audience to establish so-called employee involvement programs, offering them examples from his own company's plants. He then issued this challenge:

As I mentioned at the beginning, you are the people on the front lines of the Employee Involvement Revolution. If you win the battle of getting employee involvement accepted as a company concept, your company wins. And if your company or organization succeeds, we all succeed.

It won't happen overnight, but next week may be too late in these days of economic and corporate uncertainty. Any journey, no matter how long, must begin with a first step. I encourage you to take that first step now! Believe me, it's a step you won't regret. I promise![8]

Summary of Major Points or Ideas

As noted earlier, you should summarize, especially when your speech contains several points. A summary allows the audience to pull together the main strands of your informative speech and to evaluate its significance. In a persuasive speech, a summary gives you a final opportunity to present, in brief form, the major points of your argument. For example, Everette E. Dennis, Executive Director of the Gannett Center for Media Studies, tried to persuade the Virginia Associated Press Newspaper Council to alter some of its methods of covering the 1988 presidential campaign. She gave many examples of poor or insensitive reporting practices that lead to what she considers unfair reporting. To pull her ideas together, she used the following summary:

> To me fairness means:
>
> 1. Coherent presentation of the facts, of the basic elements and information required to know and understand the subject being reported.
>
> 2. A context and background that provides connections to the past and to concurrent issues, events and personalities.
>
> 3. More systematic information-gathering, making as efficient use as possible of many sources of information and in enough depth to enhance understanding. No critical stone should be left unturned or, if it is, the reader or viewer should be told.
>
> 4. Quality control of information. The role of the news media is to distinguish the important from the unimportant, reputable sources from unreliable ones. The media should make it clear whether information is being cited and quoted with approval or not.
>
> 5. More equitable sense-making and interpretation.
>
> There is a profound need for the reporter and editor to be a mapmaker, to offer a perspective on the many viewpoints and interests that shape the news and to render those voices with the right intensity and pitch.
>
> Finally, I think we need to reconcile our standards of news and the public's sense of fair play.[9]

Pertinent Quotation

At times, someone else's words can help you focus the end of your speech. If the quotation is relevant to you, your subject, and the emotional atmosphere you are attempting to create, it can help your audience form a pow-

A reference to the occasion, pertinent quotation, or personal greeting can remind listeners of the significance of an event.

erful final impression of your ideas. Notice how the Reverend F. Forrester Church, speaking against the U. S. bombing of Libya, quoted his father, a former U. S. senator who had also spoken against the use of terrorist tactics:

> I have been thinking a great deal this week about my father, Frank Church, who served in the U. S. Senate for 24 years. I miss him intensely right now. I miss his voice. So let me close, not with my own words, but with his.

> In 1975 the Senate Intelligence Committee, which he chaired, uncovered evidence of five unsuccessful CIA-sponsored assassination plots against foreign leaders. In issuing his report my father wrote, "The United States must not adopt the tactics of the enemy. Means are as important as ends. Crisis makes it tempting to ignore the wise restraint that makes us free; but each time we do so, each time the means we use are wrong, our inner strength, the strength which makes us free, is lessened."

Elsewhere he said, speaking of the founders of our country, "They acted on their faith, not their fear. They did not believe in fighting fire with fire; crime with crime; evil with evil; or delinquency by becoming delinquents." Amen.[10]

The quotations not only said what the Reverend Church wanted to say, but, with the emotional tie between father and son, they added even more depth to his words.

If a quotation is used at the beginning of a speech, you can tie the whole speech together with a direct reference back to it. Chui Lee Yap began a speech on ethnocentrism by quoting from Aldous Huxley: "Most ignorance is vincible ignorance. We don't know because we don't want to know." After explaining the reasons for American ignorance of other cultures, Chui Lee concluded by noting that "As Huxley implied, cure of our not knowing—is our wanting to know.[11]

Epitomizing Illustration

Just as an illustration that epitomizes your leading ideas can be used to open a speech, so may it come at the end. A closing illustration should be both *inclusive* and *conclusive:* inclusive of the main focus of your speech and conclusive in tone and impact. As with quotations, you also can use an illustration to frame a whole speech. This is what Michael Twitchell, a student at a speaking contest, did when talking about the causes and effects of depression:

Opening

Have you ever felt like you were the little Dutch boy who stuck his finger in the leaking dike? You waited and waited but the help never came. The leak became worse and the water rushed around you and swept you away. As you fought the flood, gasping and choking for air, you realized that the flood was inside yourself. You were drowning and dying in your own mind. According to the *American Journal of Psychiatry*, as many as half the people in this room will be carried away by this devastating flood. What is this disaster? Mental depression.

Closing

Let's go back to my illustration of the little Dutch boy. He was wise to take action and put his finger in the dike, preventing the flood. In the case of depression, each one of us must be like the little Dutch boy—willing to get involved and control the harmful effects of depression.[12]

Additional Inducement

Sometimes it is helpful to combine a summary or other means of concluding your remarks with one or two additional reasons for accepting the belief or taking the actions you propose. In his speech, Michael Twitchell elaborated at length on the effects of depression on the family of David Twitchell.

Besides tying the introduction and conclusion together with an illustration (see the reprinted excerpts), Mr. Twitchell added an inducement:

> Why should you really care? Why is it important? The depressed person may be someone you know—it could be you. If you know what is happening, you can always help. I wish I had known what depression was in March of 1978. You see, when I said David Twitchell could be my father, I was making a statement of fact. David is my father. I am his son. My family wasn't saved; perhaps now yours can be.[13]

Expression of Personal Intention or Endorsement

A statement of the speaker's intention to follow his or her own recommendations is particularly valuable when the speechmaker's prestige with the audience is high, or when a concrete proposal needing immediate action has been offered. If the speaker can indicate an intention to take immediate action, that lends credibility both to the speaker and to the ideas presented. When asking an audience to give blood, the following conclusion would be appropriate:

> Today I have illustrated how important healthy blood is to human survival and how blood banks work to ensure the possibility and availability of blood for each of us. It is not a coincidence that I spoke on this topic on the same day that the Red Cross Bloodmobile is visiting campus. I want each of you to ensure your future and mine by stopping at the Student Center today or tomorrow to make a donation. The few minutes that it takes may add up to a lifetime for a person in need. I believe in giving life to others. I'm going to the Student Center to give my donation as soon as this class is over. I invite those who care to join me.

Regardless of the means you choose for closing your speech, remember that your conclusion should focus your listeners' thoughts on your central theme. In addition, a good conclusion should be consistent with the mood of your speech and should convey a sense of completeness and finality.

Selecting Introductions and Conclusions

The preceding sections have concentrated on the functions of introductions and conclusions and the means of fulfilling them. In general, each of the means can be an effective way of satisfying the functions of introductions or conclusions. Thus, a pertinent quotation or a hypothetical illustration may gain attention, create goodwill, or clarify the scope of your speech. Likewise, a challenge or appeal to listeners may signal an ending or answer a "so what?" question. Obviously, some means are better suited than others for fulfilling a particular function. A real illustration works better than a hypothetical one in stating your qualifications, for instance, while a personal reference may be the most direct means of all. Conclusions that contain pertinent quotations or epitomizing illustrations may be more effective in creating an appropriate mood than would a summary of major points.

As you approach each facet of the total speech, think through what you want to accomplish and adopt the approach that has the best chance of meeting your goal. As noted in Chapter 1, creating a speech involves a *rhetorical sensitivity* to the situation in which you find yourself. There are some natural constraints on what you can and should do:

1. *What are your experiences and abilities?* The best source for real illustrations is your own life. Stories of your experiences come across naturally as you tell them. Stories that you have discovered through research, on the other hand, need to be rehearsed so that they sound "natural." Your experiences also may be the best basis for claiming qualifications in an area; otherwise, you need to illustrate, through explicit statements or the quality of your research materials, that you know what you are talking about. Your abilities as a speaker also may constrain your choices. If you do not tell funny stories in a natural, relaxed manner, attempting a humorous anecdote may not be wise. On the other hand, if you are known as a clown and want to be taken seriously for a change, you need to set forth your qualifications explicitly and, in concluding, create a serious mood for the consideration of your views. Humor may not be your best vehicle under these circumstances.

2. *What is the mood and commitment of the audience?* If you are speaking on a subject already announced and known to be controversial, gaining attention through a startling statement or a humorous anecdote may seem highly inappropriate. If, on the other hand, the audience is indifferent or has already heard several presentations on the same subject, a direct reference to the subject may be perceived as dull and unoriginal. Overcoming audience apathy may require originality and creativity. If listeners are in a lighthearted mood and do not wish to be serious, you have a major problem on your hands. A rhetorical question that forces them to think for a moment or a startling statement that creates curiosity may be appropriate in this circumstance. Both induce listeners to participate directly, rather than to listen passively.

3. *What does the audience know about you and your commitment to the subject?* If you are already known as an expert in an area, stating your qualifications would be repetitious and may even convey conceit. If, on the other hand, your personal experience and depth of feeling are generally unknown, you will want to reveal these through personal reference, or, as Michael Twitchell did (see page 243), through an additional inducement at the close of your address. Either approach establishes both your knowledge and your personal involvement in the subject. Allow time to pass before you attempt to bring deeply felt experiences before

an audience, however, especially those involving loss of life. If you appear emotionally shaken or teary-eyed, the tension level will increase as the audience shares your personal discomfort. The effectiveness of your personal revelation will be correspondingly decreased. The use of a challenge or statement of personal intent also is an effective means of demonstrating your commitment to the subject.

4. *What constraints are imposed by the situation or setting?* A somber occasion, such as a funeral or a dedication of a war memorial, is hardly the place for hilarious stories. On the other hand, some serious occasions, such as commencements, can be enlivened by timely, well-chosen humor. The student speaker who ended his high-school address by waving a beer bottle and proclaiming "This Bud's for you" quickly discovered that his attempt at humor was received well by only part of his audience. The faculty and parents did not react as pleasantly as did his peers. Not everything goes, even when *you* see nothing wrong with the story or allusion. A reference to the occasion or personal greeting may be an appropriate reminder to the audience that you, as well as they, appreciate the significance of the occasion. Pertinent quotations and epitomizing illustrations, whether used at the beginning or end, also can convey a sense of the event's meaning for everyone present.

This discussion of the use of appropriate introductions and conclusions is not intended to be exhaustive. Rather, it illustrates the general approach to *thinking through* possible audience reactions as you select various means of introducing and concluding your speech. A "thought-through" speech will be perceived as well prepared by your listeners, whether they ultimately agree with you or not. If you convey that you have thought about them and the setting in preparing your remarks, you will increase the likelihood that they will accept your information and your way of thinking about issues. Although they may not agree with you, they at least have been given reason to respect your attempt to communicate. That may be the necessary first step in obtaining their eventual approval of your ideas.

Sample Outline for an Introduction and a Conclusion

An introduction and a conclusion for a classroom speech on MADD and SADD, anti–drunk driving organizations, might take the following form. Notice that the speaker uses one of the factors of attention—suspense— together with startling statements to lead the audience into the subject and concludes by combining a final illustration with a statement of personal intention.

Introduction
I. Many of you have seen the "Black Gash"—the Vietnam War Memorial in Washington, DC.
    A. It contains the names of more than 40,000 Americans who gave their lives in Southeast Asia between 1961 and 1973.
    B. We averaged over 3000 war dead a year during that anguishing period.
II. Today, another enemy stalks Americans.
    A. The enemy kills, not 3000 per year, but over 20,000 citizens every twelve months.
    B. The enemy is not hiding in jungles but can be found in every community in the country.
    C. The enemy kills, not with bayonets and bullets, but with bottles and bumpers.
III. Today, I want to talk about organizations that are trying to contain and finally destroy the killer.
    A. Every TV station in this town carries a public service ad that says "Friends Don't Let Friends Drive Drunk."
    B. Those ads are trying to rid our streets of that great killer, the drunk driver.
    C. In response to that menace, two national organizations—Mothers Against Drunk Driving and Students Against Drunk Driving—have been formed and are working even in this community to make the streets safe for you and me.
IV. [Central Idea] MADD and SADD are achieving their goals with your help.
V. To help you understand what these familiar organizations do, first I'll tell you something about the founders of MADD and SADD; then, I'll describe their operations; finally, I'll mention some of the ways community members get involved with them.

[Body]

Conclusion
I. Today, I've talked briefly about the Lightners and their goals for MADD and SADD, their organizational techniques, and ways you can get involved.
II. The work of MADD and SADD volunteers—even on our campus, as I'm sure you've seen their posters in the Union—is being carried out to keep you alive.
    A. You may not think you need to be involved, but remember, after midnight one in every five or fewer drivers on the road is probably drunk.
    B. You could be involved whether you want to be or not.
    C. That certainly was the case with Julie Smeiser, a member of our sophomore class, who just last Friday was hit by a drunk driver when going home for the weekend.
III. If people don't take action, we could build a new "Black Gash"—this time for victims of drunks—every two years, and soon fill Washington, DC, with monuments to needless suffering.
    A. Such monuments would be grim reminders of our unwillingness to respond to enemies at home with the same intensity with which we attacked enemies abroad.
    B. Better would be a positive response to such groups as MADD and SADD, which are attacking the enemy on several fronts at once in a war on motorized murder.

IV. If you're interested in learning more about MADD and SADD, stop by Room 324 in the Union tonight at 7:30 to hear the president of the local chapter of SADD talk about this year's activities. I'll be there; please join me.

Chapter Summary

Introductions function *to raise interest, to indicate the speaker's qualifications, to recognize the demands of the occasion, to create goodwill,* and *to forecast the development of the speech.* The types of introductions include *referring to the subject, referring to the occasion, using a personal reference or greeting, asking a rhetorical question, making a startling statement of fact or opinion, using a quotation, telling a humorous anecdote,* and *using an illustration.* In concluding a speech, you should decide how strong a *summary* you need, consider the *"so what?"* question, think about an appropriate final *mood* for your speech, and *signal a sense of finality.* Useful techniques for ending a speech involve *issuing a challenge or appeal, summarizing, using a quotation, using an illustration, supplying an additional inducement to belief or action,* and *stating a personal intention.* Which techniques for beginning and ending a speech you use usually depend upon *your experiences and abilities, the mood and commitment of your audience, the audience's knowledge of you and your commitments,* and *situational constraints.*

Reference Notes

1. Russell J. Love, "The Barriers Come Tumbling Down," a speech given at the Harris-Hillman School Commencement, Nashville, Tennessee, May 21, 1981.

2. William J. Byron, S.J., "Life in General," *Vital Speeches of the Day* 54 (May 15, 1988).

3. Edward M. Kennedy, "The Worsening Crisis in Health Care," in Owen Peterson, ed., *Representative American Speeches* (New York: H. W. Wilson Company, 1987).

4. Clifton R. Wharton, Jr., "Pubic Higher Education and Black Americans," in Owen Peterson, ed., *Representative American Speeches* (New York: H. W. Wilson Company, 1987).

5. Warren Manshel, "The U.S. Constitution," *Vital Speeches of the Day* 54 (June 1, 1988).

6. David T. Kearns, "Economics and the Student: Business Must Be Involved in Education," *Vital Speeches of the Day* 52 (July 1, 1986).

7. Deanna Sellnow, "Have You Checked Lately?" *Winning Orations* (1983).

8. Allen A. Schumer, "Employee Involvement," *Vital Speeches of the Day* 54 (July 1, 1988).

9. Everette E. Dennis, "Memo to the Press," *Vital Speeches of the Day* 54 (June 1, 1988).

10. F. Forrester Church, "Terrorism," in Owen Peterson, ed., *Representative American Speeches* (New York: H. W. Wilson Company, 1987).

11. Chui Lee Yap, "Ethnocentrism," *Winning Orations* (1983).

12. Michael A. Twitchell, "The Flood Gates of the Mind," *Winning Orations* (1983).

13. Ibid.

Key Terms

introduction
conclusion

Problems and Probes

1. After listening to one or more of the following types of speeches, evaluate the introduction and conclusion that the speaker used in (*a*) a classroom lecture; (*b*) a sermon; (*c*) an open hearing at a meeting of the city council; (*d*) remarks made at a club or dormitory council meeting; and (*e*) a formal address, live or televised, made by a political candidate. In reporting your evaluation, supply sufficient information about the speaker and speaking situation so that someone who was not present could understand why you evaluated a particular beginning or ending as you did.

2. Assume you have been asked to speak on the topic "The Pros and Cons of Television Advertising Aimed at Children" (or another controversial topic that interests you). Further, you are to present this speech in a variety of settings: as a classroom lecture; before an audience favorable to the pro arguments you will present; before an audience hostile to the pro arguments; as a televised address exposing you to an audience with a variety of attitudes on the topic. Write a brief report in which you indicate how these different situations would affect your approach in introducing and concluding your remarks. Indicate which techniques in this chapter would be most and least beneficial to use, and explain why.

Communication Activities

1. To emphasize the different ways of introducing and concluding a speech, choose a topic and prepare two different one-minute introductions and conclusions to be delivered in an impromptu round of classroom speeches. The class should analyze the varying approaches and compare their benefits and disadvantages.

2. Assume that you have been asked to speak on the topic "The Importance of Self-confidence." This speech is to be given to the following three audiences:

    a. the graduating class of a local high school
    b. a regularly scheduled meeting of the Parent-Teachers Association
    c. the local Kiwanis Club luncheon

Write a brief introduction for the speech that you think would be appropriate for each audience and identify those factors that would influence the way in which you prepared the three introductions. Be prepared to present your introductions orally in class.

3. Participate in a class discussion concerning introductions and conclusions to public speeches. The discussion might be structured as follows: One student leads off by suggesting a topic for a possible speech to this class. A second student then suggests an appropriate type of introduction and conclusion, justifying those choices. A third student, in turn, challenges that selection, proposing alternative introductions and/or conclusions. Continue this discussion until everyone has proposed and defended the different types of introductions and conclusions that would be appropriate for the speech topics discussed.

CHAPTER ELEVEN

Outlining the Speech

A speech outline serves the same function as a blueprint for a building. When the major structural components of the speech are clear—the main ideas selected and the general pattern identified—you are ready to move to the drawing board. By sketching the structure of your speech in advance of delivery, you can determine whether the major sections fit together smoothly, whether each main idea receives its proper emphasis, and whether all the important subject areas are covered. Just as a blueprint identifies the essential building materials, an outline highlights relationships between main points and supporting material. If you have failed to substantiate any of your leading ideas, your speech blueprint will show this. If information that is obviously needed to support your main idea is missing—statistical data or specific instances, for example—you will notice this, too, in a careful review of your completed outline. Finally, just as careful analysis of a finished blueprint fixes the overall structure in the builder's mind, a thorough study of your outline can help you recall its pattern as you speak. A visual plan of your speech can be a valuable aid to remembering what comes next in your presentation.

Requirements of Good Outline Form

The amount of detail and type of arrangement you use in an outline depends upon the complexity of your subject. It also depends upon the speaking situation and your prior experience in composing outlines. To be useful in building your speech, a good outline must satisfy four basic requirements:

By sketching the structure of your speech in advance of delivery, you can determine whether the major sections fit together smoothly.

1. *Each item in the outline should contain only one unit of information.* Outlines that combine a series of phrases or that run together several statements under one heading cannot show relationships between and among ideas. The following examples illustrate incorrect and correct ways to meet this requirement:

Incorrect

I. Athens, Greece, should be the permanent site for the Olympic Games because they have become more and more politicized in recent years.
   A. The U.S. decision to avoid the 1980 Summer Olympics is an example.
   B. The U.S.S.R. decision to avoid the 1984 Summer Olympics is an example.
   C. Also, costs are prohibitive and returning the Games to their homeland would place renewed emphasis on their original purpose.

Correct

I. Athens, Greece, should be the permanent site for the Olympic Games.
   A. The Games have become more and more politicized in recent years.
      1. The U.S. decision to avoid the 1980 Summer Olympics is an example.
      2. The U.S.S.R. decision to avoid the 1984 Summer Olympics is an example.
   B. Costs for building new sites in new locations each four years are becoming prohibitive.
   C. Returning the Games to their homeland would place renewed emphasis on their original purpose.

Note that, in the correct version, the main point is divided into its respective parts, and the subordinate points (*A* and *B* in the incorrect version) are placed under their logical heading. Also, *C* in the incorrect version is divided, creating two new subheadings in the revised outline.

2. *Less important ideas in the outline should be subordinate to more important ones.* Because a subordinate idea is a subdivision of the larger heading under which it falls, it should rank below that heading in scope and importance. It should also directly support or amplify the statement made in the superior heading.

Incorrect
I. The cost of medical care has skyrocketed.
   A. Operating-room fees may be as much as $1200 or $1500.
      1. Hospital charges are high.
      2. A private room may cost as much as $1500 a day.
   B. X rays and laboratory tests are extra.
   C. Complicated operations may cost several thousand dollars.
      1. Doctors' charges constantly go up.
         a. Office calls usually cost between $30 and $50.
      2. Drugs are expensive.
      3. Most antibiotics cost $2.50 per dose.
   D. The cost of nonprescription drugs has mounted.

Correct
I. The cost of medical care has skyrocketed.
   A. Hospital charges are high.
      1. A private room may cost as much as $1500 a day.
      2. Operating-room fees may be as much as $1200 or $1500.
      3. X rays and laboratory tests are extra.
   B. Doctors' charges constantly go up.
      1. Complicated operations may cost several thousand dollars.
      2. Office calls usually cost between $30 and $50.
   C. Drugs are expensive.
      1. Most antibiotics cost $2.50 per dose.
      2. The cost of nonprescription drugs has mounted.

The incorrect version makes little logical sense. Main points are treated as subordinate, and subordinate points are elevated to the status of main points. The basic logic governing subordination is whether an item "fits" as a part of a larger whole. In this sense, the main points fit together as part of the total purpose of the speech; the subordinate points are directly related to (as part to whole) the main point that they are placed under.

3. *The logical relation of items in an outline should be shown by proper indentation.* The greater the importance or scope of a statement, the nearer it should be placed to the left-hand margin. If a statement takes up more than one line, the second line should be indented the same as the first.

I. Choosing edible wild mushrooms is no job for the uninformed.
    A. Many wild species are highly toxic.
        1. The angel cap (*amanitas verosa*) contains a toxin for which there is no known antidote.
        2. Hallucinogenic mushrooms produce short-lived euphoria, followed by convulsions, paralysis, and possibly death.
    B. Myths abound regarding methods for choosing "safe" mushrooms.
        1. Mushrooms with easily peeled skins are not necessarily safe.
        2. Mushrooms eaten by animals are not necessarily safe.
        3. Mushrooms that do not darken a silver coin (placed in a pan of hot water containing mushrooms) are not necessarily safe.
        4. Mushrooms that do not produce a reaction in one person are not necessarily safe for others to consume.[1]

4. *A consistent set of symbols should be used.* One such set is exemplified in the outlines printed in this chapter. Whether you use this set or another, however, be consistent; do not change systems in the middle of an outline. Unless items of the same scope or importance have the same type of symbol throughout, your mental blueprint will be confused, and the chances of a smooth and orderly presentation will be impaired. The following example demonstrates the correct usage of this set of symbols:

I. Our penal system should be reformed.
    A. Many of our prisons are inadequate.
        1. They fail to meet basic structural and safety standards.
        2. They lack facilities for effective rehabilitation programs.
    B. The persons who manage our prisons are ill equipped.
        1. All too often they have had little or no formal training for their jobs.
        2. Low rates of pay result in frequent job turnover.

The four requirements just named apply to any outline. An additional requirement, however, applies to the final draft of a complete, formal outline: *all main points and subordinate ideas in such an outline should be written as full sentences.* Especially as you prepare outlines for your classroom speeches, you will find that putting the items of the outline into sentence form will help clarify the meaning of each point and will show its exact relation to the other points. You also will find that carefully framing a statement of each point and recognizing its place in the overall structure of your speech will help you remember what you want to say when it is time to speak.

Types of Outlines

The outline can be considered a midpoint in the thought process involved in constructing and presenting a speech. By this point, you have selected some major ideas, several specific items of supporting material, and a possible way of arranging them into a coherent structure. Your outline will change as the patterns of internal organization change. A need or satisfaction step organized chronologically, for example, may have several main points, while a causal pattern may require only two main headings.

As your thoughts about putting all of the pieces together begin to take shape in your mind, the outline begins to "write itself." Problems may emerge if you attempt to force materials to fit a predetermined shape. Thus, the act of composing an outline is a significant check on the mental map you have drawn in shaping the organization of your speech. Moreover, once you have completed the outline, it may serve as the basis for oral presentation. Unless you are in a situation where very precise language is required, it normally is not essential that you write out a speech in full. As you speak, the outline keeps you on track and reminds you of points that you want to cover.

There are two types of outlines; each fulfills a different purpose. The full-sentence outline helps make the process of speech preparation more systematic and thorough. The phrase outline serves as a memory aid in the early stages of oral practice.

The Full-Sentence Outline

As its name implies, a **full-sentence outline** represents the factual content of the speech in outline form. Whether you use the traditional divisions of the speech (introduction, body, conclusion) or the steps in the motivated

An outline can serve as the basis for oral presentation. As you speak, the outline keeps you on track and reminds you of points you want to cover.

sequence (attention, need, satisfaction, visualization, action), each division or step is set off in a separate section. The principal ideas are stated as main heads, and subordinate ideas—properly indented and marked with the correct symbols—are entered in their appropriate places. Each major idea and all subordinate ones are written in complete sentences. In this manner, their full meaning and their relation to other points within the speech are clearly established. Sources for supporting material may be placed in parentheses at the end of each piece of evidence or combined in a bibliography at the end of the outline. The complete outline creates a clear, comprehensive picture of the speech. The only missing features are the specific words you will use in your presentation and the visible and audible aspects of your delivery. By bringing together all the material you have gathered and by phrasing it in complete sentences and in detail, you ensure thoroughness in the preparation of your speech. The following is an example of a full-sentence outline:

Steps in Preparing a Good Outline

I. The first step in preparing a good outline is to determine the general purpose of the speech for the subject you have selected.
  A. You will need to limit the subject in two ways.
    1. First, limit the subject to fit the available time.
    2. Second, limit the subject to ensure unity and coherence.
  B. You also will need to phrase the specific purpose in terms of the exact response you seek from your listeners.
II. The second step is to develop a rough outline of your speech.
  A. First, list the main ideas you wish to cover.
  B. Second, arrange these main ideas according to the methods discussed in Chapters 8 and 9.
  C. Third, arrange subordinate ideas under their appropriate main heads.
  D. Fourth, fill in the supporting materials to be used in amplifying or justifying your ideas.
  E. Finally, review your rough draft.
    1. Does it cover your subject adequately?
    2. Does it carry out your specific purpose?
III. The third step is to put the outline into final form.
  A. Begin this process by writing out the main ideas as complete sentences or as key phrases.
    1. State the main ideas concisely, vividly, and—insofar as possible—in parallel terms.
    2. State the major heads so that they address directly the needs and interests of your listeners.
  B. Write out the subordinate ideas in complete sentences or in key phrases.
    1. Are they subordinate to the main idea they are intended to develop?
    2. Are they coordinate with other items at the same level (that is, are all *A–B–C* series roughly equal in importance; are all *1–2–3* series roughly equal in importance)?

C. You now are ready to fill in the supporting materials.
　　1. Are they pertinent?
　　2. Are they adequate?
　　3. Is there a variety of types of support?
D. Finally, recheck the completed outline.
　　1. Is it written in proper outline form?
　　2. Does the speech, as outlined, adequately cover the subject?
　　3. Does the speech, as outlined, carry out your general and specific purposes?

The Phrase Outline

The phrase outline and the full-sentence outline use the same indentation and symbol structure. The major difference between the two is that each item of a **phrase outline** is referred to by a phrase—key words (on occasion, a single word will suffice) that may be more easily remembered. This outline can be used as a basis for your **speaking outline**, as the key words are easy to see as you stand at a lectern. You are not distracted as you might be if you used a full-sentence outline. Be sure, however, that when you look down and see a key word or phrase, you know what to say. Another advantage of the phrase outline is that it can be used to practice the speech. By reading through a phrase outline several times, you fix the sequence of ideas in your mind. Then, as you speak, you will be able to recall the structure of your presentation.

If you use a phrase outline and want to ensure accuracy when citing statistics or quoting authorities, you might place them on separate notecards and key them to the appropriate place in the speaking outline. If this seems cumbersome, you might insert each item into the appropriate place in your phrase outline. This lengthens your outline but ensures that you do not misplace items that you want to cite.

The previous sample outline, if developed as a phrase outline, would look like this:

I. Determine general purpose.
　　A. Limit subject.
　　　　1. Fit available time.
　　　　2. Assure unity and coherence.
　　B. Phrase in terms of listener response.
II. Develop rough draft.
　　A. List main ideas.
　　B. Arrange main ideas.
　　　　1. Motivated sequence
　　　　2. Traditional pattern
　　C. Arrange subordinate ideas.
　　D. Add supporting materials.
　　E. Review rough draft.
　　　　1. Adequacy?
　　　　2. Meet specific purpose?

III. Final outline form.
    A.   Complete sentences or key phrases
        1. Concise, vivid, parallel phrasing
        2. Address needs and interests of listeners.
    B.   Subordinate ideas—complete sentence or key word
        1. Under appropriate main head
        2. Coordinate with subordinate ideas of equal weight.
    C.   Add supporting materials.
        1. Pertinent
        2. Adequate
        3. Variety
    D.   Review outline.
        1. Good form
        2. Adequate coverage
        3. Meets purpose.

Steps in Preparing a Good Outline

Three major steps—selecting and limiting the speech subject, developing a rough outline, and preparing the outline in final form—are essential in outlining your speech.

Selecting and Limiting the Speech Subject

Suppose your instructor asks you to prepare a persuasive speech on a subject in which you are interested. You decide to talk about the dangers of suntanning because you know that many think a tan is essential to looking healthy. You also know that tanning can be dangerous. Your broad topic, therefore, is "The Effects of the Sun on Your Health." In the five to seven minutes that you have to speak, you will not be able to cover all the aspects of this subject. Therefore, recalling what you learned in Chapter 4 about adapting your material to your listeners and to the time limit, you decide to focus your discussion on some of the results of overexposure, spending proportionately more time on sun-related skin cancers and on some preventive measures. You are now prepared to limit the topic to "Suntanning: Not As Healthy As You Might Think" (a description of the results of overexposure and the preventive steps that might be taken).

Developing the Rough Outline

In determining the limits of your subject, you already have made a preliminary selection of some of the principal ideas to be dealt with in your speech. By listing these points, you can see how they might be modified and fitted into a suitable sequence. Your list may look something like this:

1.   Prematurely aged skin
2.   Keratoses

3. Minor skin cancers—basal and squamous cell cancers
4. Major skin cancer—melanomas
5. Who is at risk
6. Some drugs promote sunburning.
7. Preventive drugs
8. Clothing helps prevent sunburn.

This list covers most of the points you want to include, but in random order. As you think further about the order of these items, you might review the patterns of organization discussed in Chapter 9. Within the need step, a topical pattern may be the best approach. The satisfaction step can be organized in a similar manner. In both cases, the topical pattern allows flexibility in ordering the items you want to cover. You can determine, for example, which of the topics seems the most or least crucial or which should be covered in more rather than less detail. As you work with the major themes you want to cover, you rearrange and modify your ideas until the following general pattern emerges:

Effects of Suntanning
sunburn, aging skin, keratoses, types of skin cancer

Preventive Measures
sunscreens, sunblocks, timing exposure, light clothing

As you think about this general pattern, you note that the individual items can be arranged as subpoints. In enumerating effects, you can order the ideas from least to most severe consequences. In discussing preventive measures, you can discuss the items in terms of the amount of protection they provide. The resulting outline looks like this:

I. The effects of suntanning
    A. Sunburn
    B. Prematurely aging skin
    C. Keratoses
    D. Skin cancers
II. Protective measures
    A. Timing exposure
    B. Sunscreens
    C. Sunblocks
    D. Light clothing

You now have prepared a rough outline. You have identified your topic; clarified your purpose; considered various subtopics and settled upon a reasonable number of them; and decided upon a coherent, cohesive method for organizing your speech. The main points have been arranged in a "need-satisfaction" or "problem-solution" arrangement, and the subpoints, although presented in a topical pattern, also have an internal logic to their order of appearance. You would not, for example, talk about skin cancer before keratoses, since the latter is often a precancerous stage of skin reaction. When you have chosen your major and subordinate points and have arranged them in a suitable fashion, you are prepared to develop the remainder of the outline. The attention, visualization, and action steps also need to be filled in.

Developing the Technical Plot.   As you work on the full-sentence outline, it often is helpful to work out a **technical plot** of the speech. In the left margin of your outline, note the types of introduction and conclusion, supporting material, visual aids, and other devices you are using. You also can note the function of certain points in the speech ("beginning of main point," "details of early warning signs"). Used as a testing device, a technical plot can help you determine whether your speech is structurally sound. It also can pinpoint whether there are weaknesses in supporting material, whether one or more forms are overused or should be used, and whether your appeals are clearly formed.

The advantage of the technical plot is that it highlights what you are doing and why you think you are doing it. By forcing your attention on the functions of your ideas and supporting materials, the technical plot becomes an early warning system for flaws in the planned presentation. As you gain more experience, you may be able to check these items visually, without writing out the technical plot; once this checklist approach becomes second nature, you will find yourself asking such questions as you write your full-sentence outline.

A Sample Full-Sentence Outline.   You are now ready to assemble the full-sentence outline. The following sample shows both the form for the outline and the technical plot:

Suntanning: Not As Healthy As You Might Think

TECHNICAL PLOT	**FULL-SENTENCE OUTLINE**
	Attention Step
	I. "Gee, your suntan looks great!" "He must live in a darkroom; his arms and legs are so pale!"
☐ *Rhetorical question*	Have you ever heard, or used, these or similar expressions?
	A. Many people think that a suntan makes them look more attractive.
	B. Some people think that getting a "good" suntan makes them healthy.
	C. The truth is that too much sun can be harmful to your health.
☐ *Forecast*	II. In convincing you of the truth of this claim, I will concentrate on two main tasks.
	A. I will discuss the major effects of suntanning.
	B. I will explain some preventive measures that you can take to avoid these ill effects.

Need Step

☐ *Cause-effect arguments*

I. Three of the main effects range from the uncomfortable to the potentially health damaging.
   A. First, you can receive a severe sunburn.
      1. Many of us have already experienced this discomforting condition.
      2. In its more severe forms, sunburn must be treated just as a burn received from being scalded with hot water or from burning your hand on a hot stove.
   B. Another result of too much sun is prematurely aged skin.

☐ *Descriptive materials*

      1. The skin looks leathery.
      2. The skin loses its elasticity.
   C. A third result of too much sun might be a condition known as *keratoses*.
      1. These are dark patches or scaly, grey growths.
      2. They often are precancerous.

☐ *Statistics*

II. The fourth effect is the most severe: skin cancer strikes 300,000 Americans annually.
   A. There are several early warning signs.
      1. A sore may not heal.
      2. A wart or mole may change size or color.
      3. An unusual pigmented (colored) growth may appear.

☐ *Descriptive materials*

   B. Basal and squamous cell skin cancers often appear as waxlike, pearly nodules.
      1. They may also appear as a red, scaly, sharply outlined patch.
      2. If detected and treated early, these forms are almost always curable.
   C. Melanoma is the most serious form of skin cancer.
      1. These begin as small mole-like growths that increase in size and change color.
      2. If malignant, these can cause death within five years.
   D. Melanoma can be treated through several means.
      1. Surgery can be performed.
      2. Radiation therapy can be prescribed.
      3. A heat process can destroy the affected tissue.
      4. Freezing can destroy the tissue.

Satisfaction Step

I. If you still must have sun, at least take the following precautions.

☐ *Attack on the causes to eliminate the need*

   A. Control the amount of time you absorb the sun's rays, especially at the beginning of the sunning season.
      1. Sun before 10 A.M. and after 3 P.M. when the sun's rays are at their weakest.

  2. Sun only fifteen minutes the first day during high radiation hours.

  3. Sun only five minutes each day thereafter during high radiation hours until you have a good base tan.

 B. Use a sunscreen that contains PABA (para-aminobenzoic acid)

  1. Sunscreens work best when applied forty-five minutes before exposure.

  2. Sunscreens come in varying strengths.

 C. A sunblock may be an effective supplement to sunscreens.

  1. Sunblocks do not absorb ultraviolet rays from the sun.

  2. Sunblocks help shield lips, nose, and previously burned areas.

  3. Lifeguards and others constantly exposed to the sun use zinc oxide as a blocking agent.

 D. Light, cool clothing also is an effective preventive measure.

  1. Loose-fitting robes for beachwear can help.

  2. Hats can help shield you from the sun.

Visualization Step

□ *Negative and positive visualization*

 I. Is carefree and careless pursuit of the sun worth tomorrow's damaged skin or next month's keratoses or skin cancer?

 II. Careful, consistent use of the preventive measures will leave you with a suntan and less chance of skin damage.

Action Step

□ *Short action step*

 I. Plan your time in the sun with care—the skin you save is your own![2]

Developing the Speaking Outline

As noted earlier, you probably would not use a full-sentence outline in an actual speech because it is too dense to manage effectively from a lectern. One danger a full-sentence outline poses is that it can be simply read aloud to an audience. After all, it contains virtually everything you want to say. To preserve the naturalness and sense of spontaneity that enable you to maintain contact with the audience, you can compress the full outline into a phrase outline. This involves rewording the main heads into phrase form on a sheet or series of notecards. Whether you use sheets of paper or cards, be comfortable with your choice of notes.

 Your speaking outline should provide you with reminders of the overall structure of your speech as well as the subpoints you want to cover. In addition, it should include any material that you want to present in a verbatim or accurate fashion (for example, testimony from authorities or sta-

Memory and Organization

*I*f you lost your outline, would you remember the major items? Even with the outline present, could you give your speech without complete reliance upon it, trusting your memory of the points and their sequence? Further, how many points should a speech attempt to cover? What difficulty would the audience have if you were to offer seventeen reasons for the rejection of nuclear power? These issues are answered in part by research relating organizational processes to human memory. In a classic study, Miller concluded that there is a limit to the number of items a person can easily recall; according to Miller, the "magic number" is seven, plus or minus two. More recent research has suggested that a more manageable number is five plus or minus two. Using this research as a guideline would suggest that your list of seventeen items on nuclear power should be reduced to no more than five to seven points.

We routinely recall more than seven items, however (otherwise how would you pass a test in biology?). How is this possible, given the assumption that there is a limit on human memory? One of

tistical data). In developing a speaking outline, you can use phrases or, in some cases, single words that represent more complex thoughts or ideas you wish to convey. If you have practiced the speech using the full-sentence outline, a word or phrase should be enough to trigger your memory at critical points during your delivery. To be sure you say things precisely (when it is crucial) or quote someone accurately, include full sentences in your outline. Add directions to yourself in the margins or at appropriate points following a key word or phrase (for instance, "show visual" or "draw diagram on chalk-board"). Finally, you can indicate changes in emphasis by underlining key words or phrases or by using all capital letters. In its completed form, the speaking outline should contain all of the *content* that is critical, as well as cues to speak more forcefully or to use visual aids.

The following is a sample speaking outline for the speech on suntanning:

the ways we manage the additional data is by "chunking," or taking small bits of information and organizing them into discrete groupings. Your seventeen items on the hazards of nuclear power, for example, might be "chunked" into subsets involving internal safety procedures, mechanical failures, supervisor training issues, past violations of safety standards, and design flaws. These "chunks," which are easier to recall than the multiple items, can serve as the main points in your presentation. The more specific instances within each subset can serve as your subpoints, fleshing out the case you wish to make.

As this chapter has noted, the effective outlining of ideas involves *coordinating* concepts of equal emphasis or merit and properly *subordinating* specific items to each "coordinate" point. Thus, in an outline, level *I* and level *II*, or level *A* and level *B*, are coordinate when considered as separate sets. Items A and B are subordinate when placed under *I* or *II*. This *hierarchical* method of organizing ideas matches the human mind's approach to the recall of items. Thus, three to five coordinate points (level *I*, *II*, . . .) could easily contain additional subpoints under each (*A*, *B*, *C*, . . .). Recalling level *I* also brings to mind the relevant subpoints, while recalling level *II* brings into focus the points under that heading.

FOR FURTHER READING

Mandler, G. "Organization and Memory." In Gordon Bower, ed. *Human Memory: Basic Processes.* New York: Academic Press, 1977, 310–54; G. Mandler's articles in C. R. Puff, ed. *Memory Organization and Structure.* New York: Academic Press, 1979, 303–19; Miller, G. A. "The Magic Number Seven, Plus or Minus Two: Some Limits on Our Capacity for Processing Information." *Psychological Review* 63 (1956): 81–97.

Suntanning: Not As Healthy As You Might Think

Attention Step
I. "Gee, your suntan looks great!" "He must live in a darkroom; his arms and legs are so pale!"
   A. Suntan—attractive
   B. Suntan—healthy
   C. Truth—HARMFUL
II. Convincing—two themes
   A. Effects
   B. Preventive measures

A complex sentence outline can be distracting and confusing when used as a speaking outline, whereas the key words in a phrase outline are easy to see as you stand in front of an audience.

Need Step

I. Three effects—uncomfortable to potential harm
   A. *Severe* sunburn
      1. Familiar
      2. Severe—treat like other burns
   B. Aging
      1. Leathery
      2. Lose elasticity
   C. Keratoses
      1. Dark patches, scaly growths
      2. Often precancerous

II. Fourth—300,000 Americans annually contract skin cancer
   A. Early warning signs
      1. Sore—not healing
      2. Wart or mole—change
      3. Unusual growth
   B. Basal and squamous cell cancers
      1. Red, scaly patches
      2. Detection and treatment—cure
   C. Melanoma—worst
      1. Small, molelike growth—increase in size, change color
      2. Malignant—causes death in 5 years
   D. Melanoma treatment
      1. Surgery
      2. Radiation therapy

      3. Heat tissue
      4. Freeze tissue

Satisfaction Step

I.   Precautions
   A. Time
      1. 10 to 3 worst
      2. Day one—15 min.
      3. Days after—5 min. till base tan
   B. Sunscreen—PABA (para-aminobenzoic acid) [put term on board]
      1. 45 min. prior
      2. Varying strengths
   C. Sunblock
      1. No rays
      2. Shield lips, nose
   D. Light, cool clothes
      1. Loose robes for beach
      2. Hats

Visualization Step

I.   Today carefree, tomorrow damages: worth it?
II. Careful attention—tan, less damage

Action Step

I.   Plan your time in the sun with care—the skin you save is your own!

Fitting the Introduction and Conclusion to the Speech

The motivated sequence and more precise patterns of organization were incorporated in the full-sentence and speaking outlines in this section. By including the introduction and conclusion (attention and action steps), these elements are integrated into the total speech structure. In essence, the relationships between the motivated sequence and the terms "introduction," "body," and "conclusion" and the integration of these into an outline can be schematized as shown in the table on page 266. Of course, the arrangement of your main points and subpoints may not follow exactly the pattern shown in the right-hand column of the table, but the major divisions will be the same.

Chapter Summary

Arranging and outlining may appear to require a lot of effort, but, as you become more experienced in gathering and organizing ideas, you will discover that outlining is a tool that works beyond the immediate speech preparation situation. Outlining in advance helps ensure that your ideas for any

COMPARING TRADITIONAL SPEECH DIVISIONS
TO THE MOTIVATED SEQUENCE

Traditional Divisions	*Motivated Sequence*	*Outline*
Introduction	Attention step	I. _____
		A. _____
		B. _____
Body	Need step	I. _____
		A. _____
		B. _____
		1. _____
		2. _____
		II. _____
		A. _____
		B. _____
	Satisfaction step	I. _____
		A. _____
		B. _____
		C. _____
		D. _____
Conclusion	Visualization step	I. _____
		II. _____
	Action step	I. _____

oral or written project are communicated in a coherent manner. There are four requirements for good outline form: (1) *each unit should contain only one idea,* (2) *less important ideas should be subordinate to more important ones,* (3) *the logical relationship between units should be shown by proper indentation,* and (4) *a consistent set of symbols should be used throughout the outline.* These requirements can be met either in developing a *full-sentence* outline or in a *phrase* outline. In preparing an outline that meets your needs, begin by selecting and limiting the speech subject, then develop a *rough* outline. With this as a basis, you can determine whether more specific information is required or whether you need to reorder main points or subpoints in the outline. A *technical plot* helps you think through this stage of speech development. Finally, you will need to develop your *speaking* outline. Arranging and outlining your ideas, therefore, helps you check on the speech's *form,* its *coverage* of the subject, and its *suitability* to your purpose and the needs of the audience.

Reference Notes

1. Information taken from Vincent Marteka, "Words of Praise—and Caution—About Fungus Among Us," *Smithsonian* (May 1980): 96–104.

2. Information adapted from a student outline by Sandra Ginn, University of Maine-Orono. Sources used include pamphlets from the American Cancer Society ("Sense in the Sun," "Cancer Facts and Figures"); Kushio Michio, *Cancer and Heart Disease* (Japan Publishing Co., 1982) 41, 46; Mark Renneker, *Understanding Cancer* (Bull Publishing Co., 1979) 4, 28.

Key Terms

full-sentence outline   speaking outline

phrase outline   technical plot

Problems and Probes

1. Revise both *a* and *b* below, following the guidelines for correct outline form.
   a. The nuclear freeze concept is a good idea because it allows us to stop nuclear proliferation and it will help make us feel more secure.
   b. I. We should wear seatbelts to protect our lives.
       II. Studies indicate seatbelts protect children from serious injury.
       III. Studies indicate seatbelts reduce risk of head injury.
2. Select a speech from this text or from a speech anthology available in the library. Develop a full-sentence outline for the speech, then an abbreviated phrase outline. Add to these outlines a technical plot in which you indicate the forms of support, attention factors, and motivational appeals used by the speaker. Hand in your written outlines and technical plot. Your instructor may have you meet in small groups to compare your analyses of a single assigned speech.

Communication Activities

1. For a speech assigned by the instructor, draw up a full-sentence outline and a technical plot in accordance with the samples provided in this chapter. Hand in your speech outline in time to obtain feedback before presenting your speech.
2. Working in small groups, select a controversial topic for potential presentation in class. Brainstorm possible arguments that could be offered on the pro and con sides. With these as a basis, develop a phrase outline of the main points to be presented on both sides.
3. For the next round of classroom speeches, your instructor will divide the class into groups and ask each student to outline the presentations of their respective group members. Working in groups, compare and contrast the outlines of what was heard with the speaker's own outline.

PART THREE

Channels

"*It may therefore be fairly concluded, that to neglect all or any part of the labour which constitutes correct delivery; whether it be the due management of the voice, the expression of the countenance, or the appropriate gesture, is so far an injury to the cause in which the speaker is engaged, and so far deprives his composition of its just effect.*"

Gilbert Austin
Chronomia; Or a Treatise on Rhetorical Delivery *(1806)*

CHAPTER TWELVE

Using Language to Communicate

*S*o far, we have focused on the process of creating speeches: preparing, organizing, and adapting messages to their intended audiences. We will turn our attention in the next three chapters to the **encoding** of these messages— that is, to the means by which public speakers give expression and form to their ideas, attitudes, feelings, and values. These means include the choice of language, the use of visual aids, and the control of bodily and vocal behaviors. As you will see, each channel is not a conduit, an empty pipe through which "content" flows. On the contrary, each channel helps shape and complete that content, which includes not only ideas but also the emotional shadings added by voice, the graphs used in visual aids, the readiness apparent in the speaker's posture, and the knowledge the speaker demonstrates when he or she makes precise word choices.

This discussion of channels, or modes, of communication will begin by examining language—the choices of wording and style you make when you express your ideas and feelings to others. Language is both a referential and a relational medium of communication.[1] Language is *referential* when it identifies persons, places, things, feelings, or other characteristics of people and their environments. The referential dimension of language includes both its **denotations** (what it refers to, as the word "horse" refers to the equine animal) and its **connotations** (the additional associations carried by a word, as when the seductive word "caress" is used instead of the more neutral word "touch"). Through its denotative aspects, language allows you to label persons, places, and things, and, through its connotative aspects, it expresses attitudes, emotions, and other reactions we have to the world. Language also is *relational.* Many linguistic constructions encode our relationships to each other. When you say "May I please have the . . . ," you signal that you are to some degree subordinate to the person being addressed, whereas when you rephrase that question to "Give me the . . . ," you are implicitly indicating your ability to command another person.

All of these dimensions of language come together when you try to say something to someone else. To put ideas into language publicly is to *style* them. A **speaking style** is a set of verbal and nonverbal cues that speakers and listeners understand represents a particular mode of human interaction. Commonly identified styles include "an evangelical style," "an academic style," "a cool style," and "a telegraphic or staccato style." A speaking style is composed of numerous features of words and delivery that set a *social-psychological relationship* between speaker and audience.

That relationship is "social" because style is partly conventionalized—that is, determined by the ways groups interpret symbols. Thus, musical styles—Baroque, jazz, rap—are composed of melody, chord, rhythm, and sound characteristics that groups of people identify as particular styles. Similarly, a speaking style is composed of specific aspects of word and vocal choices that, when used together often enough, become identified as an oratorical or speech style. That relationship, though, is also "psychological" or individualized; each person has a style, or *signature*,[2] that marks his or her identity as a communicator. Both the social and the psychological aspects of style are strongly associated with word choice and larger units of language.

Essentials of Effective Word Choices

Communicating with precision is not easy, yet rhetorical and communication theorists have known for centuries that speakers can help listeners understand their message better if they keep certain virtues of oral language in mind. The virtues of accuracy, simplicity, coherence, language intensity, and appropriateness are primary features of effective word choices.

Accuracy

Careful word choice is an essential ingredient in transmitting your meaning to an audience. The man who tells a hardware store clerk that "I have broken the hickey on my hootenanny and need a thingamajig to fix it" had better have the hootenanny in his hand to procure the right thingamajig. When you speak, your goal should be precision. Leave no doubt as to your meaning. Words are symbols that represent concepts or objects. Your listener may attach to a symbol a meaning quite different from the one you had intended to convey. "Democracy," for example, does not mean the same thing to a citizen of the United States as it does to a citizen of the Soviet Union, or, in fact, to one American citizen and another. The term "democracy" elicits different meanings in those belonging to the Moral Majority and those belonging to the American Communist party.

It is also imprecise to discuss people or objects in a particular class as though they were no different from other members of the same class. Asian-American A differs from Asian-Americans B and C; one Oldsmobile may be an excellent car and another may be a lemon. Students of General Semantics continually warn us that many errors in thinking and communication arise from treating words as if they were the actual conditions, processes, or objectives and were fixed and timeless in meaning. From their perspective, the phrase "once a thief, always a thief" is an imprecise and inaccurate reference to all persons convicted of theft; a person is more than a label.[3]

To avoid vagueness in definition and elsewhere, choose words that express the exact shade of meaning you wish to communicate. While the verb "shine" may refer to, or denote, a ray of light to speakers of the English language, you may wish to indirectly communicate other aspects (connotations) of that light; such verbs as "glow," "glitter," "glisten," "gleam," "flare," "blaze," "glare," "shimmer," "glimmer," "flicker," "sparkle," "flash," and "beam" are familiar enough to be used in your speech. They allow you to communicate more precise features of the ray.

Simplicity

"Speak," said Lincoln, "so that the most lowly can understand you, and the rest will have no difficulty." This advice is as valid today as when Lincoln offered it, and because modern electronic media create audiences that are vaster and more varied than any Lincoln dreamed of, there is even more reason for contemporary speakers to follow it. Say "learn" rather than "ascertain," "try" rather than "endeavor," "use" rather than "utilize," "help" rather than "facilitate." Never use a longer or less familiar word when a simpler one is just as clear and accurate. Billy Sunday, the famous evangelist, gave this example:

> If a man were to take a piece of meat and smell it and look disgusted, and his little boy were to say, "What's the matter with it, Pop?" and he were to say, "It is undergoing a process of decomposition in the formation of new chemical compounds," the boy would be all in. But if the father were to say, "It's rotten," then the boy would understand and hold his nose. "Rotten" is a good Anglo-Saxon word, and you do not have to go to the dictionary to find out what it means.[4]

Simplicity does not mean that your language must be simplistic or that you should talk down to your audience; it does suggest that you consider the advantages of short, easily understandable words that convey precise, concrete meanings.

Coherence

Transmitting ideas orally requires attention to the perceived **coherence** of your message. Audiences do not have the luxury of going back over your points as they do in reading an essay; nor do they have punctuation marks

Abraham Lincoln said, "Speak so that the most lowly can understand you, and the rest will have no difficulty."

to help them distinguish one idea from another. Hence, speakers use **sign-posts** in the form of carefully worded phrases and sentences to help listeners follow the movement of ideas within a speech and perceive the overall message structure.

Summaries are useful signposts in ensuring that your audience is able to see the overall structure. **Preliminary** and **final summaries** are especially helpful in laying out or pulling together the major divisions or points of the speech:

Preliminary Summaries	*Final Summaries*
Today I am going to talk about three aspects of . . .	I have talked about three aspects of . . .
There are four major points to be covered in . . .	These four major points—(restate them)—are the . . .
The history of the issue can be divided into two periods . . .	The two periods just covered—(restate them)—represent the significant . . .

In addition to these summarizing strategies, signposts may be **connectives** that move an audience from one idea to another within the speech. The following are typical *transition* statements you might use:

In the first place . . . The second point is . . .
In addition to . . . notice that . . .
Now look at it from a different angle. . . .
You must keep these three things in mind in order to understand the
    importance of the fourth. . . .
What was the result? . . .
Turning now . . .

The preceding signposts are *neutral*—they tell the audience that another idea is coming but do not indicate the more subtle relationships that exist between the points being made. You can improve the clarity and coherence of your message by being precise about such relationships as *parallel/hierarchical*, *similar/different*, and *coordinate/subordinate*. Expressing these relationships requires connectives such as:

Not only . . . but also . . . (*parallel*)
More important that these . . . (*hierarchical*)
In contrast . . . (*different*)
Similar to this . . . (*similar*)
One must consider X, Y, and Z . . . (*coordinated*)
On the next level is . . . (*subordinated*)

Your use of preliminary or final summaries and signposts is important to your audience. The summaries—elements of *macrostructure*—give listeners an overall sense of your entire message; if they can easily see the structure, they will better understand and remember your speech. The signposts are elements of *microstructure*, and, hence, lead your listeners step-by-step through the speech, signaling specific relationships between ideas.

Language Intensity

Your word choice is partially determined by the way you feel about the object you are describing and by the strength, or intensity, of that feeling. That is, through your choice of words or phrasing you communicate your *attitude* toward the object. Consider, for example, the following "attitudinally weighted" terms:

Highly Positive
- "savior"
- "patriot"
- "defender"

Relatively Neutral
- "G.I."
- "soldier"
- "mercenary"

Highly Negative
- "enemy"
- "murderer"
- "foreign devil"

LANGUAGE INTENSITY CHART

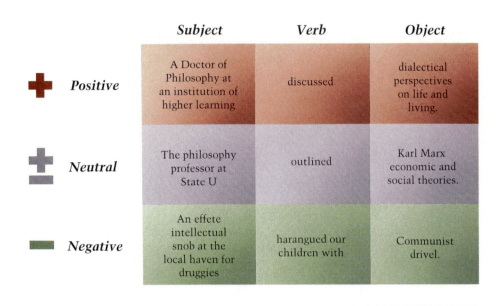

	Subject	*Verb*	*Object*
Positive	A Doctor of Philosophy at an institution of higher learning	discussed	dialectical perspectives on life and living.
Neutral	The philosophy professor at State U	outlined	Karl Marx economic and social theories.
Negative	An effete intellectual snob at the local haven for druggies	harangued our children with	Communist drivel.

These nine terms are roughly ranked according to their intensity, ranging from the highly positive "savior" to the highly negative "foreign devil." Notice that we tend to add even religious connotations when getting to the extremes of language intensity. Generally, then, such language choices signal to your listeners the intensity of your feelings toward your subject.

How intense should your language be? John Waite Bowers has suggested a useful rule of thumb: let your language be, roughly, one step more intense than the position or attitude of your audience.[5] If your audience already is committed, say, to your positive position on academic reform, then you can afford to make your language quite intense. If not, you had better use comparatively neutral language. Intense language can help create intense reactions, but only if you suit your word choices to the listeners' beliefs and tastes.

Appropriateness

Besides being accurate, clear, and properly intense, your language should be appropriate to the topic and to the situation. Solemn occasions call for diction that is restrained and dignified, joyful occasions for word choices that are informal and lively. Just as you would never use slang in a speech dedicating a memorial, so should you never phrase a humorous after-dinner speech in a heavy style, unless you are using irony. Suit your language to the tone of the occasion. Be sure, as well, that your language is appropriate to the audience you are addressing. Your slang, for example, differs in many ways from that of your parents, so even if the occasion allows for informal language, you will want to see whose informal verbal constructions are appropriate by noting who is in the audience. "Gee whiz," "Wow," "Good grief," "Far out," and "Awesome" are pieces of slang that came into English in different eras; if you use any of them, be sure that people from that era comprise a major segment of your audience and, of course, that you can say the expression without laughing.

Selecting an Appropriate Style: Strategic Decisions

Thus far, we have discussed the general qualities of an effective style—accuracy, simplicity, coherence, language intensity, and appropriateness. Those qualities are necessary for clear, understandable oral communication. Next we will consider the aspects of speaking style that more particularly control audience members' impressions of you as a person, the nature of your message, and even the occasion itself. The combination of these aspects of oral communication is generally called **tone.** Are you basically an informal, happy-go-lucky person or someone talking seriously and formally about important matters? Are you presenting an argument to the audience members or telling them stories? Are you principally concerned with yourself and what listeners think of you, or are you trying to focus their attention primarily on your ideas?

While tone is an elusive quality of speech, nevertheless it is possible to identify some of its primary aspects, or dimensions. Five dimensions will receive special attention in this section: *written vs. oral style, serious vs. humorous atmosphere, person-centered vs. material-centered emphasis, gendered vs. gender-neutral nouns and pronouns,* and *propositional vs. narrative form.*

Written vs. Oral Style

Oral speech developed long before written language. That may appear to be a simple and obvious fact, but its implications are far reaching. It is presumed that oral speech sprang directly from early humanity's contact with a harsh environment, and it still retains features of its origin. Generally, spoken language is looser and less complicated because we use it more in informal settings (at the grocery store, over the back fence, around the supper table) than we do written language. While you might write someone a note requesting him or her to "please depart from this area," the spoken version might be an order to "Get outta town!" Such words as "honey," "sweetie," and "dear" look terrible on the printed page, yet when spoken by intimates can elicit highly positive reactions. For instance, the stereotyped waitress' "Whut-kinahgitcha?" makes no sense in this book, yet it certainly is effective at 7:25 A.M. in the local greasy spoon.

Because we are usually tense about speaking in public, we often err in the direction of formality. This is especially likely to be true if we have written out the whole speech. Because we are used to composing on paper for the eye (for a reader) rather than for the ear (for a listener), most of us compose speeches in a written rather than oral style. The speeches sound stilted and stiff. They are likely to have sentences such as these:

> I am most pleased that you could come this morning. I would like to use this opportunity to discuss with you a subject of inestimable importance to us all—the impact of inflationary spirals on students enrolled in institutions of higher education.

Translated into the kind of oral style preferred in most speaking situations, those sentences would run something like this:

> Thanks for coming. I'd like to talk today about something that everyone here has had experience with—the rising costs of going to college.

Notice the differences in the two versions: the first is wordy, filled with prepositional phrases, larded with complex words, and formal in addressing the audience. The second contains shorter sentences, a more direct address of the audience, and a simpler vocabulary. The first is in a written style; the second, in an oral style.

On most occasions, you will want to cultivate an oral style. To be sure, there are some highly ceremonious occasions and situations, such as news conferences, in which you will read from a prepared text, but even at those times, you will want to strive for an oral style.[6]

Serious vs. Humorous Atmosphere

Related to the matter of written vs. oral style is another dimension of speech quality: the seriousness with which a speaker expects an audience to take a speech and a speaking situation. Your word choice, demeanor, tone of voice, and the like combine to create either a serious or a humorous atmosphere.

Sometimes the speaking situation dictates the appropriate atmosphere. We do not expect a light, humorous speaking style to be used during a funeral. This is not to say that jokes are never told during a funeral; often a minister, priest, or rabbi will tell a heartwarming, even humorous, story about the deceased, yet the overall tone of a funeral speech is somber, meditative, and respectfully serious. In contrast, a speech after a football victory, election win, or successful fund drive is seldom heavy, philosophical, or penetrating in its analysis of the human condition. Victory speeches are times for celebration, humor, warmth, joy, applause, and a feeling of unity with others who have worked on the cause.

This is not to say that "humorous" means there are no audience-centered, nonfrivolous purposes for speaking. As we will see in Chapter 18, even speeches to entertain have worthy purposes; they can be persuasive in their goals, and they can be given in grave earnestness. The political satirist who throws humorous but barbed comments at pompous, silly, or corrupt politicians is very concerned about political reform.

We are not talking here about serious or humorous speaking *purposes*, but, rather, a serious or humorous linguistic *atmosphere*—the mind-set, or mental attitude, a speaker attempts to create in audiences. A speech urging individuals to be and think for themselves, cast in a serious atmosphere, might contain a section such as: "Be yourself. Trust in your own decision-making powers. Whenever you turn over your decision-making powers to a group, you become a dependent human being." That same section of a speech offered within a humorous atmosphere might sound like this: "Remember that a camel is a horse built by a committee. And when God put the universe together, she didn't consult with the angels and the archangels, the cherubim, seraphim, and the other folks hanging around heaven. If God had done that, they'd all still be arguing to this day, trying to figure out who should be in charge of stars, and of planets, and of moons—and you and I would still be dustballs in the back pocket of God. Socrates said, 'Know thyself,'

A speaker may wish to create a sober atmosphere, a time for personal reflection and commitment. Any attempts to create such a mind-set should be undertaken with the speaking situation and the speaker's purposes in mind.

and he could have added, 'Get off your duff and do something with that knowledge!'"

Sometimes you will want to create a serious, sober atmosphere, a time for personal reflection and commitment on the part of your listeners. At other times, you will wish to loosen them up, to penetrate their defenses, and to share humor and joy with them. Make sure the atmosphere you attempt to create is appropriate to the speaking situation and to your purposes.

Person-Centered vs. Material-Centered Emphasis

Another important variable in one's speaking style is the degree to which the *speaker* is the object of attention. Most speeches are either primarily person centered or primarily material centered. That is, the speech can feature the personality, talents, experience, and wisdom of the speaker as its central engines of persuasion, or it can feature facts, figures, other sorts of evidence, and social values in its emphasis upon the world and society. Since Aristotle wrote his *Rhetoric* in the fourth century B.C., rhetoricians have wondered whether the strategy-conscious speaker should stress self (*ethos* in Greek) or material (*logos*).

Of course, a speaker always is mixing the two, making both self references and material references, yet one often dominates sections of speeches or even entire discourses. Consider, for example, the following two passages from speeches by the same man, Revolutionary War hero Patrick Henry. The first is the opening of his famous "Give Me Liberty or Give Me Death" speech in 1775 to the Virginia Convention:

> No man thinks more highly than I do of the patriotism, as well as the abilities of the very worthy gentlemen who have just addressed the house. But different men see the same subject in different lights; and therefore, I hope it will not be thought disrespectful to those gentlemen, if, entertaining as I do opinions of a character very opposite to theirs, I shall speak forth my sentiments freely and without reserve. This is no time for ceremony. The question before the house is one of awful moment to this century. For my own part, I consider it as nothing less than a question of freedom or slavery; and in proportion to the magnitude of the subject ought to be the freedom of the debate. It is only in this way that we can hope to arrive at truth, and fulfill the great responsibility which we hold to God and our country. Should I keep back my opinions at such a time, through fear of giving offense, I should consider myself as guilty of treason toward my country, and of an act of disloyalty toward the Majesty of Heaven, which I revere above all earthly kings.[7]

Note Henry's use of the first person singular "I," as well as his use of personal verbs ("I do," "I shall speak," "I consider," "I should consider," "I revere"). Attention is directed to Patrick Henry, to his rights, his obligations, his thinking. The *persona* of Henry as a clear-thinking, morally indignant, freely speaking citizen dominates the language and style of this paragraph.

Views of Women's Communication

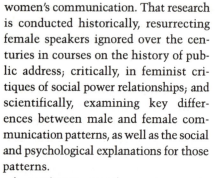

*I*n the wake of the women's and feminist movements of the last three decades has come an increasingly prominent body of research on women's communication. That research is conducted historically, resurrecting female speakers ignored over the centuries in courses on the history of public address; critically, in feminist critiques of social power relationships; and scientifically, examining key differences between male and female communication patterns, as well as the social and psychological explanations for those patterns.

A persistent question not easy to answer, however, is this: How can researchers most usefully conceive of "women's communication"? That is, what theoretical, cultural, or political assumptions do we make when discussing female talk? Several answers have been given—some only implicitly, some explicitly. These have been reviewed by Spitzack and Carter, who argue that five conceptualizations of women's place in communication have been used by researchers:

1. *Womanless communication.* Much research simply leaves women out of the study of communication. Histories of public address often ignore women; women who attain national prominence (for example, Geraldine Ferraro in 1984) are talked about as females with family roles more than as political communicators; social scientists more often than not ignore gender variables.

2. *Great women speakers.* Some study great female orators: the Grimke sisters in the first half of the nineteenth century, Susan B. Anthony in the second half, Eleanor Roosevelt in the first half of the twentieth century, and so on. While valuable, such studies can leave the impressions that (a) few women ever made it in "male" social and political realms, (b) few women had the talent to "rise above" the rest of society's females, and (c) women in general do not compare well when measured by traditional (neoclassical) standards of oratory. "Great

women" studies often are done within traditionally male standards for communicative greatness.

3. *Woman as other.* Male-female differences have been emphasized in much social-scientific research on gender. Among communication researchers, numerous studies have focused on language and paralanguage differences (in phonology, pitch, intonation, vocabulary), "male" and "female" language behavior (aggressiveness vs. passivity, rudeness vs. politeness, self-assertiveness vs. politeness), and variations in standards for communication competence. The problem with such research can be that perceived differences can lead to perceived deficiencies; in comparisons of male and female talk, women often are found to be inferior communicators—with a more limited vocabulary, more unfinished sentences, improper enunciation, superficial word usage, and so on. Too often, men's speech is taken as the norm against which to measure women's speech.

4. *The politics of woman as other.* Some researchers have sought to turn around those negative judgments by discovering positive attributes in female speech patterns. Such politicized research involves seeing women's talk as noncritical, supportive, enhancing of self-worth, maintaining of horizontal rather than up-down power relationships, and aimed at mutual understanding. Another part of this research attempts to remake even the research procedure so that it can suit women's modes of communicating. Such research is based on the assumption that women's talk differs significantly from men's talk and, hence, needs to be studied with different assumptions.

5. *Women as communicators.* A final view attempts to unite the study of male and female talk, recognizing that, while women communicate from often-inferior social positions, they nonetheless are part of the culture, "insiders" empowered to have an impact upon society. Women may communicate differently than men, but they have communicative characteristics that can be understood and valued by the whole.

In Spitzack and Carter's reading of gendered communication research, therefore, politicization is inevitable. The question is not whether there is politically neutral research, but, rather, whether we can study the politicization itself and use that research to understand relationships between men's and women's communication habits. We need to heed their analysis and open up our conversations about women's communicative roles and styles in society.

FOR FURTHER READING

Spitzack, Carole, and Kathryn Carter. "Women in Communication Studies: A Typology for Revision." *Quarterly Journal of Speech* 72 (November 1987): 401–23. See additional readings in reference note 9 of this chapter.

Speaking styles vary greatly. Some are highly propositional, whereas others are narrative.

Propositional vs. Narrative Form

Finally, speaking styles can differ greatly in another way: some styles are highly *propositional*—that is, they involve the presentation of arguments— whereas other styles are highly *narrative*—they are dominated by storytelling. When using a propositional form of speaking, the speaker offers a series of claims or assertions and supports each one with evidence. When using a narrative form, the speaker offers a story that contains a compelling message, or "moral."

Suppose, for example, that you wished to persuade your classmates to make appointments to see their academic advisors regularly. Such a speech, in propositional form, might be developed like this:

I. You ought to see your advisor regularly because he or she can check on your graduation requirements.
    A. Advisors have been trained to understand this school's requirements.
    B. They also probably helped write the departmental requirements for your major, so they know them, too.
II. You ought to see your advisor regularly because that person usually can tell you something about careers in your field.
    A. Most faculty members at this school regularly attend professional meetings and find out what kinds of schools and companies are hiring in your field.

    B.   Most faculty members here have been around a long time and, thus, have seen what kinds of academic backgrounds get their advisees good jobs after school.

III. You ought to see your advisor regularly to check out your own hopes and fears with someone.
    A.   Good advisors help you decide whether you want to continue with a major.
    B.   If you do decide to change majors, they often will help you find another advisor in another department who can work with you.

This same speech could be cast into narrative form as a story about some-one's successes and difficulties:

I.   I thought I could handle my own advising around this school, and that attitude got me into trouble.
    A.   I could read, and I thought I knew what I wanted to take.
    B.   I decided to steer my own course, and here's what happened.

II.   At first, I was happy, taking any course I wanted to.
    A.   I skipped the regular laboratory sciences (chemistry, biology, physics) and took "Science and Society" instead.
    B.   I didn't take statistics to meet my math requirement but instead slipped into remedial algebra.
    C.   I piled up the hours in physical education so I could have a nice grade-point average to show my parents.

III. When I was about half done with my program, however, I realized that:
    A.   I hadn't met about half of the general educational graduation requirements.
    B.   I wanted to go into nursing.

IV. Therefore, I had to go back to freshman- and sophomore-level courses even though I was technically a junior.
    A.   I was back taking the basic science and math courses.
    B.   I was still trying to complete the social science and humanities requirements.

V.   In all, I'm now in my fifth year of college, with at least one more to go.
    A.   My classmates who used advisors have graduated.
    B.   I suggest you follow their examples rather than mine if you want to save time and money.

Most of the time, speakers rely on propositional forms of speaking—most audiences expect them; however, in situations in which a story or a personal illustration allows you to make all of your points, you might wish to use a narrative form. It naturally catches up an audience in a situation—if you are a good storyteller—and usually is easier for people to remember than a bundle of arguments.

Ultimately, selecting an appropriate style is a matter of assessing your self, your audience, the situation or context, and your purposes as a speaker. Thinking through those aspects of the communication model will help you select an appropriate style—formal or informal, serious or humorous, person centered or material centered, gender neutral, and propositional or narrative in form.

Rhetorical Strategies

By selecting an appropriate speaking style, you can not only help listeners comprehend and retain what you are saying, but also control the general atmosphere. This section will deal more specifically with **rhetorical strategies**—the particular words you choose to increase the comprehensibility and impact of your speeches.

There are countless rhetorical strategies available to speakers. We will look at four of the most common and discuss ways they are used by effective speakers. These categories are *definition, restatement, imagery,* and *metaphor.*

Definition

In most speaking situations, audience members need fundamental definitions of concepts. You cannot expect them to understand ideas if the words are unfamiliar or if you are using words in a manner different from their generally accepted definition. Eight types of definitions are useful to speakers.

Defining from Dictionaries.   A dictionary definition is a **reportive definition,** which indicates how people in general use a word. Dictionary definitions categorize an object or concept and specify its characteristics: "An orange is a *fruit* (category) which is *round, orange* in color, and a member of the *citrus family* (characteristics)." Dictionary definitions sometimes help you learn an unfamiliar or technical word, but they are seldom helpful to speakers because they tend to describe meanings in fairly general terms. Thus, dictionary definitions normally must be followed by other kinds of definitions that more precisely clarify a concept.

Defining in Your Own Words.   Occasionally a word has so many meanings that speakers have to indicate which one they wish to use. In that case, you must use a **stipulative definition**—one that stipulates the way you will use a word: "By 'speech' I mean the act of offering a series of ideas and arguments to a group of listeners in a face-to-face situation." Such a definition orients the audience to your subject matter. Furthermore, if you think an audience respects an authority or expert, you can use that person's stipulative definition (an **authoritative definition**): "Hyman Smith, president of this school, defines a 'liberal arts education' as one in which students are taught not merely technical operations and job-related skills but also ways of thinking and reasoning. Today, I want to explore that definition and what it means to you in your four years here."

Defining Negatively.   Further clarity can be added by telling an audience how you are *not* going to use a term or concept—by using a **negative definition.** Along with the stipulative definition of speech, for example, one could say: "By 'speech' I do not mean to refer to the production of the 'correct' sounds and words of the English language, even though that is a common meaning of the word; rather, I will mean . . ." Defining negatively can clear away possible misconceptions. Using a negative definition along with a stipulative definition is a technique that is especially useful when you are trying to treat a familiar concept in a new or different way.

Defining from Origins.   Sometimes you can reinforce a series of feelings or attitudes you wish audience members to have about a concept by telling them where the word came from: " 'Sincere' comes from two Latin words: *sine*, meaning 'without,' and *ceres*, meaning 'wax.' In early Rome, a superior statue was one in which the artisan did not have to cover his mistakes by putting wax into flaws. That statue was said to be *sine ceres*—'without wax.' Today, the term 'a sincere person' carries some of that same meaning." This is called an **etymological definition** when you trace a word's meaning back into its original language. It is termed a **genetic definition** when you explain where the idea rather than the word comes from. You could, for instance, explain the American concept of freedom of speech by looking at important discussions of that idea in eighteenth-century England, and then showing how the American doctrine took its shape from our ancestors' British experiences. Defining from original sources, either of the word or of the idea, gives an audience a sense of continuity and, at times, explains certain nuances of meaning we cannot explain in any other way.

Defining by Examples.   Particularly if a notion is unfamiliar or technical, one of the best ways to define is by an **exemplar definition,** which simply points to a familiar example: "Each day, most of you stroll past Old Capitol on your way to classes. That building is a perfect example of what I want to talk about today—Georgian architecture." Be careful to pick only defining examples that your audience members will be familiar with.

Defining by Context.   You also can define a word or concept by putting it in its usual context through a **contextual definition.** This can be done verbally, as when a speaker says, "The difference between the words 'imply' and 'infer' is best understood in this way: The person generating a message *implies* a meaning; a listener *infers* an interpretation. Thus, *you* imply a certain idea or feeling in what you say, while *I* draw inferences about what you meant." A contextual definition also can go beyond such verbal descriptions, and, like a definition that uses examples, can point to a "real" context: "While there are many possible meanings of the word 'revolution,' today I want to use it to describe the events that produced the American Revolution." You then would go on to specify those events. Defining by context gives an audience a sense of meaningfulness and is a good tactic for making certain kinds of concepts concrete.

Defining by Analogy.   Still another means for making technical or abstract notions easier to understand is the **analogical definition.** An analogy compares a process or event that is unfamiliar or unknown with something that is familiar or known:

Remember when you were a kid and you got into shouting matches with other kids? You'd begin with an "am, too/are not" argument: "I'm a better baseball player than you." "You are not." "Am, too." "Are not." "Am too." Then you would up the ante by making it an "are, too/are not" match. "Well, your parents aren't as rich as mine." "They are, too!" "Are not." "Are, too." "Are not." And, finally, the argument would reach its peak with an "-ist" section: "Yeah, well, Methodists aren't real Christians." "They are, too—you're just a Communist." "Am not—I'm a Congregationalist." Those children's shouting matches are analogous to what we see in our country today. We are playing games very much like we did when we were kids, arguing over people's places in society. And today, as well, the strongest arguments in those struggles are "-ist" arguments, centered on such words as "racist," "sexist," "Americanist," "Communist," "Rightist," and "ageist." I want to discuss the destructive power of "-ist" accusations, and . . .

By relying on a familiar experience or process, the analogical definition can make the new or abstract much easier to grasp. Just make sure the analogy fits.

Defining by Describing Operations.   Some words or concepts are best defined by reviewing the operations or procedures used in making or measuring something—by offering an **operational definition.** Scientists do this often so they can translate abstract verbal concepts into observable or measurable things. Thus, a social scientist is most comfortable when defining "intelligence" not abstractly but operationally: " 'Intelligence quotient' is a person's performance on the Wechsler-Bellevue Intelligence Test compared with the performance of other members of the population." Along with exemplar and analogical definitions, operational definitions are especially good for making an audience "see" an idea or process.

Restatement

If accuracy and simplicity were your only criteria as a speaker wishing to convey clear meanings, messages might resemble a famous World War II bulletin: "Sighted sub, sank same." Because you are working face-to-face with listeners in oral, not written, language, however, another criterion is important. *Restatement* is intentional repetition of two kinds: (1) *rephrasing* of ideas or concepts in more than one set of words or sentences and (2) *reiteration* of ideas or concepts from more than one point of view. Because words literally disappear into the atmosphere as soon as you speak them, as an oral communicator you do not have the writer's advantage when transmitting ideas to others. Instead, you must rely heavily on rephrasing and reiteration.

Rephrasing.   The effect of skillful rephrasing to clarify a message and make it more specific can be seen in the following passage from John F. Kennedy's inaugural address:

John F. Kennedy's inaugural address is an example of the effect of skillful rephrasing to clarify a message and to make it more specific.

Let the word go forth from this time and place, to friend and foe alike, that the torch has been passed to a new generation of Americans—born in this century, tempered by war, disciplined by a hard and bitter peace, proud of our ancient heritage—and unwilling to witness or permit the slow undoing of those human rights to which this nation has always been committed, and to which we are committed today at home and around the world.

Let every nation know, whether it wishes us well or ill, that we shall pay any price, bear any burden, meet any hardship, support any friend, oppose any foe to assume the survival and the success of liberty.[10]

Reiteration.   Reiterating an idea from a number of perspectives can usually be done by reforming the elements that make it up or by redefining the basic concept. You can see this principle of reiteration at work in the following excerpt from a student speech. Note how the speaker defined and redefined "political image" in a variety of ways, thereby providing metaphorical, psychological, and sociological perspectives:

A "politician's image" is really a set of characteristics attributed to that politician by an electorate [*formal perspective*]. A political image, like any image which comes off a mirror, is made up of attributes which reflect the audience's concerns [*metaphorical perspective*]. An image is composed of bits and pieces of information and feelings which an audience brings to a politician [*psycho-*

logical perspective], and therefore it represents judgments made by the electorate on the bases of a great many different verbal and nonverbal acts a politician has engaged in [*sociological perspective*]. Therefore, if you think of a political image only in terms of manipulation, you are looking only at the mirror. Step back and examine the beholder, too, and you will find ways of discovering what a "good" image is for a politician.

If carefully handled, restatement in the form of rephrasing or reiteration can help you clarify your ideas and can help your listeners remember them more readily. Be careful of mindless repetition however; too many restatements, especially of ideas already clear to any alert member of your audience, are boring.

Imagery

We receive impressions of the world through the sensations of sight, smell, hearing, taste, and touch. If your listeners are to experience the object or state of affairs you are describing, you must appeal to their senses; however, you cannot punch them in the nose, spray exotic perfume for them to smell, or let them taste foods that are not present. The primary senses through which you can reach your listeners *directly* are the visual and the auditory: they can see you, your movements, your facial expressions, and objects you use as visual aids, and they can hear what you say.

Despite this limitation, however, you can *indirectly* stimulate all of their senses by using language that has the power to produce imagined sensations or that causes them to recall images they have previously experienced. Through image-evoking language, you can help your listeners create many of the sensory pictures and events that you have experienced. Through vivid words, you can project the desired image swiftly into the mind's eye of your listeners. The language of imagery is divided into seven classes, or types, each related to the particular sensation that it seeks to evoke:

1. Visual *(sight)*
2. Auditory *(hearing)*
3. Gustatory *(taste)*
4. Olfactory *(smell)*
5. Tactual *(touch)*
   a. Texture and shape
   b. Pressure
   c. Heat and cold
6. Kinesthetic *(muscle strain)*
7. Organic *(internal sensations)*

Visual Imagery.   Try to make your audience "see" the objects or situations you are describing. Mention *size, shape, color,* and *movement.* Recount events in vivid visual language. For example, in a time of cold war between the United States and Russia, General of the Army Douglas MacArthur knew he had to steel the cadets of the United States Military Academy for their uncertain future. His central theme—"duty, honor, and country"—was a refrain through the speech. To give that theme life, however, General MacArthur relied on a variety of visual images, as well as on many of the other types of imagery we shall discuss. Note particularly his stress on images of size, shape, color, and movement:

> In twenty campaigns, on a hundred battlefields, around a thousand campfires, I have witnessed that enduring fortitude, that patriotic self-abnegation, and that invincible determination which have carved his statue in the hearts of his people.
>
> From one end of the world to the other, he has drained deep the chalice of courage. As I listened to those songs in memory's eye I could see those staggering columns of the First World War, bending under soggy packs on many a weary march, from dripping dusk to drizzly dawn, slogging ankle deep through mire of shell-pocked roads; to form grimly for the attack, blue-lipped, covered with sludge and mud, chilled by the wind and rain, driving home to their objective, and for many, to the judgment seat of God.
>
> . . . Always for them: Duty, honor, country. Always their blood, and sweat and tears, as they saw the way and the light. And twenty years after, on the other side of the globe, again the filth of dirty foxholes, the stench of ghostly trenches, the slime of dripping dugouts, those boiling suns of relentless heat, those torrential rains of devastating storms, the loneliness and utter desolation of jungle trails, the bitterness of long separation of those they loved and cherished, the deadly pestilence of tropical disease, the horror of stricken areas of war.
>
> Their resolute and determined defense, their swift and sure attack, their indomitable purpose, their complete and decisive victory, always through the bloody haze of their last reverberating shot, the vision of gaunt, ghastly men, reverently following your password of duty, honor, country.[11]

Auditory Imagery.   To create auditory imagery, use words that help your listeners "hear" what you are describing. Auditory imagery may be used to project an audience into a scene. Author Tom Wolfe, for example, described a demolition derby by recounting the chant of the crowd as it joined in the

---

THE TYPES OF IMAGERY

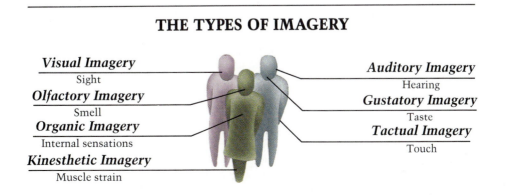

Visual Imagery
Sight

Olfactory Imagery
Smell

Organic Imagery
Internal sensations

Kinesthetic Imagery
Muscle strain

Auditory Imagery
Hearing

Gustatory Imagery
Taste

Tactual Imagery
Touch

countdown, the explosion of sound as two dozen cars started off in second gear, and finally "the unmistakable tympany of automobiles colliding and cheap-gauge sheet metal buckling."[12]

Gustatory Imagery.   Sometimes you may even be able to help your audience "taste" what you are describing. Mention its saltiness, sweetness, sourness, or spiciness. Remember that foods have texture as well as taste. In a speech demonstrating how to make granola, you might mention the mealiness of rolled oats, the firmness of whole-grain wheat and flax seeds, and the stringiness of coconut. Such descriptions allow your audience to make positive or negative judgments about the experience.

Olfactory Imagery.   Help your audience "smell" the odors connected with the situation you describe. Do this not only by mentioning the odor itself but also by describing the object that has the odor or by comparing it with more familiar ones. If you grew up in the country, think of the confusion of contrasting smells on a spring day—the fragrance of lilacs or cherry blossoms on the breeze, mingled with the odor of decaying manure as the barn is cleaned out. If you are a city person, what about the variety of smells that assault your nose as you stroll past a row of ethnic restaurants: Greek, Italian, East Indian, and Mexican?

Tactual Imagery.   Tactual imagery is based on the various types of sensation that we get through physical contact with objects. In particular, it gives us sensations of texture and shape, pressure, and heat or cold.

- *Texture and shape.* Let your listeners "feel" how rough or smooth; dry or wet; or sharp, slimy, or sticky a thing is.
- *Pressure.* Let them "sense" the pressure of physical force on their bodies: the weight of a heavy laundry bag, the pinch of jogging shoes that are too tight, the blast of a high wind on their faces.
- *Heat or cold.* Sensations of heat or cold are aroused by what is sometimes called *thermal imagery.*

Review the excerpt from Douglas MacArthur's speech for some vivid examples of all of these types of tactual imagery.

Kinesthetic Imagery.   Kinesthetic imagery describes the sensations associated with muscle strain and neuromuscular movement. Phrase your speech on the agonies and joys of jogging in such a way that your listeners "feel" for themselves the muscle cramps, the constricted chest, the struggle for air—and the magical serenity of getting a second wind and thinking they will be able to "fly like this forever."

Organic Imagery.   Hunger, dizziness, nausea—these are a few of the feelings organic imagery calls forth. There are times when an image is not complete without the inclusion of specific details likely to evoke these inner feelings. The sensation of dizziness as you struggled through the rarefied mountain air to reach the summit is one example. Another is the way the bottom dropped out of your stomach when the small plane dropped sharply, then righted itself. Be careful, however, not to offend your audience by overdoing this type of imagery. Develop the sensitivity required to measure the detail necessary for creating vividness without making the resultant image gruesome, disgusting, or grotesque.

Combinations of Imagery. The seven types of imagery we have considered—*visual, auditory, gustatory, olfactory, tactual, kinesthetic,* and *organic*—may be referred to as "doorways to the mind."[13] They open the audience to new levels of awareness in understanding and believing speakers and acting on their messages. Because people differ in their degrees of sensitivity to different types of imagery, you should try to build into your messages as many appeals to their senses through these perceptual "doorways" as possible.

In the following example, note how the speaker combined various sensory appeals to arouse listener interest and reaction:

> The strangler struck in Donora, Pennsylvania, in October of 1948. A thick fog billowed through the streets enveloping everything in thick sheets of dirty moisture and a greasy black coating. As Tuesday faded into Saturday, the fumes from the big steel mills shrouded the outlines of the landscape. One could barely see across the narrow streets. Traffic stopped. Men lost their way returning from the mills. Walking through the streets, even for a few moments, caused eyes to water and burn. The thick fumes grabbed at the throat and created a choking sensation. The air acquired a sickening bittersweet smell, nearly a taste. Death was in the air.[14]

In this example, college student Charles Schaillol used vivid, descriptive phrases to affect the senses of his listeners: *visual*—"thick sheets of dirty moisture"; *organic*—"eyes to water and burn"; *olfactory, gustory*—"sickening bittersweet smell, nearly a taste."

To be effective, such illustrations must appear plausible; the language must convey an impression that what is being described did or could happen in the way the speaker chose to relate it. The speaker who described the "strangler" that struck Donora offered a plausible account of the event. More importantly, he did so in a fashion that aroused feelings. Audiences would not be as likely to share the experience if the speaker had simply said, "Air pollution was the cause of death in Donora."

Metaphor

The images created by appealing to the various senses are often the result of using a *metaphor*—a comparison of two dissimilar things. Charles Schaillol's "fog . . . thick sheets" is one example of a metaphor used to illuminate the image he wished to create of the fog's effect. To be successful, as Michael Osborn notes, the metaphor should "result in an intuitive flash of recognition that surprises or fascinates the hearer."[15] Furthermore, good metaphors should extend our knowledge or increase our awareness of a person, object, or event. A reference to a table's "legs" may illuminate the object, but it lacks fascination. When they are fresh or vivid, metaphors can be powerful aids in evoking feelings (for example, "balanced on four obese toothpicks, the antique table swayed under the heavy load").

While vividness and freshness can make metaphors highly appealing to audiences, on other occasions you will want to use metaphors drawn from everyday experiences. In almost every public speech he delivered, for example, Martin Luther King, Jr., appealed to our experiences of light and darkness, as he did in the following quotation:

> With this faith in the future, with this determined struggle, we will be able to emerge from the bleak and desolate midnight of man's inhumanity to man, into the bright and glittering daybreak of freedom and justice.[16]

This simple light-dark metaphor was important to King's thinking and speechmaking because it allowed him to suggest (1) sharp contrasts between inhumanity and freedom and (2) the inevitability of social progress (as "daybreak" always follows "midnight"). In other words, the metaphor worked—it communicated King's beliefs about justice and injustice and urged his followers to act.

One of the most effective metaphors in recent years, however, was the one Jesse Jackson used at both the 1984 and the 1988 Democratic National Conventions. The power of an everyday object—here, a quilt—to organize ideas and appeals is demonstrated in the following quotation from his 1988 address:

> America's not a blanket woven from one thread, one color, one cloth. When I was a child, growing up in Greenville, S.C., and grandmother could not afford a blanket, she didn't complain and we did not freeze. Instead, she took pieces of old cloth—patches, wool, silk, gabardine . . .—barely good enough to wipe off your shoes with.
>
> But they didn't stay that way very long. With sturdy hands and a strong cord, she sewed them together into a quilt, a thing of beauty and power and culture.
>
> Now, Democrats, we must build such a quilt. Farmers, you seek fair prices and you are right, but you cannot stand alone. Your patch is not big enough. Workers, you fight for fair wages. You are right. But your patch, labor, is not big enough. Women, you seek comparable worth and pay equity. You are right. But your patch is not big enough. Women, mothers, who seek Head Start and day care and pre-natal care on the front side of life, rather than jail care and welfare on the back side of life, you're right, but your patch is not big enough.
>
> Students, you seek scholarships. You are right. But your patch is not big enough. Blacks and Hispanics, when we fight for civil rights, we are right, but our patch is not big enough. Gays and lesbians, when you fight against discrimination and [for] a cure for AIDS, you are right, but your patch is not big enough. Conservatives and progressives, when you fight for what you believe, right-wing, left-wing, hawk, dove—you are right, from your point of view, but your point of view is not enough.

But don't despair. Be as wise as my grandmama. Pool the patches and the pieces together, bound by a common thread. When we form a great quilt of unity and common ground we'll have the power to bring about health care and housing and jobs and education and hope to our nation.

We the people can win.[17]

Metaphors of unity always are present in times of division and crisis, but few have been more powerful than this homely image from the mouth of America's premier orator.

In summary, words are not neutral conduits for thought. Words not only reflect the "real" world outside your mind, but they also, as rhetorical critic Kenneth Burke suggests, help *shape* our perceptions of people, events, social contexts, and the world. It is clear that language has a potent effect on people's willingness to believe, to feel, and to act.

Sample Speech

William Faulkner (1897–1962) presented the following speech on December 10, 1950, in accepting the Nobel Prize for Literature. As he had no reputation as a lecturer, the public might well have expected a lesser speech filled with the kind of pessimism so characteristic of his novels. Instead, he greeted his listeners with a stirring challenge to improve humankind.

Notice in particular Mr. Faulkner's use of language. Although known for the tortured sentences of his novels, he expressed his ideas clearly and simply. His tone was closer to a written rather than an oral language, yet his use of organic imagery and powerful metaphors kept the speech alive. The atmosphere was generally serious, befitting the occasion. While he relied primarily on male pronouns, he at least opened his talk with a reference to "the young man or woman writing today," otherwise following the gender conventions of the early 1950s. Also, while one might expect a Nobel Prize winner to offer a person-centered emphasis, Mr. Faulkner did just the opposite, stressing his craft—writing—and what audience members must be committed to in order to practice that craft; this material emphasis led naturally to an essentially propositional rather than narrative form. Overall, William Faulkner offered in 1950 a speech that meets even today's oral language requirements and challenges.

On Accepting the
Nobel Prize for Literature
William Faulkner

I feel that this award was not made to me as a man, but to my work—a life's work in the agony and sweat of the human spirit, not for glory and least of all for profit, but to create out of the materials of the human spirit something which did not exist before. So this award is only mine in trust. It will not be difficult to find a dedication for the money part of it commensurate with the purpose and significance of its origin. But I would like to do the same with the acclaim too, by using this moment as a pinnacle from which I might be listened to by the young men and women already dedicated to the same anguish and travail, among whom is already that one who will some day stand here where I am standing. /1

Our tragedy today is a general and universal physical fear so long sustained by now that we can even bear it. There are no longer problems of the spirit. There is only the question: When will I be blown up? Because of this, the young man or woman writing today has forgotten the problems of the human heart in conflict with itself which alone can make good writing because only that is worth writing about, worth the agony and the sweat. /2

He must learn them again. He must teach himself that the basest of all things is to be afraid; and, teaching himself that, forget it forever, leaving no room in his workshop for anything but the old verities and truths of the heart, the old universal truths lacking which any story is ephemeral and doomed—love and honor and pity and pride and compassion and sacrifice. Until he does so, he labors under a curse. He writes not of love but of lust, of defeats in which nobody loses anything of value, of victories without hope and, worst of all, without pity or compassion. His griefs grieve on no universal bones, leaving no scars. He writes not of the heart but of the glands. /3

Until he relearns these things, he will write as though he stood among and watched the end of man. I decline to accept the end of man. It is easy enough to say that man is immortal simply because he will endure: that when the last ding-dong of doom has clanged and faded from the last worthless rock hanging tideless in the last red and dying evening, that even then there will still be one more sound: that of his puny inexhaustible voice, still talking. I refuse to accept this. I believe that man will not merely endure: he will prevail. He is immortal, not because he alone among creatures has an inexhaustible voice, but because he has a soul, a spirit capable of compassion and sacrifice and endurance. The poet's, the writer's, duty is to write about these things. It is his privilege to help man endure by lifting his heart, by reminding him of the courage and honor and hope and pride and compassion and pity and sacrifice which have been the glory of his past. The poet's voice need not merely be the record of man, it can be one of the props, the pillars to help him endure and prevail.[18] /4

Chapter Summary

Successful speeches generally are characterized by *accurate, simple, coherent, properly intense*, and *appropriate* language choices. In selecting a speaking style appropriate to you, the occasion, your subject matter, and the audience, you must make decisions about *written vs. oral language*, a *serious vs. humorous atmosphere*, a *person-centered vs. material-centered emphasis, gendered vs. gender-neutral nouns and pronouns*, and *propositional vs. narrative forms of presentation*. As far as your rhetorical strategies are concerned, consider: (1) *definition* (in your own words, negatively, from original sources, by examples, by context, by analogy, by describing operations), (2) *restatement* (both rephrasing and reiteration), (3) *imagery* (visual, auditory, gustatory, olfactory, tactual, kinesthetic, and organic), and (4) *metaphor*. Language choices, and the resulting speaking styles, form speakers' most crucial channels of substantive communication.

Reference Notes

1. These dimensions are also called the *content* and *relationship* dimensions of language by Simons and by Watzlawick, Beavin, and Jackson. See Herbert W. Simons, *Persuasion: Understanding, Practice, and Analysis*, 2nd ed. (New York: Random House, Inc., 1986), 78, working from P. Watzlawick, H. J. Beavin, and D. D. Jackson, *Pragmatics of Human Communication: A Study of Interaction Patterns, Pathologies and Paradoxes* (New York: W. W. Norton & Co., Inc., 1967).

2. For a discussion of the idea of *signature*, see Anthony Hillbruner, "Archetype and Signature: Nixon and the 1973 Inaugural," *Central States Speech Journal* 25 (Fall 1984): 169–81.

3. For more extended treatments of this subject, see Doris B. Garey, *Putting Words in Their Places* (Glenview, IL: Scott, Foresman and Company, 1957); and Roger Brown, *Words and Things* (Glenview, IL: Scott, Foresman and Company, 1968).

4. Quoted in John R. Pelsma, *Essentials of Speech* (New York: Crowell, Collier, and Macmillan, 1934), 193.

5. John Waite Bowers, "Language and Argument," in *Perspectives on Argumentation*, ed. G. R. Miller and T. R. Nilsen (Glenview, IL: Scott, Foresman and Company, 1966), esp. pp. 168–72.

6. For a summary of several technical studies distinguishing between oral and written styles and for a discussion of sixteen characteristics of oral style, see John F. Wilson and Carroll C. Arnold, *Public Speaking as a Liberal Art*, 5th ed. (Boston: Allyn and Bacon, Inc., 1983), 227–29. For a theory of what makes orality wholly different from writing as a communication medium, see Walter J. Ong, *Orality and Literacy*, New Accents Series (London: Methuen, Inc., 1982).

7. Patrick Henry, "Give Me Liberty or Give Me Death," (March 23, 1775), as reprinted in *The World's Best Orations: From the Earliest Period to the Present Time*, ed. David J. Brewer (St. Louis: Ferd. P. Kaiser, 1899), VII, 2475.

8. Patrick Henry, " 'We the People' or 'We the States,' " (June 4, 1788), as reprinted in Brewer, VII, 2479.

9. Women's and feminist studies have exploded upon the scene in communication studies. For deep background, see Barbara and Gene Eakins, *Sex Differences in Human Communication* (Boston: Houghton Mifflin Co., 1978); Barrie Thorne and Nancy Henley, eds., *Language and Sex: Difference and Dominance* (Rawley, MA: Newbury House, 1975); and Robin Lakoff, *Language and Women's Place* (New York: Harper & Row Pubs., Inc., 1975). For more current overviews, see H. M. Hacker, "Blabbermouths and Clams: Sex Differences in Self-disclosure in Same-Sex and Cross-Sex Friendship Dyads," *Psychology of Women Quarterly* 5 (1981): 385–401; Judith C. Pearson, *Gender and Communication* (Dubuque, IA: Wm. C. Brown, Publishers, 1985); Barbara Bate, *Communication and the Sexes* (New York: Harper & Row Pubs., Inc., 1987); Lea P. Stewart, Pamela J. Cooper, and Sheryl A. Friedly, *Communication Between the Sexes: Sex Differences and Sex-Role Stereotypes* (Scottsdale, AZ: Gorsuch Scarisbrick Pubs.,

1986); and Carole Spitzack and Kathryn Carter, "Women in Communication Studies: A Typology for Revision," *Quarterly Journal of Speech* 73 (November 1987): 401–23.

10. *Public Papers of the Presidents of the United States: John F. Kennedy* (Washington, DC: U.S. Government Printing Office, 1961).

11. Douglas MacArthur, "Duty, Honor and Country," in *The Dolphin Book of Speeches*, ed. George W. Hibbitt (New York: Doubleday & Company, Inc., 1965).

12. Thomas K. Wolfe, Jr., *The Kandy-Kolored Tangerine-Flake Streamline Baby* (New York: New York Herald Tribune, Inc., 1963).

13. Victor Alvin Ketcham, "The Seven Doorways to the Mind," in *Business Speeches by Business Men*, William P. Sandford and W. Hayes Yeager, eds. (New York: McGraw-Hill Book Company, 1930).

14. Charles Schaillol, "The Strangler," *Winning Orations*.

15. Michael Osborn, *Orientations to Rhetorical Style* (Chicago: Science Research Associates, 1976), 10.

16. Martin Luther King, Jr., "Love, Law and Civil Disobedience," 1961.

17. Jesse Jackson, "Common Ground and Common Sense," *Vital Speeches of the Day* 54 (August 15, 1988).

18. William Faulkner, "On Accepting the Nobel Prize for Literature," in *The Faulkner Reader*, (New York: Random House. Inc.. 1954).

Key Terms

encoding	*negative definition*
denotations	*etymological definition*
connotations	*genetic definition*
speaking style	*exemplar definition*
signposts	*contextual definition*
coherence	*analogical definition*
preliminary summaries	*operational definition*
final summaries	*visual imagery*
connectives	*auditory imagery*
language intensity	*gustatory imagery*
tone	*olfactory imagery*
rhetorical strategies	*tactual imagery*
reportive definition	*kinesthetic imagery*
stipulative definition	*organic imagery*
authoritative definition	*metaphor*

Functions of Visual Aids

Visual materials enhance your presentation in two ways: (1) th
comprehension and memory and (2) they add persuasive i
message.

Comprehension and Memory

The truth of the old saying "A picture is worth a thousand v
upon whether the picture adds information that is more ea
visually than aurally. Visual research has demonstrated that b
cially, make statistical information more accessible to an a
larly, simple drawings enhance recall, and charts and such
visuals as photographs help listeners process and retain
accompanying a story being read aloud to children have sig
on listener recall and comprehension.[3] Thus, visuals can
value if your purpose is to inform or teach an audience.

Persuasiveness

In the process of enhancing comprehension and memory, v
you time in persuasive situations. Visuals can heighten the p
of your ideas. Lawyers, for example, have taken advantage
effects that accompany the visual evidence of injuries or cr
elicit a favorable response from juries. Some lawyers are exp
the use of video technology to create dramatic portrayals
condition of a road in an involuntary manslaughter case or a
sense of caring in a custody battle—in order to influence
Undeniably, your credibility as a speaker, as well as the c
message, is positively affected by the effective use of appr
Visual materials satisfy listeners' "show-me" attitude; in
provide a crucial means of meeting listener expectations.[5]

Types of Visual Aids

Visual materials can be divided into two broad classes: ac
symbolic representations of objects. As we discuss both bro
will examine specific tips on how you can use them to supp
presentation of ideas.

Actual Objects

The objects you bring to a presentation, including your o
discussed under two headings: animate objects and inanin

Problems and Probes

1. Make a list of ten neutral words or expressions. Then for each word in this list find (a) an attitudinally weighted synonym that would cause listeners to react favorably toward the object or idea mentioned and (b) an evaluative synonym that would cause them to react unfavorably toward the same object or idea. (Example: neutral word—"old"; complimentary synonym—"mellow"; uncomplimentary synonym—"senile.")

2. Using varied and vivid imagery, prepare a written description of one of the following:

Sailboats on a lake at sunset
Goldfish swimming in a bowl
Traffic at a busy intersection
Sitting in the bleachers at a football game in 15-degree weather
The hors d'oeuvre table at an expensive restaurant
The city dump
A symphony concert

Communication Activities

1. Prepare a description of a process with which you are familiar, such as how to ride a bicycle, how to operate a machine, how to prepare a meal, or another process of your choice. Prepare and deliver a speech for each of the following audiences: (a) a group of first-graders, (b) your peers, (c) a group of college graduates. How does your choice of language differ for each group? How do your word choice, sentence structure, and overall approach differ? For example, do you need to repeat more for younger audiences? Does your language need to be more vivid?

2. Write a three-to-four-minute speech narrating your feelings about a particular location. For instance, you might describe the town in which you grew up, a building you have always dreamed of seeing, or a place made famous by one of your favorite authors. Present the speech from manuscript. Carefully revise your manuscript to take advantage of the suggestions made in this chapter. In particular, make generous use of varied and vivid imagery, appropriate words with connotative effect, and clear and graceful connective phrases.

3. Describe orally to your class a mundane object, such as a paper clip, brick, or pen, and the purposes to which it might be put. Use vivid imagery in describing this object to help your audience visualize it.

CHAPTER THIRTEEN

Using Visual Aids in a Spee

*T*elevision, film, transparencies, VCRs and videotape and opaque projectors, billboards, banners trailing fro tables with samples from a store's "today only" sale—t visual communication media. Ours is a visual age se United States is undoubtedly the most visually oriente Entire companies—from such famous ones as the ma studios down to small-town graphics production sh ments—exist because of our willingness to pay for communication.

The public speaker, of course, always has been in cation business, at least partially. Your physical prese ence as a public speaker is a powerful visual statemer visual aids makes visual communication an essentia munication transaction; from objects a second grade "show and tell" to the flipcharts sales trainers use, s communication messages when they use visual aids.

Research on visual media, learning, and attitude ch thing about the impact of visual aids on audiences.[1] still is a matter of veteran speakers' passing on their In this chapter, we will mix advice from social-scient dom from old pros. First, we will deal with the gene aids; then we will examine various types and look a to use them to greatest effect.

Animate Objects.   Live animals or plants can, with appropriate discretion, be brought into a speaking situation. If you are demonstrating the "care and feeding of laboratory mice," bringing one or two in a cage may be useful in clarifying points of your speech. Describing the differences between two varieties of plants may be easier if you use real plants; however, you might be stretching your luck a bit by bringing a real horse into class and showing how one is saddled. Although demonstrating with animate objects is a useful way of clarifying a procedure, choose the objects carefully. Common sense about what is possible and in good taste will help make such visuals work for you rather than against you.

As is true of other visuals, you will want to maximize audience attention on your commentary *about* the actual object, rather than allowing the audience to become absorbed *by* the object. A registered Persian cat may be perfect for a speech illustrating what judges look for in cat shows, but if it gets loose or is passed around the class, your message may be lost in the process. Keeping the animal firmly in your possession will help focus attention on your message.

Speeches on yoga positions, various ways of loosening up before running, ballet steps, or tennis strokes gain concreteness and vitality from speakers who illustrate them physically. The entire speech need not be devoted to a "physical" subject in order to use your body effectively in illustrating action, but plan those actions carefully. A yoga position may be well executed, but it will not help if you are on the floor and the audience members in the back rows cannot see you (use the top of a sturdy table). Slow the tempo so the audience can see discrete movements; swinging a tennis racket quickly will not help the audience understand correct form. One advantage of visual action is that you can control the audience's attention to your demonstration.

Inanimate Objects.   Demonstrations can often be enhanced by the presence of the actual inanimate object being discussed. You can help your audience understand how to string a tennis racket by bringing one in to illustrate the process. You can show the best means of repairing rust holes in a car more easily if you have samples of the work required in the separate stages. As in television cooking shows, you do not have the time to do the actual work. By preparing samples before the presentation, you save time and illustrate what must be done.

As noted, you will want to keep audience attention focused on the message. Moving objects to "center stage" and then removing them helps you control the flow of attention from the object to your narrative. Keeping the object between you and the audience, as much as possible, also allows greater visual contact. If you stand in front of the object or to the side, you run the risk of blocking the audience's view.

Symbolic Representations

When you cannot bring the actual objects in or use your own movement to clarify your meaning, you can resort to using symbolic representations of the objects or concepts you discuss. These representations may be relatively *concrete*, as in the use of photographs, slides, films, or videotapes. *Abstract* drawings, graphs, charts, and models can also depict the objects or concepts.

Concrete Representations.   *Photographs* can give the audience a visual sense of what you are talking about. You can illustrate flood damage by using photos of ravaged homes and land, for instance, or depict the beauty of an area threatened by a new dam. One problem with photographs is that audiences may not be able to see what is being shown as you hold up a small picture. If you need to pass pictures around, try to limit the number and hand out each one after discussing the point that the photo helps you make. This will minimize audience distraction as photos are passed from one person to another. Enlarging a small photograph so that people can see it more easily also will help you control audience attention.

Slides (35-mm transparencies) also allow you to depict color, shape, texture, and relationships. If you are presenting a travelogue, slides are virtually a necessity in discussing buildings and landscape. A speech on the days of the steam engines can be more interesting and informative if you obtain appropriate slides of various machines in operation. The persuasive impact of a speech against the construction of a dam can be enhanced by slides depicting the white water that will be destroyed. Slides of the work of famous artists enable you to illustrate differences in their work. Slides require some familiarity with projection equipment, however, as well as some forethought about how to set up the presentation so that people can see. Attention to small, seemingly inconsequential details makes a major difference in how smoothly the presentation goes. Do you know how to change the projection lamp (and did you bring a spare bulb just in case)? Will you need an extension cord, or will the projector's cord reach the outlet? Do you know how to remove a jammed slide? If you operate on the assumption that "whatever can go wrong, will," you will be prepared for most circumstances.

Videotapes and *films* can illustrate the point you want to make. For example, segments from current sitcoms can dramatically illustrate your claim that child stars are forced into adult roles. A tape of two or three political ads can help you illustrate the packaging of a candidate. Again, familiarity with the operation of a videocassette recorder and monitor helps ensure a smooth presentation, and, if you are using films, be sure you can thread the machine and change a projection lamp. Too often, speakers bring films with them, assuming that a projector and technician will be provided, only to find that no one can get the machine running properly. Such delays increase

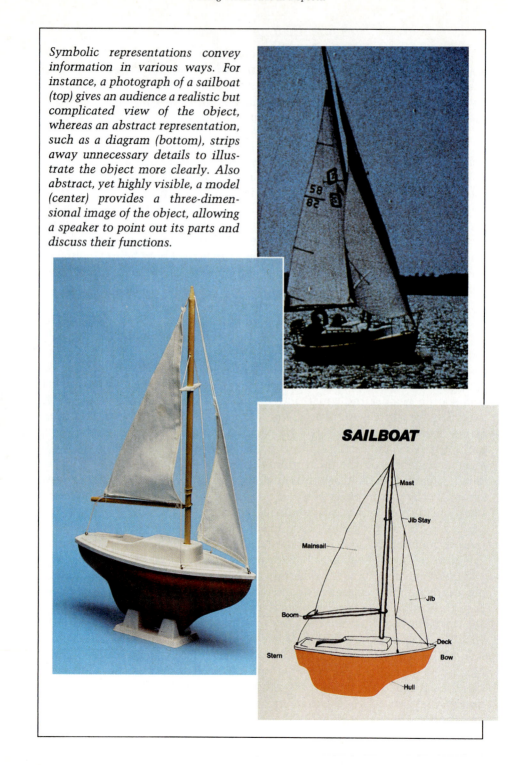

Symbolic representations convey information in various ways. For instance, a photograph of a sailboat (top) gives an audience a realistic but complicated view of the object, whereas an abstract representation, such as a diagram (bottom), strips away unnecessary details to illustrate the object more clearly. Also abstract, yet highly visible, a model (center) provides a three-dimensional image of the object, allowing a speaker to point out its parts and discuss their functions.

SAILBOAT

Mast

Jib Stay

Mainsail

Jib

Boom

Deck

Stern

Bow

Hull

your nervousness and make it more difficult to get the audience to concentrate on your presentation once the equipment problems have been solved.

Abstract Representations. If you need to illustrate the growth or decline of inflation or to show how revenue will be spent in the next six months, you can resort to more abstract representations than those previously discussed. The form and style of the representation—drawings, charts, graphs—depend upon the formality of the situation. If you are discussing a building plan for a prospective client, a quick sketch may suffice; however, if you are meeting with the client's board of directors, a rough drawing would be inadequate. The board would expect a polished presentation, complete with a professionally prepared prospectus. Similarly, a chalkboard drawing may be sufficient to explain the process of cell division to a group of classmates, but when presenting the same information as part of a formal project, you will want to refine the visual support materials. The care with which you prepare these visuals conveys to the audience an attitude of either indifference or concern.

Chalkboard drawings are especially valuable when you want to unfold an idea step-by-step. By drawing each stage as you come to it, you can control the audience's attention to your major points. Coaches often use this approach in showing players how a particular play works. Time lines and size differences also can be depicted with rough sketches on a chalkboard. The relatively short history of our civilization can be shown visually by a time line showing approximations of when life began, when recorded history began, and the time elapsed since Columbus discovered America.

Overhead projectors are often used like chalkboards; although it can be somewhat distracting to see such movement across a light source, some speakers draw with a grease pencil on an acetate sheet while they talk. Better is the practice of preparing transparencies beforehand. One advantage of an overhead projector is that you can turn it off when you have made your point, thereby removing a competing stimulus from the environment.

When using either a chalkboard or an overhead projector, make your drawings large enough to be clear to the audience. You can continue to talk to the audience as you draw, as long as you are brief; attention will wander if you talk to the board or to the light source for three or four minutes while drawing. Also, consider the visual field while you draw: where should you stand to avoid blocking the audience's view? Finally, when you are through talking about the illustration, erase the board or turn off the projector.

Graphs require more attention than quick drawings, as they normally are used to show relationships among various parts of a whole, or between variables across time. In these cases, accuracy is critical in visually illustrating the degree of difference. Graphs can take several forms:

1. ***Bar graphs*** *show the relationships between two or more sets of figures.* If you are indicating the discrepancy between income earned by various

groups of professionals, or between men and women in the same occu-pations, a bar graph would be an appropriate visual support for your oral presentation.

2. **Line graphs** *show relations between two or more variables.* If you are trying to explain a complex economic relationship involving supply and demand, a line graph is a useful tool.

3. **Pie graphs** *show percentages by dividing a circle into the proportions being represented.* A charity may use a pie graph to show how much of its income is spent on administration, research, and fund-raising cam-

---

BAR GRAPH

Bar graphs illustrate relationships.

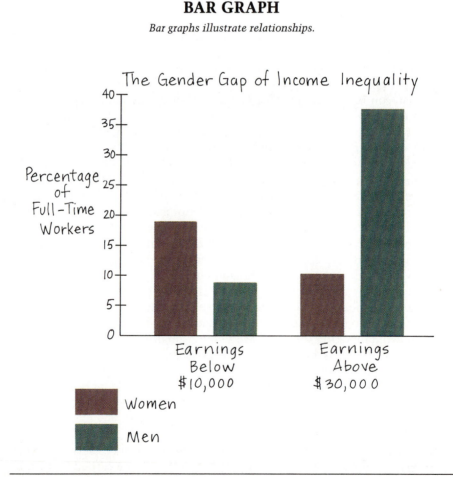

Source: U.S. Bureau of the Census, 1986 figures.

LINE GRAPH

*Line graphs can reveal relationships, but they can also deceive the unwary.
These graphs show the same data but use different spacing along the axes to
change the visual image.*

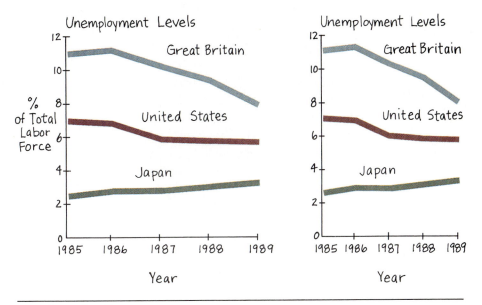

Source: Data Resources.

paigns. Town governments use pie graphs to show citizens what proportion of their tax dollars go to municipal services, administration, education, recreation, and so on.

4. **Pictographs** *signify size or number through the use of symbols.* For example, a representation of U.S. vs. Soviet missile strength would use drawings of missiles (one symbol representing 1000 actual missiles), allowing viewers to see at a glance the disparity between the two countries.

Your choice of bar, line, pie, or pictorial graphs depends upon the subject and the nature of the relationship you wish to convey. A pie graph, for example, does not illustrate discrepancies between two groups, nor does it show effects of change over time. To visually represent these relations, a bar graph or a line graph might be used. A bar graph can, however, create a misleading impression of the difference between two items if one bar is short and wide while the other is long and narrow. Line graphs can distort time if the units of measurement are not the same for each time period. These problems can be avoided by using consistent measurements in creating the graphs. Using computer-generated graphs (see page 313) can help you remain consistent.

PIE GRAPH

A pie graph shows percentages of a whole; this graph reveals the percentages of survey respondents who rated U.S. airline service.

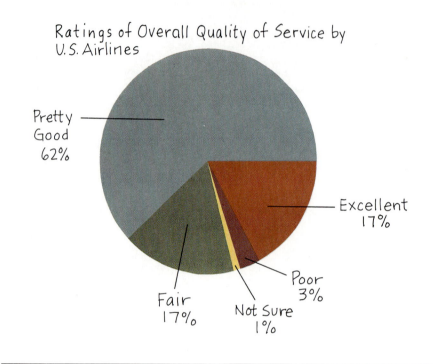

Ratings of Overall Quality of Service by U.S. Airlines

Pretty Good 62%

Excellent 17%

Poor 3%

Not Sure 1%

Fair 17%

Source: Business Week/Harris Poll conducted December 12–16, 1988.

Charts and *tables* also lend support and clarity to your ideas. If you are trying to indicate the channels of communication or lines of authority in a large company, your presentation will be much easier to follow if each listener has an organizational chart to refer to. If the organization is large and complex, you may want to develop a series of charts, each one focusing on a smaller subset of the original. A dense chart showing all the major and minor offices may simply overwhelm the listeners as they try to follow you through the maze. Unveiling successive charts, through the use of a *flip-chart*, also focuses audience attention on specific parts of the speech. If you hand audience members a complete chart, they will tend to stray from your order of explanation as they read it. A *flow chart* can help indicate the actions that might be taken across time; planners can indicate what will be done by whom and in what order. If you are explaining a fund-raising campaign, a flow chart will allow audiences to visualize the stages of the campaign. As long as the information is not too complex or lengthy, tables can indicate changes in inventory over time. They also can rank lists of items and their

PICTOGRAPH

Speakers with artistic skills can create interesting visual aids, such as this graphic representation of U.S. wine exports.

U.S. Wine Exports

1985

1986

1987

1988

= One Million Gallons

Source: Wine Institute.

cost, frequency of use, or relative importance. As with charts, tables should be designed so that they can be seen and so that they convey data simply and clearly; too much information forces the audience to concentrate more on the visual support than on your oral explanation.

Models of real objects that cannot be brought into a room or cannot be seen because of their small size can help dramatize your explanation. Architects construct models of new projects to show to clients. Developers of shopping malls, condominiums, and business offices use models when persuading zoning boards to grant needed rights-of-way or variances. An explanation of the complexity of the DNA molecule would be aided by a model.

Models need to be manageable and visible to the audience. If you are using a model that will come apart so that different pieces can be explained, practice removing and replacing the parts beforehand.

Strategies and Determining Factors in Selecting and Using Visual Aids

Your decisions of which visual materials to use, and to your best advantage, should be based on four considerations: (1) the communicative potential of various visual materials, (2) your ability to integrate verbal and visual materials effectively, (3) the characteristics of the audience and the occasion, and (4) your evaluation of available computer-generated visuals.

Consider the Communicative Potential of Various Visual Aids

Keep in mind that each type of visual material has the potential to communicate particular kinds of information and that each type interacts with your spoken presentation as well as with your audience's state of mind. In general, primarily pictorial or photographic visuals can make an audience *feel* the way you do. Slides, movies, sketches, and photographs often can be used effectively to accompany travelogues or reports of personal experiences because they illustrate or reproduce in others the kinds of feelings you experienced in another place, situation, or time.

Visuals containing descriptive or verbal materials, on the other hand, can help an audience *think* the way you do. Such aids as models, diagrams, charts, and graphs frequently add rational support to claims you are attempting to defend. Your topic and communicative purpose, therefore, play major roles in determining the best kinds of visuals to use in a given circumstance. For instance, a speech informing listeners of your experiences in Indonesia should probably be accompanied by slides or films and even some household artifacts. A speech to persuade your listeners that the United States ought to sever all association with NATO probably should be supported by maps, charts, and chalkboard drawings.

Integrate Verbal and Visual Materials

To be effective, visual aids should be relevant to your topic and to your communicative purpose. You use visuals in order to save time, to enhance the impact of your message, to clarify complex relations, and to generally enliven your presentation. The following suggestions build upon, and, in some cases, reinforce those already presented in our discussion of specific aids.

1. *Design abstract symbolic representations with care.* Use contrasting colors (red on white, black on yellow) to highlight the information in an organizational chart or table. Segments of a pie graph can be differenti-

ated by using contrasting colors. A bar graph can use the same color for two or more bars, or it can be designed so that each bar is highlighted by using a new color.

2. *Keep charts and other graphic aids clear and simple.* Research has demonstrated that using plain bar graphs—probably because they offer not only numbers but also a visualization of those numbers—is the single most effective method for displaying statistical comparisons.[6] Make sure the essential information you want your audience to focus on stands out clearly from the background. Let simplicity be your watchword in the preparation of all visual aids.

3. *Make your visuals—especially those with materials that must be read or scrutinized closely—large enough to be seen clearly and easily.* Listeners get frustrated when, in the middle of a speech, they have to lean forward and squint in order to see a detail on a sketch or graph. Follow the example of John Hancock, who, when signing the Declaration of Independence in 1776, wrote his name large enough to "be seen by the King of England without his glasses."

4. *Take enough time in preparing visuals to make them presentable.* Draw neatly; spell correctly; make bar graph lines proportional; make all letters the same size. Such advice may seem juvenile, but beginning speakers often throw together visual materials at the last minute, forgetting that *everything* they present to an audience contributes to an assessment of their credibility. Misspelled words and sloppy graphs lower listeners' estimation of your competence.

5. *Decide well in advance whether to bring animate or inanimate objects with you and, if you do, how you will handle them.* This is especially true for so-called demonstration speeches, in which you show listeners how to do something. For example, if you do tombstone dabbing (making paper casts of old tombstone faces), should you bring one in? (Tombstones are heavy.) How much of the process should you show? (It is time consuming and messy.) How detailed should you get? (Should you include discussions of the chemicals used for cleaning stone surfaces, of the different kinds of paper, or of various dabbing techniques? Should you just describe the basic processes?) Unless you think through such questions in advance, you are liable to find yourself making hasty decisions in midspeech, when you have other things to worry about.

6. *Be prepared to compensate orally for any distraction your visual aid may inadvertently create.* If you pass around a sample of your work—a leather purse or silver ring you have made—remember that an actual object or detailed model is a complex, potent visual stimulus. This makes it a message maker in its own right, and you must compete with it for your listeners' attention, so tell your audience what aspects of the object to examine closely and which ones to ignore. If, despite your cautions, the object or full-scale model proves distracting, build enough reiteration

into your speech to make reasonably certain your listeners can follow your train of thought even while they are studying the object and passing it around. As added insurance, you might also provide a rough sketch of it on the chalkboard, visually reinforcing the verbal message you are trying to communicate.

7. *When using slides, films, overhead projectors, or videotapes, be prepared to make the verbal and physical adjustments necessary to coordinate the visual materials with the spoken materials.* With these aids, you often darken the room, thereby compelling your audience to concentrate on a source of light: the silver screen in the case of slides and films, the 19-inch screen in the case of a TV monitor. At such times, you—the *oral* communicator—must compete with the *mechanical* or *electronic* communicator. If, as often happens, your audience begins to concentrate harder on the flow of light than on the flow of words, you defeat your own purpose. Therefore, when using projected materials as visual support, either (a) talk more loudly and move more vigorously when communicating simultaneously with the machine or (b) refuse to compete with it at all. That is, show the film or the slides either *before* or *after* you comment on their content. Whatever strategy you use, however, make sure the projected visual materials are well integrated into the rest of your presentation.

8. *Hand your listeners a copy of those materials you wish them to think back on or carry away from your speech.* If, for example, you are making recommendations to a student council, you may provide copies of a proposal for the council's subsequent action. If you are reporting the results of a survey, the most pertinent statistics will be better understood and remembered if you give each listener a copy of them. Few people can recall the seven warning signs of cancer, but they could keep a list of them in a handy place if you give a copy to each member of your audience. Remember that we are referring here only to speech material that is a legitimate *visual aid.* Obviously, you will not put everything you have to say on a photocopied page. Select only elements or items that have lasting value.

These suggestions should enable you—with careful planning—to take advantage of the communicative potential of various visual media. Good visual material is not distracting. It "fits," is essential to the verbal message, and leaves an audience with a feeling of completeness.

Consider the Audience and Occasion

In choosing the types and content of the visual supporting materials you use, common sense dictates that you must also consider the *status* of the subject in the minds of your audience. Ask yourself: Do I need to bring a map of the United States to an audience of American college students when discussing the westward movement of population in this country? If I am going to discuss offensive and defensive formations used by a football team, should I provide diagrams of such formations? Can I really expect an audience to understand the administrative structure of the federal bureaucracy without an organizational chart?

How much an audience *already knows, needs to know,* and *expects to find out* about you and your subject are clearly determinants that weigh heavily when you choose the types and numbers of visual supports you will use in a speech. How readily that audience can comprehend *aurally* what you have to say is another. Granted, it is not always easy to assess any of these conditions or capabilities. It may be exceedingly difficult, in fact, to decide how much an audience of college freshmen and sophomores knows about college or governmental structures, and, certainly, you cannot easily judge how well acquainted a Rotary Club audience is with football plays. That being the case, probably the best thing you can do is to check out your speculations by asking around among your potential listeners well ahead of the time you are scheduled to deliver your speech. In other words, before making any final decisions about visual supporting materials, do as much audience research and analysis as you possibly can.

As a part of your advance planning for the use of visuals, also take into account the nature of the occasion or the uniqueness of the circumstances in which you will be speaking. Certain kinds of occasions cry out for certain types of graphic supporting materials. The corporate executive who presents a projective report to the board of directors without a printed handout or diagrams probably would find his or her credibility questioned. The military advisor who calls for governmental expenditure for new weapons without offering pictures or drawings of the proposed weapons and printed technical data on their operations is not likely to be viewed as a convincing advocate. At halftime, an athletics coach without a chalkboard may succeed only in confusing team members, not helping them. In classroom settings, students who give demonstration speeches without visuals frequently feel inadequate, even helpless—especially when they realize that most of the other speakers are well fortified with such support. In short, if you are to speak in a situation that demands certain kinds of visual media, plan ahead and enhance your message by taking full advantage of them. If the speech occasion does not appear to require visual supports, analyze it further for possibilities. Use your imagination. Be innovative. Do not overlook opportunities to make your speech more meaningful, more exciting, and more attention holding in the eyes of your listeners.

Evaluate Computer-Generated Visual Materials

Computer-generated visual materials are easily available on college campuses, and you may wish to consider using them. Given that availability, a few words of advice are in order.

1. *Think of ways computer graphics can help you create an atmosphere.* For example, you easily can learn to make computer banners with block lettering and pictures printed across several sheets on continuous-feed computer paper, which you can hang in the front of the room to set a

Well thought out computer-generated visual aids can give your presentation a level of professionalism and class and enhance your credibility.

mood or theme. For example, a student urging her classmates to get involved with a United Way drive created a banner containing a United Way slogan: "Thanks to you, it works, for all of us." The banner captured the listeners' attention, as most did not initially know what it referred to, and the slogan served as a regular refrain through the speech.

2. *Be ready to enlarge small computer-generated diagrams.* Most diagrams made on computer paper are too small to be seen by an audience. A photoduplicating machine that enlarges images (sometimes to 140–200 percent of the original size) will help, although you will have to fit several sheets of paper together to complete the original image.

3. *Likewise, do not be afraid of enhancing the computer-generated image in other ways.* Use felt-tip pens to color in pie graphs or to darken the lines of a line graph. Use press-on type, available at bookstores, to make headings for those graphs, as the lettering done by computers usually is faint or small. Take pictures of your graphs so you can convert them to transparencies for projection during your speech. Mixing media in such ways can give your presentations a professional look.

4. *Alternatively, hand out copies of a computer-generated diagram to audience members.* Especially when you are working with a lot of numbers—for example, income tax rates and the usual deductions for people with different incomes—a handout is probably necessary; if you generate it by computer and print it out with a near-letter-quality or laser printer, you will have a useful and good-looking visual aid. Also, if you have enough computer experience and access to a sophisticated machine, you can create three-dimensional "see through" images of buildings, machines, and the like. Putting three-dimensional diagrams in your listeners' hands gives them something useful to take away from your speech.

5. *Know the limitations of computer technologies.* Remember that computers do their best work processing numerical data and converting them to bar, line, and pie graphs. While computers can build pictures for you, they are usually small, black-and-white approximations. You may find that it is more effective to use tag board, markers, and press-on lettering. Always remember that visual aids must fit your purpose, physical setting, and audience needs.

Well thought out computer-generated visual aids can give your presentations a level of professionalism and class that enhance your credibility.

Chapter Summary

Visual aids, as a discrete mode, or channel, of communication, can *aid listener comprehension and memory* and *add persuasive impact* to a speech. There are two main types of visual aids—*actual objects* and *symbolic representations*. Actual objects include both *animate and inanimate objects*. The types of symbolic representation include concrete representations (*slides, videotapes, films*) and abstract representations (*chalkboard drawings, graphs, charts and tables, models*). In selecting and using visual aids, consider their *communicative potential,* find ways to *integrate verbal and visual materials,* adapt them to *the audience and the occasion,* and *evaluate the possible use of computer-generated visual material.*

Reference Notes

1. The general theories of Gestalt psychology (which undergird much of our visual theory) are reviewed understandably in Ernest R. Hilgard, *Theories of Learning* (New York: Appleton-Century-Crofts, 1956). Their applications in areas of visual communication can be found, among other places, in Rudolph Arnheim, *Visual Thinking* (Berkeley: University of California Press, 1969); John M. Kennedy, *A Psychology of Picture Perception* (San Francisco: Jossey-Bass, Inc., Pubs., 1974); Leonard Zusne, *Visual Perception of Form* (New York: Academic Press, 1976); and John Morgan and Peter Welton, *See What I Mean: An Introduction to Visual Communication* (London: Edward Arnold, Pubs., Ltd., 1986). For discussions of research on media and learning, see E. Heidt, *Instructional Media and the Individual Learner* (New York: Nichols, 1976) and Gavriel Salomon, *Interaction of Media, Cognition, and Learning* (San Francisco: Jossey-Bass, Inc., Pubs., 1979).

2. William J. Seiler, "The Effects of Visual Materials on Attitudes, Credibility, and Retention," *Speech [Communication] Monographs* 38 (November 1971): 331–34.

3. Joel R. Levin and Alan M. Lesgold, "On Pictures in Prose," *Educational Communication and Technology Journal* 26 (1978): 233–44; Marilyn J. Haring and Maurine A. Fry, "Effect of Pictures on Children's Comprehension of Written Text," *Educational Communication and Technology Journal* 27 (1979): 185–90.

4. For more specific conclusions regarding the effects of various sorts of visual materials, see F. M. Dwyer, "Exploratory Studies in the Effectiveness of Visual Illustrations," *AV Communication Review* 18 (1970): 235–50; G. D. Feliciano, R. D. Powers, and B. E. Kearle, "The Presentation of Statistical Information," *AV Communication Review* 11 (1963): 32–39; Seiler; M. D. Vernon, "Presenting Information in Diagrams," *AV Communication Review* 1 (1953): 147–58; and L. V. Peterson and Wilbur Schramm, "How Accurately Are Different Kinds of Graphs Read?" *AV Communication Review* 2 (1955): 178–89.

5. For a clear exploration of the relationship between ideas and visuals, see Edgar B. Wycoff, "Why Visuals?" *AV Communications* 11 (1977): 39, 59.

6. Feliciano et al.; Vernon; and Peterson and Schramm.

Key Terms

concrete representations	*line graphs*
abstract representations	*pie graphs*
bar graphs	*pictographs*

Problems and Probes

1. Think of several courses you have taken in high school and/or college. How did the instructors use visual aids in presenting the subject matter of these courses? Were such materials effectively used? Was there a relationship between the subject matter and the type of visual aid used? Give special consideration to proper and improper uses of the chalkboard by the instructors. What communicative functions are best served by the chalkboard? least served? Are there special problems with the use of visuals when audience members are taking notes while listening? Prepare a brief written analysis of these questions, including several illustrations from the classes. How might your instructors have expanded or improved the visual presentation of information?

2. Visual aids capture appropriate moods, clarify potentially complex subjects, and sometimes even carry the thrust of a persuasive message. Examine magazine advertisements and "how-to" articles in periodicals, look at store windows and special displays in museums and libraries, and observe slide-projection lectures in some of your other classes. Then (a) using the types considered in this chapter, classify the visual materials you have encountered; (b) assess the purposes these materials serve—clarification, persuasion, attention focusing, mood setting, and others; (c) evaluate the effectiveness with which each of the materials you have examined is doing its job; and, finally, (d) prepare a report, a paper, or an entry in your journal on the results of your experiences and observations.

Communication Activities

1. Present a short oral report in which you describe a speech you will give and the ways you will incorporate visual materials and coordinate them with the verbal materials. Specify the characteristics you might try to build into each visual aid to maximize clarity. If you can, bring in some rough-draft examples of the visuals for the purpose of illustrating your intentions.

2. Prepare a short speech explaining or demonstrating a complex process. Use two different types of visual aids. Ask the class to evaluate which aid was more effective. Try this same speech without the use of any visual materials. What new pressures do you feel as a speaker? How can you deal with them? Can you still give an effective presentation?

3. Repeat activity #2 with a classmate. Working together, develop two different visual aids to enhance your joint presentation. Plan a performance in which the two of you share the delivery responsibilities. When one speaker talks, the other may be in charge of displaying visual aids. How effective are these duet performances? How does having a thoroughly initiated partner increase the speaking options?

CHAPTER FOURTEEN

Using Your Voice and Body to Communicate

*H*istory tells us that many famous speakers had to overcome severe problems of delivery before others would listen to their ideas. Abraham Lincoln suffered from extreme speechfright; Eleanor Roosevelt appeared awkward and clumsy. John F. Kennedy had a strong regional dialect and repetitive gestures. Each of these famous speakers, and many others, realized that the effectiveness of a speech depends not only upon careful research and organization, but also upon the presentation of ideas.

The manner in which a speech is presented affects its reception. If you have heard a recording or seen a video of Martin Luther King, Jr.'s, "I Have a Dream" speech, you are aware of the dramatic difference between hearing him speak and simply reading a copy of the speech. The same is true of Jesse Jackson: his delivery adds to the impact of his ideas. His use of repetition does not read nearly as well as it sounds. It is important to be aware that oral presentation adds to the impact of the ideas.

As a speaker, you must be aware of the impact of each potential channel of communication, including the meaning and delivery of your words. Your voice and bodily movements—the *aural* and *visual* channels of communication—help transmit your feelings and attitudes toward your self, your audience, and your topic. You may see speakers who approach the platform reluctantly with downcast eyes and grimacing faces, dragging their feet and fussing with their notes on the way to the front of the room. Their sense of self-confidence and their attitude toward the audience and the occasion betray them before they even begin. These speakers unwittingly establish audience predispositions that work against them. Even if their ideas are important and their speech is well crafted, the audience members will have difficulty in listening because they expect the worst. Conversely, if a speaker moves with apparent confidence, takes a moment at the platform to organize notes, and glances at the audience as if to say "I'm ready, are you?" the audience will be more favorably disposed to listen to what the speaker has to say.

Your speech reflects self-confidence and personal competence if you present it well. To help you achieve this objective, we will discuss ways to effectively use your voice and body to communicate.

Using Your Voice to Communicate

Your voice is an instrument that helps convey the meaning of language. As previously noted, it affects your listeners' perception and interpretation of your message.[1]

You can communicate enthusiasm for your ideas to listeners through your voice. An awareness of the characteristics of **vocal quality** can help you make

The most successful speakers of our time have possessed the vocal quality of conversationality, the ability to make listeners feel they are being directly, personally addressed.

ideas more interesting. Listen to a stock market reporter rattle off the daily industrial averages. Even though every word may be intelligible, the reporter's vocal expression may be so repetitive and monotonous that the ideas are not very exciting. On the other hand, recall a play-by-play account of a sports event by your favorite announcer (such as the Celtics' Johnny Most or baseball announcer Joe Garagiola). The enthusiasm and vividness created depends, in large part, upon the way the announcer uses his or her voice. The most effective announcers create an infectious enthusiasm in their listeners.

Our culture seems to prize one essential vocal quality above all others—a sense of **conversationality.**[2] The most successful speakers of our time have cultivated the ability to make listeners feel they are being directly, personally addressed. Even speakers who address millions through the mass media on evening newscasts or nightly talk shows can speak as though they are in a personal conversation with each one of us. Such conversational quality comes primarily from the realization that you are talking "with" not "at" an audience. Your principal concern, then, as you consider the vocal channel, should be mental rather than physical. You should adapt your voice to the public-speaking situation without losing the interpersonal qualities expected in everyday conversation.

This chapter will begin by reviewing some of the general characteristics of an effective speaking voice and by considering ways the voice can be adapted to particular speaking situations.

The Effective Speaking Voice

A successful speaker is able to use the voice to emotionally color the ideas captured in the words of the message. These vocal attributes contribute to the meanings that public speakers convey to audiences through the vocal channel. A flexible speaking voice has intelligibility, variety, and understandable stress patterns.

Intelligibility. In everyday conversations with friends, we all tend to articulate sloppily and to speak more rapidly and softly than we would in public-speaking situations. We can usually get by with inadequate articulation because we know the persons we are talking with and because we are probably only three to five feet from them. In public speaking, however, you may be addressing people you do not know, often from twenty-five feet or more away. In such situations, to ensure maximum **intelligibility,** you must consider four independent but related factors: (1) the overall level of loudness at which you speak, (2) the rate at which you speak, (3) the care with which you enunciate important words, and (4) the standard of pronunciation you observe.

Adjust your loudness level. Probably the most important single factor in intelligibility is the loudness level at which you speak as related to the *distance* between you and your listeners and the amount of **noise** present.[3] Obviously, the farther away your listeners are, the louder you must talk for them to hear you well. Most of us unconsciously adjust our loudness level when projecting our voice over extended distances. What we often forget is that a corresponding adjustment is required when the listeners are only a few feet away. You must realize also that your own voice always sounds louder to you than to your listeners.

In addition to distance, the amount of surrounding noise with which you compete has an effect on the required loudness level. Even in normal circumstances, some noise is always present. For example, the noise level of rustling leaves in the quiet solitude of a country lane (ten decibels) is louder than a whisper at six feet away. The noise in an empty theater averages twenty-five decibels, but with a "quiet" audience it rises to forty-two. In the average factory, a constant noise of about eighty decibels is characteristic. This is just about the same level as very loud speaking at a close range.

How can you determine the proper strength of voice to use in order to achieve sufficient loudness for the distance and noise conditions of a particular speech situation? You can always use your eyes to see if your auditors appear to be hearing you, or, even better, you can *ask* them. Get your instructor's advice on this point. Ask your friends to report on the loudness of your voice as you talk in rooms of various sizes and under varying noise conditions. Listen to the sound of your voice to correlate your own vocal production with their reports. You will soon learn to gauge the volume you must use in order to be heard.

Control your rate. In animated conversation, you may well jabber along at a **rate** of 200 to 250 words per minute. This rate is especially characteristic of people raised in the North, Midwest, Southwest, or West. As words tumble out of your mouth in informal conversational situations, they usually are intelligible because the distance they must travel is short. In large auditoriums or outdoors, however, rapid delivery can impede intelligibility. Echoes can distort or destroy sounds in rooms. In outdoor situations, words often seem to drift and vanish into the open air.

When addressing larger audiences, then, most of us must slow down to an average of 120 to 150 words per minute. Obviously, you do not go around timing your speaking rate, but you can remind yourself of potential rate problems as you rise to speak. You can also get feedback from your instructors and classmates regarding their perceptions of your speaking rate.

All of this is not to say, of course, that you should never speak rapidly. There are situations in which a quickened delivery helps you stir and intensify your listeners' emotions. If you find yourself in such a situation, you must compensate. As your rate increases, for example, adjust your volume and take more care in your enunciation of sounds and words.

Enunciate clearly. **Enunciation** refers to the crispness and precision with which we form words vocally. Most of us are "lip lazy" in normal conversation: we tend to slur sounds, dropping syllables from words, and skip over beginnings and endings of words. Careless enunciation may not inhibit communication between intimate friends, but it can seriously undermine a speaker's intelligibility to an audience.

When speaking publicly, you may have to force yourself to say *"going"* instead of *"go-in,"* *"just"* instead of *"jist"* (which can aurally be mistaken for "gist"), and *govern*-ment instead of *"guv*-ment." Physiologically, this means opening your mouth a bit more widely than usual and forcing your lips and tongue to form the consonants firmly. If you are having trouble making your vocal mechanism enunciate well, ask your instructor for some exercises to improve your performance.

Meet standards of pronunciation. **Pronunciation** and dialect depend upon enunciation, or *articulation.* To be intelligible, you must form sounds carefully and meet audience expectations regarding acceptable pronunciation. If your words cannot be understood because they are slurred, garbled, or otherwise inarticulate, your listeners will not be able to grasp what you say, and, even if your words are recognizable, any peculiarity of pronunciation is sure to be noticed by some listeners. This may distract their attention from your ideas and undermine your credibility as a speaker.

Standards of pronunciation, or **dialects,** differ among geographic regions and cultural groups. A dialect is a language use—including vocabulary, grammar, and pronunciation—that sets a group apart. Your pronunciation of words, together with the ways in which you arrange them grammatically, or syntactically, determines your dialect. You may have a "foreign accent," a white Southern or black Northern dialect, a New England "twang," or a Hispanic trill. Since dialects have unique rules for vocabulary, grammar, and pronunciation, a clash of dialects can result in confusion and frustration for both speaker and listener. Recall trying to understand the words and meanings of someone from another region of the country. You may have been distracted from the message by the way the words sounded.

Unfortunately, the use of a particular dialect also may produce *negative judgments* about the speaker's credibility—his or her education, reliability, responsibility, and capabilities for leadership.[4] Such judgments of credibility occur because dialects and even professional jargon contribute heavily to what paralinguists call **vocal stereotypes.**[5] News anchors, for example, have reacted to the potential for negative judgments by adopting a midwestern American dialect—a manner of speech broadly accepted across the country. This dialect avoids calling attention to itself, as would a "downeast" or deep–South accent. You need to analyze each speaking situation to determine whether your regional dialect is appropriate, or whether its use will create negative judgments. Should you, for example, learn to use the grammar, vocabulary, and vocal patterns of middle America when addressing a particular audience? Many speakers are forced to become "bilingual," using their own regional dialect when facing local audiences but switching to midwestern American when addressing more varied audiences.

Variety. As you move from intimate conversation to the enlarged context of public speaking, you may discover that listeners accuse you of monotony of pitch or rate. When speaking in a large public setting, you should compensate for the greater distance that sounds travel by varying certain characteristics of your voice. You should learn to vary rate, pitch, force, and pauses.

Vary the rate. Earlier we discussed the overall rate at which we normally speak. Consider ways to alter your speaking rate in accordance with the ideas you are expressing. The emotional character of your subject matter, likewise, should affect variations in rate, so you should consider slowing down to add emphasis to a particular point or to indicate your own thoughtfulness and quickening the pace when your ideas are emotionally charged. Observe, for example, how a sports announcer varies speaking rate from play to play or how an evangelist changes pace regularly. A variable rate helps keep an audience's attention riveted on the speech.

Change the pitch. Three aspects of pitch (the musical "notes" in your speaking voice) are relevant to effective vocal communication. First, your **pitch level**—your habitual pitch, whether in the soprano, alto, tenor, baritone, or bass range—is normally adequate for most of your daily communication needs.

People who frequently speak in public, however, should use a broader **pitch range.** In normal conversation, you may use only a few notes, sometimes even less than an octave, but if you use such a limited range from a podium, you may sound monotonous. Given the distances that sounds must travel between speaker and audience and the length of time speakers talk, you should exaggerate your range of sounds in order to communicate effectively. Raise your pitch "highs" and lower your "lows." Usually, the more emotionally charged your ideas, the more you should vary your pitch. Obviously, you can get carried away. Just as a narrow pitch range communicates boredom, an extremely wide pitch range can communicate artificiality or uncontrolled excitement or fear.

The key to successful control of pitch ultimately depends upon understanding the importance of **pitch variation.** As a general rule, use higher pitches to communicate excitement and lower pitches to create a sense of control or solemnity. Use different parts of your range, in other words, for different kinds of emotions. As a second rule, let the sense of a particular sentence control pitch variations. Thus, move your voice up at the end of a question; change to higher or lower notes to add emphasis within a particular sentence. An abrupt change in pitch is called a *step.* When a more gradual or continuous pitch inflection accompanies the production of the sound, it is termed a *slide.* Television announcer Ed McMahon uses both of these techniques in his famous introduction of Johnny Carson:

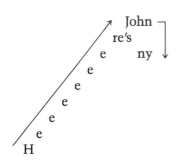

A listener's judgment of a speaker's personality and emotional commitment often centers on that speaker's vocal quality—the fullness of the tones and whether the voice is harsh, husky, mellow, nasal, breathy, or resonant.

Ed successively slides his voice up until he reaches a high pitch level on the beginning of "Johnny"; then, he steps down the scale on the end of the word. Such vocal slides and steps add emphasis. By mastering their use, you can call attention to your word choices, making your meaning clearer and more precise.

Stress.   A third significant aspect of vocal behavior is **stress**—the ways in which sounds, syllables, and words are accented. Without vocal stress, everything in a speech would sound the same, and the resulting message would be both incomprehensible and emotionless. Without vocal stress, you would sound like a computer. Vocal stress is achieved in two ways—through vocal emphasis and through the judicious use of pauses.

Add emphasis. **Emphasis** refers to the points in a sentence where, principally through increased vocal energy (loudness), changes in intonation (pitch), or variations in speed (rate), one vocally makes particular words or phrases stand out. "Emphasis" is the way you accent or "attack" words; it is most often achieved through changes in loudness or energy; variations in loudness can affect the meanings of your sentences. Consider the sentence "Tom's taking Jane out for pizza tonight." Notice how the meaning varies with the word being emphasized:

1. TOM's taking Jane out for pizza tonight. (not John or Bob)
2. Tom's taking JANE out for pizza tonight. (not Sue or Wanda)
3. Tom's taking Jane OUT for pizza tonight. (rather than staying home as usual)
4. Tom's taking Jane out for PIZZA tonight. (not seafood or hamburgers)
5. Tom's taking Jane out for pizza TONIGHT. (not tomorrow or next weekend)

Without careful control of vocal force, a speaker is liable to utter messages subject to many possible meanings. A lack of vocal stress, therefore, not only creates an impression of boredom but can also cause needless misunderstandings.

Emphasis is also fostered through changes in pitch and rate. Relatively simple changes in pitch, for example, can be used to "tell" an audience where you are in an outline, as when a speaker says,

"My ^{second} point is this: We must not forget ^{temporary} workers."

In this sentence, the audience can hear that the speaker has completed one idea and has moved on to the next, and that temporary workers will be the principal concern of that section. Variations in rate can operate in the same way. Consider the following sentence:

> We are a country faced with . . . [moderate rate] balance of payments deficits, racial tensions, an energy crunch, a crisis of morality, unemployment, government waste . . . [fast rate] and-a-stif-ling-na-tion-al-debt. [slow rate]

This speaker has built a vocal freight train. The ideas pick up speed through the accelerating list of problems and then come to an emphatic halt when the speaker's main concern—the national debt—is mentioned. Such variations in rate essentially communicate to an audience what is and is not especially important to the speech. Emphasis is achieved through the control of speaking rate.

Use helpful pauses. **Pauses** are intervals of silence between or within words, phrases, or sentences. Pauses punctuate thought by separating groups of spoken words into meaningful units. When placed immediately before a key idea or the climax of a story, they can create suspense; when placed immediately after a major point or central idea, they add emphasis. Introduced at the proper moment, a dramatic pause can express your feeling more forcefully than words. Clearly, silence can be a highly effective communicative tool if used intelligently and sparingly, and if not embarrassingly prolonged.

Sometimes speakers fill silences in their discourse with sounds—"umms," "ahs," "ers," "well-ahs," "you-knows," and other meaningless fillers. You have probably heard speakers say, "Today, ah, I would like, you know, to speak to you, umm, about a pressing, well-uh, like, a pressing problem facing this, uh, campus." Such vocal intrusions convey feelings of hesitancy and lack of confidence. You should make a concerted effort to remove these intrusions from your speaking behavior.

On the other hand, do not be afraid of silences. Pauses allow you to achieve stress for important ideas, as when the audience waits for the "punch line" in a story or argument. Pauses also intensify listeners' involvement in emotional situations, as when Barbara Walters or William F. Buckley, Jr., pauses for reflection. Avoid too many pauses or those that seem artificial, however; they can make you appear manipulative or over-rehearsed. Use strategic silence as an important weapon in your arsenal as an effective communicator.

Emotional Quality

A listener's judgment of a speaker's personality and emotional commitment often centers on that speaker's vocal quality—the fullness or thinness of the tones and whether the voice is harsh, husky, mellow, nasal, breathy, or resonant. Depending upon your vocal quality, an audience may judge you as being angry, happy, confident, fearful, sincere, or sad.

Fundamental to a listener's reaction to your vocal quality are **emotional characterizers**—their sense of a speaker's laughing, crying, whispering, inhaling or exhaling, and so on.[6] Emotional characterizers combine in various ways with your words to communicate different shades of meaning. Consider a few of the many ways you can say the following sentence:

I can't believe I ate that entire pizza.

You might say it as though you were *reporting* a fact, as if you *cannot believe* you just ate it all, or as though it were an *impossible* achievement. Finally, you might say it as though you were *expressing doubts* about the truth of the action. As you say the sentence to express these different meanings, you not only vary your pitch and loudness, but probably also alter your emotional characterizers. Such changes are important determiners of how meaning is communicated to listeners.

Your vocal qualities are of prime importance in determining the impression you make on an audience. While you cannot completely control such qualities, you can be alert to the effects they are likely to produce in your listeners. Keep in mind your repertoire of vocal qualities as you decide how to express key ideas for an audience.

Vocal Control

Do not assume that you will be able to master in a day all of the vocal skills that have been described. Take time to review and digest these ideas. Above all, *practice.* Ask your instructor to provide exercises designed to make your vocal apparatus more flexible—breathing; phonation; resonance; articulation; and control of rate, pause, and inflection. When you are able to control your vocal mechanism to make it respond to your desires, you can achieve vocal intelligibility, variety, and stress. You can add the emotional coloring of a well-tuned vocal instrument. Remember that any vocal skill, before it can be natural and effective with listeners, must be so much a habit that it works for you with little conscious effort when you begin to speak and continues to do so throughout your oral message. Once your voice can respond as you want it to in the enlarged context of public speaking, you will be able to achieve the sense of conversationality so highly valued in our society.

Using Your Body to Communicate

Just as your voice gives meaning to your message through the aural channel, your physical behavior carries meaning through the visual channel. While audience members are using the aural channel to grasp your ideas, they are simultaneously using the visual message you send to add clarity. You can use these two complementary channels to help create a better understanding of your presentation.[7] To help you explore ways of enhancing your use of the visual channel, we will examine the speaker's physical behavior on the platform.

Dimensions of Nonverbal Communication

In recent years, research has re-emphasized the important roles of physical, or nonverbal, behaviors in effective oral communication.[8] Basically, those roles can be reduced to three generalizations:

1. *Speakers reveal and reflect their emotional states by their nonverbal behaviors in front of audiences.* Your listeners read your feelings toward your self, your topic, and your audience from your facial expressions; from the way you stand and walk; and from what you do with your head, arms, shoulders, and hands. Summarizing a good deal of research into nonverbal communication processes, communications scholar Dale G. Leathers has noted: "Feelings and emotions are more accurately exchanged by nonverbal than verbal means. . . . The nonverbal portion of communication conveys meanings and intentions that are relatively free of deception, distortion, and confusion."[9]

2. *Speakers' nonverbal cues enrich or elaborate the message that comes through words.* A solemn face can reinforce the dignity of a funeral eulogy. The words "either you can do this or you can do that" can be illustrated with appropriate arm-and-hand gestures. Taking a few steps to the left or right tells an audience that you are moving from one argument to another.

3. *Nonverbal messages create a reciprocal interaction sent from speaker to listener and from listener back to speaker.* Listeners frown, smile, shift nervously in their seats, and engage in many types of nonverbal

CLASSIFICATION OF
INTERHUMAN DISTANCE

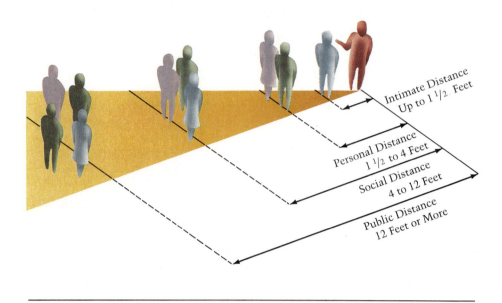

behavior already noted in Chapter 2. In this chapter, we will concentrate on the speaker's control of "body language." There are four areas of nonverbal communication that concern every speaker: (1) proxemics (the use of space), (2) movement and stance, (3) facial expressions, and (4) gestures.

Proxemics. One of the most important but perhaps least recognized aspects of nonverbal communication is **proxemics,** or the use of space by human beings. Two components of proxemics are especially relevant to public speakers:

1. *Physical arrangements*—the layout of the room in which you are speaking, including the presence or absence of a podium, the seating plan, the location of chalkboards and similar aids, and any physical barriers between you and your audience

2. *Distance*—the extent or degree of separation between you and your audience[10]

Both of these components have a bearing on your message. Most public-speaking situations involve a speaker facing a seated audience. Objects in the physical space—the lectern, a table, flags—tend to set the speaker apart from the listeners. This "setting apart," you must remember, is both *physical* and *psychological*. Literally as well as figuratively, objects can stand in the way of free communicative exchange. If you are trying to create a more informal and direct atmosphere, you will want to reduce the physical barriers in the setting. You might stand beside or in front of the lectern instead of behind it. In very informal settings, you might even sit on the front edge of a table while talking.

There is no single rule for using space; however, there are several guidelines for helping you determine your use of space in creating a particular physical and psychological impact:

1. *The formality of the occasion affects your impact—the more solemn or formal the occasion, the more distance and barriers.* Lectures, prepared reports, and the like are better suited to presentations from behind the lectern.

2. *The nature of the material may require the use of a lectern, such as when you have extensive quoted material or statistical evidence.* The use of visual aids often demands special equipment, such as an easel, table, or overhead projector.

3. *Finally, your personal preference can be considered.* You may feel more at ease speaking from behind rather than in front of the lectern.

The distance component of proxemics adds a second set of considerations. Speakers in most situations talk over what Edward T. Hall has termed a "public distance"—twelve feet or more away from their listeners.[11] To communicate with people at that distance, you obviously cannot rely on your normal speaking voice or small changes in posture or muscle tone. Instead, you must compensate for the distance by using larger gestures, broader shifts of your body from place to place, and increased vocal energy. These changes make it easier for audience members to see and hear as if you were sitting next to them. When the audience is relatively small, you may be able to decrease the distance by creating a more informal setting (for example, placing chairs in a circle) and modifying your physical movements and vocal energy accordingly. Experience with a variety of formal and informal settings will make it easier for you to refine the techniques of nonverbal delivery and to use them to enhance your message.

Movement and Stance.   How you move and stand provides a second set of nonverbal cues for your audience. **Movement** includes shifts you make from one spot to another during the delivery of a speech; **posture** refers to the

PHYSICAL ARRANGEMENTS
FOR PUBLIC SPEAKING

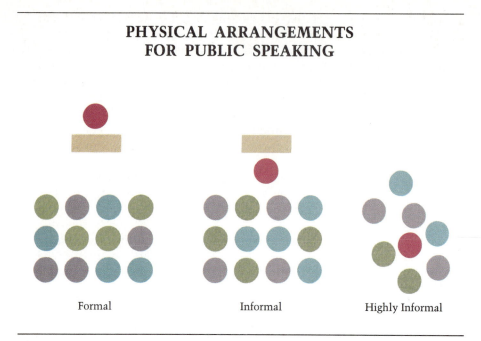

| Formal | Informal | Highly Informal |

relative relaxation or rigidity of your body, as well as to your overall stance (erect, slightly bent forward or backward, or slumping).

Purposive movements can communicate ideas about yourself to an audience. The speaker who stands stiffly erect may, without uttering a word, be saying either (a) "This is a formal occasion" or (b) "I am tense, even afraid, of this audience." The speaker who leans forward, physically reaching out to the audience, is saying silently but eloquently, "I am interested in you. I want you to understand and accept my ideas." Sitting casually on the front edge of a table and assuming a relaxed posture communicate informality and a readiness to engage in a dialogue with your listeners.

Movements and postural adjustments *regulate* communication. As a public speaker, you can, for instance, move from one end of a table to the other to indicate a change in topic, or you can accomplish the same purpose simply by changing your posture. At other times, you can move toward your audience when making an especially important point. In each case, you are using your body to signal to your audience that you are making a transition in your subject or are dealing with a matter of special concern.

Along with all of this, an equally important point to remember is that your posture and movements can not only work for you but also against you. Aimless and continuous pacing is distracting. A nervous bouncing or swaying makes the audience tense and uneasy, and if you adopt an excessively erect stance, you may lose rapport with your listeners. Your movements, in other words, should be *purposive*. Only then do stance and movement help your communicative effort and produce the sense of self-assurance and control you want to exhibit.[12]

Facial Expressions.   Your face is another important nonverbal message channel. When you speak, your facial expressions function in a number of ways. First, they communicate much about your self and your feelings. What Paul Ekman and Wallace V. Friesen call **affect displays** are given to an audience through the face. That is, audience members scan your face to see how you feel about yourself and how you feel about them.[13] Second, facial details provide listeners with cues that help them *interpret the contents* of your message: Are you being ironic or satirical? How sure are you of your conclusions? Is this a harsh or a pleasant message? Psychologists tell us that a high percentage of the information conveyed in a typical message is communicated nonverbally. Psychologist Albert Mehrabian has devised a formula to account for the emotional impact of a speaker's message. Words, he says, contribute 7 percent, vocal elements 38 percent, and facial expressions 55 percent.[14] Third, the "display" elements of your face—your eyes, especially—establish a *visual bonding* between you and your listeners. The speaker who looks down at the floor instead of at listeners, who reads excessively from notes or a manuscript, or who delivers a speech to the back wall has severed visual bonding. Our culture has come to expect eye-to-eye contact as a sign that a speaker is "earnest," "sincere," "forthright," and "self-assured." In other words, it is in part through regular eye contact with individuals in your audience that you establish your credibility.[15]

Of course, you cannot control your face completely, which is probably why listeners search it so carefully for clues to your feelings, but you can make sure that your facial messages do not belie your verbal ones. In practical terms, this means that when you are uttering angry words, your face should be communicating anger; when you are sincerely pleading with your listeners, your eyes should be looking at them intently. In short, use your face to maximum communicative advantage.

Gestures.   **Gestures** are purposive movements of the head, shoulders, arms, hands, or other areas of the body. They support and illustrate the ideas you are expressing. Fidgeting with your clothing and notecards or clutching the sides of the lectern are not gestures because they are not purposive. They distract from the ideas you are communicating. The effective public speaker commonly uses three kinds of gestures:

1. **Conventional gestures**—physical movements that are symbols to which specific meanings have been assigned by custom or convention. These gestures *condense* ideas. They are shorthand movements for things or ideas it would take many words to describe fully. The raised-hand "stop"

Facial Expression

A person's facial expression can reveal or conceal attitudes and feelings. Ekman and his colleagues have developed an entire research program around the analysis of facial movements and their potential communicative value. Their goal was to determine whether facial expressions are universal—that is, whether persons of diverse cultures identify specific expressions as revealing a particular emotion.

Ekman and his colleagues developed the Facial Action Scoring Technique (FAST) to discriminate between and among various facial expressions. The technique is based on photos representing different expressions in three areas of the face: brows/forehead, eyes/eyelids, and lower face (mouth, chin). Can we distinguish facial expressions occurring while viewing a "neutral" stimulus from expressions occurring while viewing a "stress" stimulus? The experimenters placed subjects alone in a room and played a short film showing autumn leaves (neutral) and then one showing a sinus operation (stress). The subjects were videotaped, and the tapes were then coded. Ekman found more expressions of surprise, anger, and disgust under the stress condition than

gesture of the police officer directing traffic, the manual sign language of deaf persons, and the arm signals of football referees are examples of conventional gestures.

2. **Descriptive gestures**—physical movements that describe the idea to be communicated. Speakers often depict the size, shape, or location of an object by movements of the hands and arms. Such gestures function through *pictorialization.* That is, they "draw pictures" for listeners. A speaker might use thumb and fingers to describe the "O" rings of a space shuttle, for example, or raise one arm to indicate the height of a stranger.

3. **Indicators**—movements of the hands, arms, or other parts of the body that express feelings. Thus, speakers may throw up their arms when disgusted, pound the lectern when angry, shrug their shoulders when puzzled, or point a threatening finger when issuing a warning. Such gestures encourage listeners' feelings through *arousal;* that is, they com-

under the neutral one, and that expressions of happiness were prominent during the neutral condition.

More specific studies of facial expression also have been conducted using the FAST and other coding techniques. For example, studies have isolated which areas of the face reveal which emotional states. Fear and sadness are shown, and recognized, from an analysis of the eyes and eyelids; surprise, on the other hand, is best determined by an analysis of the mouth region of the face. Studies also have linked the detection of deception to changes in facial expression. Deception may be the result of masking one's true feelings in a situation in which revealing them is inappropriate ("put on a happy face"), or it may be the result of deliberate attempts to lie.

This research is applicable to your own speaking situation, as knowledge of the relation between "face" and "emotion" helps you better understand and interpret the facial expressions of audience members. The ability to detect such emotional responses as happiness, surprise, fear, sadness, anger, disgust, and interest provides you with a more accurate assessment of your audience's reception of the message.

FOR FURTHER READING
Cody, Michael J., and H. Dan O'Hair. "Nonverbal Communication and Deception: Differences in Deception Cues Due to Gender and Communicator Dominance." *Communication Monographs* 50 (1983): 175–92; Ekman, Paul, ed. *Emotion in the Human Face*, 2nd ed. Cambridge: Cambridge University Press, 1982; Ekman, Paul. *Telling Lies.* New York: W. W. Norton & Co., Inc., 1985; Ekman, Paul, et al. "Universals and Cultural Differences in the Judgments of Facial Expression of Emotion." *Journal of Personal and Social Psychology* 53 (1987): 712–17; McDermott, Jeanne. "Face to Face, It's the Expression That Bears the Message." *Smithsonian* 16 (1986): 112–23.

municate your state of mind to your listeners and encourage similar responses in them. Your facial expressions and other body cues usually reinforce such gestures.[16]

Characteristics of Effective Gestures. Once you understand their purposes, you can perfect your gestures through practice. As you practice, you will obtain better results if you keep in mind three characteristics of effective gesturing: (1) *relaxation*, (2) *vigor and definiteness*, and (3) *proper timing*.

If your muscles are tense, your movements will be stiff and your gestures awkward. You should make a conscious effort to relax your muscles before you start to speak. You might "warm up" by taking a few unobtrusive steps, by rearranging your notes, or even by breathing deeply.

Good gestures are lively, vigorous, and definite. They communicate the dynamism associated with speaker credibility. You should put enough force into your gestures to show your conviction and enthusiasm; however, avoid

Nonverbal behaviors play an important role in effective oral communication. Facial expressions and gestures, for instance, convey cues to help listeners interpret the contents of a message.

exaggerated or repetitive gestures (such as pounding the table or chopping the air) for minor ideas in your speech. Vary your gestures as the ideas in your speech demand.

Timing is crucial to effective gestures. Try making a gesture after the word or phrase it was intended to reinforce has already been spoken and observe the ridiculous result. The *stroke* of a gesture—that is, the shake of a fist or the movement of a finger—should fall exactly on, or slightly precede, the point the gesture is used to emphasize. Practice making gestures until they have become habitual and then use them spontaneously as the impulse arises. Poor timing is often the result of an attempt to use "canned," or preplanned, gestures.

Nonverbal Channels: Strategic Choices

Although you never can completely control your vocal and bodily behavior, you can gain skills in orchestrating your movements and voice. Although we have talked in Part Three about language, visual aids, voice, and body as separate channels, you must remember that they work together while you are speaking to others. You should not attempt to control your messages in each channel separately and continuously; however, you should make fundamental choices about how to present your oral messages. As we conclude this chapter and section, let us review some of those choices.

1. *Start with your self.* You must always begin, of course, with your self—with self-directed questions about whether you are basically quiet and reticent or excitable and extroverted, whether you enjoy vigorous physical activity or avoid exertion, whether you talk easily on your feet or prefer to sit while talking, whether you are comfortable with broad movements or not, whether you feel silly shouting at an audience or not. The point is, you should (a) not try to copy a speaker you admire if your personality is very different from that person's, and (b) not reach for delivery techniques that are unnatural to your self-image. In our culture, there is a rather broad range of acceptable modes of public speaking—from the energetic, rhythmic delivery patterns of Jesse Jackson or Joan Rivers to the soothing, contemplative delivery patterns of Charles Kuralt or Barbara Walters. Do not model yourself on someone else; learn to work publicly as the person you really are.

2. *Plan a proxemic relationship with your audience that reflects your own needs and attitudes toward your subject and listeners.* If you feel more at home behind the lectern, plan to have it placed accordingly. If you want your whole body visible to the audience yet feel the need to have notes at eye level, stand beside the lectern and arrange your cards on it. If you want to relax your body—and are sure you can compensate for the resulting loss of action by increasing your vocal volume—sit behind a table or desk. If you feel physically free and want to be wholly "open" to your audience, stand in front of a table or desk. As far as possible, make the physical arrangements work for you.

3. *The farther you are from your listeners, the more important it is for them to have a clear view of you.* The speaker who crouches behind a lectern in an auditorium of 300 people loses contact with them. The farther away your audience is, the harder you must work to project your words, and the broader your physical movements must be. Think about large lecture classes you have attended, sermons you have heard in large churches, or political rallies you have attended. Recall delivery patterns of speakers who worked well in such situations, and choose and modify those that might also work for you.

4. *Insofar as practical, adapt the physical setting to the visual aids you plan to use.* If you are going to use such visual aids as a chalkboard, flipchart, working model, or process diagram, remove the tables, chairs, and other objects that would obstruct the listeners' view and, therefore, impair their understanding of your message.

5. *Adapt the size of your gestures, the amount of your movement, and the volume of your voice to the size of the audience.* Keeping in mind what Edward Hall noted about public distance in communication, you should realize that subtle changes of facial expressions, small movements of your fingers, and small changes of vocal characteristics cannot be detected when you are twenty-five feet or more from your listeners.

Although many auditoriums have a raised platform and a slanted floor to allow a speaker to be seen and heard more clearly, you should, nonetheless, adjust to the physical conditions.

6. *Continuously scan your audience from side to side and from front to back, looking specific individuals in the eye.* This does not mean, of course, that your head is to be in constant motion; "continuously" does not imply rhythmical, nonstop bobbing. Rather, it means that you must be aware—and must let an audience know you are aware—of the entire group of human beings in front of you. Take them all into your field of vision periodically and establish firm visual bonds. Such bonds enhance your credibility and keep your auditors' attention from wandering.

7. *Use your body to communicate your feelings about what you are saying.* When you are angry, do not be afraid to gesture vigorously. When you express tenderness, let that message come across a relaxed face. In other words, when you are communicating publicly, use the same emotional indicators you do when you talk on a one-to-one basis.

8. *Use your body to regulate the pace of your presentation and to control transitions.* Shift your weight as you move from one idea to another. Move more when you are speaking rapidly. When you are slowing down to emphasize particular ideas, decrease bodily and gestural action accordingly. These changes in movement and action allow your listeners to receive the same message across multiple communication channels. Your words, your vocal characteristics, and your physical movements, when orchestrated, reinforce each other and emphatically drive home your ideas.

9. *Adjust both vocal characteristics and head movements when you must use a microphone.* When you find yourself in a situation in which a microphone is necessary, there are several things to consider in making sure it complements your natural delivery. Since the mike tends to explode certain sounds if you are too close and does not pick up others when you are too far away, you need to find an optimum distance—one that can remain fairly well fixed while you are speaking. Given the variety of microphones and sound systems, experiment with distance as you begin to speak to determine what will be optimum for you. Asking if the audience can hear you is a simple, yet effective, way to test the microphone and sound system before getting into your own remarks. Besides determining the appropriate distance, there are other guides to assist you in adapting to a microphone, and letting it help carry your message to the audience:

   • Practice with mikes before you go on live. Especially if you are doing an interview, practice at home, with any object playing the part of the microphone. If you are going to talk over a public address system,

By selecting the appropriate method of presentation and by using your voice and body productively, you can enhance audience reception of your message. For instance, adapt the size of your gestures, the amount of your movement, and the volume of your voice to the size of your audience.

see if you can get into the room ahead of time to practice maintaining the right distance from the mike.

- Slow down a bit when talking to others via a public address system. If you slow down, your first two words already will have reverberated before you say the third and fourth words. Soon you will not even notice your own voice coming back to your ears.

- Remember to decrease your volume and to minimize variations in volume. Think of speaking into a microphone as speaking at an intimate distance—the equivalent of five or six inches from someone's ear. At the intimate distance, you talk more softly than in normal conversation, and you usually do not vary your volume (from quiet whispers to overpowering shouts) so much.

- Likewise, pay special attention to articulation. If you are normally a bit "lip lazy," form words more carefully into a mike. If you normally "pop your plosives"—vocally hit your *p*'s and *b*'s—hold back. Practice keeping the build-up of air behind those sounds under conscious control. Soon you will "naturally" control them. (If you are not under control, you will hear the mike "explosions" and remember to adjust.)

10. *Finally, use your full repertoire of descriptive and regulative gestures while talking publicly.* You probably do this in everyday conversation without even thinking about it; re-create that same attitude when addressing an audience. Physical readiness is the key. Keep your hands and arms free and loose so that you can call them into action easily, quickly, and naturally. Let your hands rest comfortably at your sides, relaxed but ready. Occasionally rest them on the lectern. Then, as you unfold the ideas of your speech, use descriptive gestures to indicate size, shape, or relationship, making sure the movements are large enough to be seen in the back row. Use conventional gestures to give visual dimension to your spoken ideas. Keep in mind that there is no "right" number of gestures to use; however, during the preparation of your talk, think of the kinds of bodily and gestural actions that complement your personality, ideas, language, and speaking purposes.

Selecting the appropriate method of presentation and using your voice and body productively enhance the chances of gaining support for your ideas. Practice is the key to the effective use of these elements. Through practice, you can judge your method of presentation. You can also see how your voice and body complement or detract from your ideas. The more confident you feel about presenting the speech, the more comfortable you will be, and confidence is built through careful preparation and practice. Remember that the nonverbal channel of communication creates meaning for your audience.

Chapter Summary

Every speaker should effectively use the *aural and visual channels* of communication. A good voice enables a speaker to present a clear message. A flexible speaking voice has *intelligibility, variety,* and *understandable stress patterns.* Loudness, rate, enunciation, and *pronunciation* interact to determine intelligibility. Varying standards of pronunciation create regional speech differences known as *dialects.* Changing *rate, pitch, stress,* and *pauses* influence the variety of presentation and help eliminate monotonous delivery. *Emotional characterizers* communicate shades of meaning to listeners.

Physical movements complement vocal quality to add clarity to the message. Speakers can use space, or *proxemics,* to create physical and psychological intimacy or distance. *Movement* and *stance* regulate communication. *Facial expressions* communicate feelings, provide important clues to meaning, establish visual bonding with listeners, and influence perceived speaker credibility. Finally, *gestures* enhance listener responses to messages, if the gestures are relaxed, definite, and properly timed.

Selecting the appropriate method of presentation and using your voice and body to communicate enhance your chances of gaining support for your ideas and communicating meaning to your listeners.

Reference Notes

1. R. Geiselman and John Crawley, "Incidental Processing of Speaker Characteristics: Voice as Connotative Information," *Journal of Verbal Learning and Verbal Behavior* 22 (1983): 15–23.

2. W. Barnett Pearce and Bernard J. Brommel, "Vocalic Communication in Persuasion," *Quarterly Journal of Speech* 58 (1972): 298–306; Thomas Frentz, "Rhetorical Conversation, Time, and Moral Action," *Quarterly Journal of Speech* 71 (1985): 1–18.

3. The term *loudness* is used synonymously with *intensity* here because the former term is clearer to most people. Technically, of course, loudness—a distinct function in the science of acoustics—is not strictly synonymous with intensity. To explain the exact relationship between the two terms is beyond the scope of this textbook because the explanation involves many complicated psychophysical relationships. For a full discussion of these relationships, see Giles W. Gray and Claude M. Wise, *The Bases of Speech*, 3rd ed. (New York: Harper & Row, Pubs., Inc., 1959), Chapter 3.

4. Mark L. Knapp, *Essentials of Nonverbal Communication* (New York: Holt, Rinehart & Winston, Inc., 1980).

5. Klaus R. Scherer, H. London, and Garret Wolf, "The Voice of Competence: Paralinguistic Cues and Audience Evaluation," *Journal of Research in Personality* 7 (1973): 31–44; Jitendra Thakerer and Howard Giles, "They Are—So They Spoke: Noncontent Speech Stereotypes," *Language and Communication* 1 (1981): 255–61; Peter A. Andersen, Myron W. Lustig, and Janis F. Andersen, "Regional Patterns of Communication in the United States: A Theoretical Perspective," *Communication Monographs* 54 (1987): 128–44.

6. Bruce L. Brown, William J. Strong, and Alvin C. Rencher, "Perceptions of Personality from Speech: Effects of Manipulations of Acoustical Parameters," *Journal of the Acoustical Society of America* 54 (1973): 29–35.

7. Haig Bosmajian, ed., *The Rhetoric of Nonverbal Communication* (Glenview, IL: Scott, Foresman and Company, 1971).

8. Much of this research is summarized in Mark L. Knapp, *Nonverbal Communication in Human Interaction*, 2nd ed. (New York: Holt, Rinehart & Winston, Inc., 1978).

9. Dale G. Leathers, *Nonverbal Communication Systems* (Boston: Allyn & Bacon, Inc., 1975), 4–5.

10. For a fuller discussion of each of these components, see Leathers, 52–59.

11. Hall divides interhuman communication distances into four segments: *intimate distance*—up to 1½ feet apart; *personal distance*—1½ to 4 feet; *social distance*—4 to 12 feet; and *public distance*—12 feet or more. On the basis of these distinctions, he has carefully noted how people's eye contact, tone of voice, and ability to touch and observe change from one distance to another. See Edward T. Hall, *The Hidden Dimension* (New York: Doubleday & Co., Inc., 1969), Chapter X.

12. Albert E. Scheflen, "The Significance of Posture in Communication Systems," *Psychiatry* 27 (1964): 321.

13. Paul Ekman, *Emotion in the Human Face*, 2nd ed. (Cambridge: Cambridge University Press, 1982).

14. Robert Rivlin and Karen Gravelle, *Deciphering the Senses: The Expanding World of Human Perception* (New York: Simon & Schuster, Inc., 1984), 98; Flora Davis, "How to Read Body Language," *Glamour Magazine* (September 1969).

15. For a difficult but rewarding essay on the management of demeanor, see Erving Goffman, *Interaction Ritual: Essays on Face-to-Face Behavior* (New York: Doubleday & Co., Inc., 1967), 5–46.

16. For a more complete system of classifying gestures, see Paul Ekman and Wallace V. Friesen, "Hand Movements," *Journal of Communication* 22 (1972): 360.

Key Terms

vocal quality	*stress*
conversationality	*emphasis*
intelligibility	*pauses*
noise	*emotional characterizers*
rate	*nonverbal communication*
enunciation	*proxemics*
pronunciation	*movement*
dialects	*posture*
vocal stereotypes	*affect displays*
pitch level	*conventional gestures*
pitch range	*descriptive gestures*
pitch variation	*indicators*

Problems and Probes

1. The instructor will divide the class into small groups. Given the physical constraints of your classroom (size, furniture, and so on), each group will design a speaker-audience configuration that differs from the way in which the chairs and lectern or table are traditionally arranged. A representative from each group will explain his or her group's alternative room arrangement. The class then will discuss the pros and cons of the different suggestions in terms of the effective use of space.

2. The instructor will divide the class into small groups. Each group will be given an excerpt from a speech or a play, or a short piece of fiction (selected by the instructor). In working on an oral presentation of the material, each group will be assigned a different facet of vocal presentation (rate, pitch, stress; different dialects; expanded gestures and physical movement) to implement. After a representative of each group presents his or her group's rendition of the material to the class, the class as a whole will discuss the influence of shifts in vocal presentation on the impact or meaning of the material.

Communication Activities

1. Can your speaking voice be easily understood? As a test of your intelligibility, the instructor may ask you to deliver a short speech with your back to the audience. Stand in approximately the same place you normally do when speaking to the class.

2. Your instructor will provide the class with a list of emotions. Each student is to choose one emotion and to decide on a number. Using only vocal cues and speaking only that number, each student is to try to express that emotion. The class should try to guess what emotion is being expressed. After each attempt, the class should suggest additional cues that will help the speaker express the emotion.

3. Prepare and present a short speech describing an exciting event you have witnessed—an automobile accident, a political or campus rally, a sporting event. Use movement and gestures to render the details clear and vivid. That is, make the audience "see" and "feel" the event as you integrate words/ideas and movements/actions for maximum impact. Successful completion of this assignment should demonstrate your ability to use all of the available message systems.

PART FOUR

Types

> "*All the ends of speaking are reducible to four; every speech being intended to enlighten the understanding, to please the imagination, to move the passion, or to influence the will. Any one discourse admits only one of these ends as the principal.*"

George Campbell
The Philosophy of Rhetoric *(1776)*

CHAPTER FIFTEEN

Speeches to Inform

O urs is a society that almost worships facts. Particularly because of such technological developments as electronic media, photostatic printing, miniaturized circuitry, and computerized data storage and retrieval systems, a staggering amount of information is available. Mere information, however, does nothing, tells us nothing; information is simply there until human beings shape, interpret, and act upon it. That is why public speakers often are called upon to assemble, package, and present information to other human beings.

One theme will be sounded throughout this chapter: *"Mere information" is useless until someone has put it together in ways that make it clear and relevant to the lives of others.* Informative speeches are needed to clarify and make data and ideas relevant to audiences. In this chapter, we will discuss various types of informative speeches, as each type has its own purpose and internal rhetorical dynamics; we then will outline the essential features of all informative speeches, to make your challenges clearer; and finally we will review some of the standard ways of structuring each type.

Types of Informative Speeches

Informative speeches take many forms, depending upon the situation, the level of knowledge possessed by audience members, and your own abilities as a presenter of data. Four of these forms—speeches of definition, instructions and demonstrations, oral reports, and lectures—occur so frequently, however, that they merit special attention.[1]

Speeches of Definition

"Mommy, what's a 'knucklehead'?" "Professor Martinez, could you tell me what a 'quark' is?" "Joanne, before we can decide whether to buy this house, you're going to have to answer a dumb question for us: What's 'earnest money'?" You have been asking these sorts of questions all of your life. As you can see, a speech of definition is not something that merely asks for a dictionary definition of something; you could look up the word if that were all that is involved. Rather, a **speech of definition** seeks to define concepts or processes in ways that make them relevant to a situation or a problem an audience faces. Once five-year-old Sarah knows what a "knucklehead" is, she will know she has a human relations problem she had better work on; once you know what a "quark" is, Professor Martinez's lecture will make a good deal more sense; and, once you know that "earnest money" is simply a sign of good faith in a purchase agreement, your anxiety will disappear.

Notice that these examples have two characteristics: (1) you are offered a *vocabulary*—"knucklehead," "quark," "earnest money"—for dealing with the objects, people, and processes under consideration and (2) you are given an *orientation*, a way of thinking about a phenomenon. The idea behind "earnest money," for example, forces you to think about property sale as a two-way street, a transaction in which the seller is risking as much as the buyers. A notion such as "the welfare syndrome" demands that you look beyond food stamps, unemployment compensation, and social security checks in order to visualize what is essentially a separate subculture in this country, one with its own ways of thinking and acting. A good definitional speech, therefore, provides listeners with a vocabulary they can attach to ideas and situations and with orientations that organize bits of information into coherent wholes.

Instructions and Demonstrations

Throughout your life, classroom instructions, job instructions, and instructions for the performance of special tasks have played vital roles. Not only have you gone through many "tell" sessions with others, but you have also had people "show" you how to execute desired actions—how to implement a special procedure in chemistry class, how to conduct a voter registration drive, how to make a never-fail soufflé. **Instructions** are verbal communications that explain complex processes, while **demonstrations** are verbal and nonverbal messages explaining and illustrating such processes.

Speeches of demonstration and instruction have two essential features. Both involve the *serial presentation* of information, usually in clearly defined steps or phases. They normally are organized, therefore, in chronological or spatial patterns. Also, both demand *utter clarity*, simply because your listeners are expected to be able to repeat or reproduce the steps through which you take them.

Informative speeches take many forms. A speech of definition seeks to define concepts and processes in ways that make them relevant to a situation or problem. Instructions are verbal communications that explain complex processes, whereas demonstrations are verbal and nonverbal messages explaining and illustrating such processes. In an oral report, a speaker assembles, arranges, and interprets information in response to a request by a group. Finally, an explanatory speech is one in which the speaker either clarifies a concept, process, object, or proposal or offers a supporting rationale for a contestable claim.

Oral Reports

An **oral report** is a speech in which one assembles, arranges, and interprets information gathered in response to a request made by a particular group. A business firm may ask one of its members to assemble statistics relative to employment, sales, or cost overruns; a congressional committee may call in outside experts to offer testimony; a club may ask its treasurer to report on patterns or trends in its finances over a specified period; a college might wish its registrar to report to the faculty on steps the school can take to

recruit more students with particular backgrounds or interests. As these examples indicate, there are two basic types of reportive speeches: the **factual report** concentrates upon assembling, arranging, and interpreting raw information and the **advisory report** makes a set of recommendations relative to information that has been prepared.

As a reporter, you should be aware of certain restrictions. Above all, bear constantly in mind your role as an *expert*—the source of predigested information for an assemblage of people who, in turn, will act upon it. That role carries tremendous responsibilities. It demands that you prepare with special care and that you present your material with clarity and balance. The success of a business firm, the government's legislative program, or your club's future all may depend upon your reporting abilities. Therefore, keep the following guidelines in mind as you prepare and deliver your report:

1. *The information you present must be researched with great care.* Although you may be asked only to present a series of statistical generalizations in a five-minute report, your research must be extensive and solid. You must assemble your material cleanly, free of bias or major deficiency. The quarterly report for a business that relies upon material gathered from only one of the territories in which it operates may not only be partial, but also skewed. Furthermore, even though you may be asked only to report the bare facts of your information, you could be asked to expand upon what you say—to supply the figures on which you based your statistical conclusions—in a question-and-answer session. Have all of your information available, even if you are allotted only a short time for your presentation.

2. *When making recommendations rather than merely reporting information, be sure to include a complete rationale for the advice you present.* Suppose, for example, that you have been called upon by your student-government council to recommend how certain unappropriated monies should be spent. First, you will need to gather information on specific needs: Does this campus require additional buses (and should you, therefore, recommend further subsidy for public transportation)? Could it use more student-sponsored scholarships? Might it profit from a "careers week" during which recruiters from various businesses, industries, and other endeavors hold special seminars for interested students? To make recommendations on these needs, you must have financial information on the cost of each proposal. Second, you will need to assemble data on student interest, based upon interviews and patterns of usage observed in the past. Third, in order to make sound recommendations, you will have to rank the options open to the group. Fourth, you will need to build a rationale for your ranking, including answers to such questions as: What student needs will each course of action meet? Why do you consider one need more pressing than the other? Why should student government, and not another college or university agency, act to meet that need? Were student government to act on a specific need, what other kinds of university, community, and/or governmental support would be forthcoming over the short and long term? Answers to such questions in each case provide the rationale for decision. This is important for two reasons. Such a rationale enhances your image, or credibility, because it demonstrates your ability to think through and rationally solve problems. Unless your credibility is strong, your rec-

ommendations have little chance for action. More importantly, if your rationale is a good one, it probably will be adopted by the audience as a whole, for the audience, in turn, has constituencies—the student body, specific organizations represented on the government council, and so on—to which it must answer when it takes action. In other words, by making recommendations and also offering reasons, you allow your auditors to meet objections, to urge the action, and so on in the important second step of persuasion—the appeal to secondary audiences.

3. *Make full use of visual aids when giving reports.* Because reports often have to be short and to the point and yet contain a great amount of information, the reporter must decide how to present a maximum amount of useful material in the shortest period of time. The advice on using visual aids presented in Chapter 13 is germane.

4. *Stay within the boundaries of the charge you were given.* As a reporter, you are a primary resource on the audience's subject of interest. You, therefore, must be highly sensitive to the audience's expectations: Were you charged with gathering information only or were you told what kind of information to bring in? Were you instructed to assemble recommendations for action? Were you to include financial and impact analyses along with those recommendations? Most reporters are given a charge, a duty to perform. If you depart too far from that charge—if you make recommendations when you are expected only to gather information, or if you only gather information when you have been asked to make recommendations—you are likely to create ill will among your listeners. When this occurs, your work will be for naught; you will have failed as a reporter. Clarify the boundaries within which you are operating; when given a task, ask for relevant instructions. In that way, as you discharge your duties, you probably will satisfy the group and, consequently, will also increase (or at least not diminish) your own credibility and status.

Explanations

An **explanatory speech** is one in which the speaker either clarifies the nature of a concept, process, object, or proposal or offers a supporting rationale for a contestable claim. The notion of "clarifying" means that speeches of explanation have much in common with definitional messages, because one function of a definition is to clarify. Normally, though, an explanatory speech is less concerned with the word or vocabulary than it is with connecting one concept with a series of others. For example, a speech of definition on political corruption would concentrate on the term, telling what sorts of acts committed by politicians are comprehended by the term. An explanatory speech on corruption, however, would go into more depth, perhaps indicating the social-political conditions likely to produce corruption or the methods that are available for eliminating it. The clarification involved in an explanatory speech, therefore, is considerably broader and more complex than that demanded of a speech of definition.

The key to most explanatory speeches, however, lies in the second notion—"offering a rationale." Most explanations explain from a particular point of view. Suppose, for example, you wanted to tell an audience how the American Revolution came to be. You could offer a great number of explanations, depending upon your point of view. One explanation might be economic, stressing that the Revolution was the result of disagreements between Americans and Britons over trade and taxation policies. Another might be political, noting that the Americans felt a strong need for self-government. A third might be social or cultural, for surely the Revolution could not occur until the colonists had a strong sense of their own social identity as separate from the mother country. In a speech on public health, you could offer several explanations of how contagious diseases spread. You could talk about the biochemical processes of contagion; the physiological processes of debilitation; the environmental means by which diseases spread; or even the sociological relationships between subgroups of people, which allow viruses to spread through some parts of a population but not others. The point is, each of these explanations of the American Revolution and of the spread of communicable diseases is "correct"; each explains satisfactorily how war or pestilence spreads through a country. There are probably as many different explanations of phenomena as there are vantage points. By now you have probably heard economic, sociological, and political explanations of urban decay; moral, educational, and sociological ramifications of the country's high divorce rate; and every explanation possible of the effects of excessive TV viewing.

Explanations, therefore, represent some of the most sophisticated and complicated kinds of informative speeches you will ever give. They are needed whenever an audience is in confusion or ignorance. An explanation is called for any time concepts are fuzzy, information is only partial, effects cannot easily be attributed to their causes, or competing claims are at loggerheads. Explanatory speeches arise whenever people ask the questions "what," "how," and "why" when trying to understand ideas and physical processes.[2]

Essential Features of Informative Speeches

Four qualities should characterize any speech to inform: (1) clarity, (2) the association of new ideas with familiar ones, (3) coherence, and (4) motivational appeal.

Clarity

The quality of clarity is largely the result of effective organization and the careful selection of words. Informative speeches achieve maximum clarity when your listeners can follow you and understand what you are saying.

In organizing your speech, observe the following rules:

1. *Do not try to cover too many points.* Confine your speech to three or four principal ideas, grouping whatever facts or ideas you wish to consider under these headings. Even if you know a tremendous amount about your subject matter, remember that you cannot make everyone an expert in a single speech.

2. *Clarify the relationship between your main points by observing the principles of coordination.* Word your transitions carefully—"*Second,* you must prepare the chair for caning by cleaning out the groove and cane holes"; "The Stamp Act Crisis was *followed by* an *even more important* event—The Townshend Duties"; "To test *these* hypotheses, we set up the *following* experiment." Such transitions allow auditors to follow you from point to point.

3. *Keep your speech moving forward according to a well-developed plan.* Do not jump back and forth between ideas, charging ahead and then backtracking.

In wording your speech, follow the advice offered in Chapter 12:

1. *Use a precise, accurate vocabulary without getting too technical.* In telling someone how to finish off a basement room, you might be tempted to say, "Next, take one of these long sticks and cut it off in this funny-looking gizmo with a saw in it, and try to make the corners match." An accurate vocabulary helps your listeners remember what supplies and tools to get when they approach the same project: "This is a ceiling molding; it goes around the room between the wall and the ceiling to cover the seams between the paneling and the ceiling tiles. You make the corners of the molding match by using a mitre box, which has grooves that allow you to cut 45-degree angles. Here's how you do it."

2. *Simplify when possible, including only as much technical vocabulary as you need.* Do not make a speech on the operation of a two-cycle internal combustion engine sound as if it came out of a lawn mower mechanic's operational manual. An audience bogged down in unnecessary detail and vocabulary can become confused and bored.

3. *Use reiteration when it clarifies complex ideas, but avoid simply repeating the same words.* Rephrase to help solidify ideas for those who had trouble getting them the first time: "Unlike a terrestrial telescope, a celestial telescope is used for looking at moons, planets, and stars; that is, its mirrors and lens are ground and arranged in such a way that it focuses on objects thousands of miles, not hundreds of feet, away from the observer."

Televised Information

*P*ublic-speaking textbooks discuss the importance of shaping and interpreting information so that listeners are given not only the facts but also ways of understanding them. In public speaking, the shaping and interpreting processes occur in words, in things you say about facts or ideas. In the case of television news, however, meaning is also communicated in other ways, a fact that bothers critic and communications scholar Neil Postman of New York University. His 1985 book *Amusing Ourselves to Death* expresses his concerns about televisual discourse and the meanings it makes for us.

Postman calls the eighteenth century the Age of Exposition. That century witnessed the peak of printing's power. The printed word, in the forms of books, newspapers, pamphlets, and political broadsides, surrounded the citizens of the western world. Print taught people to read ideas one at a time, to link them together with the kinds of verbal transitions discussed in Chapter 12, and even to criticize each other in logical and relevant ways.

He terms the twentieth century, however, the Age of Show Business. With the advent and dominance of television in our lives, according to Postman, information and ideas come to us chopped into little pieces, into the sound bites and video clips of televised news. The average length of a network tele-

Association of New Ideas with Familiar Ones

Audiences grasp new facts and ideas more readily when they can associate them with what they already know. Therefore, in a speech to inform, try to connect the new with the old. To do this, of course, you need to have done enough solid audience analysis so that you know what experiences, images, analogies, and metaphors to use in your speech.

Sometimes the associations you ought to make are obvious. A college dean talking to an audience of manufacturers on the problems of higher education might present her ideas under the headings of raw material, casting, machining, polishing, and assembling. She thus translates her central ideas into an analogy her listeners, given their vocations, would be sure to

vision shot is 3.5 seconds; the average length of network news stories is 45 seconds. When continuing stories, such as a presidential campaign, are involved, as Professor Kathleen Jamieson of the University of Texas-Austin noted at the 1988 Speech Communication Association convention, coverage of a particular candidate's activities is closer to 18 seconds a night.

Postman argues that all of this leads to a "peek-a-boo world," in which information pours down upon us in extremely small units, in which discontinuity rather than coherence and continuity is a fact of life (with television's main transition being "And now . . . this"), and in which the credibility of the information giver is more important than reason or logic. Reminding us that people often pointed out contradictions between what then-President Ronald Reagan said from one day to the next, Postman notes that Reagan's illogic did not really bother the American people very much because they have become conditioned to absorb information in unconnected bits.

In one sense, then, Postman's research suggests that we may be swimming upstream in our battle to demand of public speakers logical coherence—carefully described and explicitly interpreted ideas. Should we then give up the fight to improve public communication? That view is too cynical. Better is Postman's own effort: to return in face-to-face speaking situations to older practices, where people spoke to each other via well-chosen words with clear and adequate information appropriately interpreted for five, ten, or twenty minutes at a time. While the speed and razzmatazz of MTV is entertaining, it should not be mistaken for informative communication.

FOR FURTHER READING

Postman, Neil. *Amusing Ourselves to Death: Public Discourse in the Age of Show Business.* New York: Penguin Books, 1985.

understand and appreciate. At other times, if you cannot think of any obvious associations, you may have to rely on common experiences or images. For instance, you might explain the operation of the human eye pupil by comparing it to the operation of a camera lens aperture.

Coherence

Coherence is, in part, a matter of organization—of finding a pattern that fits your subtopics together in a meaningful manner. Sometimes it is relatively easy to create a sense of coherence, as when giving a speech on the structure of the federal government, for there are only three branches. At other times,

ASSOCIATION OF NEW IDEAS
WITH FAMILIAR ONES

Snail Shell
(Single Unit)

House
(Single Unit)

Honeycomb
(Multi-Unit)

Condominium
(Multi-Unit)

especially when you are not covering all components of a subject, you have to manufacture coherence.

Occasionally, you may have to do a little forcing. Suppose you decide to give a speech on the Nielsen television program rating system. You might discuss only three aspects of the system—what it is, how it works, and how it is used by network executives to determine which programs to continue and which to drop. To give the speech coherence, you could use a question-answer organizational pattern and move into the body of your speech in this fashion: "People who worry about the effect of the Nielsen ratings on what they watch usually ask three questions: 'What *is* a Nielsen rating, anyway?' 'How is the rating done?' 'Why do the networks rely on it for making decisions on shows?' To answer these common questions and to explain the 'what,' 'how,' and 'why' of television ratings, today I will . . ." Notice that the speaker used a common trio of words—"what," "how," and "why"—as an organizing principle to give coherence to this explanatory speech.

Motivation of the Audience

Finally, and perhaps most important, you must be able to motivate the audience to listen. Unfortunately, many people ignore this essential feature of good informative speeches. Many of us blithely assume that because we are interested in something, our audience also will want to hear about it. To you, stamp collecting may be an interesting, relaxing, and profitable hobby, but until your listeners are likewise convinced, they will yawn through your speech on American commemoratives.

Keep in mind, therefore, what you have learned about attention and motivation when preparing informative speeches. Use the factors of attention to engage the members of your audience. Be sure to build in motivational appeals, reasons they should want to know what you are about to tell them. If you indicate that your talk will increase their interpersonal effectiveness, provide them with additional income, reduce their confusion about important matters, or the like, you make your speech relevant and compelling.

Structuring Informative Speeches

Now that we have discussed the various types of informative speeches and their essential features, it is time to examine ways to structure each of those types. Of course, it is possible to use any of the organizational patterns mentioned earlier, but some patterns are better suited to particular types than others.

Speeches of Definition

Speeches of definition usually are easy to structure. The main problem speakers face is in finding ways to engage the audience members psychologically.

Introduction. Because speeches of definition treat either unfamiliar or familiar concepts in a new light, their introductions must create curiosity and need in listeners. Curiosity is a special challenge in speeches on unfamiliar concepts, for we all are tempted to say, "Well, if I've made it this far through life without knowing anything about black holes, carcinogens, or trap blocking, why should I bother with learning more about these ideas now?" The answer, to a large extent, depends upon your ability to make people wonder about the unknown. You may want to concentrate part of your introduction to a definitional speech, therefore, on making listeners desire to know more about unknown aspects of their everyday environment or of far-away segments of life.

Speeches on both unfamiliar and familiar concepts must be attentive to listeners' needs or wants. This means that the introduction should include motivational materials—explicit statements that indicate how the information can affect the audience. Thus, you might say, "Understanding the dynamics of trap blocking will help you better appreciate line play in football and, therefore, increase your enjoyment of the games you attend in our stadium."

Body. Most speeches of definition use a topical pattern (see Chapter 9) because such speeches usually describe various aspects of a thing or an idea. It seems natural, for example, to use a topical pattern when giving a speech on a career in computer programming and to organize the body of the speech around such topics as "the duties of a computer programmer," "skills needed by a computer programmer," and "training you will need to become a computer programmer."

There are occasions, too, when other patterns serve your specific purpose well. You might use an effect-cause pattern, for example, when preparing an informative speech on the laws of supply and demand. You could enumerate a series of effects with which people are already familiar—soaring prices coupled with seemingly fantastic sales, interest rates that apparently change every other week—and then discuss the laws of supply and demand that account for such confusing fiscal patterns in society.

A speech on cancer could be outlined as follows.

What Does Cancer Mean?

I. "You have cancer" is a phrase that can strike fear into the hardiest among us. Fear of the unknown is the most difficult to accept. Thus, if we are to understand cancer, we must know more about what the term means.
   A. My intent is to acquaint you with several terms that, together, will give us a better understanding of cancer.
   B. By knowing more about what is involved in cancer, we can eliminate needless fear.
II. There are several terms used in the scientific discussion of cancer. Not all are clearly understood.
   A. "Carcinogen": Chemicals from various products (for example, cigarette smoke) may lead to cancer.
   B. "Activation": The carcinogen must be chemically changed in order to start the cancer process.
   C. "Detoxification enzymes": These are naturally occurring chemicals in the body that detoxify—take the poison out of substances ingested into the body.
      1. Most carcinogens entering the body are detoxified and can cause no harm.
      2. In some cases, the detoxification process goes wrong, and the carcinogen is rendered capable of entering a cell's nucleus and attaching itself to DNA.
   D. "DNA attachment": The DNA is the central code that determines the function of the cell, the central operating system of the human computer.
      1. The second line of defense occurs when scavenger molecules attack the activated carcinogen and render it harmless.
      2. Unfortunately, this line of defense sometimes fails.

    3.   DNA has a third line of defense, as invading activated carcinogens can be isolated by DNA repair molecules.

    4.   Unfortunately, this line of defense can also fail.

  E. "Cell mutation and division": Remember your junior-high biology? Cells divide and create exact replicas.

    1.   If the defenses have failed, an active carcinogen is attached to DNA inside a cell.

    2.   Cell division will produce two new cells with the carcinogen-affected DNA.

    3.   Mutation is not an automatic sign of cancer, for the alteration may only cripple one cell.

  F. "Promoter chemicals": These are chemicals near the mutated cell that foster its multiplication, to the detriment of other nonmutants nearby.

    1.   The mutant cell may also be attacked by a second carcinogen.

    2.   If all of the defenses fail again, a second mutation occurs.

    3.   After several cycles of mutation and promotion, a group of cells may begin to form a tumor.

III.   I hope this review of the major terms and their meanings gives you a better understanding of the term "cancer."[3]

Conclusion.   Conclusions for speeches of definition frequently have two characteristics: (1) they usually include a summary, especially if many facts, figures, and ideas have been covered and (2) they often stress the ways in which people can apply the ideas they have been given. For example, a speech on your campus' aerobics classes could conclude with a review of the main features of aerobics exercise and a list of campus buildings where noon and evening classes are held. As with all good conclusions, the ending of a speech of definition should not come abruptly, as a dictionary definition does. Rather, round it off for your listeners, tying it up in ways useful to them.

Instructions and Demonstrations

Instructions and demonstrations are easy to assemble. Your most difficult tasks are in adapting your presentation to the physical demands of the situation.

Introduction.   In most situations in which you will be called upon to give instructions or to offer a demonstration, you will need to spend little time piquing curiosity or motivating people to listen. After all, if you are instructing your listeners in a new office procedure or giving a workshop on how to build an ice boat, they already have the prerequisite interest and motivation; otherwise, they would not have come. If your listeners' attendance is not voluntary (as can be the case in speech communication classrooms), then you will have to pay attention to motivational matters. Normally, however, you must concentrate your introduction on two other tasks:

1. *Preview your speech.* If, say, you are going to take the members of your audience through the seven steps involved in making a good tombstone rubbing, give them an overall picture of the process before you start describing each operation in detail.

2. *Encourage them to follow along, even through some of the more difficult steps.* A process like tombstone rubbing, for example, looks easier than it is; many are tempted to quit listening and give up somewhere along the way. If, however, they are forewarned and are promised special help with the difficult techniques, they are more likely to bear with you.

Body.   As suggested earlier, you should package most speeches of demonstration and instruction in a chronological and/or spatial pattern, simply because you are teaching people a serial process you want them to be able to carry out on their own. A nonsequential organizational pattern would be very confusing.

In other words, speakers usually have little trouble organizing the body of a speech of demonstration or instruction. Their problems are more likely technical ones:

1. *The problem of rate.* If the glue on a project needs to set before you can go on to the next step, what do you do? You cannot just stand there and wait for it to dry. You need to have prepared some material for filling the time—perhaps additional background or a brief discussion of what problems one can run into at this stage. Plan your remarks carefully for those junctures; otherwise, you are likely to lose your audience.

2. *The problem of scale.* How can you show various embroidery stitches to an audience of twenty-five? When dealing with minute operations, you often must increase the scale of operation. In this example, you might use a large piece of plastic needlepoint canvas or even a 3' by 4' piece of cloth stretched over a wooden frame. By using an oversized needle, yarn instead of thread, and stitches measured in inches instead of millimeters, you could easily make your techniques visible to all audience members. At the other extreme, in a speech on how to make a homemade solar heat collector, you probably would want to work with a scaled-down model.

3. *The coordination of verbal and visual materials.* Both instructions and demonstrations usually demand that speakers "show" while "telling." To keep yourself from becoming flustered or confused, be sure to practice talking while doing—demonstrating your material while explaining aloud what you are doing. Decide where you will stand when showing a slide so that the audience can see both you and the image; practice talking about your aerobic exercise positions while you are actually doing them;

work a dough press in practice sessions as you tell your intended audience how to form professional-looking cookies. If you do not, you will inevitably get yourself into trouble in front of your real audience.

Thinking through such procedural and technical problems you can face might lead to an outline like the following one on planting tomatoes.

How to Plant Tomatoes

□ *Coordinate verbal and visual materials*

I. First, you must select a variety of tomato seed that is suited to various geographical, climatological, agricultural, and personal factors. [display chart, showing varieties in columns along with their characteristics]
  A. Some tomatoes grow better in hard soils; some, in loose soils.
  B. Some varieties handle shade well; some, direct sunlight.
  C. Some are well suited to short growing seasons; others, to long seasons.
  D. Each variety tends to resist certain diseases, such as blight, better than others.

II. Once you have selected a variety (or maybe even two, so that they mature at different times), next you must start the seeds.

□ *Coordinate verbal and visual materials*

  A. Prepare a mixture of black dirt, peat moss, and vermiculite as I am doing. [do it, indicating proportions]
  B. Fill germination trays, pots, or cut-off milk cartons with the germination soil, and insert seeds. [do it]

□ *Reduce time delay (rate)*

  C. With watering, sunlight, and patience, your plants will grow. I can't show you that growth here today, but I can use these seedlings to illustrate their care along the way. [bring out half-grown and fully grown seedlings]

□ *Coordinate verbal and behavioral actions*

    1. When the seedlings are about an inch or two tall, thin them. [demonstrate]
    2. At about six inches [show them], you can transplant them safely.
    3. But, you'll know more about which plants are strong if you wait until they are ten to twelve inches tall. [show them plants of different strengths]
  D. Now you are ready to transplant the seedlings to your garden.
    1. Carefully unpot the seedlings, being sure not to damage the root network. [demonstrate]

☐ *Coordinate visual and verbal materials; enlarge materials*

2. Put each seedling in a hole already prepared in your plot; this diagram shows you how to do that. [show an enlarged drawing that illustrates hole size and depth, a mixture of peat moss and vermiculite in the bottom, and spacing of plants]
3. Pack the garden soil firmly but not so hard as to crush the roots.
4. Water it almost every day for the first week.

☐ *Coordinate verbal and visual materials; reduce size of materials*

5. Put some sort of mulching material—grass clippings, hay, black sheets of plastic—between the rows if weeds are a problem. [another drawing or picture]

E. Once you know your plants are growing, cage or stake each plant. [show sketches of various styles of cages or stakes, discussing the advantages of each]

Conclusion. Conclusions for demonstration speeches usually have three parts. First, *summaries* are offered. Most audiences need this review, which reminds them to ask questions about procedures or ideas they do not fully understand. Second, some *bolstering* has to take place. People trying their hand at new processes or procedures usually get into trouble the first few times and need to be reassured that this is natural and can be overcome. Finally, *future help* should be offered. What sounded so simple in your talk can be much more complicated in execution. If possible, make yourself available for later assistance, as group leaders often do when orienting new members or employees: "As you fill out your registration form, just raise your hand if you're unsure of anything and I'll be happy to help you." Or point to other sources of further information and assistance: "Here's the address of the U.S. Government Printing Office, whose pamphlet X1234 is available for only a dollar; it will give you more details"; "If you run into a filing problem I haven't covered in this short orientation to your job, just go over to Mary McFerson's desk, right over here. Mary's experienced in these matters and is always willing to help." Such statements not only offer help, but assure your audience members that they will not be labeled as dull-witted if they actually have to ask for it.

Oral Reports

Oral reports require more difficult structuring decisions than do the types of speeches we have discussed thus far.

Introduction. Oral reports are requested by a group, committee, or class; the audience members, therefore, generally know what they expect and why. In introducing oral reports, then, you need not spend much time motivating your listeners—they already are motivated. Rather, you should concentrate on (1) reminding them of what they asked for, should their memory be short, (2) describing carefully the procedures you used in gathering the information, (3) forecasting the development of various subtopics so listeners can follow you easily, and (4) pointing ahead to any action they are expected to take in light of your information. Thus, the key to a good introduction for an oral report is *orientation*—reviewing the past (their expectations and your preparations), the present (your goal now), and the future (their responsibilities once you are done). Remember that you give the report to an audience for a purpose.

Body. The principle for organizing the body of an oral report can be stated simply: Select the internal organizational pattern best suited to the audience members' needs. Have you been asked to provide them with a history of a group or problem? Use a chronological pattern. Do they want to know how a particular state of affairs came to be? Try a cause-effect format. Have you been asked to discuss an organizational structure for the group? A topical pattern allows you to review the constitutional responsibilities of each officer. If you were asked to examine the pros and cons of various proposals and to recommend one to the group, you could use a topical pattern, enumerating and eliminating possibilities, as in the following example.

Report from the Final Examination Committee

I. My committee was asked to compare and contrast various ways of structuring a final examination in this speech class and to recommend a procedure to you. [the reporter's "charge"]
    A. First, we interviewed each one of you.
    B. Then, we discussed the pedagogical virtues of various exam procedures with our instructor.
    C. And next, we deliberated as a group, coming to the following conclusions. [orientation completed]
II. Like many students, we first thought we should recommend a take-home essay examination as the easiest way out.
    A. But, we decided our wonderful textbook is filled with so much detailed and scattered advice that it would be almost impossible for any of us to answer essay-type questions without many, many hours of worry, work, and sweat.
    B. We also wondered why a course that stresses oral performance should test our abilities to write essays.
III. So, we next reviewed a standard, short-answer, in-class final.
    A. Although such a test would allow us to concentrate on the main ideas and central vocabulary, which has been developed in lectures, readings, and discussion, it would require a fair amount of memorization.

B. And, we came back to the notion that merely understanding communication concepts will not be enough when we start giving speeches outside this classroom.

IV. Thus, we recommend that you urge our instructor to give us an oral examination this term.

    A. Each of us could be given an impromptu speech topic, some resource material, and ten minutes to prepare a speech.

    B. We could be graded, in this way, on both substantive and communicative decisions we make in putting together and delivering the speech.

    C. Most important, such a test would be consistent with this course's primary goal—and could be completed quickly, almost painlessly.

Conclusion. Most oral reports end with a conclusion that mirrors the introduction. The report's purpose is mentioned again; the main points are reviewed; committee members (if there are any) are thanked publicly; and then either a motion to accept the committee recommendations (if there are any) is offered or, in the case of more straightforwardly informative reports, questions from the audience are called for. Conclusions to reports—when done well—are quick, firm, efficient, and pointed.

Explanations

Usually, introductions and conclusions give you your greatest challenges when structuring explanations.

Introduction. Introductions to explanatory speeches can use many of the techniques described thus far. You may have to raise curiosity in some instances: how many of your classmates are wondering about the causes of the American Revolution at ten o'clock in the morning? You usually have to generate a desire to listen, too, especially if your topic seems distant or irrelevant. Also, if the explanation is somewhat complex, a forecast of coming ideas is almost mandatory. Finally, you may need to encourage people to follow along, telling them you will go into greater detail in the more difficult sections.

Body. The body of most explanations fits into causal or topical organizational patterns. If you are trying to explain how or why something operates the way it does, either cause-effect or effect-cause works very well. If you are trying to explain how a problem can be solved, you might find that a straightforward problem-solution format is your most efficient choice. These two organizational patterns are well suited to explanations because, as we noted earlier, explanations seek to interconnect phenomena and/or ideas.

Conclusion. Typically, the conclusion of a good speech of explanation develops additional implications or calls for particular actions. If, for example, you have explained how contagious diseases spread through geographical areas, you probably should conclude by discussing some actions listeners can take to halt the process of contagion. If you have explained the concept of "children's rights" to a parent-teacher organization, close by asking your listeners to consider what these rights mean to them—how they should change their thinking and behaviors toward six-year-olds.

Suppose you are a theater buff, and you decide to discuss Shakespeare's Globe Theater in a speech of explanation. Consider the following outline to see how some of this advice can be put to work for you.

The Globe Theater

General Purpose: To inform
   Specific Purposes: To increase audience interest in performances of Shakespeare by explaining how characteristics of his plays were shaped by the physical structure of the Globe Theater and vice versa

Introduction
Curiosity: Raise their curiosity by noting how odd some of the special effects and stage directions are in Shakespearean plays. [Show sketches or a model of the Globe.]
   Desire: Indicate that increasing their knowledge of Shakespearean play production will not only make them more liberally educated college students but should help them improve their performance in literature class.

Body
Organizational Pattern: Use a kind of problem-solution pattern to capture listeners up in the dynamics of theater construction, for example:
I.   External characteristics of the Globe
   A.   Shakespeare wished the audience to see better, so a round (20- or 24-sided) theater was constructed.
   B.   Shakespeare wished to accommodate both wealthy and poor patrons, so the good seats were elevated and covered, while the "groundlings" stood in the pit (open semicircle in front of the stage).
II.   Internal characteristics of the Globe
   A.   Shakespeare needed elevations to stage such scenes as the balcony scene in *Romeo and Juliet.*
      1.   A half-roof over the upper stage could be the balcony or castle top.
      2.   It also could house musicians who played drums and wind instruments to represent thunder and wind.
   B.   Because the stage was rounded, actors could not move into the wings, yet Shakespeare's plays needed to move actors on and off easily and to "hide" some actors from others, as when Polonius in *Hamlet* or Iago in *Othello* overhears someone talking.
      1.   Multiple rear exits into so-called tiring rooms were built.
      2.   Some exits led backstage, while others were covered with curtains to serve as hiding places.

C. Elizabethan plays were filled with ghosts, angels, devils, and other apparitions that needed to appear suddenly.
  1. Shakespeare accommodated the ghosts and devils by The Heavens, the upper stage noted before.
  2. For the lower spirits and disappearing magicians, he filled the main stage with trap doors so that actors could suddenly sink away in a burst of smoke.[4]

[Other points having to do with costumes, banners, dueling, and so on could be made.]

Conclusion

Implications: Point out that we usually read plays as "literature," but, in reality, they ought to be read as "performance guides"; also indicate that plays from ancient Greece, the Restoration period, and even contemporary dramatists are designed in part to fit the stage mechanisms and styles of a particular era.

Overall, informative speeches are greater challenges than most people realize. Information is not useful to listeners until it has been carefully selected, structured, and cast into motivational appeals that draw them in. "The facts" are seldom enough for human beings; as an informative speaker, you must supply the rest.

Sample Speech

The following is a student explanatory speech. Notice the attempt to convince audience members that their lives will be affected by Compact Disc Interactive (CDI) in the first paragraph; the use of a topical pattern—explanation, applications, and evaluation—in the body of the speech; and the efficient summary and final motivation of the audience in the conclusion. Ms. Seidl built a clear, smooth explanation of CDI.

The Next Electronic Revolution
Barbara Seidl

You may have seen this before. It's a CD—Compact Disc Audio, actually. It was the "miracle music technology" of 1982. But if you weren't a particularly avid music fan, it was, well, interesting, but perhaps more interesting than most anticipated. From this basic technology has come this: a system which has applications reaching far beyond the music industry into education, professional job training, home maintenance, and health care, just to name a few. This is Compact Disc Interactive, the technology that Phillips, Sony, Hitachi,

Toshiba, and a number of other companies which are difficult to pronounce, are calling "the next electronic revolution." In fact, according to a phone interview with President of International Consumer Technologies Robert Kotick: When CDI hits the market in the fall of 1988, it will change everything—from the way we learn and work to the way we buy our clothes and see our physician. So this new technology is going to have a profound effect on our lives. Perhaps we should learn more about it. /1

We'll first examine what CDI is, including what is meant by that "I" for interactive, explore some of the applications of this new electronic revolution, and evaluate the concerns of the future acceptance of compact disc interactive. /2

In order to understand what CDI is, we need to first have a working knowledge of the technology behind it, or what I like to call the ABC's of CD's. A compact disc, CD audio, or CDI, is a type of laser disc which just means that the information on it is read by a laser, or a type of light beam. The programming of a compact disc involves embedding the disc with a series of pits. For example, one disc might contain Encyclopedia Britannica's A through L; another, duplicate film footage of the Wright Brother's first flight; and a third, the Air Force theme song. So when you type "History of Airplanes" into a personal computer, amazing things happen. The laser beam passes over the pits, the screen becomes a movie screen, as you watch Wilbur and Orville give it one more shot. A recorded human voice describes the scene, and provides you with historical information while the background music of the Air Force theme song can be heard through state-of-the-art CD technology. But with Compact Disc interactive, what you see is only the beginning of what you get. It's the interactive, in Compact Disc Interactive, that makes this technology so revolutionary. Interaction means you can move and see and change anything on the screen, in the music, or in the narration. You can even put yourself on the screen. And the image you will be viewing is more than the cheap computer graphics we are so used to seeing. This image was taken from one of the latest McIntosh programs; and this is a CDI image, comparable to a high-quality Hollywood film. As stated in the March 29th, 1988 edition of the *Wall Street Journal*, "The time has come when people have a choice of watching 'Raiders of the Lost Ark' or being in 'Raiders of the Lost Ark.'" /3

Now that we have a basic understanding of CDI technology, let's briefly consider the technology required to use it. One of the key considerations in the development of CDI was its ability to piggyback on previous technology like television sets and CD players. The result is a remarkably flexible system. CDI disks can be played three different ways: by plugging a CDI disk player into your television set; by plugging one into your personal computer; or on a full-fledged CDI system which includes a keyboard, a disk drive, and a touch sensitive screen. /4

But, adaptable or not, a technology without applications does bring us right back to, uh—interesting. In a speech presented at the 1987 IEEE Convention of the Institute of Electrical and Electronic Engineers, Inc., Gordon Stober,

President of Polygram Corporation, said that CDI presently has over ninety applications. For our purposes we will narrow these to three areas. CDI's role in entertaining, in healing, and in living day-to-day. /5

CDI has created an entirely new form of entertainment—interactive movies. The August 1987 edition of *CDI News* discussed two movies: "Exposed" (an adult film which the article did not cover extensively, and so neither shall we) and "Danger in Dreamland." This film was originally produced by a Chicago comedy troop called Firesign Theatre, and follows the antics of Nick Danger. Antics—which you determine. For example, Nick would approach a door, hear a blood-curdling scream from the other side, so he'd step away from the door, and the frame freezes. You, the viewer, are asked, "Should Nick go through the door?" You respond, and the film continues until the next decision. /6

In the medical profession, CDI has both preventive and curative applications. One form of prevention is training, and Phillips International Media Corporation has recently introduced a CPR dummy that uses CDI technology. A narrative explanation and a video familiarize the student with this procedure, and then the dummy is hooked up to the machine. And the dummy is actually pretty bright. It talks, saying "your hand's in the wrong place," "the pressure's uneven," or "you're doing just fine." CDI has curative abilities, in that you can maintain records of not only medical charts and graphs, but also film footage of your surgery and your recovery process. This will allow physicians to draw more accurate diagnoses, and better serve your needs. /7

But it is CDI's role in our day-to-day lives that's most fascinating. CDI's function on the home front ranges from mundane bookkeeping to do-it-yourself disks. Reynolds and Reynolds Computer Systems of Dayton, Ohio, has introduced their latest idea at the 1987 IEEE Convention. They are producing do-it-yourself auto maintenance disks which are interactive. Now the disk essentially contains a movie of engine repair, except you can stop the movie at any time, pick parts up, turn them around, ask questions, look at the engine from a different angle, anything that would make it easier and more fun for you to do it yourself. /8

If you'd like to leave the car to the mechanics, but would stay home to do your shopping, Phillips is working the bugs out of a system that would essentially serve as a visual mail order catalog. One of the most intriguing parts of this system is that a portion of the disk has been left blank so that when you purchase it, visual images of you and your family members can be programmed onto the disk allowing you to try things on before buying. /9

Now this disk itself is going to run anywhere between fifteen and thirty-five dollars, whereas the full-fledged CDI system according to the August 1987 edition of *CDI News* is going to cost between $500 and $1,000. Now the attractiveness of these costs to the general consumer is just one of the many concerns over the future acceptance of CDI. /10

There seems to be some question over whether America wants to interact, as Gary Kilgo, President of Knowledge Set, stated in an April interview. Let's take the average person out there. Are they really going to buy a CD player and hook it up to their TV set? Most people are just interested in popping a beer and watching a game. And there's nothing wrong with that. It is responses like this that have sparked CDI producers to work all the harder on programs that might appeal to the general public, and understandably, because that appeal is very important. /11

But the greatest concern over the effect of CDI is what impact it might have on our younger society. Will the child that learns how to interact with the computer, whether at home or at school, also be able to interact with people? This is a significant concern, and consequently educators, programmers, and parents alike are keeping a close eye on CDI, and understandably. Compact Disk Interactive is estimated to hit the market in under six months. Consumer and computer experts concur as to both the negative and the positive potential of CDI. /12

Now having acquired a basic understanding of CDI technology, its applications in a number of areas, and some of the concerns over its future acceptance, you should be able to draw your own conclusions about participating in this interesting evolution, because you'll soon be encountering the grandchild of this odd little disc, this miracle music technology. Compact Disk Interactive (CDI)—it's the next electronic revolution.[5] /13

Chapter Summary

Speeches to inform include all messages that attempt to assemble, package, and interpret raw data, information, or ideas. Four common types of informative speeches are *speeches of definition, instructions and demonstrations, oral reports,* and *speeches of explanation.* No matter what type of informative speech you are preparing, you will need to strive for *clarity, ways to associate new ideas with familiar ones, coherence,* and *methods to motivate an audience.* Think carefully through the various organizational structures available to you and select one that best suits your purpose and message.

Reference Notes

1. For more detail on each of these types of informative speeches, see Bruce E. Gronbeck, *The Articulate Person; A Guide to Everyday Public Speaking,* 2nd ed. (Glenview, IL: Scott, Foresman and Company, 1983), Chapters 5 and 6.

2. For an interesting discussion of the what/how/why aspects of explanation, see W. V. Quine and J. S. Ullian, *The Web of Belief* (New York: Random House, Inc., 1970), Chapter 7, "Explanation."

CHAPTER SIXTEEN

Speeches to Persuade and Actuate

Speeches to persuade and to actuate are designed to bring about changes in people's psychological states or behaviors. In comparison, a successful *informative* speech affects listeners by increasing their understanding of an idea or event; by altering their conceptions of the world; or, in the case of instructions and demonstrations, by illustrating how to accomplish a task. For example, you could present an informative speech on the American two-party political system by describing two-party vs. multiparty coalition politics, by comparing two-party democracies with one-party totalitarian governmental systems, or even by tracing the history of two-party confrontations in various epochs of U.S. history. In each instance, the central focus of an informative speech is always on *information* and its successful (clear) transmission.

In contrast, the central focus of *persuasion* is on *change* and/or *action*. If your purpose were to present a persuasive speech about a facet of American politics, you could attempt to convince people that one party is better than the other or that a particular election was misinterpreted by some historians. An actuative speech might urge that everyone vote on the second Tuesday in November. As these examples illustrate, the persuader/actuator makes quite a different demand on an audience than does the informer. The informative speaker is satisfied when listeners understand what has been said; the persuader, however, is not successful until the audience *internalizes* or *acts upon* the message. The demand is either for personal change in beliefs, attitudes, or values or for action premised on such change.

The concept of persuasion, therefore, encompasses a wide range of communication activities, including advertising, marketing, sales, political cam-

Persuasive speaking is the process of producing oral messages that increase personal commitment; modify beliefs, attitudes, or values; or induce action.

paigns, and interpersonal relations. Because we are examining speechmaking, we will narrow our focus to the three types of speeches that will be discussed in this chapter. *Persuasive speaking is the process of producing oral messages that (1) increase personal commitment; (2) modify beliefs, attitudes, or values; or (3) induce action.* Before examining each type of speech that can flow from a persuasive or an actuative purpose, we will consider three dimensions of the general process of persuasion. We will extend and apply some material presented earlier (especially in Chapters 5 and 6) to help you accomplish a persuasive or an actuative purpose. Finally, we will consider typical approaches to structuring each major type.

The Challenge of Persuasion

Persuading others is a challenging task. People do not simply change their long-standing beliefs or values on a whim, nor do they choose to act upon the ideas of others without good reason. The speaker's task of providing "good reasons"[1] can be facilitated by considering three general dimensions of the persuasive process: (1) *adapting to an audience's psychological state*, (2) *drawing upon external reference groups*, and (3) *enhancing personal credibility*.

Adapting to an Audience's Psychological State

The phrase **psychological state** refers here to the complex of beliefs, attitudes, and values that an audience brings to a speech occasion. First, an individual's degree of *cognitive complexity* affects his or her response to messages. Second, individuals may be *predisposed* to respond favorably or unfavorably to a persuasive message. Individuals also vary in their degree of *hostility* toward the topic and in the *centrality* or *saliency* of their beliefs, attitudes, and values. They also vary in terms of the degree, or *latitude*, of change they will accept.

Cognitive Complexity. **Cognitive complexity** is a matter of an individual's sophistication, not simply the number of things a person knows, but rather his or her abilities to deal with a wide range of causes, implications, and associated notions when thinking about an idea or event. Cognitive complexity is partly intelligence, partly maturity, and partly experience. While

---

Persuading others is a challenging task. People do not simply change their long-standing beliefs or attitudes on a whim, nor do they choose to act upon the ideas of others without good reason.

there is much work remaining to be done in this area of research, the following observations are well grounded in the literature: (1) cognitively complex audiences demand and can follow relatively *sophisticated arguments*, (2) they respond better to *two-sided* than to one-sided messages (whether hostile or not), (3) they require a comparatively large amount of *evidence* before they will change beliefs and attitudes, and (4) cognitively complex *speakers* generate more *strategically sound tactics* and, hence, are (and are perceived as) more competent communicators.

In adapting to such audiences, your task as a persuader is to provide evidence, to reason cogently, and generally to offer more than simple solutions to complex problems. Petty and Cacioppo have developed a theory of persuasion, the **Elaboration Likelihood Model,** that supports this approach. They suggest that "in a persuasion context, elaboration refers to the extent to which a person scrutinizes the issue-relevant arguments contained in the persuasive communication. When conditions foster people's motivation and ability to engage in issue-relevant thinking, the 'elaboration likelihood' is said to be high."[2] Recognizing that not every audience member is in a position to make decisions about a speaker's claim on such a systematic basis, Petty and Cacioppo note that when people have *low motivation* to think about the issues, or when their ability to critique is constrained by other influences, they make decisions based on *peripheral* concerns. These might include deference to the authorities cited by the persuader, the credibility or even attractiveness of the speaker, and other concerns not central to the message itself. Individuals also vary in the degree to which they *need* to be involved cognitively in affairs going on around them. Persons relatively high in cognitive need tend to pay more attention to a systematic appraisal of what they hear. Individuals lower in a need for cognitive activity tend to rely on peripheral concerns in decision making. One advantage of addressing individuals who will give your ideas intense scrutiny is that any alteration in their beliefs and attitudes will last longer and be more resistant to attempts to change their new position.[3]

Predisposition Toward the Topic. As noted in Chapter 5, there are five possible attitudes that an audience can have toward your topic and purpose: (1) favorable but not aroused to act; (2) apathetic toward the situation; (3) interested in it but undecided what to do or think about it; (4) interested in the situation but hostile to the proposed attitude, belief, value, or action; or (5) hostile to any change from the present state of affairs. Furthermore, these predispositions may be relatively fixed or tentative and may be either uniformly present or only held by some individuals. Given the potential variability, consider the following suggestions as you design your message.

First, if you sense that audience members are *hostile* toward your *message*, adjust your content by presenting *both sides* of the issue under discussion. A one-sided speech offers only arguments for your claim, while a *two-sided* message acknowledges opposing ideas and refutes them. If you expect resistance, this strategy is more effective than simply ignoring the audience's position. If the hostility is extreme, deal with it early in the speech. By doing so, you let audience members know that you are aware of their disagreement with your ideas. You can defuse their initial hostility by appealing to their sense of fair play—their willingness to hear you out, to agree to disagree without being disagreeable.

Second, if your analysis indicates that listeners' beliefs are relatively well fixed and important to them or are the result of their own direct experiences, they are going to be more resistant to change. The more central or highly significant beliefs, attitudes, and values are, the greater the likelihood they are part of a *network* of interconnected concepts. A study by Prescott demonstrated clearly, for example, that people who are against abortion are likely to be in favor of physical punishment for children and capital punishment for criminals and against prostitution, nudity, premarital sex, and drugs.[4] In your role as a persuader, therefore, you must assess the degree to which your position runs counter to such a network of interconnected beliefs or attitudes. When your analysis suggests that it does, you can try to deal with the whole complex. If this seems impossible, you can try separating one issue from the others by demonstrating its uniqueness. By stressing the unique problems encountered by physically abused children, for example, you can put some distance between reactions to this issue and a person's beliefs about other potentially related issues.

Third, attitudes may not only be central but highly salient at a given moment. **Saliency** refers to the relevance and interest level of a belief, attitude, value, or issue for an individual. For example, topics currently on the front page of a local or national newspaper often are highly salient for people. Beliefs and attitudes that are regularly invoked in our daily interactions, direct experiences, and relationships are highly salient. In general, the more salient attitudes and beliefs are for a person, the more "accessible" they are to both the listener and the persuasive speaker.[5] The following suggestions will help you adjust your persuasive strategies to take saliency into account:

1. *When topics are highly salient, listeners are more likely to be familiar with the central issues.*[6] You do not need to spend a lot of time gaining audience attention or developing the background or reasons for the importance of a highly salient issue. Conversely, topics low in salience require much more development of an attention step that highlights the significance of the topic.

2. *Similarly, as noted, when topics are highly salient, listeners are more likely to resist changes in their beliefs and attitudes.*[7] Treat this situation as you would a hostile one, by acknowledging the audience's resistance in the need step and then demonstrating in the satisfaction step why the new or different beliefs and attitudes you propose are essential to a positive solution of the problem.

3. *When saliency is high, increasing the number of cogent or strong arguments you offer on behalf of your ideas has a positive influence on*

listeners; when saliency is low, increasing the number of both *strong and weak arguments enhances the persuasive effect.*[8] Thus, strong, cogent arguments for your position are essential in either case.

4. *Audience members are more likely to be highly critical if your position challenges their central values.*[9] Decriminalizing drugs, protecting the rights of persons with alternate life-styles, and promoting an equal rights amendment are all issues that elicit strong positive or negative reactions from many people. Advocating change in any of these areas challenges accepted values and asks people to rethink their most cherished and centrally held assumptions about human relations. The tactics of separating values from one another and gaining small concessions in a prolonged campaign are appropriate in dealing with the saliency of central values.

5. *Quote salient* authorities *in your persuasive and actuative speeches.* Citing Lyndon LaRouche rather than Jesse Jackson on an issue concerning social welfare makes a difference. The expertise of the individuals aside, one may be far more salient with respect to the issue, as well as to the listeners' feelings about the issue. There is some evidence to suggest that citing salient authorities is more influential with those who use peripheral cues to judge persuasive outcomes; those less involved with the issue are affected more by sources than those highly involved. The more a person is willing to take the time to process the information presented, the less influential specific sources become.[10]

Degrees of Change.   In addition to adapting to the cognitive complexity and predispositions of an audience, recognize that people will change only so much in response to a speech. It is extremely difficult, except in the rarest of circumstances (for example, radical religious experiences), to make wholesale changes in people's beliefs, attitudes, and values, especially if they are hostile to your ideas or their views are of central importance. Generally, you should strive for **incremental change**—step-by-step movement toward a particular goal. The distance you can move audience members is determined by (1) their *initial attitude* and (2) the *latitude of change* they can tolerate.

Assume that you have been asked to indicate your present attitudes toward a topic on a scale ranging from "extremely favorable" to "extremely unfavorable." If the topic were legalized abortion, the scale might look like this:

1	extremely favorable toward legalized abortion
2	moderately favorable
3	mildly favorable
4	neutral
5	mildly unfavorable
6	moderately unfavorable
7	strongly unfavorable toward legalized abortion

INCREMENTAL APPROACH TO ATTITUDE CHANGE

Incremental Attitude Change

1 2 3 4 5 6 7

An attempt to convince someone who is strongly unfavorable (*7*) that abortion should remain legal (*1*) would probably fail, even though you presented both sides of the argument. Even in the face of credible speakers and well-thought-out arguments, most radical "anti's" could only be moved a short way toward the pro position, if at all (for example, from 7 to 6). Trying to change them too much in a single speech can produce a boomerang effect; the persuasive attempt backfires and creates more rather than less resistance to your ideas. In the face of a strong *1* speech, most 7's will be even more committed to their position.[11] You can avoid a boomerang effect by working toward a small change; ask audience members to accept a small deviation from their current position by accepting a modest proposal. An opposite approach also might work; begin with a strong message that is likely to be rejected and follow it with a more moderate proposal. Be sure that your initial request cannot be deemed absurd, however, or the audience will not bother to listen to your next proposal.[12]

The precise degree of change people will tolerate varies from individual to individual and from topic to topic. *Authoritarian* individuals, for example, tend to support more conservative political candidates, to defer to higher authority, and to express strong aversion to what they see as "social deviants"—those who violate the normal social, moral order of a community.[13] Such people have a narrow **latitude of acceptance;** in terms of the numerical scale used in the legalized abortion example, we can assume their views are firmly anchored in one number, whether it is *2, 5,* or *7.* Individuals who are more "open-minded" would be receptive to a message that fell within a 3–5 range on the numerical scale; they would be easier to persuade or to move to action.[14] By assessing the degree of your audience's latitude of acceptance, you will be in a good position to determine your chances of success with a "one-shot" message. The more authoritarian the listeners, the more likely that incremental change will be in order, with a sustained campaign to change their thinking; if the audience is relatively open-minded, you will have greater flexibility in the degree of change you can advocate.

Obviously, it is impossible for a speaker to interview all audience members, noting their degree of cognitive complexity, writing down their predispositions toward the topic on a numerical scale, and determining their degrees of change. Good audience analysis, however, allows you to guess shrewdly, at least, and to adjust your appeals and plans of action accordingly. In a controversial situation, you can get a feel for the mood of the people from prior public expressions by members of the community, either in letters to the editor, in comments to a television news reporter, or in public speeches. Advance planners for a presidential candidate, for example, visit a community days in advance of a planned speech to assess community feeling on a broad range of issues. By reading the newspaper and listening to the evening news, as well as talking to community leaders, they are able to identify the salient issues and tell the candidate the best ways to address them. With careful attention to the audience's internal psychological state, you can select strategies that will maximize your chances of successful persuasion.

Drawing upon External Reference Groups

Reference groups, as we have seen, are collections of people and organizations that affect individuals' beliefs, attitudes, and values. You may or may not hold actual membership in such groups; you may belong to the Young Republican Club and not to a Peace Action Committee, yet each group can influence your beliefs. Membership can be voluntary (for example, you might join a group because it espouses a cause) or involuntary (you are either male or female and you were born into a particular ethnic group). Groups whose values are similar to yours generally have a positive effect on your attitudes or behavior, while those whose values are dissimilar may produce negative reactions. Given these possible associations, we can think of reference groups as *membership* and *nonmembership groups, voluntary* and *involuntary groups,* and *positive* and *negative groups.*

Our beliefs, attitudes, and values are based, in part, on the traditions and customs of reference groups, although we all differ in our degree of direct reliance. The content of your persuasive message can reflect alliances with the audience's reference groups. The following suggestions can help you adjust your message to take maximum advantage of reference group information:

Beliefs, attitudes, and values are based, in part, on the traditions and customs of reference groups, although people differ in their degree of direct reliance.

1. *You can cite the opinions of voluntary, positively viewed groups whose values* coincide *with the positions you are taking.* You also can use the approach of "praising Athens to the Athenians," by stressing the positive characteristics of a reference group when speaking to members of that group or when some members are present in the audience.

2. *You can make effective use of voluntary, negative, nonmembership groups when they* oppose *the position you are advocating.* Such groups can be thought of as the "devils" to which people react; if the claims you are defending go counter to the thinking and actions of "devil-groups," your audience will be more likely to be responsive to your ideas.

3. *The more significant a person's* roles *are in any group, the more the group's norms and beliefs influence that person's thoughts and behavior.* Corporate executives, for example, tend to have more important roles in business than do new, relatively powerless workers. Hence, it is more difficult to produce radical business-oriented attitude changes in executives than in front-line workers.[15]

4. *Reference groups may provide a sense of security, of "belonging to the majority."* When your position reflects that of the majority, audience members are more disposed to process the views systematically; their acceptance tends to be more lasting.[16]

Enhancing Personal Credibility

The issue of authority brings us to the third essential dimension affecting the persuasive process. A good deal of your potential effectiveness depends upon your perceived credibility, or ethos. In Chapter 1, we outlined several factors that can determine listeners' perceptions of your credibility—their sense of your expertise, trustworthiness, competency, sincerity or honesty, friendliness and concern for others, and personal dynamism. While you should work to maximize the potential impact of all of these factors whenever speaking, regardless of purpose, they are especially important when you seek to change someone's mind or behavior. The following guidelines can assist you in making decisions about the use of credibility as an effective tool in persuasion.

First, when speaking to people who are relatively unmotivated and who do not have enough background information to critically assess what they hear, the higher your credibility the better your chances of being a successful persuader. Conversely, if your credibility is low, even strong arguments will not overcome your initial handicap.[17] This fact should give you a clear sense of why your own credibility is an important component in your chances for success.

Second, you can increase the likelihood of being judged credible when seeking to persuade an audience by taking steps to enhance your image of *competence* and *sincerity*. People who do not take the time to weigh your reasons and evidence are unlikely to change their beliefs and values if they think you have done a poor job of researching the issues or are insincere. There are several things you can do to increase the audience's perception of your competence: (1) carefully set forth all of the competing positions, ideas, and proposals relevant to a topic *before* you come to your own judgment; (2) review various criteria for judgment to show that your recommendations or positions flow from accepted and generally held criteria; and (3) show that the recommendations you offer actually will solve the problems you identified in the need step of your speech. You can increase the audience's sense of your sincerity by: (1) showing yourself to be open to correction and criticism should any listener wish to question you (a calmly delivered, relevant response does more to defuse hecklers than responding in kind);[18] (2) exuding personal warmth in your relations with the audience; (3) maintaining direct eye contact with listeners; and (4) recognizing anyone who has helped you understand and work on the issue or problem. Using these tactics is simply good common sense if you wish to be believed as a competent and sincere speaker.

Third, heighten audience members' sense of your *expertise, friendliness,* and *dynamism,* especially when seeking to move them to action. People are unlikely to change their routines on your recommendation unless they feel that you know what you are talking about, that you have their best interests in mind, and that you are excited about your own proposal. Expertise can be demonstrated by: (1) documenting your sources of information; (2) using a variety of sources as cross-checks on each other; (3) presenting your information and need analyses in well-organized ways; (4) using clear, simple visual aids when they are appropriate or necessary; (5) providing adequate background information on controversial issues; (6) separating causes from effects, short-term from long-term effects, hard facts from wishes or dreams, and one proposal from others in a competent manner; and (7) delivering your speeches in a calm and forthright manner. A sense of friendliness and concern for others can be created by: (1) treating yourself and others as human beings, regardless of how controversial the topic is and how intensely you disagree with others, and (2) depersonalizing issues, talking in terms of the "real-world" problems rather than in terms of personalities and ideologies. Finally, an audience's sense of your dynamism can be enhanced by: (1) speaking vividly, drawing clear images of the events you describe; using sharp, fresh metaphors and active rather than passive verbs; and expressing your ideas with a short, hard-hitting oral style rather than a long, cumbersome written style and (2) using varied conversational vocal patterns, an animated body, direct eye contact rather than reliance upon your notes, and a firm upright stance.[19]

A public speaker's principal communicative virtue is the presence of a living, active human being behind the lectern—a person who *embodies* a message, whose own values are expressed in and through the message. People command more attention and interest than written words, and people, unlike films and videotapes, can feel, can react to audience members, and can create a sense of urgency and directness. Hence, personal credibility is an extremely valuable asset for the persuader and actuator.

The three dimensions of persuasion do not, of course, tell the whole story of persuasion and its effects. Nonetheless, by understanding the principles involved and the strategies to use—*adapting to an audience's internal psychological state, drawing upon external reference groups,* and *enhancing personal credibility*—you will be a more effective persuader. With this information as a theoretical and practical backdrop, we now turn our attention to some specific ways of organizing a persuasive speech around a specific purpose.

Types of Persuasive and Actuative Speeches

Although there are many ways to classify persuasive and actuative speeches, we will examine them in terms of their psychological and behavioral force. That is, in classifying these speech types, we are concerned with the *demands* each type makes upon an audience's mental state and level of activity. This focus allows us to identify three principal types of persuasive and actuative speeches and some specific subtypes that are easily differentiated in terms of more precise demands they make upon audiences. We will examine speeches of reinforcement, modification, and actuation.

Speeches of Reinforcement

Americans are joiners. To get our political, economic, social, and personal work done, we constantly organize ourselves into groups and associations. Action-oriented groups serve you by gathering and packaging the latest information, by keeping on top of issues that are important to the members of the group and proposing solutions to specific problems. Service groups organize charities, perform volunteer work, and provide support for other activities in communities.

An inevitable fact of group life is that, as time goes by, members' interest in activities declines, membership drops, and the cause for which the group was formed gets lost in the myriad of causes competing for the attention and support of the people in the community. Periodically, people need to be reminded of why they joined the group, what its services are, and how the group helps them meet their personal goals. On other occasions, the group may be relatively healthy and active but about to undertake a project that will test individuals' commitment to the group. On these occasions, persuasive speakers can convince members to endure sacrifice and hardship to see the struggle to its end with messages that remind them of their common goals. In both cases, the reminders are matters of reinforcement.

In public speaking, **reinforcement** is a process of calling up the original beliefs and values that caused people to join a group in the first place and of reinvigorating audience members so they once more contribute their time, energy, and finances to the tasks needing to be done. In a practical sense, reinforcement speeches are *epideictic*—they seek to increase adherence to, or rejection of, a particular set of values. As Perelman and Olbrechts-Tyteca observe, "epideictic discourse sets out to increase the intensity of adherence to certain values, which might not be contested when considered on their own but may nevertheless not prevail against other values that might come into conflict with them. . . . In epideictic oratory, *the speaker turns educator*" (emphasis added).[20]

Reinforcement speeches are called for when listeners are mentally apathetic and physically lethargic. People behave as though they are unconcerned about the problem. This is often the case with fund-raising drives for charitable causes: every fall the United Way asks you to contribute; public lobbies, such as Common Cause or the Nature Conservancy, periodically send out appeals for financial assistance. In cases in which apathy is less extreme, the committed still need an extra nudge to dip into their pockets and give assistance. Televangelists crusade for dollars on behalf of their continuing ministries. Political candidates hold fund-raising dinners to support their campaigns. Whether the state of apathy and lethargy is extreme or moderate, the message is oriented toward reaffirming basic verities, reeducating audience members about the values that attracted them to the group in the first place.

The key to reinforcement speaking is motivation. While people may say, "Sure, I support the Republican party," or "Yeah, I agree with SADD's efforts to control drug and alcohol use in the schools," they may not be motivated to act upon the basis of their convictions. They need to have their original commitment resurrected. Jesse Jackson's speech to the delegates at the 1988 Democratic National Convention is one example of a speech designed to serve an educative function and gain active support for the Democratic party.

Speeches of Modification

Unlike speeches of reinforcement, speeches of **modification** seek specific psychological changes in one's belief state, attitudes toward an object, or basic values. Speeches of this type have been the central feature in the art of rhetoric since the time of the early Greeks. Whether your present or future role is that of a student, businessperson, lawyer, minister, sales clerk, doctor, or parent, the task of changing the views of others is a constant demand of your daily life. Using the categories of beliefs, attitudes, and values described in Chapter 5, we can examine three subtypes of speeches aiming at modifying the views of listeners.

Changing Beliefs. The psychological basis for most speeches aimed at changing someone's beliefs about the world is *differentiation*. That is, one can get you to change your beliefs about anything from eating seaweed to the balance of power between the U.S. and the U.S.S.R. by persuading you to perceive those matters in different ways. Persuaders who want you to differentiate between your old way of looking at something and a newer way of seeing it may use one or more of three basic strategies:

1. *Selective description.* A persuader may accentuate the positive and ignore the negative. Someone might persuade you to consider tofu an acceptable food by assuring you that its vitamin and mineral content is superior to that of foods in your normal diet, while ignoring your questions about its taste or processing costs. As we have seen, because it is a one-sided strategy, selective description would not be an advisable tactic in those situations where the audience is strongly hostile toward the message.

2. *Narrative.* A persuader may use narrative forms, as we discussed them earlier, by telling a story about the United States preparedness level going into the Korean Conflict, with the moral that the country can never let its guard down. Two features of storytelling are essential if the narrative is to have persuasive force. First, listeners must perceive the story to be probable; it must make coherent sense to them. Second, the story must possess what Fisher terms "narrative fidelity"—it must appear consistent with other stories listeners have heard.[21] When both features are present, a story can function as a powerful image to move an audience.

3. *Appeals to uniqueness.* Someone attempting to get you to change your beliefs about a politician may convince you that the candidate is "not like all the others," pointing to unique aspects of her background, experience, public service, honesty, and commitment to action.

These three strategies are effective to the extent that listeners perceive the message to be important, novel, and plausible. The message must be one that is not already well internalized by the audience members (they are not already convinced), and the rationale for change must appear credible to them. Finally, the change itself must be seen as feasible or practical.[22]

Changing Attitudes. Attitude change is probably the most heavily researched psychological change of this century.[23] Given the previous discussion of attitude as predisposition, you are aware that this form of change involves modifying one's evaluation of an object from "good" to "bad," or at least to "neutral." Because attitudes are attached to beliefs ("Opportunities for women are increasing in this country [belief] and that is good [attitude]"), sometimes persuaders attempt to change an attitude by attacking a belief. If a speaker can show that opportunities for women are *not* increasing, or even demonstrate that the rate of increase is minimal or insignificant, he or she then can link that assertion to a negative attitude ("The slow rate of increase is harmful to women"). Because attitudes are organized into clusters around a value, they can sometimes be changed by getting people to think in different valuative terms. For instance, persons interested in advancing the cause of gay rights could argue in terms of equal access to the work place (a political value) instead of human rights (a sociological value).

Attitudes can be changed not only by attacking underlying beliefs or overarching values, but also by direct assault. Parents attempt to instill any number of attitudes in their young children by repeatedly offering short "lectures" (for instance, "Spinach is good for you" and "Don't give in to peer pressure—be an individual"). Repetition often has the desired effect, as children accept the attitude as their own and live by its creed. Recall Michael Dukakis at the 1988 Democratic National Convention repeating his parents' refrain "Much has been given you; you have much to give" as an attitude that became his personal rationale for seeking public office. Such direct assaults can be termed *brainwashing* when "they" (enemies or malicious people) use this technique and *education* when "we" (friends or "right-thinking people") use it. From our perspective, the cult members who committed suicide in Jonestown, Guyana, in 1978 were victims of brainwashing. From their perspective, they may have felt in the presence of a "right-thinking" individual who had taught them well; hence, they went willingly to their deaths.

Changing Values. Perhaps the most difficult challenge for any persuader is to change people's value orientations. As noted in earlier chapters, values are fundamental anchors, basic ways of organizing our view of the world and our actions in it. They are difficult but not impossible to change. Three techniques often are used:

1. *Valuative shifts.* Like differentiation, this technique asks an audience member to look at an issue or a proposal from a different valuative van-

Resistance to Counterpersuasion

*I*n this chapter, we have concentrated on the issue of persuading—increasing or otherwise changing people's acceptance of certain beliefs, attitudes, and values. We have not, however, focused on the ways in which you can increase your listeners' resistance to ideas that run counter to your own. Besides persuading them to accept your beliefs or attitudes, you also may need to protect them against *counterpersuasion*, attempts by others to influence your audience away from your position. By protecting your listeners from counterpersuasion, you can strengthen their adherence to your claim.

McGuire and his associates con-ducted a research program on resistance to ideas. They argue that "cultural truisms"—audience-held attitudes that appear so basic and correct as to seem invulnerable to attack—are, in fact, very vulnerable to counterpersuasion. Because people have not had to defend these attitudes, they have not developed the appropriate defensive skills; because they believe these cultural truisms to be invulnerable, they lack the motivation to develop strong defenses against counterpersuasive attempts. Consider, for example, the statement "Democracy is the best form of government." How well prepared are you, for instance, to present specific arguments in defense of this claim? If

tage point. The person asking you to buy insurance, for example, tells you to look at it not simply as financial protection (a pragmatic value) but as family protection and a source of peace of mind (sociological and psychological values). Such appeals can persuade people to shift their valuative orientation and see an issue or proposal in a new way. While the issue remains unchanged, its relationship to the audience member is transformed from a negative one ("*I* don't need financial protection") to a positive one ("You're right, the *family* will need protection if something happens to me").

2. *Appeals to consistency.* When you hear such appeals as "The American Legion favors . . ." you as a member of that organization are being asked

you are ill prepared, you are far less resistant to counterpersuasion than you might think. The antidote for your lack of preparation might involve an *inoculation* strategy: hearing refutations of the arguments that might be advanced in attacking your attitude. Inoculation provides you with a basis for responding to an attack, thereby increasing your resistance to counterpersuasion.

In addition to creating an inoculation strategy, you can increase resistance to counterpersuasive attempts either by forewarning audience members or by simply encouraging them to think seriously about their own behaviors and attitudes. *Forewarning* means letting audience members know in advance that they will be exposed to a counterpersuasive attempt—that someone will try to change their beliefs or values in ways that you, and they, may not desire. Time is a crucial variable; the more time between forewarning listeners and an attack on their attitudes, the stronger will be their resistance to the counterpersuasive message. Time allows them to formulate reasons to support their own attitudes and to reject possible arguments against them. Thinking about their beliefs and attitudes focuses attention on the actions that they are comfortable with retaining, and, like forewarning, gives them time to develop reasons to resist change.

A third strategy that increases resistance involves the amount of knowledge that people bring to a situation. For example, Hirt and Sherman found that individuals with greater knowledge are more resistant to refutational arguments. Thus, you can increase potential resistance to messages that are contrary to your own by adding to the audience's knowledge about the issues involved.

FOR FURTHER READING

Hirt, E. R., and S. J. Sherman. "The Role of Prior Knowledge in Explaining Hypothetical Events." *Journal of Experimental Social Psychology* 21 (1985): 519–43; Petty, Richard E., and John T. Cacioppo. *Communication and Persuasion: Central and Peripheral Routes to Attitude Change.* New York: Springer-Verlag, 1986.

to approve a certain measure in order to remain consistent with others in your reference group. Those for whom peripheral cues are important are likely to respond to this type of appeal. When someone projects a value orientation from the present to the future ("If you like horror films, you'll positively love the Friday the Thirteenth series"), he or she is appealing to cognitive consistency. As we have seen, people with a well-developed "need for cognition" are particularly affected by an appeal that includes a systematic appraisal of the reasons for accepting a certain value.

3. *Transcendence*. This sophisticated method for getting you to change your values approaches the issue from the perspective of a "higher" value.

The transcendence technique for altering values approaches the issue from the perspective of "higher" values. Oliver North used such appeals in his defense during the 1988 Iran-Contra hearings.

Oliver North used such appeals in defense of his actions during the Iran-Contra hearings. By appealing to "patriotic duty," he defended what appeared to many to be direct violations of the law. In this way, he sought to redefine his actions as consistent with higher national values, and, therefore, as excusable. Senator George Mitchell responded to North during one phase of the hearings by presenting a different hierarchy of values: patriotic duty does not stand above adherence to the law, regardless of the situation. From Mitchell's perspective, the actions were deemed inexcusable.

The dominance of central values impacts upon the potential for influencing people. For example, individuals who value freedom more than equality approach problems in fundamentally different ways than those who operate from an opposite perspective. Political conservatives tend toward freedom, while liberals focus more on issues of equality. Thus, a message that argues from an appeal to equality ("equal pay for equal work") will not be as well received by audiences that lean heavily toward the freedom pole. Conversely, a message that argues from an appeal to freedom ("A strong national defense is essential") will be less influential with an ultra-liberal (socialist, Marxist) audience. People who value both, or are less extreme in their preference for one over the other, demonstrate a more complex value structure (and one with potentially greater latitude for acceptance of proposals that are moderately divergent).[24] Knowing listeners' political values, thus, can be of enormous assistance in assessing the degree of value complexity they bring to the situation.

Thus, speeches of modification may seek a change in beliefs, attitudes, or values. Speeches designed to bring about these kinds of changes in listeners demand a higher level of communicative competence than most other types of speeches. As you know from experience, however, these competencies can be acquired by speakers willing to think through situations calling for such kinds of persuasion and willing to spend time on thorough speech preparation.[25]

Speeches of Actuation

Moving uncommitted or apathetic people to action is a chore many prefer to avoid. For example, you may have heard such expressions from friends and acquaintances as "I don't like to ask people to contribute money to a cause, even if it's worthy," "Don't ask me to solicit signatures for that petition—I feel like I'm intruding on others' privacy," or "I'm just not persuasive enough to get people to volunteer to work at the Kiwanis Auction—ask Mary." If all of us felt this way, little would be accomplished. In some cases, simply making a living requires that we move others to action. Even if you take one of these positions, some day you will have to engage in the task of creating a speech of **actuation.**

Consistent with our earlier definition of persuasion, *an actuative speech seeks, as its final outcome, a set of specifiable actions from its audience.* These actions may be as diverse as giving personal time to an activity (visiting a local nursing home), contributing money to a cause or product (donating to the Wildlife Fund), or changing a habit (stopping smoking). There are two types of audiences for whom actuative speeches are generally appropriate: (1) those who believe in the idea or action but are lethargic about doing anything and (2) those who doubt the value of the action and are uninformed or uninvolved. The second situation is our concern here.

Actuative speeches addressed to the uninvolved listeners or "Doubting Thomases" among us demand significant behavioral change. The goal might be as short range as making a profit the next quarter of the fiscal year or as long range as sociopolitical transformation of society. Whatever the extent or loftiness of the goal, all actuative speeches depend upon making a set of needs salient for an audience and then demonstrating that a certain course of action will satisfy those needs. Structurally, actuative speeches fit into the motivated sequence (discussed in Chapter 8) and use the other organizational patterns (discussed in Chapter 9) as appropriate to present a need for change and to illustrate how the solution remedies the problem addressed.

As in the case of speeches of reinforcement and modification, the key to effective actuation is motivation. No matter how wonderful the new product, how exciting the political candidate, or how worthy the cause, unless a listener is personally convinced that the product, candidate, or cause will make a significant change in his or her life, your speech will fail to have its intended effect.

With the discussion of the three dimensions of persuasion and the identification of three types of speeches (reinforcement, modification, and actuation) as a base, we can turn our attention to a practical issue: using the motivated sequence to organize these speeches into meaningful presentations.

Structuring Persuasive and Actuative Speeches

The overall structure of a persuasive or an actuative speech incorporates the features of the motivated sequence—attention, need, satisfaction, visualization, and action—relevant to the specific type of speech. Within each step, as appropriate to the topic and occasion, other patterns of organization can be used to bring a sense of coherence and cohesiveness to each step. (See Chapters 8 and 9 for more details on organizing speeches.)

The Motivated Sequence and Reinforcement Speeches

The visualization and action steps are the crucial elements in most reinforcement speeches. This is because the listeners are already convinced of the importance of the problem and are predisposed to accept particular solutions. The most important goal in a reinforcement speech is to get listeners to renew their previous commitments and to charge once more into the public arena to accomplish a common objective. Thus, a typical reinforcement speech following the motivated sequence usually has a short attention step, a need step that documents recent gains and losses (especially losses, as they illustrate the desirability of reengagement), little or no satisfaction step, a more fully developed visualization step (which lets listeners "see" themselves as reengaged with the issues), and an action step that focuses on particular actions to take now or in the near future (as audiences for these speeches are usually ready to respond quickly to appeals for renewed efforts).

In the following brief outline, the speaker is urging her players to rededicate themselves as they initiate a week of practice prior to playing for the league championship. There is little reason for a lengthy attention or need step, as the players are committed to the game and its role in their lives; the major emphasis is on reminding them of what they have done to get to this point and what remains to be done.

You're Already Winners

Specific Purpose: To reinforce the listeners' previous commitment to the team and to their own involvement in the sport

Attention Step
I. "Winning isn't everything; it's the only thing." For us, this will not mean "win at all costs."
II. Integrity and commitment yield winners.

Need Step
I. The way we use our time during our last practices is critical.
   A. "You play as you practice."
   B. Work ethic determines results.
II. Academically, you're already winners.
   A. You are proven student-athletes with the highest academic average of any team on this campus.
   B. The seniors will graduate.
III. Athletically, you're already winners.
   A. We can win the league championship.
   B. Integrity has earned positive recognition.

Satisfaction/Visualization Step (combined, as the solution [win the game] is accepted)
I. Why not quit now while you're ahead?
   A. It insults commitment to excellence.
   B. It lets your fans down.
   C. It lets me down.
II. Renew commitment to hard work, fun, and a winning attitude.
   A. These are the ingredients that led to our past success.
   B. They will be sufficient to carry us through this week, into the game, and beyond.
III. What does winning this final game mean?
   A. It means being satisfied with your own participation as a player and team member.
   B. It means recognition for you and the university.

Action Step
I. Now is the time to do what has to be done.
   A. Practice hard.
   B. Play the championship game with all your heart.
II. Win or lose, be satisfied with your individual effort.
   A. Individual and team integrity and discipline count.
   B. "Winning is everything" if done for the right reasons.

you read the speech, notice how he attempted to break down the attitudes of apathy and complacency through a combination of statistics, specific instances, and authoritative testimony; pay particular attention to his personal appeal to listeners to take care of their own books.

The Burning Question of Our Nation's Books
Jay W. Brown

Attention Step

□ *Pertinent quotation*

"Books are the legacies left to mankind, delivered down from generation to generation, as presents to the posterity of those yet unborn." Joseph Addison poetically hints at the relationship between a reader and a book. As we sit in front of the fire with Shakespeare or curl up in bed with a romance novel, reading becomes a tactile, aesthetic relationship. But more than that, through the written word we have preserved all those things which are important to us: from the Old Testament to Einstein. We've made their relationship to ourselves concrete by means of the printed page. So when something violates this relationship, it means the loss of a part of ourselves. John Steinbeck argues that "A book is somehow sacred. A dictator can kill and maim people and only be hated. But when books are burned, the ultimate in tyranny has happened." /1

□ *Testimony*

□ *Startling statement*
□ *Testimony*

□ *Specific instance/ statistics*

The ultimate in tyranny *is* happening. Our books are burning as they sit on our library shelves. The Minneapolis *Star and Tribune* writes, "There are no flames. No smoke. But the paper is burning, nonetheless. It turns yellow, then brown. It becomes crisp and eventually crumbles to dust." The Library of Congress, the world's largest depository of books which is founded on the philosophy that every book is invaluable, recently reported that 40% of its collection is no longer usable. The New York Public Library estimates that one half of its five million books are on the brink of disintegration. And according to a study done in 1978 by the William Barrow Laboratories, 97% of all books published in the first half of the century will be unusable by 1990. /2

□ *Claim*

□ *Forecast speech development*

The dramatic deterioration of our nation's library holdings is a crisis which affects all of us who depend on books for information, entertainment, or aesthetic pleasure. Let me first explain what causes this deterioration and then discuss why current methods for dealing with it are inadequate. Thirdly, I'll explore why we are ignoring our written legacy, and finally, suggest what we must do to protect it in the future. /3

Need Step

□ *Explanation*

The crisis of book deterioration is paradoxic. You see, volumes printed during the Middle Ages—from the Gutenberg Bibles on—are in better condition than books published 30 years ago. Why? Because older books were printed on better paper. Manufactured from linen and cotton rags mixed with animal and vegetable oils, such paper was not only strong, it had a high alkaline content. But as the demand for paper increased in the late 19th century, paper manufacturers searched for cheaper and faster ways to produce it, settling on the process which is used today: wood pulp mixed with various chemicals. These chemicals give the paper a high acid content. And this acid is rapidly eating up our intellectual heritage. /4

□ *Testimony*

□ *Specific instance*

□ *Testimony*

Now, if you're like most people you've already said to yourself, "So we'll just computerize or microfilm all these books and then it won't be a problem." Though many libraries rely on these easy electronic methods, *Publishers Weekly* pointed out last year that such "preservation techniques" are inadequate because they don't really preserve anything. Magnetic computer tapes are subject to easy erasure. And the National Archives reported in 1981 that 750,000 microfilmed documents have been damaged or destroyed because of deteriorating microfilm. And while the chemical preservation techniques advocated by some librarians do add 100 to 200 years to the life of a book, *Science News* pointed out last year that chemical techniques are so time-consuming and expensive that they are impractical. /5

□ *Appeal to saving*

□ *Testimony*

But regardless of their effectiveness, the fundamental inadequacy of these "preservation" methods is that they are merely means of treating symptoms, not curing the disease. We clearly need to do what we can to preserve what we have now, but more importantly, we need to get at the root of the problem and change the way paper is manufactured. If that sounds impossible to you, it isn't. A manufacturing process developed 30 years ago produces highly alkaline paper equal in quality to acidic paper. There is a capital cost to convert the manufacturing equipment, but according to *Chemistry* magazine, the alkaline paper is actually cheaper to make than the acidic! And if estimates are correct, it will last about ten centuries longer. /6

Satisfaction Step

□ *Rhetorical question*

If the solution is so simple, why are we still ignoring our written legacy? The underlying cause of the problem is *our* attitude. We can hardly expect paper manufacturers to care about the longevity of their product if we, the users, ignore

□ *Testimony*

it. And as a New England-based paper wholesaler explains, "I have no demands about the longevity of paper . . . it never comes up." The paper makers will only have motivation to switch to alkaline paper when we change our attitude. We *are* arrogant consumers. Unless something has sentimental or commercial value, when it's old, we throw it away. Of course, the classics will always be with us because consumers will continue to buy them and publishers will continue to reprint them. Unfortunately, there are an awful lot of important books which don't retain that commercial value. The thing we tend to forget is that what is burning is not merely a sheaf of paper, but an idea. Ideas, like humans, are ephemeral. But through books, both endure. /7

Visualization Step

You may argue that not all books are worth saving. *Perhaps* not. But by continuing to print all books on acidic paper, we preclude the possibility of saving any of them. And it would be the height of arrogance for us to choose what future generations will read about us. If we only preserve books which *we* consider important, we enter the very dangerous realm of social censorship. *Our* society would be radically different if the societies which produced the Dead Sea Scrolls or Charles Darwin's notes had decided one of them wasn't worth saving. /8

Action Step

If we and our ideas are to endure, we must see that our books—the physical manifestations of our ideas and our culture—are preserved. Not just for our own ego satisfaction, but because we owe it to our children. At present, we are committing our ideas to a medium which we ourselves will outlive. We need to do something about the way paper is manufactured. Norman Shaffer, Director of the Library of Congress Preservation Office, says that pressure from the reading public does make a difference. Because of such pressure, a few small mills have switched from acidic to alkaline manufacturing. Shaffer believes additional pressure from us will force the major mills to make the switch and he argues that the best way to apply that pressure is to write a letter—not to our Congressmen, but to our Congressional Librarian. The Library of Congress has asked for indications of public concern about book deterioration. I have their address if any of you would like it now, or it can be found in any government [publication] and, most importantly, to convince the paper industry to make the switch to alkaline paper. /9

But that's not all. We can do something our parents and teachers have been telling us for years, and which most of us—and

□ *Appeals to pride, saving*

□ *Testimony*

□ *Appeal to pride*

most of them—have ignored: we can take care of the books we use. Even books printed on acidic paper will last 50 or 60 years if handled properly. That means turn the pages with care, don't fold down corners to mark your place, and definitely don't write in them. The pressure from writing and the acid in ink and pencil simply accelerate the deterioration. /10

It's simple for you and me to care for the books we use and, by supporting the Library of Congress, it would be almost as simple for us to ensure that all books are printed on alkaline paper. But because of our society's attitude that books are disposable, the paper industry continues to produce a product that will only last for 50 years, when it could easily last for a thousand. I think it's a tremendous irony that we spend billions of dollars yearly to build libraries to house our books, to catalogue them and store them; and then we print them on paper that won't last as long as we do. The problem is that not many of us think about the consequences of deterioration until a book falls apart in our hands. /11

☐ *Testimony*

☐ *Pertinent quotation*

One person described such an experience this way: "The front part of the book I took from the shelf was in my left hand, the back was in my right hand, and in between was this yellow snow drifting to the floor." That yellow snow is an idea that has been destroyed, not debunked, but destroyed. As Gilbert Highet asserts, "Books are not lumps of lifeless paper, but *minds* alive on the shelves . . . so by taking one down and opening it up, we call this range the voice of a (person) far distant from us in time and space, and hear (them) speaking to us. Mind to mind, heart to heart." Unless, of course, that voice falls fractured to the library floor in a flurry of yellow snow.[27] /12

Chapter Summary

The arts of persuasion and actuation are fundamental to any democratic society. Unless enough citizens are skilled both in preparing and in listening to appeals for changes of mind and action, a nation is vulnerable to the influences of the unscrupulous and self-serving. As noted in this chapter, effective persuasive speaking is a complex task enhanced by close attention to the three dimensions of persuasion: *adapting to an audience's psychological states, drawing upon external reference groups,* and *enhancing personal credibility*. The strategies discussed under each of these topics are not exhaustive, but they do present a solid foundation on which to develop a persuasive or an actuative speech. Your precise goal in speaking persuasively may be to *reinforce* an audience's commitment to shared values; to *modify* a listener's specific *beliefs, attitudes,* or *values;* or to move a listener to *action.* An overall presentation that meets any one of these goals may be structured according to the motivated sequence.

Reference Notes

1. Walter R. Fisher, *Human Communication as Narration* (Columbia, SC: University of South Carolina Press, 1987).

2. Richard E. Petty and John T. Cacioppo, *Communication and Persuasion: Central and Peripheral Routes to Attitude Change* (New York: Springer-Verlag, 1986), 7.

3. Petty and Cacioppo, 20–21.

4. The classic research on audience predisposition and order of ideas in the face of those predispositions is summarized in Carl I. Hovland et al., *The Order of Presentation in Persuasion* (New Haven, CT: Yale University Press, 1961). More recent research is summarized in Kay Deaux and Lawrence S. Wrightsman, *Social Psychology,* 5th ed. (Pacific Grove, CA: Brooks/Cole Publishing Co., 1988) and in Erwin P. Bettinghaus, *Persuasive Communication,* 3rd ed. (New York: Holt, Rinehart & Winston, Inc., 1980), esp. 141–43. The main source of research on central and peripheral beliefs, attitudes, and values is Milton Rokeach, *Beliefs, Attitudes, and Values* (San Francisco, CA: Jossey-Bass, Inc., Pubs., 1968); Rokeach's main findings also are summarized in Bettinghaus, 23–26. The study of attitudinal networks referred to in this chapter is J. W. Prescott, "Body Pleasure and Origins of Violence," *The Futurist* (1975): 64–74.

5. Russell H. Fazio and Carol J. Williams, "Attitude Accessibility as a Moderator of the Attitude-Perception and Attitude-Behavior Relations: An Investigation of the 1984 Presidential Election," *Journal of Personality and Social Psychology* 51 (1986): 505–14. The theoretical work is presented in Russell H. Fazio, David Sanbonmatsu, Martha C. Powell, and Frank R. Kerdes, "On the Automatic Activation of Attitudes," *Journal of Personality and Social Psychology* 51 (1986): 229–38.

6. Petty and Cacioppo, 83.

7. Petty and Cacioppo, 129.

8. Petty and Cacioppo, 153.

9. Petty and Cacioppo, 87.

10. Petty and Cacioppo, 143.

11. The view that attitudes, in part, are cognitions that can be thought of as existing on a continuum is central to most "balance theories" of attitudes. The classic source is R. P. Abelson et al., *Theories of Cognitive Consistency: A Sourcebook* (Chicago, IL: Rand McNally & Co., 1968). For a contemporary summary, see Deaux and Wrightsman, 182–209.

12. Michael Burgoon and Erwin P. Bettinghaus, "Persuasive Message Strategies," in M. Roloff and G. R. Miller, eds., *Persuasion* (Beverly Hills, CA: Sage Publications, 1980), 141–69. When presenting a strong and then more modest proposal, the persuasive situation cannot be a "one-shot" deal, where you address the audience on only one particular occasion. The tactic is best used when you are negotiating with others opposed to your ideas and have several opportunities to present and alter proposals.

13. Deaux and Wrightsman, 391–95.

14. The basic research on latitudes of acceptance and rejection is covered in Muzafer Sherif, Carolyn Sherif, and Roger Nebergall, *Attitude and Attitude Change* (Philadelphia, PA: W. B. Saunders Co., 1965).

15. The general notions behind reference group theory are developed in H. H. Kelley, "Two Functions of Reference Groups," in H. Prohansky and B. Seidenberg, eds., *Basic Studies in Social Psychology* (New York: Holt, Rinehart & Winston, Inc., 1965), 210–14. The idea of positive and negative groups is developed in Theodore M. Newcomb's essay "Attitude Development as a Function of Reference Groups," in the same book, 215–25. The conclusions about the effects of reference groups on beliefs and attitudes are defended in Bettinghaus, 70–88.

16. Diane M. Mackie, "Systematic and Nonsystematic Processing of Majority and Minority Persuasive Communications," *Journal of Personality and Social Psychology* 53 (1987): 41–52.

17. Petty and Cacioppo, 205.

18. R. E. Petty and T. C. Brock, "Effects of Responding or Not Responding to Hecklers on Audience Agreement with a Speaker," *Journal of Applied Social Psychology* 6 (1976): 1–17.

19. A complete summary of research on credibility, which supports these conclusions, is found in Stephen Littlejohn, "A Bibliography of Studies Related to Variables of Source Credibility," in Ned A. Shearer, ed., *Bibliographical Annual in Speech Communication: 1971* (New York: Speech Communication Association, 1972), 1–40. Research which shows that credibility tends to vary from situation to situation and topic to topic is represented by such studies as Jo Liska, "Situational and Topical Variations in Credibility Criteria," *Communication Monographs* 45 (1978): 85–92. For a contemporary account of the relationship between source credibility and attitude change, see Petty and Cacioppo.

20. Chaim Perelman and L. Olbrechts-Tyteca, *The New Rhetoric: A Treatise on Argumentation*, trans. John Wilkinson and Purcell Weaver (Notre Dame, IN: University of Notre Dame Press, 1969), 51.

21. Walter R. Fisher, "Narration as a Human Communication Paradigm: The Case of Public Moral Argument," *Communication Monographs* 51 (1984): 1–22.

22. Donald Dean Morley and Kim B. Walker, "The Role of Importance, Novelty, and Plausibility in Producing Belief Change," *Communication Monographs* 54 (1987): 436–42. The theory is presented in Donald Dean Morley, "Subjective Message Constructs: A Theory of Persuasion," *Communication Monographs* 54 (1987): 183–203.

23. Deaux and Wrightsman, 160–209; Petty and Cacioppo; Gerald R. Miller, Michael Burgoon, and Judee K. Burgoon, "The Functions of Human Communication in Changing Attitudes and Gaining Compliance," in Carroll C. Arnold and John Waite Bowers, eds., *Handbook of Rhetorical and Communication Theory* (Boston, MA: Allyn and Bacon, Inc., 1984), 400–474.

24. Philip E. Tetlock, "Cognitive Style and Political Belief Systems in the British House of Commons," *Journal of Personality and Social Psychology* 46 (1984): 365–75; Philip E. Tetlock, "A Value Pluralism Model of Ideological Reasoning," *Journal of Personality and Social Psychology* 50 (1986): 819–27.

25. For additional discussion of the strategies involved in changing people's beliefs, attitudes, and values, see Bruce E. Gronbeck, *The Articulate Person: A Guide to Everyday Public Speaking*, 2nd ed. (Glenview, IL: Scott, Foresman and Company, 1983), Chapters 7 and 8.

26. Adapted from a speech by Fran Biersman, in R. R. Allen and R. E. McKerrow, *The Pragmatics of Public Communication*, 3rd ed. (Dubuque, IA: Kendall/Hunt Publishing Co., 1985), 351–53.

27. Jay W. Brown, "The Burning Question of Our Nation's Books," *Winning Orations* (1984).

Key Terms

psychological state   *latitude of acceptance*

cognitive complexity   *reinforcement*

Elaboration Likelihood Model   *modification*

saliency   *actuation*

incremental change

Problems and Probes

1. Analyze the differences between an appeal to persuade and an appeal to actuate in relation to the essential features of persuasion discussed in this chapter (adaptation to psychological state, change by degrees, saliency, credibility) for each of the following situations: (a) you want your parents to stop smoking; (b) you try to convince your best friend not to drop out of school; (c) you want a stranger to donate money to the local Hospice program. In what ways do your appeals differ? What variables account for the differences? Which factors are the most difficult to analyze in each of these situations and why?

2. Comment on this statement: "Most people act out of desire rather than reason; they only use reason to justify to themselves and others what they want to do anyway." If this statement has merit, how would it affect the development of a speech to actuate (develop at least three specific principles that a speaker might consider if the statement is true).

Communication Activities

1. Develop and present to the class a five-to-seven-minute speech. Follow the steps in the motivated sequence appropriate to the type of speech chosen: reinforcement, modification, or actuation. As you construct your speech, keep in mind the strategies discussed in this chapter, both in terms of the essential features of all persuasive speeches and those specific to your speech. Adapt to the audience members as you deem appropriate from your analysis of their beliefs, attitudes, and values.

2. Present a five-to-eight-minute speech with the specific goal of persuading audience members to take an action you recommend. Show that a problem or situation needing remedy exists and that they should be personally concerned about potential solutions. In presenting the solution, indicate why you believe that action on their part will be a concrete, influential move toward a remedy (do not simply say, "Write your . . ."; indicate why it would help). On a future "checkup" day, see how many listeners have taken the recommended action.

This task can be an assignment for the entire class with a questionnaire used on "checkup" day to see which recommended actions were taken. As possible speeches, you might urge an audience to sign a petition asking for a specific change on your campus (for example, establishing a day-care center), or you might ask class members to write letters to the editor of the local newspaper urging that a particular community action be taken or avoided (be sure to provide the address). You also might ask them to attend an informational meeting of a newly organized campus group or a meeting of the student government to protest its position on an issue important to you.

CHAPTER SEVENTEEN

Argumentation and Critical Thinking

*T*he ability and desire to think critically is central to your participation in a social world. You are constantly being bombarded with requests, appeals, and pleas to change your beliefs or to adopt new behaviors or actions. Sorting through this myriad of requests (and sometimes commands) to determine which beliefs or actions you are justified in accepting requires skills in the analysis and evaluation of reasons offered by others. If you are not comfortable accepting everything others say to or ask of you, you have developed what might be called a "critical spirit"—a desire to apply your reasoning skills to others' ideas and requests (as well as to your own).[1]

As you engage in critical evaluation, you also become an *arguer*, a person who argues with others or even with your self, in assessing reasons or offering counterreasons for denying a claim or proposed action. As in the critical evaluation of others' ideas, you also become an arguer when you propose your own ideas or rationales for action. Through **argumentation,** a speaker offers reasons supporting particular claims; through critical thinking, a listener evaluates such claims. In this chapter, we will examine the nature of argumentation as a social process involving the central elements of critical thinking. From this discussion, we will focus on the elements of an **argument** and the strategies for evaluating arguments.

Argumentation As a Social Process

When you engage in an argument with others, you commit yourself to following certain social conventions, or expectations, of conduct. These often implicit rules govern the way you develop your argument and your own reaction to the arguments of others. When you offer an opinion, others have the right to expect you to support that belief or judgment with something other than "that is what I feel." The right to hold an opinion is not, by itself, sufficient reason for others to accept the belief or judgment. Similarly, when you critically evaluate your own reasons or those of others, you adhere to often unstated assumptions about what it means to be "reasonable" or "rational." The following social conventions generally apply to argumentation, as well as to thinking critically about your own and others' arguments.

Bilaterality

Argumentation is inherently bilateral: it requires at least two people or two competing messages. Even when arguing with your self, you assume two opposing positions. There is an element of controversy inherent in this exchange between two people: we do not argue about what is self-evident. Others will undoubtedly have different, somewhat opposing views to our own. When candidates for public office present their campaign ideas, they expect counterargument from opposing candidates. Usually, candidates invite and receive reasoned response to their ideas. On some occasions, formal debates or other forums for a structured exchange of views will result. In your own immediate environment, arguments may occur in a variety of settings—in dormitory rooms, classrooms, or coffee shops. While these are not as formal as debates, they nonetheless share many of the same features: reasons are given and refuted, claims are advanced and withdrawn.

Self-risk

When you engage in argumentation and open your ideas to the critical assessment of others, you assume certain risks. There is always a chance that your ideas will not be adequately justified, but that is a risk you must be willing

---

Argumentation is inherently bilateral: it requires at least two competing messages. Reasons are given and refuted; claims are advanced and withdrawn.

to take when you advance claims in a public setting. For example, if you argue that all athletes should be subject to random drug testing, you may face the charge that such a proposal is discriminatory and, therefore, unfair. If opponents succeed in showing that it would be discriminatory, and if audience members already accept the notion that any action that discriminates is inherently unjustified, you will have to acquiesce or find other, stronger reasons to support your proposed policy. You must be willing to accept a "moral obligation" to yield to a stronger argument.[2]

Reasonableness

Reasonableness in argumentation depends upon the commonly accepted standards of a social group; it entails allowing others to "have their say." Either party to a dispute has the right to say, "You may reject my claims and reasons, but first hear me out." For this reason, most legislative bodies are reluctant to cut off debate. In small groups, where a standard set of procedural rules is followed (such as *Robert's Rules of Order*),[3] a rule of thumb to apply is "When in doubt, let people debate." In situations where competing interests are being debated, the procedural rules help ensure that both minority and majority views are given a fair hearing.

Being reasonable is as much an *attitude* as a specific *ability* that one takes into an argumentative situation.[4] Besides being perceived as fair to others' opinions, an attitude of reasonableness implies a willingness to attack *ideas* rather than persons. Finally, reasonableness implies that the content of your argument—the reasons and evidence you advance on behalf of a claim—are perceived as being relevant to the issues involved. The plea "Be reasonable!" often is the result of a perception that your idea or proof is "out of sync" with what people are normally conditioned to accept.

Rationality

Rationality is the central element in both the assessment of reasons (critical thinking) and their advancement (argumentation). When you argue, you are committed to offering "good reasons" for the ideas or actions you propose. If you argue, for instance, that international peace requires a "strategic defense initiative," others have the right to dispute that claim. They might argue that implementing a "Star Wars" project actually encourages further development of the arms race, rather than controlling or curtailing its growth. No matter what a speaker says, others have the right, and obligation, to critically assess the grounds for the claim and to hold the speaker accountable for producing sufficient justification for another person's adopting a belief or engaging in an action. In particular, rational argumentation follows rules that guarantee its **validity** and **soundness.** An argument is considered *valid* if its pattern of reasoning adheres to the applicable rules for its development. An argument is *sound* if its content offers good reasons for the adoption of the claim being advanced. As covered later in this chapter, applying the tests of reasoning and detecting fallacies in your own arguments, as well as in those advanced by opponents, will make you both a competent arguer and an astute critical thinker.

Within the context of assessing reasons, either before advancing them or as offered by others, you often will argue in accordance with procedural rules. A presidential debate, for example, is conducted in accordance with a unique set of rules governing who may speak and for how long. A legislative body argues issues in accordance with agreed-upon **parliamentary procedures** (such as those set forth in *Robert's Rules of Order*). In a courtroom, technical rules governing who may speak and what evidence may be introduced in support of an argument ensure that the rights of both parties to a dispute are protected. Since such technical rules are an important feature of argumentation in small-group or deliberative settings, a section on parliamentary procedure is included in the *Speaker's Resource Book* at the end of this textbook.

In other settings, arguers are expected to follow somewhat different but analogous technical rules. A social scientist who has studied the effect of source credibility on the persuasiveness of messages must report the results in a specific format. In every discipline, conventions govern the conduct and reporting of research. Researchers who violate the standard formats for arguing within their discipline will find that their work is not accepted for presentation at regional or national meetings. There is, for example, a great difference in style and format for reporting results of a communication experiment in *Communication Monographs* and *Psychology Today*. Even though the information is the same, one generally does not accept a report suitable for the other until it is cast in the proper argumentative format, because the audiences for scholarly journals and popular magazines differ. Academic and business disciplines, thus, lay out their own rules for arguing, rules that must be followed if you are to engage in argumentation in a given profession or field.[5]

These features—bilaterality, self-risk, reasonableness, and rationality—comprise the essential conventions of argumentation. When one of these is absent, the quality of the argument, and of any decisions that might result, will be less than optimum. In the absence of bilaterality, there simply is no argument. If communicators are not open to the possibility of changing their mind as a result of argumentation, they are engaged in a deceptive act of communication. If they are not willing to argue as reasonable people, in accordance with the social standards of the group or community, there is little to be gained from continuing the dialogue. Finally, if they are not willing to present reasons for their beliefs, there is little ground for acceptance of their views. Thinking critically simply means being willing to analyze or evaluate ideas according to these conventions and determining whether you are justified in following the lead of another.

Elements of Argumentation

At its most general level, argumentation consists of proponents and opponents taking turns addressing each other and a mutual audience. This process is initiated with an **argumentative,** or **constructive, speech;** it progresses when someone offers a **refutative speech;** it then continues through a series

Argumentativeness and Verbal Aggression

*I*s being an arguer a positive or negative trait? How about the individual who argues by attacking the person rather than the substance of the argument? Isn't he or she violating the conventions of argumentation outlined in this chapter? Don't some people really like to engage in argumentation, while others seem to acquiesce in order to avoid an argument?

Infante and his colleagues conducted a series of studies on *argumentativeness* and *verbal aggression*. They conceptualized *argumentativeness* in positive terms, as a socially desirable trait that predisposes an individual to assess reasons and to present arguments in accordance with appropriate social conventions. Students strongly oriented toward arguing with others were found to have experienced greater training in argumentation. They also reported a higher overall grade point, were born earlier in the family birth order (which is consistent with other research on the assertiveness of first-borns), preferred smaller classes (presumably because it is easier to engage in argumentation), and tended to be more liberal. More importantly, Infante et al. found that "high argumentatives" are *not* less likely than "low argumentatives" to value the importance of maintaining general social relations or getting along with peers. Enjoying a good argument does not mean a person cannot respect others. In actual argumentation, those who scored high on an "Argumentativeness Scale" displayed less flexibility in the positions they advocated, appeared

of **rebuttals** or **rejoinders** until a decision is reached by majority vote or consensus, surrender, or other event.

At a more specific level, we can analyze the structure of a specific argumentative speech in terms of these characteristics:

1. The attention and need steps should establish the claim and suggest criteria for judging the quality of support offered.
2. The satisfaction step should be organized around a series of reasons supporting the claim.
3. The visualization step should summarize the position and indicate why it is superior to the opposing view.

more interested in arguing and willing to argue, were perceived as more skillful arguers, and were more enthusiastic in their conduct of the argument.

While argumentativeness is linked to assertive behavior, verbal aggressiveness is related to hostility and reflects a willingness to verbally abuse a person in the act of arguing. While argumentatively oriented people may resort to verbal aggression under some circumstances, the two "traits" are distinct psychological responses. People higher in argumentativeness are no more likely than others to engage in aggressive behavior. Two sources of verbal aggression are frustration with the way another person is arguing or with a recognition of one's own skill deficiencies and prior experience or social conditioning to respond aggressively. A person scoring high on a "Verbal Aggressiveness" scale is more likely to use aggressive language (calling an opponent a name instead of responding to the issue) than those who score lower.

As this research suggests, argumentation can be a constructive, positive activity when it adheres to the social conventions. Whereas arguing well with others can be personally enjoyable regardless of the outcome, using verbal aggression is destructive to other people and diminishes the quality of any decisions that might be reached.

FOR FURTHER READING

Infante, Dominic A. "The Argumentative Student in the Speech Communication Classroom: An Investigation and Implications." *Communication Education* 31 (1982): 141–48; Infante, Dominic A. "Trait Argumentativeness as a Predictor of Communicative Behavior in Situations Requiring Argument." *Central States Speech Journal* 32 (1981): 265–72; Infante, Dominic A., and Andrew Rancer. "A Conceptualization and Measure of Argumentativeness." *Journal of Personality Assessment* 46 (1982): 72–80; Infante, Dominic A., and Charles J. Wigley III. "Verbal Aggressiveness: An Interpersonal Model and Measure." *Communication Monographs* 53 (1986): 61–69; Infante, Dominic A., J. David Trebing, Patricia E. Shepherd, and Dale E. Seeds, "The Relationship of Argumentativeness to Verbal Aggression." *Southern Speech Communication Journal* 50 (1984): 67–77.

If the speech seeks to refute an opposing position, your first task is to explain the claim you are attacking. Then, set forth specific reasons and evidence to support the refutation. In both initial constructive and subsequent refutative speeches, your central aim is to provide reasons for the claims you wish an audience (and sometimes an opponent) to accept.

Finally, at the most specific or "unit" level, you should focus on the construction and evaluation of a single argument. Each argument has three essential features: the *claim* being defended; the relevant *evidence* offered in support of that claim; and the *reasoning pattern* (sometimes referred to as the *inference*) that connects the evidence to the claim. This level will be of primary concern in the remainder of this chapter. In this section, we will consider the various types of claims that can be advocated, the nature of evidence used to support claims, and the major types of inferences, or reasoning patterns, that are used to connect evidence to claims.

Types of Claims

Most argumentative speeches assert that in the opinion of the speaker (1) something is or is not the case, (2) something is desirable or undesirable, or (3) something should or should not be done. Such judgments or recommendations, when formally addressed to others, are the speaker's *claims*. The first step in constructing a successful argument is to clearly determine the nature of the claim you wish to establish.

Claims of Fact. If you were trying to convince your listeners that "price controls on raw agricultural products result in food shortages," you would be presenting a **claim of fact**—asserting that a given state of affairs exists or that something is indeed the case. When confronted with a claim of this sort, two questions are likely to arise in the mind of a critical listener:

1. *By what criteria or standards of judgment should the truth or accuracy of this claim be measured?* If you were asked to determine a person's height, you would immediately look for a yardstick or other measuring instrument. Listeners likewise look for a standard when judging the appropriateness of a factual claim. In the price controls example before agreeing that controls result in shortages, your audience would probably want to know what you mean by "shortages." Do you mean "the disappearance, for all practical purposes, of a given kind of food" or merely "less of that food than everyone might desire"? Against what standard, precisely, is the accuracy of the claim to be judged?

2. *Do the facts of the situation fit the criteria as set forth?* Does the amount of produce and other raw agricultural products presently on supermarket shelves fall within the limits set by your definition of "shortages"? First, get your listeners to agree to certain standards or measurements for judgment and then present evidence to show that a given state of affairs meets these standards. Then you will, in most instances, be well on your way toward winning their belief.

Claims of Value. When, instead of asserting that something is or is not so, you assert that something is good or bad, desirable or undesirable, justified or unjustified, you are advancing a **claim of value**—a claim concerning the intrinsic *worth* of the belief or action in question. As in the case of claims of fact, a critical listener can ask: (1) By what standards or criteria is something of this nature to be judged? (2) How well does the item in question measure up to the standards specified? We may, for example, assert that the quality of a college is to be measured by the distinction of its faculty, the excellence of its physical plant, the success of its graduates in securing positions, and the reputation it enjoys among the general public and then proceed

THE LEVELS OF ARGUMENTATION

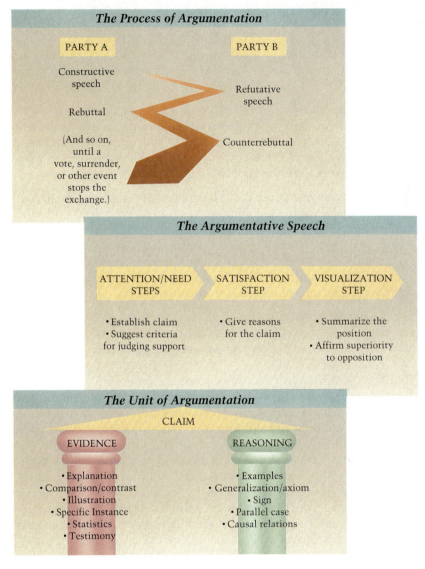

The Process of Argumentation

PARTY A

PARTY B

Constructive speech

Refutative speech

Rebuttal

(And so on, until a vote, surrender, or other event stops the exchange.)

Counterrebuttal

The Argumentative Speech

ATTENTION/NEED STEPS

SATISFACTION STEP

VISUALIZATION STEP

• Establish claim
• Suggest criteria for judging support

• Give reasons for the claim

• Summarize the position
• Affirm superiority to opposition

The Unit of Argumentation

CLAIM

EVIDENCE

REASONING

• Explanation
• Comparison/contrast
• Illustration
• Specific Instance
• Statistics
• Testimony

• Examples
• Generalization/axiom
• Sign
• Parallel case
• Causal relations

to argue that because the college we are concerned with meets each of these tests, it is a good one.

Claims of Policy.   A **claim of policy** recommends a course of action you want the audience to approve. Typical examples are "Federal expenditures for pollution control *should be* substantially increased" and "The student senate *should have* the authority to expel students who cheat." In both instances, you are asking your audience to endorse a proposed "policy," or course of action. When analyzing a policy claim, four subsidiary questions are relevant:

1. *Is there a need for such a policy or course of action?* If your listeners do not believe that a change is called for, they are not likely to approve your proposal.

2. *Is the proposal practicable?* Can we afford the expenses it would entail? Would it really solve the problem or remove the evil it is designed to correct? Does such a policy stand a reasonable chance of being adopted? If you cannot show that your proposal meets these and similar tests, you can hardly expect it to be endorsed.

3. *Are the benefits your proposal will bring greater than the disadvantages it will entail?* People are reluctant to approve a proposal that promises to create conditions worse than the ones it is designed to correct. Burning a barn to the ground may be a highly efficient way to get rid of rats, but it is hardly a desirable one. The benefits and disadvantages that will accrue from a plan of action always must be carefully weighed along with considerations of its basic workability.

4. *Is the offered proposal superior to any other plan or policy?* Listeners are hesitant to approve a policy if they have reason to believe that an alternative course of action is more practicable or more beneficial.

From what you have learned about the three types of claims, you should be able to see the importance of knowing exactly the kind of claim you are seeking to establish. Is it a claim of policy, fact, or value? If it is a claim of policy, do you need to answer all four of the basic questions listed above, or is your audience likely to accept one or more of them without proof? If yours is a claim of fact or value, what criteria should you use as bases for judgment, and how well are they met by the evidence?

Finally, unless there are sound reasons for delay, you should announce early in your speech the claim you are going to support or oppose. If your listeners do not see the precise point on which they will be asked to make a judgment, your strongest arguments and appeals probably will prove useless.[6]

Evidence

As you discovered in Chapter 7, supporting materials are the items you use to clarify, amplify, and strengthen the ideas in your speech. They provide evidence for the acceptance of your claim and its supporting points. Evidence is a crucial part of developing a clear, compelling argument. It can be presented in any of the forms of supporting materials with which you are already familiar: explanation, comparison and contrast, illustration, specific instance, statistics, and testimony.

You have already engaged in the research required to find the supporting materials necessary to reinforce the ideas in your speeches. The *selection of relevant evidence* is particularly important in constructing good arguments. There is no single or easy rule for selecting relevant evidence. Supporting material that is relevant to one claim may not be relevant to another, or it may be relevant as logical proof but not as a compelling reason for action. You should consider both the *rational* and the *motivational* characteristics of good evidence selection.

Rationally Relevant Evidence. The type of evidence you choose should reflect the type of claim you advocate. For example, if you are defending the claim that censorship violates the First Amendment guarantee of freedom of speech, you will probably choose testimony by noted authorities or definitions of terms to advance your claim. On the other hand, examples, illustrations, and statistics work better for showing that a problem exists or a change is needed. If nine out of ten Americans believe that taking adult literature off public library shelves is a violation of their rights, there is popular support for a change. As you can see, the claim you present requires a logically relevant type of evidence. As you plan your arguments, you should ask yourself, "What type of evidence is logically relevant in support of my claim?"

Motivationally Relevant Evidence. If you hope to convince your listeners to adopt your attitudes or actions, your claim must be supported by more than logically relevant evidence. Your evidence must also create in your listeners a desire to become involved. That is, it must be motivationally relevant to them. In order to best determine what evidence works for specific audiences, you should ask two questions:

1. *What type of evidence will this audience demand?* Whenever Congress proposes a new form of taxation, taxpayers usually demand that it also supply statistical evidence, financial reports, an explanation of underlying key concepts, testimony from experts in economics, examples of the ways the new laws will affect taxpayers, and comparisons and contrasts with this law and other potential tax legislation. "Mere" examples or illustrations are not compelling enough to garner public support for higher taxes. On the other hand, if you were reviewing a recent film for a group of friends, an example from the plot, a figurative analogy, or an illustration of dialogue would be more forceful as proof than statistical counts of words, box office receipts, or testimony from published movie critics. Careful audience analysis will help you determine what type of evidence is needed psychologically to move your particular group of listeners.

2. *Which specific pieces of evidence will your listeners be most responsive to?* This is a question you should pose once you have determined the type of evidence required in your argument. For example, if you have

decided to use expert testimony to support your argument, whom should you quote? If you are using an illustration, should you use a factual example from the local group or develop one of your own? Will your listeners be more moved by a personal story or by a general illustration?

To answer these and similar questions about your listeners, you need to analyze them. A homogeneous audience may be suspicious of outsiders. It might react best to local experts or to illustrations from its community or range of experience. A heterogeneous audience, on the other hand, requires more generally recognized authorities and geographically varied examples because such listeners do not share experience and background. While you cannot always tailor your evidence to your audience's demographic or psychological characteristics, you can at least attempt to consider them. It is one thing to discover evidence but quite another to select it wisely. Select evidence with both your claim and audience in mind.

Reasoning (Inference)

The third element of a unit of argumentation "connects" the evidence with the claim. This is called *reasoning*, or inference. Reasoning is a process of connecting something that is known or believed (evidence) to a concept or idea (claim) you wish others to accept. *Patterns of reasoning* are habitual ways in which a culture or society uses inferences to connect that which is accepted to that which is being urged upon it. Basically, there are five reasoning patterns.

Reasoning from Examples.   Often called *inductive reasoning,* reasoning from instances or examples is a matter of examining a series of examples of known occurrences (evidence) and drawing a general conclusion (claim). The inference in this reasoning pattern can be stated: "What is true of particular cases is true of the whole class." This represents a kind of mental inductive leap from specifics to generalities. For example, the National Cancer Institute has studied hundreds of individual case histories and discovered that people whose diets are high in fiber are less prone to contract cancers of the digestive tract. With an inductive leap, the Institute then moved to the factual claim "High fiber diets prevent certain types of cancer." Commuters use a similar pattern of reasoning every time they drive during rush hour. After trial and error, they may decide that a residential street is the best route to take home between 5:00 and 5:30 P.M. and the expressway between 5:30 and 6:00 P.M. In other words, after enough instances, they arrive at a generalization and act upon it.

Reasoning from Generalization or Axiom.   Applying a general truth to a specific situation is a form of *deductive reasoning.* In a high-school consumer education class, you may have learned that buying goods in large quantities saves money (the generalization or evidence). You might shop at discount stores because they purchase goods in quantity, thereby saving money and passing that savings on to you (the claim deduced from the evidence).

You may believe that getting a college education is the key to a better future (the generalization or axiom); therefore, if you get a college degree, you will get a better job (claim). This inference gathers power because of experience (you learned it through observation) or by definition (one of the characteristics of education is self-improvement). You ultimately accept this inference because of the uniformities you believe exist in the world.

Reasoning from Sign. A third reasoning pattern uses an observable mark, or symptom, as proof of the existence of a state of affairs. You reason from sign when you note a rash or spots on your skin (the evidence) and decide you have measles (the claim). The rash does not "cause" measles; rather, it is a sign of the disease. Detectives are experts at reasoning from sign. When they discover that a particular suspect had motive, access, and a weapon in his possession (the signs), they move to the claim that he might be the murderer. Your doctor works the same way every time she asks you to stick out your tongue and looks for signs of trouble. These signs, of course, are circumstantial evidence—and could be wrong. The inference "This evidence is a sign of a particular conclusion" is one you have to be careful with. Such reasoning works well with natural occurrences (ice on the pond is always a sign that the temperature has been below 32 degrees Fahrenheit); however, reasoning from sign can be troublesome in the world of human beings (as when we take people's skin color as a sign that they have certain characteristics). Yet, we often must use signs as indicators; otherwise we could not project the economy, predict the weather, and forecast the rise and fall of political candidates.

Reasoning from Parallel Case. Another common reasoning pattern involves thinking solely in terms of similar things and events. Your college or university, for example, probably designed its curriculum by examining the curricula of similar colleges or universities. These curricula functioned as evidence; the claim was that similar courses should be offered at your school. The inference that linked the evidence and the claim was probably something like this: "What worked at Eastern University will work here at Western University because they are similar institutions." Your instructors might use parallel reasoning every time they tell you, "Study hard for this exam. The last exam was difficult; this one will be too." Obviously this is not a generalization, since every exam will probably not be the same; however, your instructors are asserting that the upcoming examination and past ones are similar cases—they have enough features in common to increase the likelihood that careful study habits will pay off.

Reasoning from Causal Relations. The assumption of causal reasoning is that events occur in a predictable, routine manner with a cause that accounts for each occurrence. Reasoning from causal relations involves associating events that come before (antecedents) with events that follow (consequents). If the drug problem, for example, appears to be increasing in this country, there is an immediate inquiry into the cause or causes for the increase. Is it the result of activities by organized crime, is it affected by lower moral standards within society, or is it caused by the breakup of the traditional family? Pointing to one or more of these as a cause sets the stage for a particular solution designed to remove or alleviate the harm that would continue if nothing were done. When children have difficulty in classes, educators often look for the root of the problem in family difficulties, physical problems, or social trauma. Educators might even predict that weak performance in the classroom is the antecedent for such future problems as juvenile delinquency or underemployment. In this instance, effects can become causes. The inference in causal reasoning is simple and constant: every effect has a cause.

The five forms of reasoning are judged "logical" or "rational" in this culture. They provide the primary means by which we connect evidence to claims.

Evaluating Arguments

In order to present "good reasons" for others to adopt your claim, you need to evaluate your own reasoning patterns. In addition, as a critical thinker, you must assess the reasons offered by others. An assessment of the adequacy of your reasoning can take one of two forms: (1) an analysis of the specific form of reasoning or (2) an analysis of possible fallacies in reasoning.

Tests for Reasoning

Each form of reasoning has its own tests or questions that can be used to determine its soundness. Within the context of each pattern of reasoning, apply the questions both to your own arguments and to those of others.

Reasoning from Examples

1. *Have you looked at enough instances to warrant generalizing?* (You do not assume spring is here because of one warm day in February.)

2. *Are the instances fairly chosen or representative?* (You certainly hope your neighbors do not think you have an unruly child just because he or she picked one of their flowers; you want them to judge your child only after seeing him or her in many different situations.)

3. *Are there important exceptions to the generalization or claim that must be accounted for?* (While it is generally true, from presidential election studies, that "As Maine goes, so goes the nation," there have been enough exceptions to that rule to keep Maine losers campaigning hard even after that primary.)

Reasoning from Generalization or Axiom

1. *Is the generalization true?* (Remember that sailors used to set certain courses on the assumption that the world was flat and that for years

parents in this country accepted as gospel Benjamin Spock's generalizations about child rearing.)

2. *Does the generalization apply to this particular case?* (Usually, discount stores have lower prices, but if a small neighborhood store has a sale, it may offer better prices than discount houses. While the old saying "Birds of a feather flock together" certainly applies to birds, it may not apply to human beings.)

Reasoning from Sign

1. *Is the sign "fallible"?* (As we have noted, many signs are merely circumstantial. Be extremely careful not to confuse sign reasoning with causal reasoning. If sign reasoning were infallible, weather forecasters would never be wrong.)

Reasoning from Parallel Case

1. *Are there more similarities than differences between the two cases?* (City A and City B may have many features in common—size, location, and so on—yet they probably also have many different features, perhaps in the subgroups that make up their populations, the degree of industrial development, and the like. Too many differences between two cases rationally destroy the parallel.)

2. *Are the similarities you have pointed out the relevant and important ones?* (There are two children in your neighborhood who are the same age, go to the same school, and wear the same kinds of clothes; are you, therefore, able to assume that one is well behaved simply because the other is? Probably not, because more relevant similarities would include their home life, their relationships with siblings, and so forth. Comparisons must be based on relevant and important similarities.)

Reasoning from Causal Relation

1. *Can you separate causes and effects?* (We often have a difficult time doing this. Do higher wages cause higher prices, or is the reverse true? Does a strained home life make a child misbehave, or is it the other way around?)

2. *Are the causes strong enough to have produced the effect?* (George Bush's assertion that Michael Dukakis was a "Liberal" gave him an edge in the 1988 presidential election, but was it *the* determining factor? There probably were much stronger and more important causes.)

3. *Did intervening events or persons prevent a cause from having its normal effect?* (If a gun is not loaded, you cannot shoot anything, no matter how hard you pull the trigger. Even if droughts normally drive up food prices, that might not happen if food has been stockpiled, if spring rains left enough moisture in the soil, or if plenty of cheap imported food is available.)

4. *Could any other cause have produced the effect?* (Although crime often increases when neighborhoods deteriorate, increased crime rates can be caused by any number of other changes—alterations in crime reporting methods, increased reporting of crimes that have been going on for years, or closing of major industries. We rationally must sort through all of the possible causes before championing one.)

Detecting Fallacies in Reasoning

As suggested, one of your jobs as a critical listener and as a person who engages in argumentation is to evaluate the claims, evidence, and reasoning of others. Whether you are a listener or a participant in public debate, you must be able to think carefully about the arguments. On one level, you are looking for ways in which the ideas and reasons of others are important to your own, and, on another level, you are examining the logical soundness of their thinking. A *fallacy* is a flaw in the rational properties of an argument or inference. As you detect these fallacies in your own or in others' arguments, you should note and point them out. We can divide fallacies into three categories: *fallacies in evidence, fallacies in reasoning,* and *fallacies in language.*

Fallacies in Evidence.   As the label suggests, fallacies in evidence occur in the way we use supporting material to reach our claims. Three of them stand out: hasty generalization, false division, and genetic fallacy.

Hasty generalization (faulty "inductive leap"): A hasty generalization is a claim made on the basis of too little evidence. You should ask, "Has the arguer really examined enough typical cases to make a claim?" If the answer is no, then a flaw in reasoning has occurred. Urging the ban of aspirin because several people have died of allergic reactions to it or the closure of a highway because of a traffic fatality are examples of hasty generalization.

False division: A false division occurs when someone argues that there is only one way to divide a process or idea. In fact, there may be many ways to view the process or idea. Be on the lookout when someone argues that the only ways to treat the mentally handicapped are to confine them to institutions or to place them with guardians. "Only" often signals a false division; there may well be other options worth our attention.

Genetic fallacy: Many people argue for an idea by citing its origins, history, or sacred tradition. They assume that if an idea has been around for a long time, it must be true. Many people who defended slavery in the nineteenth century referred to the Biblical practices of slavery and to those of the earliest American settlers. Times change, however; new values replace old ones. Genetic definitions can help us understand a concept, but they are hardly proof of its correctness or justice.

Fallacies in Reasoning.   Logical flaws often occur in the thought process itself. Five fallacies of reasoning should be mentioned.

Appeal to ignorance (argumentum ad ignoratiam): People sometimes argue with double negatives: "You *can't* prove it *won't* work!" They may even attack an idea because information about it is incomplete: "We can't use radio beams to signal UFOs and extraterrestrials because we don't know what languages they speak." Both of these are illogical claims because they depend upon what we do not know. Sometimes we simply must act on the basis of the knowledge we have, despite the gaps in it. In countering such claims, you can cite parallel cases and examples to overcome this fallacy.

Appeal to popular opinion (argumentum ad populum): A frequent strategy is to urge "jumping on the bandwagon." This argument assumes that if everyone else is doing or thinking something, you should too. For example: "But Christopher, everyone knows the world is flat!" or "But Dad, everyone else is going!" While these appeals may be useful in stating *valuative* claims, they are not the basis for *factual* claims. Even if most people believe or think something, it still may not be true. The world has witnessed hundreds of widely believed but false ideas, from the belief that night air causes tuberculosis to panic over an invasion by Martians.

Sequential fallacy (post hoc, ergo propter hoc): Literally translated from the Latin "after this, therefore because of this," the sequential fallacy is often present in arguments from causal relations. It is based on the assumption that if one event follows another, the first must be the cause. Thunder and lightning do not cause rain, although they often occur sequentially, and, even if you usually catch colds in the spring, the two are not causally related. That is, the season of the year does not cause your cold; a virus does.

Begging the question (petitio principii): Begging the question is rephrasing an idea and then offering it as its own reason. It is a *tautology,* or circular thought. If someone asserts, "Abortion is murder because it is taking the life of the unborn," he or she has committed a fallacy by rephrasing the claim (it is murder) to form the reason (it is taking life). Sometimes questions can be fallacious, such as "Have you quit cheating on tests yet?" The claim, phrased as a question, assumes that you have cheated on tests in the past. Whatever your answer to the question, you are guilty. Claims of value are especially prone to *petitio principii.*

Appeal to authority (ipse dixit): Ipse dixit fallacies ("because he says it") occur when someone who is popular but not an expert urges the acceptance of an idea or a product. Television advertisers frequently ask consumers to purchase products because famous movie stars or sports heroes endorse them. Thus, celebrities promote everything from blue jeans to beer. The familiar figure provides name recognition but not expertise. You can detect this fallacy by asking, "Is he or she an expert on this topic?"

Fallacies in Language.   Finally, some fallacies creep into our arguments simply because of the ways in which we use words. Word meanings are flexible, so language can be used sloppily or manipulatively. Five linguistic fallacies are frequent in public debate.

Ambiguity: A word often has two or more meanings. Because of this, such words, used in the same context, can cause confusion and inaccurate claims. Suppose you hear: "Some dogs have fuzzy ears. My dog has fuzzy ears. My dog is *SOME* dog!" The problem here rests in the word "some." In its first

Converse. An 80-year winning streak.

Advertisers frequently ask consumers to purchase products because celebrities endorse them. In detecting fallacies in reasoning, consumers need to ask, "Is the celebrity an expert on the topic?"

usage, it means "not all." The word shifts meanings, however, so in the second usage it becomes "outstanding/exceptional." Such shifts of meaning can result in flawed claims.

Nonqualification: It is all too easy to drop out some important qualifications as an argument progresses. If such words as "maybe," "might," and "probably" fall by the wayside, the meaning of the argument can change. Advertisers often claim: "Our brand *may* result in fewer cavities *if* you follow a program of regular hygiene and professional dental care." When the qualifications are underplayed, the argument becomes verbally distorted.

Is-Faults: One of the trickiest verbs in English is "is." "John is a man" and "John is a radical" are grammatically equivalent sentences; however, gender is a permanent characteristic of John, while his political leanings are not. We might expect political orientation to change, but not gender. Learn to distinguish between the "is" of classification and the "is" of attribution. Condemnatory speeches and advertisements often contain such fallacies.

Persuasive definition: In the heat of an argument, many advocates attempt to win by offering their own definitions of ideas or concepts. Value terms or abstract concepts are most open to special or skewed definitions. "Liberty means the right to own military weapons." "A good university education is one that leads to a good job." "Real men don't wear cologne." Each of these definitions sets up a particular point of view; each is capricious or arbitrary. If you accept the definition, the argument is over.[7] In order to challenge this fallacious argument, you can substitute a definition from a respected source.

Name calling: Name calling is the general label for several kinds of attacks on people instead of on their arguments. *Argumentum ad hominem* is an attack on the special interests of a person: "Of course, you're defending her. You voted for her." *Argumentum ad personam* is an attack on a personal characteristic of someone rather than on his or her ideas: "You're just a dweeb" (or yuppie or chauvinist). Even dweebs, yuppies, and chauvinists sometimes offer solid claims. *Ideological appeals* link ideas or people with emotional labels: "Social security is really a Communist plot to overthrow America." This appeal links social security to something the listener considers sinister rather than examining it on its own merits. Claims ought to be judged on their own features, not on their sources.

These are some of the fallacies that creep into argumentation. A good basic logic book can point out additional fallacies.[8] Armed with knowledge of such fallacies, you should be able to construct sound arguments to protect yourself against unscrupulous demagogues, sales personnel, and advertisers.

Strategies for Developing Arguments

As you begin to develop arguments for public debates, you should consider the following practical suggestions:

1. *Organize your arguments, using the strongest first or last.*[9] This takes advantage of the **primacy/recency effect.** That is, researchers have found that people more readily retain information that is presented first or last. Information or arguments presented first set the agenda for what is to follow (the primacy effect). If you use your strongest argument first, it is likely that your listeners will judge what follows to be equally as strong. On the other hand, you may want to take advantage of the recency effect. Listeners also tend to retain the most recently presented idea. Since your last argument is most recent in their mind, they will probably remember it. It makes good sense to place a strong argument either first or last.

2. *Use a variety of evidence.* You should present a variety of evidence as you construct each argument; take advantage of both relevance and motivation. For example, if you decide to argue for capital punishment, you can use statistics to alert your listeners to the widespread problem of premeditated violence; however, to clinch such an argument, more than cold, hard facts are necessary. It would be wise to provide a moving example of a crime victim to involve your listeners in the human drama of the problem.

3. *Avoid personal attacks on your opponent.* It is important to maintain the argument at an intellectual level. This indirectly enhances your credibility. If you can argue without becoming vicious or personal, you will earn the respect, if not the convictions, of your listeners. You may also discourage the tendency for your opponent to attack you on a personal level.

Often the best advocates know their opponent's arguments better than their opponent does. Such knowledge enables them to prepare a response and boosts their confidence in their ability to argue well.

4. *Know the potential arguments of your opponent.* Often the best advocates know their opponent's arguments better than their opponent does. It is important at least to understand what your opponent might say during an argument. This will not only enable you to prepare a response, it will boost your confidence in your own ability to argue well.

5. *Finally, practice constructing logical arguments and detecting fallacious ones.* Ultimately, argumentation is a skill based on logic. The common denominator of all arguments, despite their different content, is the patterns of reasoning people use. If you have a clear grasp of the basic building blocks of argumentation, including the material presented in this chapter, you will develop your understanding and skill.

Sample Speech

Policies are supported by particular factual assertions, as well as values. The advisability of a policy is based on the credibility of the facts offered in its support, and on the audience's willingness to accept the value judgments being made. In many cases, it is necessary to attack conclusions drawn on the basis of factual data in order to argue for a reconsideration of a policy. Jenny Clanton of Southeastern Illinois College faced this problem in her analysis of NASA's continued willingness to use Plutonium 238 as its "fuel of choice" in launching space flights.

In developing her position that NASA's policy is flawed, Ms. Clanton used a combination of testimony from experts and argument from cause to demonstrate the level of risk that exists every time the shuttle is launched under current policy. Underlying her analysis is the value assumption that the level of risk is unacceptable. She began the speech with the startling observation that the *Challenger* disaster, in fact, saved future lives. The next scheduled launch, in which the O-rings could have just as easily failed, would have produced a nuclear disaster.

In paragraphs 6–9, she demonstrated the risks attendant on the use of plutonium as a fuel. She concluded that continued use is "a crazy idea" unless all launches are perfectly safe. This led her to outline NASA's argument for safety in paragraph 10. In paragraphs 11–14, she offered a clear refutation of the presumed safety of plutonium. In the process, she highlighted the values underlying a policy that risks human life without due regard and found them inadequate as support. With the policy questioned through an analysis of factual claims about the potential hazards of plutonium use, she moved toward a resolution by using three questions to structure a discussion of what Congress has been doing, what should be done, and what listeners can do. Her personal appeal was strengthened by a final rhetorical question that focused her listeners' attention on the risk involved.

The Challenger *Disaster That Didn't Happen*
Jenny Clanton

Attention Step

□ *Reference to subject*

On January 28, 1986, the American Space Program suffered the worst disaster in its more than 30 year history. The entire world was shocked when the space shuttle Challenger exploded seconds after lift-off, claiming the lives of seven brave astronauts and crippling our entire space agenda. I suppose the oldest cliché in our culture, spoken on battlegrounds and indeed virtually anywhere Americans die, is "We must press forward so we can say they did not die in vain." Rest assured. They

□ *Startling statement*

didn't. The deaths of our seven astronauts probably saved the lives of untold thousands of Americans. /1

□ *Explanation*

For, you see, if the O-rings had not failed on January 28, 1986, but rather on May 20, 1987, the next scheduled shuttle launch,

□ *Testimony*

in the words of Dr. John Gofman, Professor Emeritus at the University of California at Berkeley, you could have "kissed Florida good-bye." /2

□ *Specific instance*

Because the next shuttle, the one that was to have explored the atmosphere of Jupiter was to carry 47 lbs. of Plutonium 238, which is, again, according to Dr. Gofman, the most toxic

□ *Testimony*

substance on the face of the earth. Dr. Helen Caldicott corroborates Dr. Gofman's claim in her book, *Nuclear Madness*, when she cites studies estimating one ounce of widely dispersed Plutonium 238 particles as having the toxicity to induce lung cancer in every person on earth. /3

Today, when you leave this room, I want you to fully understand just what impact NASA's plans could have on this planet. I want you to become cynical. I want you to be a little scared. I want you to become angry. But most of all, I want you to begin to demand some answers. /4

□ *Forecasting*

□ *Statement of claim*

To move you in this direction I would first like to explore with you just what plutonium is and what could happen if it were released in our atmosphere. Second, let's consider NASA's argument for the safety of the plutonium as used in the shuttle program. And finally, I want to convince you that NASA's conclusions are flawed. /5

Need Step

□ *Significance of issue*

□ *Explanation*

So now, let's turn our attention to the nature of plutonium. Plutonium is a man-made radioactive element which is produced in large quantities in nuclear reactors from uranium. Plutonium is a chemically reactive metal, which, if exposed to air, ignites spontaneously and produces fine particles of plutonium dioxide. These particles, when dispersed by wind and inhaled by living organisms, lodge in the lungs. Lung cancer will follow—sooner or later. Once inside the human body, plutonium rests in bone tissue, causing bone cancer.

□ *Factual claim*

Plutonium 238 is so poisonous that less than one *millionth* of a gram is a carcinogenic dose. /6

□ *Qualifying expertise*

□ *Testimony*

Last July, *Common Cause* magazine contacted Dr. Gofman at Berkeley and asked him to place Plutonium 238 in perspective. Before I share Dr. Gofman's assessment, please understand he's no poster-carrying "anti-nuke." Dr. Gofman was co-discoverer of Uranium 233, and he isolated the isotope first used in nuclear bombs. Dr. Gofman told Karl Grossman, author of the article "Redtape and Radio-activity" that Plutonium 238 is 300 times more radioactive than Plutonium 239, which is the isotope used in atomic bombs. /7

□ *Testimony*

Dr. Richard Webb, a nuclear physicist and author of *The Accident Hazards of Nuclear Power Plants*, said in a similar interview that sending 46.7 lbs. of Plutonium 238 into space would be the equivalent of sending five nuclear reactors up—and then hoping they wouldn't crash or explode. /8

□ *Transition*

Dr. Gofman's final assessment? It's a crazy idea, unless shuttle launches are 100 percent perfect. Which is just about what NASA would have liked us to believe, and at first glance NASA's guarantees are pretty convincing. /9

□ *Opposing view*

□ *Specific instances*

NASA estimates the chance of releasing Plutonium into the environment, because of the possibility of a malfunction of the space shuttle, at .002 percent—that's not quite 100 percent perfect, but it's awfully close. NASA and the Department of Energy base their reliability figures on three factors: 1) the

Titan 34D launch vehicle and its high success rate, 2) Energy Department officials in the March 10th *Aviation Week and Space Technology* magazine explain that the Plutonium would be safely contained in an unbreakable, quarter-inch thick iridium canister which would withstand pressures of over 2,000 pounds per square inch, and 3) in that same article, NASA explains there is "little public danger" because the Plutonium on board would be in the form of oxide pellets, each one inch in diameter. If you'll remember, the danger of Plutonium is in fine particles. /10

□ *Refutation of NASA position*

□ *Testimony/ statistics*

Now, let's take a second glance. One month later, the April 28th issue of *Aviation Week and Space Technology* reported that two of the last nine Titans launched have blown up. Two failures in nine trips is great in baseball, but not when we're dealing with nuclear payloads. That same article estimates loss of orbiter and crew, not at .002 percent but at 1 in 25. /11

□ *Rhetorical questions*

□ *Qualifying expertise*

With odds on the launch vehicle reduced to 1 in 25, the dual questions arise: just how breach-proof is that canister and, in a worst case scenario, what could happen if the pellets of 238 were released? For the answers to those questions we go to Dr. Gary Bennett, former Director of Safety and Nuclear Operations, who not only answers those questions, but also explains why NASA is so insistent on using plutonium. /12

□ *Testimony*

□ *Causal argument*

Last July, Dr. Bennett told *Common Cause* that there is concern within NASA and the Department of Energy that an explosion aboard the Galileo spacecraft, a Titan or other rocket, would, in turn, set off an explosion of the booster rockets. Bennett admitted that government tests in 1984 and 1985 determined that if the shuttle exploded, and then the booster rockets exploded, there would be a likelihood of breaching the iridium canister. The plutonium would then be vaporized and released into the environment; and there goes Florida. /13

Satisfaction Step

□ *Rhetorical question*

□ *Explanation*

□ *Comparison/ contrast*

But why would NASA take such a risk? It's really quite simple. On the one hand, Plutonium 238 is the one fuel that would enable space exploration beyond the limit of Mars. Without it, distant space exploration must wait for research to develop an equally effective, safe fuel. On the other hand, a worst case scenario would create the worst nuclear accident in history. In short, NASA weighed exploration now against the chances for disaster and opted to take the risk. The only problem is, I really don't like the idea of someone risking my life without consulting me—and I hope you don't either. By the way, there is evidence that NASA and the Department of Energy have projected some pretty horrible figures. Under the Freedom of Information Act rules, Karl Grossman was able to obtain agencies' estimates for the number of lives lost in a major accident. The only problem is that every reference to the number of people affected is blanketed out with liquid paper and the term Exempt #1 is written over the deletion. James Lombardo of the Energy Department explains the white-outs were necessary for—you've got it—national security reasons. I would contend that national security would be threatened by mass anger over the callousness of the Energy Department, and justifiably so. Representative Edward Markey agrees, and when he was head of the House subcommittee on Energy, Conservation and Power, he uncovered most of the information I share with you today. /14

□ Qualifying expertise

Visualization Step

□ Transition
□ Questions to structure following explanation

In a telephone interview last August, I asked Congressman Markey three questions. Why hasn't Congress done anything? What should be done? What can we do to help? /15

His answer to the first question was quite interesting. You may remember that shortly after the shuttle exploded and just when Congress was showing some interest in a thorough investigation of the space program, another larger, even more dramatic accident occurred—Chernobyl. The attention to Chernobyl as it related to our own power industry captured not only the attention of most Americans, but of Congress as well. Consequently, most of our nuclear experts are involved in working with Congress and the nuclear power industry. /16

And while Congress is focusing on one facet of the nuclear question, NASA and the Department of Energy are receiving much less attention. Which is why Congressman Markey helped found Space Watch. /17

Representative Markey is of the opinion that hysteria accomplishes nothing, but that all space flight should be halted until either Plutonium 238 can be made safe, which is highly unlikely, or until an alternative fuel can be found. The burden of proof should be on NASA to prove a fuel safe, and not on the public to prove it dangerous. /18

Action Step

□ Personal appeal

This is where you and I come in. First, if by now you are sufficiently scared or angry, contact Space Watch through Representative Markey's office. Then, keep abreast of developments and exert pressure through your elected officials if Congress does nothing to interfere with NASA's plans. Send your objections not only to your own legislators, but to Representative Markey as well. Allow him to walk into the House with mailbag after mailbag of letters in opposition to NASA's unbridled desire to go to Jupiter. We have a friend in Congress who solicits help. The least we can do is give it to him. /19

□ *Pertinent
 quotation*
□ *Rhetorical
 question*

One last thought; as of November, Plutonium 238 is *still* NASA's and the Department of Energy's fuel of choice. Dr. Bennett's last words in that July interview were, "I think you should understand there's a degree of risk with any kind of launch vehicle." But isn't that the point?[10] /20

Chapter Summary

Argumentation is a persuasive activity in which a speaker offers reasons and support for claims in opposition to the claims advanced by others. Arguing with others engages people in tasks central to *critical thinking:* assessing the reasons offered in support of claims. The process of arguing is governed by *social conventions*, including *bilaterality, self-risk, reasonableness,* and *rationality.*

Public argumentation, at its most general level, consists of *constructive* and *refutative* speeches, often structured in accordance with specific rules of procedure. Within single argumentative speeches, particular *arguments* consist of (1) the *claim* to be defended, (2) the *evidence* relevant to the claim, and (3) the *reasoning pattern*, or inference, used to connect the evidence to the claim. Claims of *fact* assert that something is or is not the case, claims of *value* propose that something is or is not desirable, and claims of *policy* attempt to establish that something should or should not be done. Evidence is chosen to support these claims because it is *rationally* or *motivationally relevant*. There are five basic reasoning patterns: *reasoning from example, reasoning from generalization or axiom, reasoning from sign, reasoning by parallel case,* and *reasoning from causal relation*. Each of the inferential, or reasoning, patterns can be tested by applying specific questions to evaluate the strength or soundness of the argument. Critical thinkers also should be on the alert for *fallacies* committed during an argumentative speech. Fallacies are flaws in the reasoning process and include, as general groups, *fallacies in evidence, fallacies in reasoning,* and *fallacies in language.*

Speakers seeking to develop argumentative speeches, either to initiate support for a position or to offer a refutation of an opponent's position, should consider the general strategies presented in this chapter. As you become more adept at constructing your own presentations, you also will increase your skill in critically appraising the arguments of your opponents.

Reference Notes

1. Harvey Siegel, *Educating Reason: Rationality, Critical Thinking, and Education* (New York: Routledge, 1988), 1–47. The importance of critical thinking has been underscored in two recent national reports on higher education: The National Institute on Education's *Involvement in Learning: Realizing the Potential of American Higher Education*, 1984; and the American Association of Colleges' report, *Integrity in the College Curriculum: A Report to the Academic Community*, 1985. For a summary of research on critical thinking in the college setting, see James H. McMillan, "Enhancing College Students' Critical Thinking: A Review of Studies," *Research in Higher Education* 26 (1987): 3–29.

2. Douglas Ehninger, "Validity as Moral Obligation," *Southern Speech Communication Journal* 33 (1968): 215–22.

3. Henry M. Robert, *Robert's Rules of Order Newly Revised*, ed. Sara Corbin Robert, Henry M. Robert III, William J. Evans, and James W. Cleary (Glenview, IL: Scott, Foresman and Company, 1981).

4. Walter R. Fisher, "Rationality and the Logic of Good Reasons," *Philosophy and Rhetoric* 13 (1980): 121–30; Ray E. McKerrow, "Rationality and Reasonableness in a Theory of Argument," in J. R. Cox and C. A. Willard, *Advances in Argumentation Theory and Research* (Carbondale, IL: Southern Illinois University Press, 1982), 105–22.

5. Richard Rieke and Malcolm O. Sillars, *Argumentation and the Decision Making Process*, 2nd ed. (Glenview, IL: Scott, Foresman and Company, 1983).

6. A full discussion of the logical grounding of claims in evidence and reasoning is presented in Douglas Ehninger and Wayne Brockriede, *Decision by Debate*, 2nd ed. (New York: Harper & Row Pubs., Inc., 1978).

7. Charles L. Stevenson, *Ethics and Language* (New Haven, CT: Yale University Press, 1944), Chapter 9.

8. An excellent logic textbook is Irving M. Copi, *Introduction to Logic*, 7th ed. (New York: Macmillan Publishing Co., 1986).

9. Robert Bostrom, *Persuasion* (Englewood Cliffs, NJ: Prentice-Hall, 1983), 177–78.

10. Jenny Clanton, "The *Challenger* Disaster That Didn't Happpen," *Winning Orations* (1988).

Key Terms

argumentation

argument

bilaterality

self-risk

reasonableness

rationality

validity

soundness

parliamentary procedures

argumentative (constructive) speech

refutative speech

rebuttals

rejoinders

claim of fact

claim of value

claim of policy

reasoning from examples

reasoning from generalization or axiom

reasoning from sign

reasoning from parallel case

reasoning from causal relations

fallacies in evidence

fallacies in reasoning

fallacies in language

primacy-recency effect

Problems and Probes

1. How influential are political debates in campaign years? In researching this question, consult Kathleen H. Jamieson and David S. Birdsell, *Presidential*

Debates: The Challenge of Creating an Informed Electorate. Present your critical summary in written form or as part of a class discussion on the role of argumentation in decision making.

2. Think through two or three of the informal arguments you have engaged in during the last few days: in the student union; in classroom discussion; in exchanges with an instructor, a close friend, or your roommate. (a) In any of them, did you present a relatively sustained speech? (b) What kinds of arguments and reasons for accepting those arguments did you offer as the disagreement progressed? (c) Did you or any of the other arguers become angry? If so, who handled it—and how? (d) Looking back, recall whether you or any others invoked conventions of self-risk ("How can you possibly hold that view?"), the fairness doctrine ("Come on! Give me a chance to explain!"), or a commitment to rationality ("That's the dumbest reason I ever heard! Don't you have any better reasons than that?"). Prepare a short paper summarizing the foregoing analysis and, in addition, clearly distinguishing informal arguments of this type from the more formal ones we have considered in this chapter. Hand in your written analysis to the instructor and be prepared to discuss your ideas.

3. Assume you are going to give a speech favoring the universal military to an audience of fellow students who are hostile to your proposal. Outline your speech by using Toulmin's model of argumentation as it is discussed in the *Speaker's Resource Book.* What factors do you consider as you construct and frame your argument? Assume several counterarguments are made from audience members. Rebuild your case using the Toulmin model. What new factors must you now consider?

Communication Activities

1. Prepare a ten-minute argumentative exchange on a topic involving you and one other member of the class. Dividing the available time equally, one of you will advocate a claim; the other will oppose it. Adopt any format you both feel comfortable with. You may choose: (a) a Lincoln/Douglas format—the first person speaks four minutes; the second, five; and then the first person returns for a one-minute rejoinder; (b) an issue format—you both agree on, say, two key issues, and then each speaks for two and a half minutes on each issue; (c) a debate format—each speaker talks twice alternatively, three minutes in a constructive speech, two minutes in rebuttal; and (d) a heckling format—each of you has five minutes, but during the middle of each speech the audience or opponent may ask questions.

2. Turn the class into a deliberative assembly, decide on a motion or resolution to be argued, and then schedule a day or two for a full debate. This format should use particular argumentative roles: advocate, witness, direct examiner, cross-examiner, summarizer. It allows each speaker to be part of a team; what you do affects not only yourself but also other speakers on your side of the argument. (For guidance in the use of this format, see John D. May, ed., *American Problems: What Should Be Done? Debates from "The Advocates"* [Palo Alto, CA: National Press Books, 1973]).

CHAPTER EIGHTEEN

Speeches on Special Occasions

When asked the question "Who are you?" most people respond in terms of social categories: "I'm a college student" (educational institution), "I'm a Baptist" (religious assembly), "I'm an Italian" (ethnic collectivity), "I'm a computer programmer" (work group), "I'm one of the Thomas kids from Macon, Georgia" (familial and geographical identification), "I'm an American" (societal roots). All of this is not to say, however, that there is no real "you" behind those labels; human beings tend to think of and identify themselves in terms of social groups. We also refer to ourselves in terms of social roles: "I'm Thad Gardner's son," "I'm Pedro Gonzalez's neighbor," "I'm Nancy Pei's friend."

Groups and our consciousness of roles not only present us with aspects of our identity, but they also have authority over us. They can regulate behavior upon occasion, because, after all, they often predate us; we were thrust into preexisting families, with their own rules or customs, and into social and political institutions that made claims upon us from the day we were born. Social groups and larger institutions can provide us with services, control our behaviors, and mark us for who we are. It is no wonder that people maintain very special relationships with the groups and institutions to which they belong.

In this chapter, we will look at several kinds of speeches you may give in the presence of or as the representative of some of those groups and institutions. Our focus will be on speeches that are given to or for "communities," a word, of course, directly related to the idea of *communication*. First, we will consider an individual's relationships to such communities and then examine types of **speeches on special occasions**—occasions particularly important to communities—speeches of introduction, speeches of tribute, speeches of nomination, speeches to create goodwill, and speeches to entertain.

People tend to think of and identify themselves in terms of social groups and roles.

Ceremony and Ritual in the Community

The word "community" comes from the Latin *communis*, meaning "common," or, more literally (with the *-ity* ending), "commonality." A community is not simply the physical presence of people, say, who live in the same town (often called their "local community") or who worship in the same church (although that church sometimes is called a "religious community"). Physical presence is not the key here; psychological state is. A **community** is a group of people who think of themselves as bonded together, whether by blood, locale, nationality, race, occupation, gender, or other shared experience or attribute.

As we have noted earlier, we all belong to a variety of demographic or social units—age stratum, social or work group, socioeconomic class, ethnic population, gender classification, church, and so on. In particular situations, one of those institutions becomes important to us and "reminds" us that we "belong" to it. Thus, a middle-aged professor may dismiss an opinion you have expressed by retorting, "You won't be saying that when you're forty-five," reminding you that you belong to "the younger set." On Martin Luther King Day, St. Patrick's Day, or Passover, you may celebrate your ethnic heritage. In many late-evening dorm bull sessions, your membership in a church or ethnic group may be discussed and even questioned. In such times, you will be made conscious of community: your affinity with other, like-minded people.

Reference Groups and the Individual

We have mentioned reference groups earlier, but now it is time to discuss them more fully. Social psychologist Philip Zimbardo defines reference groups as "the formal or informal groups from which an individual derives attitudes and standards of acceptable and appropriate behavior and to which the individual refers for information, direction, and support for life-style."[1] Notice in this definition the dual powers of reference groups: they give you attitudes and behavior patterns, and you turn to them when you need additional information or support. You thus are both passively and actively related to groups; you both draw self-definition from groups and seek new information or reinforcement from them. Hence, many people are born into a religious community (reference group) whose doctrines and rites make indelible marks on them; when faced in later life with such crises as unwanted children, the death of loved ones, or decisions about marriage, those people often will turn to that community for solutions. The reference group is both definer and extender of the individual.

Your relationships to groups, therefore, are complex. Even though some groups come and go in your life—you are no longer a Cub Scout, Blue Bird, gang member, or high-school glee club singer—you always have some reference groups in your life. The key to their power is *salience*—the degree to which you perceive them and their standards as relevant to a particular situation. Thus, you probably no longer see the Blue Birds as relevant to your life. That community has little salience for you; hence, it rarely affects your decision making. Other reference groups do, however. You currently are being influenced by an educational institution. You are learning how to see things you had not seen before; to question some of your everyday assumptions about the world; and to reason your way to complex aesthetic, social, political, and evaluative judgments you have never made before. School is highly salient to your thinking. Furthermore, the things—and ways of thinking about them—you now are learning will become parts of your decision-making apparatus. Your educational institution will have less effect on you in later life, although you probably will find that, even when you are being influenced strongly by other groups, something out of your school experience will come to mind occasionally and affect a decision you are making.

Thus, reference groups make claims on individuals when they are seen as salient to a problem or event. Just as your group memberships change over time, so does the power of a particular group to affect your life.[2]

Public Address As Community Building

So far, we have been talking in social-psychological terms, in terms of group-individual relationships understood mentally. We now need to extend the discussion into the realm of speechmaking. That extension is easy: your sense of community is created in large part through public address. Social communities—family and friends—take shape through interpersonal, or one-on-one, talk, but most of your reference groups influence your life through public talk. You may have memorized and learned to recite in a group the Boy Scout Law and oath, with each recitation reinforcing the Scouts' beliefs and values. Many churches have ceremonies of group confession of sins and profession of faith, and most depend upon speechmaking—preaching—to instill and reinforce doctrine and morals. Your civic education begins with pledging allegiance to the flag; broadens when you participate in Memorial Day, Fourth of July, and Labor Day ceremonies (which include public addresses); and is reviewed every time the president appears on television or hopefuls campaign for local, state, or national office.

As Michael Walzer puts it, "The state is invisible; it must be personified before it can be seen, symbolized before it can be loved, imagined before it can be conceived."[3] The same is true with most reference groups in your life. You cannot see group standards, only individuals' behavior; you cannot feel the influence of groups outside of the words and other symbols they use to define their claim upon you.

Finally, groups remind you of their claims upon you on special occasions, in special rituals. David Kertzer has described **ritual** as follows: "Ritual action has a formal quality to it. It follows highly structured, standardized sequences and is often enacted at certain places and times that are themselves endowed with special symbolic meaning. Ritual action is repetitive and, therefore, often redundant, but these very factors serve as important means of channeling emotion, guiding cognition, and organizing social groups. I have defined ritual as action wrapped in a web of symbolism."[4] Confirmation or bar mitzvah services, the act of "hooding" a new Doctor of Philosophy during graduation, reciting the Pledge of Allegiance in school—these are the kinds of ritual actions Kertzer is talking about. All rituals are structured, standardized, and repetitive, with times and places set aside for ritual observances. Ritual is imbued with symbols and with public address to provide the means of channeling, guiding, and organizing that Kretzer mentions.

Speeches on special occasions are themselves, then, ritualized, and often structured, standardized, and so on. If introductions of speakers often seem trite, that is because introducing someone into your community is a ritualized activity. If many nomination speeches sound alike from campaign to campaign, that is because few of us really want surprises in our campaign processes. Surprise could lead to change, and change, in turn, could upset our political system. In speeches for special occasions (except, as we shall see, speeches to entertain), the emphasis is upon ritualized tradition rather than revolutionary change. Let us now look at some types of special-occasion talk.

Speeches of Introduction

Speeches of introduction usually are given by a person who belongs to a community (the group that is to hear the speech). They are designed to prepare that community to accept the featured speaker and his or her message. There is a sense in which a speech of introduction asks for permission for an outsider to speak; that permission, presumably, is based upon what the nonmember can contribute to the group. The group must *want* to hear

Rituals and Power

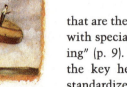

We have discussed speeches for special occasions as community building. They also are important for community maintaining, and therein lies one of their great powers. We seldom think about our routine activities as "powerful," yet a whole line of research in cultural studies is working to substantiate that claim. Of recent vintage is Kertzer's *Ritual, Politics, and Power*. A professor of anthropology at Bowdoin College, Kertzer investigates the influence of ritual in politics.

He defines "ritual" as "action wrapped in a web of symbolism," as "highly structured, standardized sequences . . . often enacted at certain places and times that are themselves endowed with special symbolic meaning" (p. 9). Symbolization is the key here. Some highly standardized sequences of behavior, such as brushing your teeth or getting dressed, have little or no symbolic significance; they are simply habits or routines. Rituals are structured actions to which we attach particular collective significance, often about how the past is related to the present and how the present should affect the future. A political ritual, Kertzer notes, "helps us cope with two human problems: building confidence in our sense of self by providing us with a sense of continuity—I am the same person today as I

the outsider before the featured speaker can be successful. If the speaker is a member of the group, the introduction may serve as a reminder of his or her role or accomplishments within the community.

Purpose and Manner of Speaking for Speeches of Introduction

The purpose of a speech of introduction is, of course, to create in the audience a desire to hear the speaker you are introducing. Everything else must be subordinated to this aim. You are not being called upon to make a speech yourself or to air your own views on the subject. You are only the speaker's advance agent; your job is to sell him or her to the audience. This task carries a twofold responsibility. First, you must arouse the listeners' curiosity about the speaker and/or subject, thus making it easier for the speaker to get the attention of the audience. Second, you must do all that you reasonably can to generate audience respect for the speaker, thereby increasing the likelihood that listeners will respond favorably to the message that is presented.

was twenty years ago and as I will be ten years from now—and giving us confidence that the world in which we live today is the same world we lived in before and the same world we will have to cope with in the future" (p. 10). As a group, thus, we celebrate our pasts and construct our futures in the present; ritual is the mechanism of that celebration.

The notion of power comes into the picture when we consider politics as the processes whereby vested interests in a society struggle for domination. Republicans fight Democrats for legislative or executive control; a section of town unrepresented on the city council fights to get a seat; a lobbyist for the American Association of Retired Persons pushes for increased state appropriations to elderly services budgets; the Hispanic voters of Texas ask presidential candidates to take stands against the "English-language only" movement. Political struggle can be harsh, even fatal, in some societies. Citizens attempt to ritualize political fighting: they invent rules of "parliamentary procedure" to ritualize partisan debate; press traditions dictate the kinds of questions that are asked of presidents in their news conferences; the transfer of power from one executive to another is ritualized in inaugural ceremonies, and coronation ceremonies for kings and queens are often lavish beyond description.

The power in such rituals, according to Kertzer, lies in their abilities (1) to control the actual struggles for power and (2) to help convince the witnesses (the populace) that authority is being wielded benevolently, in their name. The rhetoric of special occasions, thus, is a two-edged discourse of power and community maintenance.

FOR FURTHER READING
Kertzer, David I. *Ritual, Politics, and Power*. New Haven, CT: Yale University Press, 1988.

When giving a speech of introduction, your manner of speaking should be suited to the nature of the occasion, to your familiarity with the speaker, and to the speaker's prestige. If you were introducing a justice of the United States Supreme Court, for instance, it would hardly be appropriate to tell a joke about him or her. Nor would this approach be tactful if the speaker were a stranger to you, or the occasion serious and dignified. On the other hand, if you are presenting an old friend to a group of associates on an informal occasion, a solemn and dignified manner would be equally out of place.

Formulating the Content of Speeches of Introduction

The better known and more respected a speaker is, the shorter your introduction can be. The less well known he or she is, the more you will need to arouse interest in the subject or build up the speaker's prestige. In general, however, observe these principles:

At a dedication, the speaker says something appropriate about the purpose to be served by whatever is being dedicated or commemorated.

Dedications

Buildings, monuments, and parks may be constructed or set aside to honor a worthy cause or to commemorate a person, group, significant movement, historic event, or the like. At such **dedications,** the speaker says something appropriate about the purpose to be served by whatever is being set aside and about the person(s), event, or occasion thus commemorated.

Memorial Services

Services to pay public honor to the dead usually include a speech of tribute, or **eulogy.** Ceremonies of this kind may honor a famous person (or persons), perhaps on anniversaries of their deaths. For example, many speeches have paid tribute to John F. Kennedy and Martin Luther King, Jr. More often, however, a eulogy honors someone personally known to the audience and recently deceased.

At other times, a memorial honors certain qualities that person stood for. In such a situation, the speaker uses the memorial to renew and reinforce the audience's adherence to ideals possessed by the deceased and worthy of emulation by the community.

Purpose and Manner of Speaking for Speeches of Tribute

The purpose of a speech of tribute is, of course, to create in those who hear it a sense of appreciation for the traits or accomplishments of the person or group to whom tribute is paid. If you cause your audience to realize the essential worth or importance of that person or group, you have succeeded, but you may go further than this. You may, by honoring a person, arouse deeper devotion to the cause he or she represents. Did he give distinguished service to his community? Then strive to enhance the audience's civic pride and sense of service. Was she a friend to youth? Then try to arouse the audience's interest in working to provide opportunities for young people. Create a desire in your listeners to emulate the person or persons honored.

When delivering a speech of tribute, suit the manner of speaking to the circumstances. A farewell banquet usually blends an atmosphere of merriment with a spirit of sincere regret. Dignity and formality are, on the whole, characteristic of memorial services, the unveiling of monuments, and similar dedicatory ceremonies. Regardless of the general tone of the occasion, however, in a speech of tribute avoid high-sounding phrases, bombastic oratory, and obvious "oiliness." A simple, honest expression of admiration presented in clear and unadorned language is best.

Formulating the Content of Speeches of Tribute

Frequently, in a speech of tribute a speaker attempts to itemize all the accomplishments of the honored person or group. This weakens the impact because, in trying to cover everything, it emphasizes nothing. Plan, instead, to focus your remarks, as follows:

1. *Stress dominant traits.* If you are paying tribute to a person, select a few aspects of his or her personality that are especially likeable or praiseworthy, and relate incidents from the person's life or work to illustrate these distinguishing qualities.

2. *Mention only outstanding achievements.* Pick out only a few of the person's or group's most notable accomplishments. Tell about them in detail to show how important they were. Let your speech say, "Here is what this person (or group) has done; see how such actions have contributed to the well-being of our business or community."

3. *Give special emphasis to the influence of the person or group.* Show the effect that the behavior of the person or group has had on others. Many times, the importance of people's lives can be demonstrated not so much by their particular material accomplishments as by the influence they exerted on associates.

Organizing Speeches of Tribute

Ordinarily you will have little difficulty in getting people to listen to a speech of tribute. The audience probably already knows and admires the person or group about whom you are to speak, and listeners are curious to learn what you are going to say about the honoree(s). Consider the following steps in preparing your speech:

1. *Direct the attention of the audience toward those characteristics or accomplishments that you consider most important.* There are two

An educational program provides the public with desired information, while creating goodwill for the speaker's company or profession.

Special Demonstration Programs. Special programs are frequently presented by government agencies, university extension departments, and business organizations. For example, a wholesale food company may send a representative to a nutritionists' meeting to explain the food values present in various kinds of canned meat or fish products and to demonstrate new ways of preparing or serving them. Although such a speech would be primarily informative, the speaker could win goodwill indirectly by showing that his or her company desires to increase customer satisfaction with its products and services.

Manner of Speaking in Speeches for Goodwill

Three qualities—modesty, tolerance, and good humor—characterize the manner of speaking appropriate for goodwill speeches. Although you will be talking about your business or vocation and trying to make it seem important to the audience, you should never boast or brag. Let the facts speak for themselves. Moreover, show a tolerant attitude toward others, especially competitors. The airline representative, for instance, who violently attacks trucking companies and bus lines is likely to gain ill will rather than good. Finally, exercise good humor. The goodwill speech is not for the zealot or crusader. Do not try to force acceptance of your ideas; instead, show so much enthusiasm and good feeling that your listeners respond spontaneously and favorably to the information you are providing.

Formulating the Content of Speeches for Goodwill

In selecting materials for a goodwill speech, keep three suggestions in mind. First, present novel and interesting facts about your subject. Make your listeners feel that you are giving them an inside look into your company or organization. Avoid talking about what they already know; concentrate on new developments and on facts and services that are not generally known. Second, show a relationship between your subject and the lives of your listeners. Make them see the importance of your organization or profession to their personal safety, success, or happiness. Third, offer a definite service. This offer may take the form of an invitation to the audience members to visit your office or shop, to help them with their problems, or to answer questions or send brochures.

Organizing Speeches for Goodwill

Because of its close relationship to speeches to inform and to persuade, the organization of the materials we have just described can be discussed in terms of the motivated sequence.

Attention Step.   The purposes of the beginning of your speech are to establish a friendly feeling and to arouse the audience's curiosity about your profession or the institution you represent. You can gain the first of these objectives by a tactful compliment to the group or by a reference to the occasion that has brought you together. Follow this with one or two unusual facts or illustrations concerning the enterprise you represent. For instance: "Before we began manufacturing television parts, the Lash Electric Company confined its business to the making of clock radios that would never wear out. We succeeded so well that we almost went bankrupt! That was only fifteen years ago. Today our export trade alone is over 100 times larger than our total annual domestic business was in those earlier days. It may interest you to know how this change took place." In brief, you must find a way to arouse your listeners' curiosity about your organization.

Need Step.   Point out certain problems facing your audience—problems with which your institution, profession, or agency is vitally concerned. For example, if you represent a radio or television station, show the relationship of good communications to the social and economic health of the community. By so doing, you will establish common ground with your audience. Ordinarily the need step is brief and consists largely of suggestions developed with only an occasional illustration; however, if you intend to propose that your listeners join in acting to meet a common problem, the need step will require fuller development.

Satisfaction Step.   The meat of a goodwill speech is in the satisfaction step. Here is the place to tell your audience about your institution, profession, or business and to explain what it is or what it does. You can do this in at least three ways. You can relate interesting events in its history. Pick events that demonstrate its humanity, reliability, and importance to the community, to the country, or to the world of nations. You also can explain how your organization or profession operates. Pick out those things that are unusual or that may contain beneficial suggestions for your audience. This method often helps impress upon your listeners the size and efficiency of your operation or enterprise. You also might want to describe the services your organization renders. Explain its products; point out how widely they are used; discuss the policies by which management is guided—especially those you think your audience will agree with or admire. Tell what your firm or profession has done for the community: people employed; purchases made locally; assistance with community projects; or improvements in health, education, or public safety. Do not boast, but make sure that your listeners realize the value of your work *to them*.

Visualization Step.   Your object here is to crystallize the goodwill that your presentation of information in the satisfaction step initially has created. Do this by looking to the future. Rapidly survey the points you have covered or combine them into a single story or illustration. To approach this step from the opposite direction, picture for your listeners the loss that would result if the organization or profession you represent should leave the community or cease to exist. Be careful, however, not to leave the impression that there is any real danger that this will occur.

Action Step.   In this step, you make your offer of service to the audience. For example, invite the group to visit your office or point out the willingness of your organization to assist in a common enterprise. As is true of every type of speech, the content and organization of the speech for goodwill must be adapted to meet the demands of the subject or occasion. You should, however, never lose sight of the central purpose for which you speak: to show your audience that the work you do or the service you perform is of value to them, that it somehow makes their lives happier, more productive, interesting, or secure.

Speeches to Entertain

To entertain an audience presents special challenges to speakers. As you may recall, we identified "to entertain" as an independent type of speech in Chapter 4 because of the peculiar force of humor in speechmaking. Discounting slapstick (of the slipping-on-a-banana-peel genre), most humor depends primarily upon a listener's sensitivities to the routines and mores of one's society; this is obvious if you have ever listened to someone from a foreign country tell jokes. Much humor cannot be translated, in part because of language differences (puns, for example, do not translate well) and in even larger measure because of cultural differences.

Purposes and Manner of
Speeches to Entertain

Like most humor in general, **speeches to entertain** usually work within the cultural frameworks of a particular group or society. Such speeches may be "merely funny," of course, as in comic monologues, but most are serious in their force or demand on audiences. After-dinner speeches, for example, usually are more than dessert; their topics normally are relevant to the group at hand, and the anecdotes they contain usually are offered to make a point. That point may be as simple as deflecting an audience's antipathy toward the speaker, as group centered as making the people in the audience feel more like a group, or as serious as offering a critique of society.

Speakers seeking to deflect an audience's antipathy often use humor to ingratiate themselves. For example, Henry W. Grady, editor of the *Atlanta Constitution*, expected a good deal of distrust and hostility when, after the Civil War, he journeyed to New York City in 1886 to tell the New England Society about "The New South." He opened the speech not only by thanking the Society for the invitation but also telling stories about farmers, husbands and wives, and preachers. He praised Abraham Lincoln, a Northerner, as "the first typical American" of the new age; told another humorous story about shopkeepers and their advertising; poked fun at the great Union General Sherman—"who is considered an able man in our hearts, though some people think he is a kind of careless man about fire"; and assured his audience that a New South, one very much like the old North, was arising from those

Although its purpose is primarily to entertain, an after-dinner speech normally offers important information relevant to the group at hand.

ashes.[6] Through the use of humor, Henry Grady had his audience cheering every point he made about the New South that evening.

Group cohesiveness also can be created through humor. Politicians, especially when campaigning, spend much time telling humorous stories about their opponents, hitting them with stinging remarks. In part, of course, biting political humor degrades the opposition candidates and party; however, such humor also can make one's own party feel more cohesive. For example, Democrats collected Richard Nixon's 1972 bumperstickers, which said "Nixon Now," cut off the *w*, and put them on their own autos. Democrats did endless turns on the names Bush and Quayle in 1988. Likewise, Republicans poked fun at Michael Dukakis, laughing at a picture of him seated in a tank and savaging his foreign policy statements. Such zingers allow political party members to laugh at their opponents and to celebrate their membership in a "better" party.

Finally, speeches to entertain can be used not merely to poke fun at outsiders, but even to critique one's society. Humor can be used to urge general changes and reform of social practices.

Formulating the Content of Speeches to Entertain

When arranging materials for speeches to entertain, develop a series of illustrations, short quotations or quips, and stories, each following another in fairly rapid succession. Most important, make sure that each touches upon a central theme or point. An entertaining speech must be more than a comic monologue; it must be cohesive and pointed. The following sequence works well for speeches to entertain:

1. Relate a story or anecdote, present an illustration, or quote an appropriate passage.
2. State the essential idea or point of view implied by your opening remarks.
3. Follow with a series of additional stories, anecdotes, quips, or illustrations that amplify or illuminate your central idea. Arrange those supporting materials so they are thematically or tonally coherent.
4. Close with a restatement of the central point you have developed. As in step 1, you can use another quotation or one final story that clinches and epitomizes your speech as a whole.

Sample Speech

The following speech by cartoonist Garry Trudeau of *Doonesbury* fame illustrates the principles for arranging speeches to entertain and demonstrates pointedly that such speeches can have very serious purposes—in this case, a critique of American attitudes toward impertinence. Notice that he began the speech with humorous observations, but then let his point about impertinence emerge sharply, with sarcasm his primary use of humor through the latter portions of the speech. In all, this commencement speech delivered at Vassar College in 1986 suited his occupation, the times, and his audience.

The Value of Impertinent Questions
Garry Trudeau

Ladies and gentlemen of Vassar:

My wife, who works in television, told me recently that a typical interview on her show used to run 10 minutes. It now runs only five minutes, which is still triple the length of the average television news story. The average pop recording these days lasts around three minutes, or, about the time it takes to read a story in *People* magazine. The stories in *USA Today* take so little time to read that they're known in the business as "News McNuggets." /1

Now, the average comic strip only takes about 10 seconds to digest, but if you read every strip published in the *Washington Post*, as the President of the United States claims to, it takes roughly eight minutes a day, which means, a quick computation reveals, that the Leader of the Free World has spent a total of 11 days, 3 hours and 40 minutes of his presidency reading the comics. This fact, along with nuclear meltdown, are easily two of the most frightening thoughts of our times. /2

There's one exception to this relentless compression of time in modern life. That's right—the graduation speech. When it comes to graduation speeches, it is generally conceded that time—a generous dollop of time—is of the essence. This is because the chief function of the graduation speaker has always been to prevent graduating seniors from being released into the real world before they've been properly sedated. Like all anesthetics, graduation speeches take time to kick in, so I'm going to ask you to bear with me for about a quarter of an hour. It will go faster if you think of it as the equivalent of four videos. /3

I want to speak to you today about questions. About pertinent questions and impertinent questions. And where you might expect them to lead you. /4

I first learned about pertinent questions from my father, a retired physician who sued [sic] to practice medicine in the Adirondacks. Like all parents racing against the clock to civilize their children, my father sought to instruct me in the ways of separating wheat from chaff, of asking sensible questions designed to yield useful answers. That is the way a diagnostician thinks. Fortunately for me, his own practical experience frequently contradicted his worthiest intentions. /5

Here's a case in point: A man once turned up in my father's office complaining of an ulcer. My father asked the pertinent question. Was there some undue stress, he inquired, that might be causing the man to digest his stomach? The patient, who was married, thought about it for a moment and then allowed that he had a girlfriend in Syracuse, and that twice a week he'd been driving an old pick-up down to see her. Since the pick-up frequently broke down, he was often late in getting home, and he had to devise fabulous stories to tell his wife. My father, compassionately but sternly, told the man he had to make a hard decision about his personal priorities if he was ever to get well. /6

The patient nodded and went away, and six months later came back completely cured, a new man. My father congratulated him and then delicately inquired if he'd made some change in his life. /7

The man replied, "Yup. Got me a new pick-up." /8

So the pertinent question sometimes yields the impertinent answer. In spite of himself, my father ended up teaching me that an unexpected or inconvenient truth is often the price of honest inquiry. Of course, you presumably wouldn't be here if you didn't already know that. I'm confident that your education has been fairly studded with pertinent questions yielding impertinent answers. /9

But how many of you have learned to turn that around—to ask the impertinent question to get at that which is pertinent? /10

I first came across the impertinent question in the writings of that master inquisitor, Studs Terkel. He himself claims to have adopted it from the physicist Jacob Bronowski, who once told him, "Until you ask an impertinent question of nature, you do not get a pertinent answer. Great answers in nature are always hidden in the questions. When Einstein in 1905 questioned the assumption held for three hundred years that time is a given, he asked one of the great impertinent questions: "Why? How do I know that my time is the same as yours?"' /11

The impertinent question is the glory and the engine of human inquiry. Copernicus asked it and shook the foundations of Renaissance Europe. Darwin asked it and is repudiated to this day. Thomas Jefferson asked it and was so invigorated by it that he declared it an inalienable right. /12

Daniel Defoe asked it and invented the novel. James Joyce asked it and reinvented the novel, which was promptly banned. /13

Nietzsche asked it and inspired Picasso, who restated it and inspired a revolution of aesthetics. /14

The Wright brothers asked it and their achievement was ignored for five years. Steven Jobs asked it and was ignored for five minutes, which was still long enough for him to make $200 million. /15

Whether revered or reviled in their lifetimes, history's movers framed their questions in ways that were entirely disrespectful of conventional wisdom. Civilization has always advanced in the shimmering wake of its discontents. As the writer Tristan Vox put it, "Doubt is precisely what makes a culture grow. How many of what we call our classics were conceived as the breaking of laws, exercises in subversion, as the expression of doubts about the self and society that could no longer be contained?" /16

The value of the impertinent question should be self-evident to Americans, for at no time in human history has it been asked more persistently and to greater effect than during the course of the American experiment. It is at the very core of our political and cultural character as a people, and we owe our vitality to its constant renewal. /17

Today, the need for that spirit of renewal has never seemed more pressing. There is a persistent feeling in this country that many of our institutions have not measured up, that with all our resources and technology and good intentions, we as a nation are still a long way from fulfilling our own expectations. The social programs that have failed to eliminate poverty, an educational system which has seen its effectiveness seriously eroded, the chemical breakthroughs that now threaten man's environment, the exploding booster rockets, malfunctioning nuclear power plants—these are but some of the images that have shaken our confidence. According to a recent poll, the only American institution that still enjoys the trust of a majority of college students today is medicine; only 44% of those polled trust educational institutions, 29% trust the White House, 23% trust the press and only 21% say they trust religion. /18

It's difficult to think of an institution in this country that has not had to re-examine its agenda, to ask impertinent questions about the purpose and the means of its mission. Society's leaders, whose number you join today, face a wall of public cynicism. As professionals, they have to speak more clearly about what they *can* do. As citizens, they have to speak clearly about what they *should* do. /19

Nowhere is the need for accountability more urgent than in what is shaping up to be the largest coordinated national undertaking of your generation—the Strategic Defense Initiative. It may well become the most fiercely contended issue of your times. Already 6,500 college scientists, including a majority of professors in 109 university physics and engineering departments, have declared their opposition to SDI and have signed a "pledge of non-participation" in a project they have called "ill-conceived and dangerous." The group, including 15 Nobel Prize winners, maintains that the weapons system is inherently destabilizing and that further pursuit of its development is likely to initiate a massive new arms competition. /20

The actions of these scientists constitute an extraordinary repudiation of the amorality of indiscriminate weapons research. Science, since it leads to knowledge, has all too frequently led its practitioners to believe that it is inherently self-justifying, that there is nothing dangerous about splitting atoms in a moral vacuum. These attitudes are held in abundance by some of the brightest people of your generation, who are already hard at work on what nearly *all* of them concede is a dangerous fantasy. /21

Listen to these comments from the young Star Warriors still in their 20s working on particle beams and brain bombs at Lawrence Livermore National Laboratory: /22

This from the inventor of the atomic powered x-ray laser, "Until 1980 or so, I didn't want to have anything to do with nuclear anything. Back in those days I thought there was something fundamentally evil about weapons. Now I see it as an interesting physics problem." /23

His co-worker, another brilliant young physicist, says he has doubts about the wisdom of SDI but concurs that "the science is *very* interesting." /24

A third member of the team had this to say: "I think that the great majority of the lab's technical people view the President's (Star Wars) speech as somewhat off the wall and the programs being proposed as being, in the end, intrinsically rather foolish. But obviously, the lab is benefiting right now and will continue to benefit, and everybody's happy with the marvelous new work." /25

Marvelous new work, indeed. As a TRW recruiting brochure put it recently, "We're standing on the first rung of a defense development that will dominate the industry for the next 20 years." Why? Because weapons manufacturers think Star Wars will work? On the contrary, at a recent trade show, McDonnell Douglas boasted on one wall its Star Wars hardware while on a facing wall, it displayed proposed Star Wars countermeasures, including a "maneuvering re-entry vehicle" and a "defense suppression vehicle." GA Technologies is already marketing the latest in "survivable materials" to protect American missiles from a *Soviet* defensive system. /26

No one in the defense industry seriously believes in a "peace shield"; in fact they're betting against it. If an American SDI is big business, then the hardware needed to overcome the anticipated Soviet response is even bigger business. The industry is further encouraged by the mindless momentum of the program, as evidenced by the recent admission of Reagan's undersecretary of defense that he pulled the $26 billion price tag out of the air. /27

Said the official, "I tried to figure out what the hell we're talking about. [Congress] wanted a number and kept on insisting on having a number. OK. First year was $2.4 billion, and I figure, OK, best we could handle is maybe a 20%–25% growth." /28

Little wonder that during the program's first year, the money could not be spent fast enough to use up the yearly appropriation. Undeterred, the following year the administration asked for $2.5 billion, greater than its request for all the basic research financed by the National Science Foundation and Department of Energy combined. /29

It should not surprise us that so many in the scientific establishment find this obscene. Said computer scientist David Parnas, who recently quit an SDI advisory panel, "Most of the money spent will be wasted; we wouldn't trust the system even if we did build it. It is our duty . . . to reply that we have no technological magic (that will make nuclear weapons obsolete). The President and the public should know that." /30

To question the rationale of the SDI enterprise should be, as Mr. Parnas suggests, a question of simple duty. It shouldn't have to be an impertinent question, but that's exactly what it's becoming. The Star Wars juggernaut may already be unstoppable. $69 billion dollars will be spent by 1994. A representative of Hughes Aircraft recently predicted, "By 1988, it may be institutionalized." Lobbies are already being mobilized, interests are becoming entrenched, foreign governments are already being involved, on the sound theory that Star Wars will be harder to stop if it becomes part of Allied diplomacy. And all around the country, some of the most talented men and women of your generation are being recruited to solve "an interesting physics problem." /31

The impertinent question. We need it now more than ever. /32

And yet, sadly, healthy skepticism is at odds with the prevailing sentiment of our times. As Tristan Vox sees it, "arguments abound to the effect that a nation does not grow great by doubting itself, indeed the self-criticism was the trap that American democracy had laid for American greatness." /33

We've been here before. It was called the '50s. This supposedly conservative doctrine holds that the very qualities from which this country has traditionally drawn its strength—idealism, openness, freedom of expression—are naive and dangerous in a cold war struggle. It maintains that America's raucous squabbles, our noisy dissent—in short, its very heritage—have weakened us as a nation and caused it to lose its unchallenged supremacy. /34

As the *New Republic*'s Mike Kinsley put it, "Talk about blaming America first." /35

In such an atmosphere, the impertinent question comes with risks. Ask the two engineers at Morton Thiokol who protested the launch of the doomed Challenger space shuttle. Ask any Pentagon procurement whistle-blower. Ask David Stockman. The mere fact of this president's widespread popularity casts suspicions on the motives of even the loyalest of oppositions. There is, of course, no question that this president seems to have fulfilled a deep yearning in many Americans to feel positively about their country. And yet, the Reagan presidency often reminds me of a remark made by a woman to sportscaster Heywood Broun following the victories of the great racehorse Secretariat in the Triple Crown. After the trauma of Vietnam and Watergate, she told Broun, Secretariat had "restored her faith in mankind." /36

I would submit to you that Ronald Reagan is the Secretariat of the '80s. He has restored our faith in ourselves, and for that, we are all in his debt. It does not, however, exempt his administration from criticism from concerned citizens who love their nation as much as he does. One of the things that has always distinguished this country from most others is that we've always challenged ourselves to do better. As a satirist, I can't foresee any administration, Republican or Democratic, under which the basic message wouldn't be the same—that it's possible to do better. /37

This is the true glory of America. This hope is what stirs me as a patriot—not a winning medal count at the Olympics, not the ability to drop 9,000 servicemen on a Caribbean golf course, not jingoistic commercials that tell me that the pride is back, America, when for many of us the pride never left, and certainly not by the fantasy of 1,000 laser rays criss-crossing the heavens in software-orchestrated precision, obliterating a swarm of supersonic projectiles. /38

Skeptical? You bet. You're looking at a man who has attended 16 graduations, at four of which, including one technical college, the microphone failed. /39

The impertinent question. The means by which we reaffirm our noblest impulses as a people. But what about the impertinent question as it pertains to us as individuals? Bronowski had an addendum to his comments on the subject. "Ask the same kind of question," he charged Studs Terkel, "not about the outside, but the inside world; not about facts but about the self." /40

This is impertinence of the gravest sort. The inner life finds very little currency in this, the age of hustle. David Stockman has written of a leadership circle which is intellectually inert, obsessed by television, bored by introspection and ideas of substance. Meanwhile, all across town, the sad stories of sleaze abound, 110 to date, all pointing the new prevailing ethic of corner-cutting and self-advancement, whose only caveat is the admonition not to get caught. /41

It can seem a pretty grim picture. Indeed, as you look around you, you see very little to distract you from this narrow path. And yet that is exactly what your liberal education—with its emphasis on ideas, on inquiry, on humanist values—sought to do. As the president of my alma mater once observed, "The whole point of your education has been to urge you to see and feel about the connectedness among things and how that connectedness must be fostered so that civilization is sustained." /42

Our understanding of the interdependencies of the human experience is the only force which keeps a society from fragmenting. The extent to which you seek that understanding is the extent to which you will be strong enough to repudiate the callousness you see around you. /43

This won't please you, but let me share a little of what one of the more astute voices of your generation, 24-year-old David Leavitt, has written about his peers: "Mine is a generation perfectly willing to admit its contemptible qualities. But our contempt is self-congratulatory. The buzz in the background, every minute of our lives, is that detached ironic voice telling us: At least you're not faking it, as they did, at least you're not pretending as they did. It's okay to be selfish as long as you're up-front about it." /44

This is a pretty bleak portrait of the values of a generation, and my guess is I'm staring at hundreds of exceptions. My further guess is that the yearning for moral commitment is as intense as it always was, but that the generation with no rules, the generation that grew up in the rubble of smashed idealism, fallen heroes and broken marriages is deeply suspicious. /45

Columnist Ellen Goodman has speculated that this is why apartheid and the soup kitchen have emerged as the causes of choice; they offer that stark unambiguous clarity that World War II offered their grandparents, that sense that there is no good news about the other side of the argument. But Goodman, being incorrigibly of her era, also believes that micro evolves into macro; that to be involved inevitably leads to decisions between imperfect options; that many of you will take risks, make mistakes, and become citizens in spite of yourselves. /46

I'm afraid there's simply no other way. If ours becomes a society intolerant of failure and uncompassionate in the face of suffering, then surely we are lost.

With the uncertainties of the future hedging in on you, you need to assess your commonalities. You need to say how you would treat other people, and how you would have them treat you back. /47

The best your college education can do for you now is to remind you that it's one thing to be self-absorbed and quite another to be self-aware. It comes down to a matter of being open, of seeing. It comes down to a matter of remaining intrigued enough by life to welcome its constant renewal. In short, it comes down to the impertinent question. /48

From those of us floundering out here in the real world, to those of you preparing to enter it, may I just say, welcome. We need you. /49

Thank you and good luck.[7] /50

Chapter Summary

Speeches on special occasions usually are grounded in communities' ceremonies or rituals for defining and reinforcing those communities' fundamental tenets. We define ourselves and live up to standards of behavior within *reference groups*; thus, special-occasion speeches are community building in important ways. Typical speeches on special occasions include *speeches of introduction*, *speeches of tribute* (farewells, dedications, memorial services), *speeches of nomination*, *speeches to create goodwill*, and *speeches to entertain*. Most of these forms are built around community standards, although speeches to entertain often are used to critique group beliefs and practices.

Reference Notes

1. Philip G. Zimbardo, *Psychology and Life*, 12th ed. (Glenview, IL: Scott, Foresman and Company, 1985), 631.

2. For a discussion of the kinds of group activity that reinforce the power of groups over your life, see James E. Combs, *Dimensions of Political Drama* (Santa Monica, CA: Goodyear Pub. Co., 1980), "The Functions of Ritual," 20–22. Cf. Zimbardo, esp. 628–32.

3. Michael Walzer, "On the Role of Symbolism in Political Thought," *Political Science Quarterly* 82 (1967): 194.

4. David I. Kertzer, *Ritual, Politics, and Power* (New Haven, CT: Yale University Press, 1988), 9.

5. Harold Haydon, "The Testimony of Sculpture," *The University of Chicago Magazine* (1968).

6. Henry W. Grady, "The New South," *American Public Addresses: 1740–1952*, ed. A. Craig Baird (New York: McGraw-Hill Book Co., 1956), 181–85.

7. Garry Trudeau, "The Value of Impertinent Questions," *Representative American Speeches 1986–1987*, ed. Owen Peterson (New York: H. W. Wilson Co., 1987), 133–42.

Key Terms

community	*dedications*
speeches on special occasions	*eulogy*
ritual	*speeches of nomination*
speeches of introduction	*speeches to create goodwill*
speeches of tribute	*speeches to entertain*
speeches of farewell	

Problems and Probes

1. This chapter has argued that goodwill speeches usually are informative speeches with underlying persuasive purposes. Describe various circumstances under which you think the informative elements should predominate in this type of speech, and then describe other circumstances in which the persuasive elements should be emphasized. In the second case, at what point would you say that the speech becomes openly persuasive in purpose? If you prefer to work with advertisements, scan magazines to find public service ads that emphasize what a company is doing to help society with its problems or to promote social-cultural-aesthetic values. Then ask yourself similar questions about these advertisements.

2. In this chapter we have discussed speeches of introduction and tribute, but we have ignored speakers' *responses* to them. After you have been introduced, given an award, or received a tribute, what should you say? Knowing what you do about speeches of introduction and tribute, what kinds of materials might you include as attention, satisfaction, and visualization steps?

Communication Activities

1. Assume that you are to act as chairperson on one of the following occasions (or on a similar occasion):
   a. A student government awards banquet
   b. A special program for a meeting of an organization to which you belong
   c. A kickoff banquet for a schoolwide charity fund-raising program
   d. A student-faculty mass meeting called to protest a regulation issued by the dean's office

In your role as chairperson, (a) plan a suitable program of speeches or entertainment, (b) allocate the amount of time to be devoted to each item on the program, (c) outline a suitable speech of introduction for the featured speaker or speakers, (d) prepare publicity releases for the local media, (e) arrange for press coverage. Work out a complete plan—one that you might show to a steering committee or faculty advisor.

2. Your instructor will give you a list of impromptu special-occasion speech topics, such as:

   a. Student X is a visitor from a neighboring school; introduce him/her to the class.

   b. You are Student X; respond to this introduction.

   c. Dedicate your speech-critique forms to the state historical archives.

   d. You have just been named Outstanding Classroom Speaker for this term; accept the award.

   e. You are a representative for a Speechwriters-for-Hire firm; sell your services to other members of the class.

You will have between five and ten minutes in which to prepare and then will present a speech on a topic assigned or drawn from the list. Be ready also to discuss the techniques you used in putting the speech together.

3. Giving speeches to entertain is quite difficult because humor is a delicate art that only few can master; however, many audiences, as well as speakers, have come to expect the inclusion of jokes and funny stories in even the most serious presentations. Collect jokes, anecdotes, and cartoons that fit a certain genre, such as ethnic, religious, or sex-role-related. Analyze your collection with audience adaptation in mind. How might these jokes be offensive to some groups? How might they be modified so they are no longer offensive? How useful is material that is offensive even though it seems funny to you? Also collect jokes, anecdotes, and cartoons that are not offensive to anyone and suggest how they might be useful in speaking situations. Be prepared to share your observations with your classmates.

Speaker's Resource Book

*T*he *Speaker's Resource Book* is a collection of generally short presentations of materials especially relevant to some speaking situations or to particular speakers facing special problems. Some of these materials were included within the regular chapters in earlier editions of this book. Some materials have been added to this edition in response to current needs. All are relevant to the public speaker's task—to share information, experience, or ideas publicly for the common good. Use them as directed by your instructor or independently to refine your public-speaking skills.

ANALYZING AND CRITICIZING THE SPEECHES OF OTHERS

The bulk of this book has been concerned with making you a more skillful producer of oral messages. Except for some comments on listening in Chapter 2, we have not discussed explicitly the matter of analyzing and evaluating the messages of others. Because during your lifetime you will spend more hours listening than talking, however, you certainly should know something about speech analysis and criticism. In a short space, we can only introduce the subject; you might learn enough here to want to study and practice speech analysis and criticism later.

What Is Speech Analysis and Criticism?

For most people, the word *criticism* calls up images of parents lecturing their kids, of politicians shouting at each other in a "Did not! Did too!" sort of way, or of teachers telling you about your shortcomings. Those kinds of negative or corrective judgments are part of what criticism *can* be about, but they are only that—negative judgments. There is much more to a complete act of criticism.

Suppose you come out of a classroom lecture and say to a friend, "That was the worst lecture I've heard all term." Your friend replies, "How so?" You answer, "The professor was disorganized, he turned his back on us most of the time and talked to the chalkboard, and the point he made about audience analysis as the single most important part of public speaking was just plain dumb." Your friend responds, "Oh, I don't know about that. He did outline the lecture pretty well, I thought, and of course he turned his back—he had a lot to write down. And what do you mean, audience analysis is 'just plain dumb'?" "Well," you counter, "he didn't really follow the outline—remember when. . . ?" On it goes, until you both agree or get tired of discussing the topic.

In dialogues like this one, you are engaging in analysis and criticism. *Criticism is an argumentative process of analytical description and reasoned evaluation aimed at producing interpretations and judgments.* It is argumentative in that it is based on a disputable claim ("That was the worst . . ."). It is a process in that it is aimed at another party, either someone who responds or someone who simply reads what you have written. Analytical description provides the "evidence" one uses to support the claim. The evaluative aspects of criticism are not simply self-reports of likes and dislikes, but are based on accepted criteria for judgment (in the example, on the positive values of good organization, eye contact with audiences, and audience analysis).

The goals of criticism—what someone else should get from your efforts to criticize well—are twofold:

1. *Interpretation.* Critics are in the business of getting others to view something in a particular way, from a particular vantage point. In our example, you tried to get your friend to examine the professor's effort from three perspectives—organizational skills, delivery skills, and assertions about audience analysis. All three of these points of view fit under a general category one could call "technical speaker competencies"; technical speaker competencies are a kind of vantage point for evaluating that teacher's lecturing on that day. (Other vantage points, each with its own vocabulary, could have been used.)

2. *Judgment.* Also, criticism as a kind of argumentative discourse usually ends in judgment. A critic normally ends up asserting that someone or something is beautiful/ugly, useful/useless, ethical/unethical, good/bad. In a fully rounded piece of criticism, those judgments are reasoned, are argued

for in the ways we talked about argumentation earlier in this book.

All criticism, therefore, includes three elements: (1) an interpretive-judgmental assertion, (2) evidence in support of that assertion, and (3) a perspective or way of looking at something which makes the assertion in some way important or worthy of consideration. More specifically, then, rhetorical criticism or speech criticism focuses on informative and persuasive messages (often, but not only, speeches, for persuasion also can be sought via newspapers, magazines, radio and television programs, propagandistic art, and so on). The rhetorical critic or analyst seeks to interpret and judge those rhetorical messages in particular ways and from certain perspectives.

Speech Criticism vs. Speech Evaluation

As you will recall from Chapter 2, you evaluate classroom speeches and others you hear from your personal perspective and from the speaker's as well. From your personal perspective you ask, "What's in this speech for me? What can I learn? What should I be wary of? What does this person think of me?" From the speaker's perspective—as when you are giving someone feedback about his or her oral performance—you ask, "How did this person come across? Was the claim or central idea clearly stated? Was the speech well organized and easy to follow? Were the supporting materials adequate? Was the language clear and appropriate?" *Speech evaluation*, then, is aimed at oneself and at the speaker—for the listener's and the speaker's personal benefit.

Speech criticism usually is quite different. It is an *independent* message aimed at *a public*. Speech analyses and criticisms are messages about other messages. A speech seeks to accomplish an informative, persuasive, or entertaining purpose, while criticism of that speech interprets and judges that performance or transaction *with another, usually larger, purpose in mind*. That larger purpose is determined in part by what you, the analyst-critic, want other people to understand about the performance or transaction, and in part by what your readers (your public) want to learn.

Types of Speech Analysis and Criticism

That last statement leads us to consider the range of purposes critics and readers can have, which in turn produces a list of types of rhetorical criticism. Actually, there are almost as many purposes and types of criticism as are individual critics, especially when you think about specific purposes as we discussed them in Chapter 3; however, most of the specific purposes can be placed under one of the three following categories.

To Account for the Effects of Communication.
Perhaps the most common end of rhetorical analysis is to account for the effects of a message or speaker upon an audience. Almost anyone, with sense and a bit of energy, can describe many of these effects. In assessing the effects of a presidential speech, for example, you can:

- Note the amount of applause and its timing

- Read newspaper accounts and commentary on it the next day

- Check public opinion polls, especially those assessing the president's performance thus far and those dealing with the particular subject of the speech

- Notice how much it is quoted and referred to weeks, months, or even years after it was delivered

- Examine votes in Congress and election results potentially affected by the speech

- Read memoirs, diaries, and books treating the event, the speaker, and the speech

- Read the president's own accounts of the speech[1]

Mere description of effects, however, is not criticism; after all, you can do that without even reading the speech. The important phrase in this purpose, therefore, is "accounting for." Rhetorical analysts discussing the effects of a speech take that extra step, delving into the speaking process to see if they can discover what in the message, the situation, the speaker, and other elements of the speech produced those results. That is no easy task, yet it is central to improving our knowledge of speechmaking and its effects on society. Following are examples of where you might look in the communication process to find elements that can account for a message's reception by an audience:

1. *The situation.* Did the situation make certain demands the speaker had to meet? A series of events, the traditions of discourse surrounding the occasion (that is, the expectations we have about inaugurals, sermons, and the like), or even the date of the speech (it is one thing for a presidential aspirant to make promises in October, but quite another for the elected person to make them in January)—all these can provide critics with clues to situational demands.

2. *The speaker.* Did the speaker have the authority or credibility to affect the audience, almost regardless of what he or she said? Some speakers have such a reputation or carry so much charisma that they can influence an audience with the sheer power and dynamism of their words and presence. The rhetorical critic is interested in such phenomena and seeks to find specific word patterns and speech behaviors that account for listeners' reactions to these factors.[2]

3. *The arguments.* Did the speaker's message strike responsive chords in the audience? Were the motivational appeals those to which this audience was susceptible? Why? Were the beliefs, attitudes, values, and ideological orientations advanced by the speaker likely to have made impressions on this audience? Why? Were the supporting materials—and specific combinations of the various types—useful in helping an audience comprehend and accept the overall message? Why? (These "whys" usually have to be answered by assessing the temperament of the times, the dominant ideologies in the culture, and the facts of the situation, as well as the internal and external characteristics of audiences discussed in Chapter 5.)

4. *Uses of modes of communication.* Were the linguistic, paralinguistic, bodily, and visual modes of communication used effectively? In other words, as a critic you must look at more than the words on a printed page. Oral communication always needs to be explained as completely as possible, either from videotapes, films, or—if necessary—newspaper descriptions of the speaker and occasion.

5. *Audience susceptibility.* In general, why was *this* audience susceptible to *this* message delivered by *this* speaker in *this* setting at *this* time? The critic seeking to explain the effects of a speech ultimately has to answer that all-important question.

A solid analysis of communication effects, therefore, demands a careful integration of "who did what to whom, when, and to what effect."[3] It demands thoughtful assessment—the hard work of deciding which among all of the elements of the speaking process were responsible for particular aspects of audience reaction. Ultimately, your quest for "why" will lead you to look at more than the speech itself. For example, determining why the audience was particularly receptive to President Johnson's call for a "blank check" during the 1964 Gulf of Tonkin crisis will require a historical examination of public attitudes at the time. To determine the effect of President Carter's debates on his 1976 victory and 1980 defeat will require more than an analysis of his arguments or his use of the media in both campaigns.

At times, it may be necessary to combine scientific research with historical explanation.[4] An example will illustrate this point. Two teams of rhetorical analysts—Andrew A. King and Floyd D. Anderson, and Richard D. Raum and James S. Measell—were interested in techniques presumably used by Richard Nixon, Spiro Agnew, and George Wallace to polarize public opinion and divide voting groups in order to win elections in the '60s. King and Anderson examined with considerable care the speeches of Nixon and Agnew between 1968 and 1970, while Raum and Measell looked at Wallace's speeches between 1964 and 1972. Neither team felt that a mere listing of argumentative and linguistic techniques was enough, for the listing did not provide them with answers to the question "Why did these techniques work?" Both teams, therefore, read the social-psychological literature on the concept of *polarization.* King and Anderson then used this research to shed light on ways words can be used to affirm a group's identity (in this case, that of the silent majority), and on methods for isolating or negating the voting power of an opponent. The concept of polarization seemed to explain why those tactics supposedly created two different political power blocs, or "societies," in the late 1960s.

Raum and Measell, however, went further. They not only examined the tactics and psychological dimensions of polarization, but also looked at the concept as they deemed it to occur in specific situations. George Wallace's effectiveness, they concluded, lay in the kinds of people he appealed to, in his vocabulary—which charged his audiences emotionally—and in the ways in which Wallace made himself a social redeemer who could save the country from the "enemy."[5] You may not find it necessary to resort to such sophisticated strategies to explicate a message's effects. Nevertheless, your analysis of a contemporary speech may be based on information you possess about how people behave in crowds, what their attitudes are, or what a particular psychological theory would predict given certain speech strategies. This information becomes a central part of your critical evaluation. The difference is one of degree, not of kind, as you proceed to offer your interpretation of why a speaker succeeded or failed. The rigor of analysis may separate you from the professional rhetorical analyst, but the process is the same. The critical judgment in both cases is not based just on a "gut reaction" to the speech or on an uninformed response of liking or disliking.

To Explore the Critical Dimensions of Communication.

So far, we have been discussing a focus on criticism that examines the effects of speeches—changes in attitudes or behavior, voting shifts, and acknowledgment of a speaker's rhetorical expertise are potential items mentioned or examined in the process of arriving at a critical judgment. This is not, however, the only way of looking at a speech. A speech, after all, is many things on many different levels; hence, it is possible to talk about a number of different critical perspectives. A *critical perspective* is, in language we already have used, a human design or purpose. It is the reason-for-being of a piece of criticism, the particular viewpoint a critic is interested in bringing to bear on a discourse. Just as you can be looked at in a number of different ways—as a student, as a son or daughter, as an employee, as a lover—so, too, can a speech be examined from different vantages, depending upon the observer's purposes or designs. For example, speeches have been viewed critically in the following ways:

1. *Pedagogically.* You can use the speech as a model, as a way of examining public communicators who have made judicious rhetorical choices. You can learn how to speak well, in part, by looking at and listening to other speakers.

2. *Culturally.* You can examine a discourse to acquire a better understanding of the times. For example, you may look at speeches from the Revolutionary War period or from the nineteenth century to better understand *how* our ancestors thought, *how* the great American values were spread through the society, and *how* we as a nation came to be what we are.

3. *Linguistically.* Because human beings are symbol-using animals—because we are distinguished from other animals by the complexity of our symbol systems—it makes sense to be particularly interested in the language used in public discourses. Some critics look at oral language to better comprehend the communicative *force* of words—how some words plead, others persuade, still others threaten, and so on. Some critics are concerned with *condensation symbols*—the process by which certain words (for example, *communist* in the '50s, *hippie* in the '60s, *polluter* in the '70s, *yuppie* in the '80s) acquire a broad range of ideologically positive or negative connotations. Other critics are especially interested in *metaphors*—in ways we describe experiences vicariously with words ("He's an

absolute *pig*") or, in the case of *archetypal metaphors*, ways by which we can capture the essence of humanity by appealing figuratively to the great common human experiences (light and dark metaphors, birth and death metaphors, sexual metaphors, and so on). Whatever approach linguistic critics take, however, they ultimately seek to illuminate what it means to communicate as a symbol-using human being.

4. *Generically*. A great number of critics have addressed the problem of classifying speeches into types, or genres. For example, in this book we generally have classified speeches into four basic types— speeches to inform, to entertain, to persuade, and to actuate—because the groupings help you accomplish certain *purposes*. Other critics classify speeches by *situation* or *location*—for instance, the rhetoric of international conflict, the rhetoric of the used-car lot, the political-convention keynote address—in order to uncover the ways in which the location or expectations created by the occasion determine what must be said. Others argue that speeches are best categorized by *topic* because certain recurrent themes congregate around recurrent human problems. Hence, they write about the rhetoric of war and peace, the rhetoric of women's issues, of reform or revolution. Whatever approach critics use in the process of classification, however, they all generally have a single goal: to categorize speeches in order to find *families of discourses* that have enough in common to help us understand dominant modes of thought or modes of expression typical of an age, problem, or set of speakers.[6]

Pedagogical, cultural, linguistic, and generic critics, therefore, all examine specific aspects of discourses, features they think deserve special attention. They make this examination in order to learn what these aspects tell us about communication practice (*pedagogy*), the condition of humanity (*culture*), the potentials of language codes (*linguistics*), or the dominant species of discourse (*genres*).

To Evaluate the Ethics of Communication.

In an age of governmental credibility gaps, charges of corporate irresponsibility, situational ethics, and the rise of minorities who challenge the prevailing social and ethical systems of the United States, a host of ethical questions have come to concern speech analysts: Can we still speak of the democratic ideal as *the* ethical standard for speakers in this country? What are the communicative responsibilities that attend the exercise of corporate, governmental, and personal power? For example, President Nixon's speech on November 3, 1969, in which he talked about the "silent majority," his quest for peace, and three alternatives for ending the war in Vietnam—escalation, withdrawal, or gradual de-escalation—naturally aroused considerable controversy. One critic, Forbes Hill, found no special ethical problems in the speech because the president's appeals to the majority of Americans were consistent with the country's values at that time. Another, Robert P. Newman, assuming the "democratic ideal" as his standard, decried the speech because he claimed that it violated the individual's right to know fully all that a government plans and does. A third critic, Karlyn K. Campbell, argued that the standards initially set for evaluating the alternatives were violated later in the speech, and Philip Wander and Steven Jenkins accused the president of lying.[7] Thus, each critic assumed a particular ethical posture, and from that posture proceeded to evaluate the speech in accordance with his or her own views and biases.

Essential Critical Activities

Rhetorical analysis, no matter what its specific purpose, always demands certain activities of the critic. No matter what goal you are attempting to accomplish, as a critic you need a way of talking about the speech event, a plan for observing or reconstructing it, and a method for writing up your critical thoughts.

A Coherent Vocabulary for Rhetorical Evaluation.

Perhaps the most difficult task a beginning critic faces is that of settling on a rhetorical vocabulary, a way of talking. The "who? what? when? where? why? how?" questions of the journalist may provide a starting point for analysis, but they will not get a critic very far in examining a speech. Unlike the journalist, the critic is engaged in a systematic, coherent pursuit of specialized knowledge *about* communication. The description of the event itself is only a part of that process; therefore, the actual analysis demands a language that "talks about" talk. There are many such critical vocabularies. Let us look at one as an example.

Lloyd Bitzer argues that the *rhetorical situation* almost literally dictates what kinds of things ought to be said, to whom they ought to be said, and in what forms the messages should be presented.[8] More specifically, he maintains that situations are marked by *exigencies* (events, peoples, or happenings that call forth discourse from someone because they are important, serious, demanding, and so on), by *audience expectations* (thoughts of who should say what to whom, when, and where), and by *constraints* (the limits of choices speakers can make—for instance, the rules governing congressional debate, the boundaries of social propriety, the availability or not of certain audiences). If a speaker in a rhetorical situation satisfies the reasons calling forth talk, meets the audience's expectations, and abides by the constraints, the speech will be considered a *fitting response* to the situation.[9] Thus, in Bitzer's model, the main emphases are upon *the primacy of situation and the importance of speech competencies.*

Bitzer's approach to rhetorical analysis and his vocabulary are especially useful when, as a critic, you are studying the speeches of representatives of particular groups. The behaviors of heads of state, congressional politicians, leaders of churches, labor unions, and the like are in part dictated by the groups they represent. They are not speaking for themselves as individuals, but rather for groups or institutions. Hence, no matter what they believe personally, their public utterances always must be consistent with the organization's goals, reinforce its viewpoints, and voice its concerns.

They may even be pressured by the forces inherent in certain occasions—by what custom dictates *must* be said in inaugurals, in Labor Day speeches, in Easter sermons, and the like. In short, when speakers are constrained by situationally imposed roles, Bitzer's approach and vocabulary help us examine how these constraints affect the way people talk publicly and upon what bases we judge them competent speakers.

Careful Observation.
The second task you must grapple with as a critic is that of deciding *what* to look at and *how*. In part, of course, this problem is solved by your selection of a vocabulary. If, for example, you use a textbook vocabulary, you know you will have to isolate motivational appeals, look for an arrangement pattern, and see if you can find out how the speaker delivered the message. Yet, the vocabulary does not, as a rule, exhaust your task of looking. You may need to expand it to include searches for information both inside and outside the speech text itself.

Outside observation.
Often you have to look for relevant information about the speech, the speaker, the audience, and the situation *outside* the actual text of what was said. As we have already suggested, if you are interested in the effects of a presidential speech, you probably will want to check public opinion polls, memoirs, diaries, the results of subsequent voting on the issue or issues, and newspaper and magazine reactions. If you are working from the textbook vocabulary, you probably will need to see what the audience knew about the speaker beforehand (prior reputation), what kind of people made up the audience present, and what ratings were given to radio or television broadcasts of the speech. If you are doing a cultural analysis of the speech, you will have to read whatever you can find on the cultural values and mores of the era in which the speech was delivered. You cannot, for example, do a study of Daniel Webster as a typical ceremonial orator of the 1830s or 1840s without having a solid grasp of what Americans were doing and thinking about during that early national period. Webster's political generalizations, metaphors,

and sweeping vision of the Republic make little sense unless you are acquainted with political-economic expansion, the settling of the Midwest and West, the growing fight between states' righters and nationalists, the problem of slavery, and other key cultural battles that characterized the period. Many kinds of critical studies of speeches, therefore, require you to spend time in the library with newspapers, magazines, history books, and biographies.

Inside observation. As a critic, you also will have to live with the speech for a while. Often, an initial reading of it produces either a "So what?" or a "What can I say?" reaction. You should read it time and again, each time subjectively projecting yourself into the situation, into the frame of mind of the speaker and the audience. You probably should even read the speech aloud (if you do not have a recording or videotape of it), trying to capture emphases, rhythms, and sounds. Part of inside observation, then, is a process of "getting the feel" of the speech.

The other part is discovering the key points on which it turns. Certain statements or phrases in great speeches became memorable because they were pivotal. They summarized an important idea, attitude, or sentiment. As you read over, say, Cicero's "First Oration Against Cataline," you are impressed by the initial series of eight rhetorical questions, which immediately put the Roman audience into an abusive frame of mind. You may be similarly impressed by the way Queen Elizabeth I used *I* and *we* in her speeches in order to make her dominance over Parliament eminently clear, or by British Prime Minister David Lloyd George's preoccupation with light-dark archetypal metaphors, which elevate his discourse. Contemporary speeches, too—those published in *Vital Speeches of the Day*, for example—have certain elements in common: a heavy reliance upon particular forms of support, especially statistics, quotations from authorities, and explanations.

In other words, looking inside speeches intently forces your critical apparatus to operate. Your mind begins to catch points of dominance and memorability—aspects of discourse you find noteworthy and even fascinating. When those insights are coupled with research you have done on the outside—in newspapers, magazines, books, and the like—you soon find that you have something critical to say about a particular speech or group of speeches.

Composing Your Critical Evaluation.

Acts of criticism are arguments. Your critical evaluation functions as a *claim* that must be supported with specific reasons justifying its soundness. Your process of observation and the vocabulary you use come together into a cogent explanation of why the speech was effective, how certain identification strategies functioned, or why cultural symbols in a speech were ignored by the audience. The following outline of a plan for writing your critical evaluation is not the only way in which your argument may be organized. Nevertheless, it may be helpful as a general guide to the organization of your critical response. The plan also may be useful for term papers or research papers you will be asked to write.

A Plan for Writing Speech Criticism

I. Introduction
    A. As a "starter" for your paper, introduce a quotation, a description of events, a statement of communication principles, or whatever will indicate your approach to the speech or your point of view about it.
    B. Make *a statement of questions or claims*—the point or points you wish to develop or establish in the paper.
    C. Make *a statement of procedures*—how you propose to go about answering the questions or proving the claims.

II. Body
    A. After you have thus described the basic speech material or the situation with which you are dealing, take the steps of your critical analysis one point at a time, looking, for example, at *exigencies/ audience expectations/constraints/ fittingness* if you are using Bitzer's critical techniques, making sure in this approach that you have carefully described the situation around which you are building your analysis.

B. As you offer the subpoints or claims, liberally illustrate them with quotations from the speech or speeches you are analyzing, quotations that serve as evidence for your point of view or argument. Also quote from other critical observers to further support your position if you wish.

III. Conclusions

A. In your *summary*, pull the argument of your paper together by indicating how the subpoints combine to present a valid picture of public communication.

B. Draw *implications*, commenting briefly upon what can be learned from your analysis and this speech (or set of speeches) about communication generally. That is, you say in effect that this is a case study of something having larger implications.

With a coherent vocabulary for thinking about public communication, with patient and thoughtful observation, and with a plan for reporting your reactions, you should be able to produce useful and stimulating evaluations and analyses of speeches. Ultimately, your practice in communication criticism will help you better understand the ways by which public discourse affects the beliefs, attitudes, values, and behaviors of yourself and your society.

In this short appendix, we have been able to describe only *briefly* a few critical frameworks or approaches and to allude to a limited number of actual speeches and speaking events. A good general introduction to rhetorical criticism suitable for undergraduate students can be found in James R. Andrews, *The Practice of Rhetorical Criticism* (New York: The Macmillan Co., 1983).

Reference Notes

1. For an example of how skilled critics search out the effects of a controversial speech of this kind, see Paul Arntson and Craig R. Smith, "The Seventh of March Address [Daniel Webster]: A Mediating Influence," *Southern Speech Communication Journal* 40 (Spring 1975): 288–301.

2. For a discussion of ways to talk critically about charisma, see George P. Boss, "Essential Attributes of the Concept of Charisma," *Southern Speech Communication Journal* 41 (Spring 1976): 300–13.

3. For a detailed discussion of the kinds of information that can be produced by "effects studies" (also called historical studies), see Bruce E. Gronbeck, "Rhetorical History and Rhetorical Criticism: A Distinction," *The Speech Teacher* 24 (November 1975): 309–20.

4. On the relationships between rhetorical criticism and the social sciences, see John W. Bowers, "The Pre-Scientific Function of Rhetorical Criticism," in *Essays on Rhetorical Criticism*, ed. Thomas R. Nilsen (New York: Random House, Inc., 1968), 126–45.

5. Andrew A. King and Floyd D. Anderson, "Nixon, Agnew, and the 'Silent Majority': A Case Study in the Rhetoric of Polarization," *Western Speech* 35 (Fall 1971): 243–55; Richard D. Raum and James S. Measell, "Wallace and His Ways: A Study of the Rhetorical Genre of Polarization," *Central States Speech Journal* 25 (Spring 1974): 28–35.

6. Literature for these "families of discourse" abounds. For samples of cultural studies, for instance, see Ernest Wrage, "The Little World of Barry Goldwater," *Western Speech* 27 (Fall 1963): 207–15; and Theodore Balgooyen, "A Study of Conflicting Values: American Plains Indian Orators vs. the U.S. Commissioners of Indian Affairs," *Western Speech* 24 (Spring 1962): 76–83. For an example of linguistic analysis—especially as it involves condensation symbols—look at Doris Graber, *Verbal Behavior and Politics* (Urbana: University of Illinois Press, 1976), especially Chapter 7.

7. Forbes I. Hill, "Conventional Wisdom—Traditional Form: The President's Message of November 3, 1969," *Quarterly Journal of Speech* 58 (December 1972): 373–86; Robert P. Newman, "Under the Veneer: Nixon's Vietnam Speech of November 3, 1969," *Quarterly Journal of Speech* 56 (December 1970): 432–34; Karlyn Kohrs Campbell, "Richard M. Nixon," *Critiques of Contemporary Rhetoric* (Belmont, CA: Wadsworth Publishing Co., 1972), 50–57; and Philip Wander and Steven Jenkins, "Rhetoric, Society, and the Critical Response," *Quarterly Journal of Speech* 58 (December 1972): 373–86.

8. Lloyd F. Bitzer, "The Rhetorical Situation," *Philosophy & Rhetoric* 1 (Winter 1968): 1–14.

9. For a study clearly illustrating Bitzer's method of analysis, see Allen M. Rubin and Rebecca R. Rubin, "An Examination of the Constituent Elements in Presenting an Occurring Rhetorical Situation," *Central States Speech Journal* 26 (Summer 1975): 133–41.

COMMUNICATION MODELS

A model is a picture or representation of a thing or a process that identifies the key parts or elements and indicates how each element affects the operations of all of the other elements. A communication system can be reduced to such a model—in fact, to many models, depending upon what aspects of communication are of primary interest.

Before examining some communication models, however, you might legitimately ask, "Who cares?" "Of what importance or use are models?" While it undoubtedly is true that some speakers create and deliver extraordinarily powerful speeches without having seen—much less drawn up—a communication model, the fact is that most of us need help in conceptualizing the oral communication process; its primary features are not always clear. Further, armed with models that direct our attention to particular aspects or features of oral communication, we are more likely to create strategically sound and situationally sensitive speeches than if we are unaware of the importance of particular elements or aspects of communication.[1] Models can control our percep-

tion of the communication process; in turn, the way we perceive communication can govern our practice.

For example, one of the earliest definitions of communication came from the Greek philosopher-teacher Aristotle (384–322 B.C.).[2] He defined communication, then called "rhetoric," as "the faculty of observing in any given case the available means of persuasion" (*Rhetoric* 1335b). With his stress upon "observing in any given case the available means" and with his long lists of things a speaker might want to say when talking in the Greek law courts and assemblies, his was a *speaker-centered* model of communication. Translating some of his Greek concepts into more contemporary language, his model looked essentially like the figure below.

As time passed, rhetoricians, or communication theorists, became less concerned with the speaker or writer and more concerned with types and contents of actual messages. For example, in the late eighteenth and nineteenth centuries, the "belletristic" approach to communication education developed in the schools.

ARISTOTLE'S MODEL

A SPEAKER   discovers   logical, emotional, and ethical proofs,

arranges   those materials strategically,

clothes   the ideas in clear and compelling words, and

delivers   the resulting speech appropriately.

BERLO'S MODEL

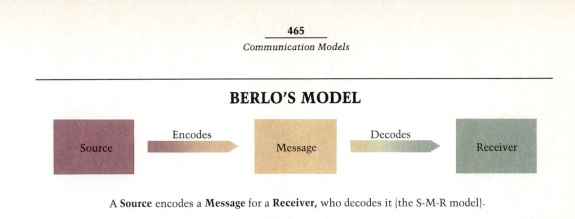

A **Source** encodes a **Message** for a **Receiver,** who decodes it (the S-M-R model).

After learning as much as they could about language—its origins, main elements, and eloquent use—students were put through a series of exercises. These began with the construction of relatively simple descriptive passages; moved on to more complicated historical narratives; and culminated in the writing of argumentative, persuasive, and literary works.

All of this emphasis upon preparing various kinds of messages led to *message-centered* theories of communication, which could be used to describe both oral and written discourse. The simplest and most influential message-centered model of our time came from David Berlo[3] (see the figure on page 465). This model was useful for the post–World War II world of communication study for several reasons. (1) The idea of "source" was flexible enough to include mechanical, electronic, or other nonhuman generators of messages. (2) "Message" was made the central element, stressing the transmission of *ideas.* (3) The model recognized that receivers were important to communication, for they were the targets. (4) The notions of "encoding" and "decoding" emphasized the problems we all have (psycholinguistically) in translating our thoughts into words or other symbols and in deciphering the words or symbols of others into terms we can understand.

The model was (and still is) popular. It does, however, tend to stress the manipulation of the message—the encoding and decoding processes; it implies that human communication is like machine communication, like signal sending in telephone, television, computer, and radar systems. It even seems to stress that most problems in human communication can be solved by technical accuracy—by choosing the "right" symbols, preventing interference, and sending efficient messages.

The problems of human communication, however, are not as simple as that. Even when we know what words mean and choose the right ones, we still can misunderstand because we all have different experiences and interests in life. Even when a message is completely clear and understandable, we often do not like it. Problems in "meaning" or "meaningfulness" often are not a matter of comprehension but of reaction; of agreement; of shared concepts, beliefs, attitudes, values. To put the *com-* back into communication, we need a *meaning-centered* theory. While there are many such theories, perhaps one of the simplest was that offered by theorist Wilbur Schramm in 1954[4] (see the figure on page 466).

This model is elegant, picturing the meaning-sharing process simply and graphically. It essentially argues that, in any given signal (message), you and I will comprehend and understand each other to the degree that our "fields of experiences" (interests, feelings, values, goals, purposes, information, ideas) overlap. That is, we can communicate in any given situation only to the degree that our *prior* experiences are similar.

Before we assume we have frozen interhuman communication in a simple process, we must take into account three other aspects of people-talk: feedback, context, and culture.

Feedback

First, we must remember that communication is usually a two-way path. Most communication systems allow receivers to feed back messages to sources. (See Chapter 2.)

SHRAMM'S MODEL

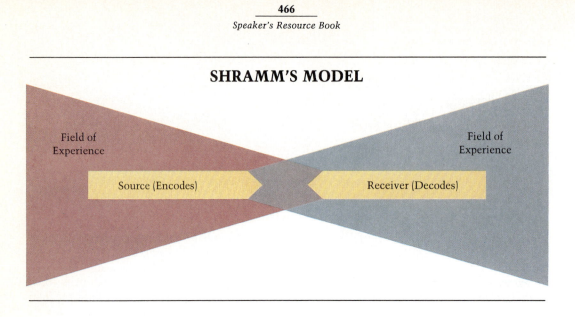

Field of
Experience

Field of
Experience

Source (Encodes)

Receiver (Decodes)

Context

A message may have different meanings, depending upon the specific context. The message "Let's get out of here" has one meaning when cooed by a member of the opposite sex at a dull party, but quite another when snarled angrily in front of a waiter who has been providing bad service. Shouting "Fire!" on a rifle range produces one set of reactions—reactions quite different from those produced in a crowded theater. Meaning depends in part upon context or situation.

Culture

Finally, a message may have different meanings associated with it depending upon the culture or society. Each culture has its own rules for interpreting communicative signals. A hearty belch after a dinner in Skokie, Illinois, is a sign of impoliteness, but it is a supreme compliment to the host or hostess in some other cultures. Negotiating the price of a T-shirt at Macy's is unheard of, yet it is a sign of active interest in an Istanbul bazaar or a neighborhood garage sale. Communication systems, thus, operate within the confines of cultural rules and expectations to which we all have been educated.

When we add the ideas of feedback, context, and culture to some of the other elements of

communication we have been discussing, we come up with a model that looks like the one on page 467.[5]

Our model now includes all the elements of a communication system that we need. To understand how systems operate, though, you also must keep in mind some of the characteristics of the elements we have alluded to:

1. *Sources* and *receivers* hold differing bundles of beliefs, attitudes, values, expectations, skills.
2. *Messages* are encoded into a variety of symbol systems (words, gestures, tones of voice, pictures, bodily postures).
3. *Contexts* provide almost innumerable cues that help receivers interpret what is being said or done.
4. *Cultures* provide even more complex rules for offering and interpreting messages.

If you look at the model on page 467 carefully and then examine the one offered in Chapter 1, you will note some important similarities. That is because this *general* model of human communication formed the basis for the *specific* model of public speaking—one kind of human communication—we have been operating from in this textbook. As a matter of fact, were you to go through the entire book with this model in hand, you would discover that the language, general advice, and even lists

A CONTEXTUAL-CULTURAL MODEL

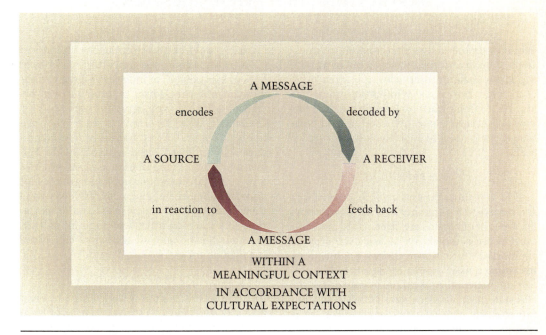

A MESSAGE

encodes   decoded by

A SOURCE   A RECEIVER

in reaction to   feeds back

A MESSAGE

WITHIN A
MEANINGFUL CONTEXT

IN ACCORDANCE WITH
CULTURAL EXPECTATIONS

of specific "do's" and "don'ts" throughout the preceding chapters are grounded in this model. The stress upon making rhetorical choices based on your assessments of situation, audience, and purpose; the references to communication rules and roles; the expressed hope that you will develop a broad range of oral communication skills are all rooted in this model.

Communication models are merely pictures; they are even distorting pictures, because they stop or freeze an essentially dynamic interactive or transactive process into a static picture. Nevertheless, a well-drawn model—and certainly you are able, if you think about it, to draw a model that reflects your own view of communication practices—can direct your attention to key aspects of human communication and, hence, affect your oral communication performance. A picture may well be worth a thousand words—especially if it helps you shape those words into a coherent, powerful speech.

Reference Notes

1. For a helpful and more sophisticated introduction to communication models, see C. David Mortensen, *Communication: The Study of Human Communication* (New York: McGraw-Hill Book Co., 1972), Chapter 2, "Communication Models."

2. Aristotle's speaker-centered model received perhaps its fullest development in the hands of Roman educator Quintilian (ca. A.D. 35–95), whose *Institutio Oratoria* was filled with advice on the full training of a "good" speaker-statesman.

3. Simplified from David K. Berlo, *The Process of Communication* (New York: Holt, Rinehart, and Winston, 1960).

4. From Wilbur Schramm, "How Communication Works," in *The Process and Effects of Communication*, ed. Wilbur Schramm (Urbana: University of Illinois Press, 1954), 3–26.

5. For an expanded discussion of this model, see Bruce E. Gronbeck, *The Articulate Person: A Guide to Everyday Public Speaking*, 2nd ed. (Glenview, IL: Scott, Foresman and Company, 1983), Chapter 1.

CONSTRUCTING INTERVIEW QUESTIONS

While everyone knows that answers to questions often determine one's success in achieving major goals in interviews, too often most of us forget how equally important questions are. We all must learn how to phrase different types of interview questions and how to organize them in order to elicit the information we seek.

Types of Interview Questions

A skill you must possess as both interviewer and interviewee is facility in asking questions. Six types of questions are often asked, and you must possess the ability to ask each type in appropriate situations. *Primary questions* introduce a topic or area of inquiry, while *follow-up questions* probe more deeply or ask for elaboration or clarification. Thus, if you are interviewing a local newspaper editor for a speech, you might begin with "What background did you have before becoming editor?" and follow up with "Would you elaborate on your experience as a copy editor—what did you do in that position?" You also will develop *direct questions* ("How long have you been the editor?") and *indirect questions* ("What is your goal for the paper five years from now?"). Direct questions allow you to gather information quickly, while indirect probes let you see interviewees "thinking on their feet," structuring materials and responses and exploring their own minds. Interviewers also use both *open* and *closed* questions. A closed question specifies the direction of the response—"Do your editorials create public concern about local issues?" An open question allows the interviewee to control the categories of response—"How do you perceive your role in the community?" Closed questions require little effort from the interviewee and are easy to "code" or record; open questions allow interviewers to observe the interviewee's habits, to let them feel in control of the interaction. Of course, these various types of questions overlap: you can use a direct or indirect question as your primary question; a closed question can be either direct ("Do you function most as editor, reporter, or lay-out specialist?") or indirect ("Of the various jobs you perform—editor, reporter, lay-out specialist—which do you enjoy the most?").

Overall, it is important to know that primary, direct, and closed questions tend to produce a lot of "hard" information quickly. Follow-up, indirect, and open questions produce more thought; interpretation; and grounds for understanding and analyzing interviewees and their motivations, capacities, and expectations. As you plan interviews, you must learn to blend questions of all six types. This blend is called an *interview schedule.*

Interview Schedules

An interview schedule is your effort to organize specific questions to systematically elicit the materials and opinions you are looking for. Like any other organizational pattern, an interview schedule should have a rationale, one that (1) permits you to acquire systematic information or opinion and (2) seems reasonable to the interviewee, avoiding confusing repetitions and detours. Interview schedules normally are built in one of two forms—the *traditional* and the *branching schedule.*

Traditional Schedule of Questions

I. "What was your background before becoming an editor?" (primary, indirect, open question)
   A. "How many journalism courses did you take in college?" (follow-up, direct, open question)
   B. "What kinds of practical experience did you obtain in your newswriting course?" (follow-up, direct, open question)
II. "How do you perceive your role in the community?" (primary, indirect, open question)
   A. "Several letters to the editor have complained about your bias in favor of the largest employer in the town. How do

you respond to these criticisms?" (follow-up, indirect, open question)

1. "Do you ignore the largest employer when writing editorials, or do you consider its position and then write what you believe in?" (follow-up, direct, closed question)
2. "Do you find it difficult to take positions counter to those of the largest employer?" (follow-up, direct, open question)

Branching Schedule of Questions

1. "Did you take courses in journalism prior to becoming a journalist?"

If yes: ⌐↓   *If no:* ————————↓

2. "Did you take courses in newswriting?"	2. "What type of practical experience did you have?"

If yes: ⌐↓   *If no:* ————————↓

3. "Did you obtain practical experience in the newswriting course?"	3. "Did you do primarily features or general news items?"

If yes: ⌐↓   *If no:* ————————↓

4. "What specific assignments did you have?"	4. [Note: Go to next area of inquiry.]

Notice that the traditional schedule of questions uses an organizational pattern that first extracts information and then follows with more probing questions. This pattern allows the interviewee to think through his or her experiences concretely before you ask for self-reflection or evaluation. Were that reversed, the interviewee might be asked to evaluate an experience before having recalled it clearly, most likely producing a less-than-complete evaluation. Notice, too, the mixing of types of questions in the traditional schedule to keep the interaction progressing.

A branching schedule is used in situations in which the interviewer knows rather specifically what he or she is looking for. Survey or polling interviewers often use this schedule. In our example, a student is using a branching schedule to explore the background of a local newspaper editor. In a complete branching schedule, the *If no* questions would likewise have "branches" beneath them; nonetheless, our illustration indicates the essential logic of the pattern.

No matter what type of questions you use and what specific organizational pattern for questions you devise, the important points to remember are these:

1. *Plan your questions* before going into an interview so that you know your goals and proceed toward them.
2. *Organize your questions* in a manner that seems rational and prepares interviewees adequately before asking them to make abstract, complex evaluations.

THE EMPLOYMENT INTERVIEW

The employment interview can be a crucial communicative experience. The outcome may enhance your career aspirations or simply ensure that the rent will be paid on time. Either way, you often have a lot at stake in an interview situation. Seldom will you enter an interview with no real concern over whether the interviewer responds positively to you, or whether you actually get the job. The suggestions offered regarding building self-confidence (see Chapter 3) apply to the interview situation as well. By being prepared in advance, you will be able to respond appropriately to the questions you are asked. The following guidelines may be helpful in preparing for and participating in an interview.

Preparing for an Interview

As you prepare for an interview, consider the following questions:

1. *Why do you want this job?* Aside from the fact that jobs mean money, what is your reason for seeking this particular job?

2. *What knowledge or skills does the job require?* What skills, talents, abilities can you contribute? List the major skills that you possess; which ones are most relevant to this particular job? What courses or work experiences would be especially meaningful in this position? What should you stress in explaining your qualifications? Keep in mind that some courses provide you with necessary technical knowledge (a course in finance, for example), while others may be relevant because they helped refine skills (a course in contemporary American literature, for example, that stressed research and writing skills).

3. *What information can you gather about the company before the interview?* What homework should you do to indicate that you are seriously interested in this company and what it offers? Check with a campus placement office or with a local employment agency; they may have useful information available. If the company is a large national firm, check business publications for relevant information. Call the company's public relations office and request an annual report or other informative materials.

4. *What working conditions (location, extent of travel, benefits, salary) are you willing to accept?* How much of this information is available in the job description? If not mentioned there or by the interviewer, what issues are important enough for you to raise during the interview? Make a short list of your key concerns; refer to the list as the interview progresses to see what important concerns still need to be raised.

5. *What is the most appropriate apparel for the interview?* How will the interviewer expect you to dress? How do you want to present yourself?

By thinking through these and similar questions, you can go into an interview with a clear idea of what you want to accomplish.

Participating in an Interview

An interviewer seldom gets down to business in the initial moments of the interview. There is a brief time for exchanging social talk about the day, last night's game, and so on. This time allows you to relax and to establish a communicative relationship with the interviewer. Does the interviewer seem to be friendly, outgoing, and relatively informal in conducting the interview? Or is the interviewer likely to be all business once the obligatory social niceties are out of the way? You will need to adapt to the social atmosphere that the interviewer seeks to establish. During this brief time, both of you are gaining first impressions of the other. If the interviewer responds positively to you in the first minutes, the interview will probably proceed smoothly.

Follow the interviewer's lead. When he or she is ready to move to more formal questions, you should be able to shift gears and begin answering and asking questions regarding the position for which you are applying. The interviewer generally will begin with background information about the position and will ask general questions about your academic and work experience. As you respond to general questions, be wary of "overtalking" a question— going on and on without end. Give precise answers, developed in sufficient detail to respond fully to the question. You can tell stories that will make a point, as long as the stories remain relatively brief and are clearly relevant to the question.

You will be expected to ask questions as well as respond to them. Appropriate questions may include asking the interviewer what he or she likes about the company, what the opportunities for advancement are, how much travel would be involved, and what kind of equipment you will be working with. Asking questions about salary and benefits can be a delicate matter. If you probe too much or spend an inordinate amount of time on details, the interviewer may get the impression that you are only interested in making a buck. If the interviewer does not offer the information, you can ask what the expected salary range will be and what benefits, in general terms, the company has for its employees. You want to appear interested in how supportive the company is; at the same time, you want to demonstrate your willingness to earn a salary.

Be sensitive to the interviewer's cues that the session is coming to an end. This might be an appropriate time to review your notes and ask if you could get some information on one or two brief points that were not covered. Asking a dozen specific questions of no clear importance, however, will not create a positive impression. As the interview closes, you can pull together your earlier statements regarding your qualifications and briefly restate them for the interviewer. This gives you a chance to express your perception of what you can contribute to, and why you are interested in working for, the interviewer's company.

Sending a follow-up note thanking the interviewer for his or her time and reiterating your interest in the position is a helpful touch. Besides being a social nicety, it gives you a chance to clarify any points made, to add information you felt was not adequately covered in the interview, or simply to say "thanks" for an enjoyable experience.[1]

Reference Notes

1. For further information on employment interviewing, consult Lois Einhorn, Patricia Hayes Bradley, and John E. Baird, Jr., *Effective Employment Interviewing* (Glenview, IL: Scott, Foresman and Company, 1982).

ETHICS AND PUBLIC SPEAKING

Four types of ethical demands are made upon the responsible speaker: the demands you make upon yourself, the demands imposed upon you by the situation, the particular audience's sense of what will be ethically proper, and constraints imposed by societal standards of conduct.

1. *Self.* You are the best judge of your personal standards of conduct. Not everyone is able to sell encyclopedias to young, struggling couples and feel good after closing the sale. Not all people are willing to sell a car they know is a lemon without mentioning the possibility of problems. While there may be a sucker born every minute, every speaker is not inclined to exploit that possibility in selling his or her ideas to an audience. Each of us has limits beyond which we are uncomfortable in advancing ideas or selling products. First and foremost, then, you need to be consistent with your own standards for the ideas you advocate, the information you dispense, and the techniques you use to convey it to others.

2. *Situation.* Some people will attempt to take advantage of a situation in order to sell an idea or a product. News stories about elderly persons who have been swindled are all too common. For this reason, there are laws that restrict conduct in particular situations. "Truth in advertising" legislation, disclosure of information by used car dealers, provisions for ensuring that estimates are given and agreed to before work is performed on your car or home, and "truth in lending" statutes all work to limit the range of unethical practices that people might otherwise be prone to commit. While they do not guarantee that frauds will not occur, they do provide recourse in the event of irresponsible behavior. Adhering to legal statutes or to situational standards dictated by custom also will help prevent irresponsible speech.

3. *Audience.* Some audiences are more gullible than others. One audience's level of knowledge, interest, or even comprehension may make it possible to capture that

audience without its realizing that you have been less than candid or honest. Another audience, in contrast, will appraise your ideas critically. What does this mean for you as a public speaker? Should you take advantage of the less critical listeners and hope to slide your ideas past them without their noticing that the reasoning and support are weak? Your own standards and those implicit in the situation should prevent you from taking this route.

4. *Society.* If your standards and those of the specific situation are not sufficient to prevent unethical practices, the standards of the society often prove potent enough to prevent abuses. Where there are no formal laws or rules to follow, communities have established general standards that a speaker violates at his or her peril. One question you might ask before embarking on a questionable practice is "What happens if I get caught?" You will recognize this as the familiar "means-ends" dilemma: is the practice justified because the end being sought is "noble" or "good"? Unfortunately, this issue cannot be answered in a simple absolute: ends do not justify means. Again, we are forced to rely on a speaker's own code of conduct, as well as on the conduct expected or required by the situation and the audience.

None of these standards operates in isolation. Taken together, they form a whole and act as a check on the excesses of ethical abuse.

Guides to Practice

Thinking about being ethical in your presentation and actually being ethical are quite different. Knowing what should be done is no guarantee against mistakes. The following guidelines will help you translate the previously mentioned cautions into actual practice.

Advocate Ethically Based Proposals.

Audiences can challenge your techniques of presentation as unethical, or they can challenge the ideas themselves. Your position on topics that evoke heightened emotional feelings (for example, abortion) may be rejected on ethical grounds. If the audience feels your proposal is questionable, how far will you get with it, regardless of the techniques you use? You have an obligation to be sensitive to community standards regarding the ideas and proposals you submit for approval and action. You are not being asked to say whatever the audience wants to hear or to refrain from advocating controversial proposals. Rather, you need to gauge audience reaction to the viability of your ideas and offer the best possible arguments you can for their adoption. You may be convinced that the proposal is ethical, but you may still need to persuade your audience that it does not violate community standards.

Protect the Rights of Others.

The language you use and the claims you advance should not be so abusive as to libel or slander others. You need to defend claims about the wrongdoing of others and state your case in clear, precise terms without resorting to loaded language or name calling. When in doubt, be very careful in your accusations regarding the behavior of other people.

Subordinate Techniques to Ideas.

You want the audience to focus upon your message, not upon the artistry of your approach, style, or delivery. Whatever techniques you use should be in the service of the message, rather than so transparent that they assume a significance of their own. Techniques perceived as "too smooth" may cause the audience to question the sincerity of your motives in persuading them. Going beyond what an audience feels is reasonable for the topic under discussion or the situation will bring attention to the techniques and damage your effectiveness.

Responsible speech, in essence, requires a sensitivity to the total communicative situation. Speaking with knowledge and skill, drawing upon your knowledge of your self, the situation, the audience, and the broader community standards and limiting the potential for abuse by following the above guidelines will help you practice ethically responsible communication.

attempt to be heard. Not only do men talk more, they also do not acknowledge comments from women in the same manner as similar comments from men.

The communication variables that differentiate male and female talk are much more complicated than can be discussed here. The solution to the problems implied by the stereotypes for both men and women are not simple—it is not the case that women should simply talk like men, or vice versa. A gender-neutral language is one way to lessen the impact of both stereotypes in the public speaking setting. Using language that is inclusive—that references both genders—equalizes individuals in terms of their gender. Given research that clearly indicates that references to "men" or "mankind" are *not* seen as inclusive of both sexes, the switch to a more inclusive, nonspecific language is an appropriate means of valuing all members of a mixed-sex audience. Adopting such language behaviors also moves a speaker closer toward what some term an "androgynous" style—a set of behaviors that is not gender-specific, but rather is open to both male and female speakers. Using language and emo-

tion appropriate to the situation, whether a speaker is male or female, is to place the demands of the rhetorical occasion first, and the "traditions" of gender second. Hesitancy and tentativeness may have their natural place in a public setting, and language should reflect these tendencies whenever appropriate, but neither gender should be locked into a feminine or masculine stereotype simply by acknowledging what the situation calls for.[1]

For Further Reading

Mulac, A., T. L. Lundell, and J. J. Bradac. "Male/Female Language Differences and Attributional Consequences in a Public Speaking Situation: Toward an Explanation of the Gender-Linked Language Effect." *Communication Monographs* 53 (June 1986): 115–29.

Reference Notes

1. This discussion is indebted to Deborah Borisoff and Lisa Merrill's *The Power to Communicate: Gender Differences as Barriers* (Prospect Heights, IL: Waveland Press, 1985) and to Judy C. Pearson, *Gender and Communication* (Dubuque, IA: Wm. C. Brown Publishers, 1985).

GROUP DISCUSSION: LEADERSHIP

Our culture has a particularly ironic way of cooling down zealots and go-getters. If you are the person in your organization, business, or classroom with ideas, enthusiasm, and commitments, you are immediately made the group's leader. Suddenly, where you once were a strong advocate and a hard worker in the trenches, you now are expected to be impartial, organized, wise, knowledgeable about procedures, politically shrewd, and able to turn out the ever-present report in forty-eight hours.

Groups sometimes make shameful demands of their leaders; yet if they did not, most groups would not get anything done. Someone ultimately has to be in charge, to execute the group's *leadership functions*—handling procedural aspects of group operation, seeing that ideas are explored fully and fairly, and taking care that

the feelings and contributions of everyone in the group are brought out. In this short review of leading meetings and of leadership functions, we will discuss a leader's job as it falls into three phases: premeeting preparation, running the meeting, and post-meeting evaluation. By examining the responsibilities in these three phases, perhaps we can demystify the leader's jobs and necessary skills.

Phase I: Premeeting Preparation

As a leader, your principal job throughout all three phases is to operate as a *facilitator*. While leadership in general is diffused among all members of a group (because all are responsible for helping produce a quality end-result), "the" leader has special duties. This is especially true in Phase I, premeeting preparation. Group members are counting on you to do what you can to make the actual discussion, committee, team, session, or meeting function smoothly. Although your tasks will vary with the precise goal and the degree of formality of the group, they may include some of the following.

Announcing the Time and Place.

You probably will be responsible for getting information about the meeting to interested parties. This may include contacting the group members (one hopes you got telephone numbers on a sign-up sheet earlier), making sure the room or facility is open and available, letting the press know of the meeting if it is open to the public. It is a small task, but overlooking it can produce disastrous results.

Assembling Background Material.

You may also have to get some general materials ready for the meeting. In a book club, the thoughtful leader looks up information on the author or on the issue being discussed to orient the group. The business team leader digs through old files to find out how the firm last approached this question and to unearth pertinent cost-benefit statistics, sales histories, or whatever. For an in-class symposium, the leader may assign specific tasks to the other members—sources to cover, kinds of articles to read, topics on which to be prepared. If these sorts of backgrounding activities are carried out carefully, you will save the group a lot of frustration and wheel-spinning during the actual discussion.

Constructing an Agenda.

Even if the topics for the upcoming meeting were announced in the previous meeting, a group usually needs more guidance. That guidance often takes the form of an *agenda*, a structured list of topics, questions, resolutions, and the like. Agendas vary, obviously, in detail and length; their completeness depends upon the specialization of the group and the expertise of its members.

Final Check of Arrangements.

Just before the meeting is to begin, you as leader may have to check on the facilities one last time. Are the seating arrangements conducive to discussion? If there are microphones, are they working? Are the refreshments prepared? Make sure your meeting is not problematic because you have overlooked the "little" details people expect leaders to care for.

Phase II:
Running the Meeting

With careful preplanning, you should have little trouble actually running the meeting. Your primary jobs are to keep the discussion progressing toward its goal and to serve the participants in whatever ways you can. To carry out these two jobs, you probably will use some of the following communication techniques in each stage of the meeting.

Beginning the Meeting.

Of course, you will have to start the meeting. This may involve nothing more complicated than a "Can I have your attention, please? It's time we begin." In other settings, you may have responsibilities for opening remarks, a short speech orienting the group to the meeting's purpose, the procedures you will follow, and the like. Prepare opening remarks carefully, so that you will not embarrass yourself, not forget anything, and *not* drone endlessly. You are a facilitator, not an orator. If this is a formal meeting of an organization, you may have to begin it in the usual parliamentary fashion:

1. Call to order
2. Review of the minutes of the previous meeting
3. Reports from committees or officers
4. Review of old business (considerations carrying over from the previous meeting)
5. New business (new resolutions and considerations)

Whatever the situation, begin the meeting crisply and clearly. Your group will thank you for your sense of organization and your concern that they have time to talk.

Leading the Discussion.

Once the discussion is launched, you should stay out of the substance of it as much as possible. Think of yourself as an interested troubleshooter. You are watching for confusion, omissions, conflict, procedural tangles, and the like. When you see any of these sorts of problems, only then do you move in. In most groups, you have several major responsibilities during the discussion.

Bringing out reticent individuals.
Except in the most formal parliamentary groups, you ought to be on the lookout for nonparticipants, people who hang back because they are hesitant or because talkative souls are dominating the group. "What do you think, Harry?" is a simple but effective way to bring someone out. If that does not work, you may need to add a bit of encouragement: "Harry, you're the person here closest to our problems in Missouri. We really could use your thoughts." If you still get no response, move on, looking back at Harry periodically to see if he is ready to talk yet.

Summarizing at key points.
Another essential job is that of objectively summarizing particular ideas, conflicts, analyses, and agenda items. A summary from a leader does several things for a group: (1) it shows them you are a fair leader, summarizing both sides of a dispute cleanly; (2) it gently reminds them to finish off a particular point and move on; (3) it catches up members whose minds have drifted off to other matters; and, (4) if well done, it can push a group to a decision. Do not be afraid to take notes to make summaries accurate and well structured.

Tying down the key facts, generalizations, and cause-effect relationships.
Even though you try to stay out of the discussion as much as possible, often you are needed to fill out the factual picture, to go after a particularly obvious causal relationship no one has mentioned, to intrude a valuative perspective needing consideration, and so forth. Because you do not want others to think you are running the meeting with a heavy hand, try to draw out the missing information, relationship, or value from the participants, if possible. Tact is all-important; if you are going to make a statement, you might even want to ask the group's permission: "Excuse me, but I was reading an article last week bearing on this point, and I wonder if it would be all right for me to . . . ." Otherwise, you can go to open calls for information: "Has anyone come across material on . . . ?" Or you might refer to a previous discussion: "During last week's session, someone mentioned that . . . . Is that idea appropriate here?" A leader can always make a direct reference to a document members supposedly are familiar with: "So far, we've not said anything about Appendix B in the Jackson Report. Should its recommendations be considered now?" Try to leave the matter up to the group; you thus preserve your objectivity and impartiality.

Handling conflict.
All methods for handling conflict are applicable here: depersonalizing the conflict, using outside authorities to undercut positions, trying to get the participants in the melee to settle it themselves, and referring to the need for dispatch. A leader is in a tricky position when it comes to conflict. On the one hand, a leader realizes that conflict can be creative and can lead to group-generated agreements. Conflict is absolutely necessary for testing ideas and exploring positions, feelings, and proposals. On the other hand, if it becomes dominant and personalized, conflict can destroy a group. The skillful leader watches to see if it is getting too bloody; watches noncombatants to see if they are getting bored, scared, or frustrated; and watches the clock. Then the leader moves in gingerly, with something like: "OK, you two certainly have demonstrated how complex and touchy this issue is. We really, however, must keep progressing, so how about the rest of you? Does anyone else have an opinion on it?" If you can succeed in getting the rest of the group to pick up on the controversy—and, hopefully, resolve it—your job is done. Go to harsher measures only if the combatants will not quit. Try to slow down the dominating individuals and more equitably spread the communicative load. Reprimand if necessary, but only in the name of the group itself.

Terminating the discussion.
It is the leader's job to terminate the discussion. You must find a way of ending it positively. Your greatest ally in this, of course, is the clock: "Excuse me, but even though I'm finding this discussion fascinating and enlightening, we've got to quit in five minutes. Any last word or two before we break?" Beyond actually stopping the proceedings, the articulate leader moves to a summary of what has been discussed and decided, what remains open, and what is left to be treated in another session. A round of

thanks (naming names, even) never hurts. A clear wrap-up sets important notions in members' minds, getting them ready for further consideration or discussion at another time.

Leading the actual discussion, therefore, does not involve too many tricks or strategies of communication. As long as you are a careful listener, sensitive to the intellectual and emotional processes that are developing, you can handle it easily. Keep your head working and your heart dispassionate, being warm but firm.

Phase III: Post-Meeting Responsibilities

Too many leaders forget their post-meeting responsibilities. Some of these duties are courtesies (thank-you notes to those who brought refreshments, for example); others are economic (paying bills if hall rental and catering were involved). Other important details have to do with the ongoing life of the organization (minutes of the meeting, plans for the next meeting, refiling of materials used, reports to others in the organization, or evaluations to be passed on to your successor).

Because, as leader, you are in so many ways responsible for the social-emotional and substantive life of the organization, be sure you carry out such duties promptly. If people do not receive minutes of the meeting for a month or more, they will think less of you and will have forgotten some of the salient features of the discussion you can only hint at in the minutes. Thank-you notes leave a good impression and probably prod the recipients to render good service the next time the group meets. If the news release detailing the results of the meeting does not get to the press the next day, your group's decisions, recommendations, or actions will be old news and hardly fit to print. Even though you are tired, finish off your post-meeting duties quickly. It will pay off in what you accomplish and in how people think of you.

Being a leader, as you can see, is not an easy job. Leadership demands forethought, anticipation, organization, impartiality, sensitivity, and good sense. By spacing your tasks, however, you can serve your club, organization, or group as an effective leader.

GROUP DISCUSSION: PARTICIPATION

Although most of this book deals with public speaking, it is important also to look at group communication as another important kind of multiperson public communicative activity. A group discussion is a shared, purposive communication transaction in which a small group of people exchanges and evaluates ideas and information in order to understand a subject or solve a problem.

As this definition suggests, there are two major kinds of discussion. In a *learning, or study, discussion*, participants seek to educate each other, to come to a fuller understanding of a subject or problem. People interested in art, computer programming, or religious study, for example, may gather monthly to share thoughts and expertise. In an *action, or decision-mak-*ing, group, participants attempt to reach an agreement on what the group as a whole should believe or do, or they seek ways to implement a decision already made. In such discussions, conflicting facts and values are examined, differences of opinion are evaluated, and proposed courses of action are explored for their feasibility or practicality in an effort to arrive at a consensus. For example, a neighborhood block association may gather periodically to decide on projects to undertake; a city council will decide what to do with its federal revenue-sharing funds; a subcommittee in a business may be asked to recommend useful ways to expand markets.

You will probably spend much personal and work-related time in group discussions. Your communicative tasks in those groups will be complicated by the fact that, as a participant, you are focusing in three directions at once: on yourself, on others in the group, and on the group's task.

Focus on Self

Because you are you and not someone else, you must focus on your own needs, desires, attitudes, knowledge, opinions, hopes, and fears. You participate in group discussions because, reasonably, you expect some sort of gain. That gain can be emotional, as you become accepted by others. It can be reinforcing, as you use others to add authority to ideas or positions you want to defend publicly. That gain also can include time or money, as your group shares the burden of a task and helps you implement a project quickly.

Focus on Others

In a group, however, you cannot be completely self-absorbed. Other members also have their biases, priorities, and experiences. If they get turned off, if they drop out, or if they strike out because of feelings of injustice or intolerance, a group can be reduced to shambles and lose its reasons for existence. As a participant, you are partially responsible for *group maintenance*— for building a supportive social-emotional atmosphere in which everyone feels comfortable even in times of conflict, in which mutual respect is a norm or expectation, and in which there is interdependence and honest openness to others.

Focus on the Task

In addition to everyone's feelings, the group purpose must be kept in mind. You have joined a group to accomplish something—to learn something, to solve a problem, to launch a plan or campaign. If you do not keep that task in mind, you are liable to run down blind alleys and around irrelevant issues, to spend more time talking about next week's fishing trip than the job to be done.

Participating in a group can be tricky business, therefore, because you are looking in these three directions at once. If you lose sight of yourself, you are a mere pawn. If you forget about "them," you are a tyrant. If you ignore the task, you are probably going to have to attend yet another meeting. In essence, as a discussant, you must engage in a mental juggling act, keeping track of your self, of others, and of the group's progress toward its goal.

Knowing and Revealing Your Self in Discussions

Let us begin with you. You have both rights and responsibilities as you consider your own head and heart. The following suggestions include both head and heart.

Preparing. Obviously, you must enter a discussion prepared to participate. This may mean reading the month's assignment in a book club, scanning recommended articles and reports for a business meeting, or working out a "telephone tree" for an action group about to launch a public campaign. Getting intellectually ready for a discussion guarantees two things. First, it ensures that you are able to offer positive contributions and, hence, uphold your end of the bargain that constitutes "groupness." Second, it protects you from glib but shallow sales pitches, silly proposals, ignorant allies, and overpowering opponents.

Getting Background on Others. You ought to have information not only on the topic but also on the other participants. This may not be a problem in a group that has a history, but it certainly can be in newly formed work teams and committees. The more you know about others, the better able you will be to separate the curd from the cream, to anticipate the sources and strengths of your opposition, to know how to object without hurting someone's feelings, to guess at how tenacious various individuals will be. You will know whom to trust, and how far. Ask around.

Introducing Ideas. As a discussion proceeds, you must calculate how and when to introduce your ideas, opinions, and feelings. That is the only way you can be true to your self. Several tactics for introducing ideas have proven successful.

Hitchhiking. In this tactic, you link your idea to one that someone else has stated. It seems perfectly natural to say, "Carl said that we needed to consider the impact of this pro-posal on our clerical staff, and I agree. As a matter of fact, I've done some thinking about this problem, and . . . ." In this way, you build on someone else's notions and probably gain an ally.

Summary. "So far, we've isolated three causes for declining school enrollments and I think they're accurate, but I wonder if there isn't a fourth reason . . . ." In this tactic, you give everyone who has contributed to the dis-cussion a psychological stroke and then seek to move the discussion into new territory—yours.

Shift in viewpoint. Consider: "We've looked at the problem of child abuse from the perspectives of the child and of the abusing par-ent. What about those teachers, doctors, social workers, and other professionals who suspect they've seen a case. What's their role in all this?" This sort of introductory statement, once more, recognizes the ideas and feelings of others while it allows you—with the group's blessing—to intrude your own position.

Disagreement. You might say, "Jean, I certainly can understand why you think no more parking ramps should be built downtown, but I think you've examined only two of the factors involved. Before we reach a decision on the issue, I think we must look at two additional factors . . . ." In this way, you express your disagree-ment softly. You leave Jean with the feeling you are accepting her analysis and integrity, yet you give yourself an entering wedge. In these tac-tics, take care that your remarks actually fit with what has been going on.

Listening to and Evaluating Others.

To protect yourself in a discussion, you must be a rapt and careful listener. You must be able to see through the swarm of words from an eloquent advocate. You must be sure you do not have mistaken impressions, for the con-sequences of misunderstanding can be great, both interpersonally and intellectually. To pro-tect yourself and to understand the full impli-cations of what others say, consider the follow-ing listening techniques.

Questioning. Do not be afraid to ask polite questions of others: "I didn't follow that; could you repeat it?" "Can you translate that for me?"

"I'm curious—where did you read that?" If you phrase the question in terms of your own needs, you will not seem to be suggesting that the other person is unclear or incorrect. Questioning in this way is relatively nonthreat-ening.

Rephrasing. To check on your own lis-tening abilities, and to make sure you know what position you are disagreeing with, try rephrasing another person's ideas: "Let's see if I followed you. First you said that . . . and then you noted that . . . , right?" Putting someone else's ideas into your own words protects you and can save the group time, especially if others also need the translation.

Recording. Take notes. If, say, you are in a decision-making group and the discussion becomes protracted, by the time you arrive at a solution stage, people may have forgotten all the problems to be solved. Keeping track throughout the discussion will save embar-rassment and make your own contributions useful later.

Reacting to Disagreement and Crit-icism.

Not only must you carefully evalu-ate the ideas of others, but you should be men-tally ready to react to their analyses of you. Your first impulse, of course, is to protect your own ego and feelings. Time and again, it may seem that others misunderstand you, imply that you are not very smart, and pick on you. You want to fight back. Unless, for some reason, you simply want to destroy the group and its task, resist that temptation to become a game-ster or a fighter. Be a debater, and focus on the disagreement rather than on the personalized attack. This goal can be accomplished in sev-eral ways.

Interpreting. "Let's see if I can figure out what part of my analysis you're having trouble with." By focusing on the substance of the dis-agreement, you are telling the group that you want to ignore personal innuendos and keep the group as a whole on track.

Turning the other cheek. In all humil-ity, you could say, "I'm sorry what I said both-ered you so much, Fred. Let's see if we can resolve this issue." Poor Fred looks pretty bad after this response, and you can come out more highly credible.

Confronting the attacker. Especially if another person seems to be disrupting and attacking everyone, you (and the rest) may have to confront that person directly: "Janet, you don't seem to be happy with the way we're handling this. What can we do to make you more comfortable and to get on with the task at hand?" In thus confronting a particularly nasty person, you are extending the group's good wishes and sympathy, attempting to return the common focus to the job to be accomplished. With all three techniques, you are protecting your self, which is essential to your own well-being.

Taking Care of Others in Discussions

Your second focal point is the other members of the group. Without that focus, you are not doing your part to keep them happy and productive. A supportive social-emotional atmosphere, even in times of disagreement, is a must. There are many ways to build a supportive atmosphere.

Stroking. It never hurts to give psychological strokes to other group members. It costs you little (unless your pride and ego get in the way), and it keeps everyone working and playing together. "That's a great idea!" "Thanks for the suggestion. It makes me see this question in a different light." "That's beautiful, Ralph." Such personal reactions to others show mutual trust and support.

Criticizing Constructively. It does not hurt, either, to do a little stroking even while you are disagreeing with someone. There are ways to fight ("That's the dumbest thing I've ever heard!"), and there are ways to criticize constructively. These can involve (1) bringing in additional authorities to erode the other person's position, (2) politely cataloguing facts that have been ignored, (3) introducing alternative statements of value ("You look at this as a political question, but I wonder if it's not more a matter of human rights"), and (4) calling for a discussion of the implications of an idea ("I think your plan sounds decent, but do you think it will alleviate the first problem we mentioned?"). The important point, as you communicate your criticisms, is to go as far as you

can in depersonalizing the disagreement. If possible, keep the focus on *authorities* (who do the attacking instead of you), on the *facts* (which we would love to think speak for themselves), on *value* positions, and on the hard-headed *implications*.

Accepting Correction. Not only must you be able to disagree positively with someone else's misrepresentation or misunderstanding of you, but you will do the group a lot of good if you can gracefully accept others' positions and ideas as correctives to your own. It is tempting to be the gamester and to fight back inch by inch, but if you see the basic logic of someone's analysis or if you note that group opinion is running counter to your own, you will have to surrender—or leave. You can get into a huff or a blue funk, or you can retreat with the aplomb of Robert E. Lee of Appomattox. Your ego cries out, "You fools! One day you'll see my wisdom!" but your sense of commitment to others demands, "OK, I'm still having a little problem with all this, but if the rest of you think we should try, then I'll certainly go along" or "I didn't realize some of those implications of my proposal, Paul. Thanks for pointing them out. Are there other proposals that won't have those bad effects?" Eating a little crow certainly leads to occasional indigestion, but sometimes it is better to cave in a bit than to be beaten to death. In this way, you will live to fight another day.

Being Patient. Patience is perhaps the essential quality in your focus on other group members. You are often forced to be an extraordinarily saintly, patient person while discussing. Just as you think you have carved out a piece of truth and wisdom, so does everyone else. Work hard at allowing them—even forcing them—to show you the error of your ways. Ask them to repeat, to go further, to extend. Keep them talking in the hope that their contributions will be given full consideration. What they say may even be good! Especially with somewhat hesitant or reticent people, you often must gently prod them along, even if you know your own ideas will triumph. Patience is a small price for ultimate victory; it might actually produce a good suggestion or two, and it certainly will promote a positive social-emotional climate. It can be inefficient at times, but that is something you occasionally have to tolerate in groups.

Achieving the Group's Goals in Discussions

Finally, you must focus on the goal or task of the group. We often think, perhaps wistfully, that it is the leader's job to keep a discussion moving forward. Of course, it is, but leaders often need help, occasionally miss important points here and there, sometimes get flustered, and perhaps let the group get bogged down in an overextended discussion of an issue. While there is usually a person designated "leader," leadership must be shared by all participants from time to time. Even if you do not have the word *boss* emblazoned on your forehead, you still have some responsibilities for moving the group ahead. A few of these responsibilities have already been suggested. Others are strictly procedural matters to which you should attend.

Knowing the Agenda.
An *agenda* is an agreed-upon list of tasks to be accomplished or questions to be answered in a particular session. Know it. Know when it is appropriate to bring up a matter you are interested in. If necessary, as the group is about to begin, ask the others whether an idea you want to talk about is appropriate to the agenda. If it does not appear to be, ask if it can be inserted somewhere. Knowing the agenda, in other words, allows you (and the rest) to keep the discussion orderly and progressive and tells you something about timing your remarks.

Asking Procedural Questions.
Never be afraid to ask questions about what is happening in a discussion: "Are we still on point three, or have we moved to point four?" "Is there some way we can resolve this question and move ahead?" "Can we consider the feasibility of Art's proposal before we move on to Brenda's?" Such questions can seem inordinately naive, and, if asked with a sneer in your voice, could reflect badly on the leader, yet sometimes naive questions are absolutely necessary.

Summarizing.
Seldom can a single leader carry out all of the summarizing that most groups need. As you may have noticed, summary is a theme of this section—summarizing your own position, summarizing those of others, and, here, summarizing so that the group can keep progressing. A good summary allows you to check bases, to see what has been agreed to and what remains to be done. Summaries form the intellectual junctures in a discussion. They can be simple: "Now, as I heard you two, Jack said this and this, and Bob said that and that, right?" or they can be elaborate attempts to trace through the whole of a discussion so that members have it clearly in mind before you adjourn.

Arbitrating.
Another important leadership function that should not fall solely on the leader's shoulders is that of arbitrating disputes. Being the peacemaker is sometimes risky business, for both parties may go for your throat, yet if a discussion is going to be mutually supportive and satisfying, and if it is going to get its job done, then each person occasionally will have to help it get over intellectual and emotional rough spots. Sometimes you can arbitrate by offering a *compromise:* "OK, is it possible for us to accept a part of Proposal A and a part of Proposal B and forge those parts into a new Proposal C? It might go this way. . . ." At other times, you are going to have to call for *clarification:* "Bill, you think Ron's idea is defective because of this, and you, Ron, seem to be saying that Bill has missed the point about the riverfront land, right?" By pointing out the idea in conflict rather than the personalities in conflict, you perhaps can deflate it. You may occasionally have to offer a *gentle reprimand:* "Whoa! If you two don't quit beating each other to death, we'll never get done in an hour! Let's see if we can get to the nub of the matter here." By thus holding out the standards of efficiency and expediency, you may succeed in getting two people to clarify, to remember the rest of the group, and to charge ahead.

Participating in a discussion can be a tremendously rewarding and efficient way of making your own ideas and feelings public, of learning new information and perspectives, of making key decisions at work or at home, and of implementing plans or proposals. You will achieve maximum satisfaction and gain, however, only if you constantly keep in focus yourself, others, and the task. Monitor all three focal points steadily. You must have some degree of trust (or even suspicion); you must do your part in bringing out the best in others; you must remember that discussion is an interdependent activity with both social-emotional and intellectual components; you must abide by faith in a quasi-democratic outlook on life.

GROUP PRESENTATIONS: PANELS AND SYMPOSIA

When a group is too large to engage in effective roundtable discussion, when its members are not well enough informed to make such discussion profitable, or when subgroups in the larger collectivity represent distinct viewpoints on important issues, a *panel* of individuals—from three to five, usually—may be selected to discuss the topic for the benefit of others, who then become an audience. Members of a panel are chosen either because they are particularly well informed on the subject or because they represent divergent views on the issue.

Another type of audience-oriented discussion is the *symposium.* In this format, several persons—again, usually from three to five—present short speeches, each focusing on a different facet of the subject or offering a different solution to the problem under consideration. Usually, the short presentations are followed by periods of discussion among the symposiasts and question-and-answer sessions with the onlooking audience. The symposium is especially valuable when recognized experts with well-defined points of view or areas of competence are available as speakers and, thus, is the discussion procedure commonly used at large conferences and conventions.

When you are asked to participate in a communication event with these types of formats, remember that the techniques you employ do not vary substantially from those used for other types of speeches. Bear in mind, however, that you are participating as a member of a group that is centering its remarks, information, and opinions upon a specific topic or problem. You,

therefore, have an obligation to function as part of a team, to coordinate your communicative behaviors with the efforts of others in order to give your audience a full range of viewpoints and options. Thus, you must sacrifice part of your individual freedom and latitude for the greater good of all. With this important caution in mind, we can discuss techniques useful in preparing for and participating in group and conference presentations.

Preparation for Panels and Symposia

Because in panels and conferences you are one of a team of communicators, it is important that you take others into account as you prepare your remarks. This taking-into-account involves considerations you do not have to face in other speaking situations. First, *you have to fit your comments into a general theme.* If, say, the theme of your panel is "The State of the U.S. Constitution at the Beginning of Its Third Century," not only will you be expected to mention "U.S. Constitution," "two hundred years," and the like, but probably you will also be expected to say something about how the Constitution has been interpreted over those two hundred years, what is happening today, and how you see the interpretation evolving. The theme, in other words, affects how you will treat your subject, and perhaps even forces you to approach it in a particular way.

Also, *remember that you may be responsible for covering only a portion of a topic or theme.* In most symposia and panels, the speakers divide the topic into parts to avoid

TYPES OF GROUP PRESENTATIONS

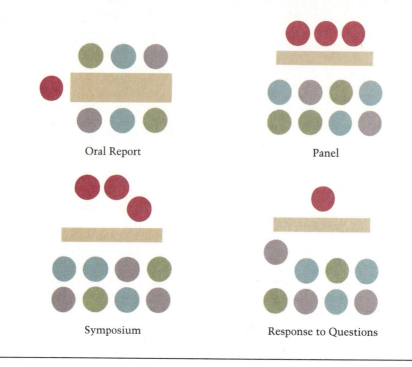

Oral Report

Panel

Symposium

Response to Questions

duplication and to provide an audience with a variety of viewpoints. For example, if the theme is the state of American culture, you might be asked to discuss education, while others will examine social relations, the state of science and technology, and leisure time, thus dividing the theme *topically*. Alternatively, you might be asked to discuss *problems* (depersonalization, the "plastic" world, the limits of the work force) while other participants examine *solutions* (individual, corporate, ethical, political). Part of your preparation, therefore, involves coordinating your communicative efforts with those of others.

The more you know about the subject under discussion, the better. To be ready for any eventuality, you must have a flexibility born of broad knowledge. For each aspect of the subject or implication of the problem you think may possibly be discussed, make the following analysis:

1. *Review the facts you already know.* Go over the information you have acquired through previous reading or personal experience and organize it in your mind. Prepare as if you were going to present a speech on every phase of the matter. You will then be better qualified to discuss any part of it.

2. *Bring your knowledge up to date.* Find out if recent changes have affected the situation. Fit the newly acquired information into what you already know.

3. *Determine a tentative point of view on each of the important issues.* Make up your mind what your attitude will be. Do you think that Hemingway was a greater writer than Faulkner? If so, exactly how and why? What three or four steps might be taken to attract new members into your club? On what medical or health-related grounds should cigarette smoking be declared illegal? Stake out a tentative position on each question or issue that is likely to come before the group, and have clearly in mind the facts and reasons that support your view. Be ready to state and substantiate the opinion at

whatever point in the discussion seems most appropriate, but also be willing to change your mind if information or points of view provided by others show you to be wrong.

4. *To the best of your ability, anticipate the effect of your ideas or proposals on the other members of the group or the organization of which the group is a part.* For instance, what you propose may possibly cause someone to lose money or to retract a promise that has been made. Forethought concerning such eventualities will enable you to understand opposition to your view if it arises and to make a valid and intelligent adjustment. The more thoroughly you organize your facts and relate them to the subject and to the people involved, the more effective your contributions to the discussion will be.

Participating in Panels and Symposia

Your style and vocal tone will, of course, vary according to the nature and purpose of the discussion as a whole, the degree of formality that is being observed, and your frame of mind as you approach the task. In general, however, *speak in a direct, friendly, conversational style.* As the interaction proceeds, differences of opinion are likely to arise, tensions may increase, and some conflict may surface. You will need, therefore, to be sensitive to these changes and to make necessary adjustments in the way you voice your ideas and reactions.

Present Your Point of View Clearly, Succinctly, and Fairly. Participation in a panel or symposium should always be guided

by one underlying aim: to help the group think objectively and creatively in analyzing the subject or solving the problem at hand. To this end, you should organize your contributions not in the way best calculated to win other people to your point of view, but rather in the fashion that will best stimulate them to think for themselves. Therefore, instead of stating your conclusion first and then supplying the arguments in favor of it, let your contribution recount how and why you came to think as you do. Begin by stating the nature of the problem as you see it; outline the various hypotheses or solutions that occurred to you as you were thinking about it; tell why you rejected certain solutions; only after all this, state your own opinion and explain the reasons that support it. In this way, you give other members of the group a chance to check the accuracy and completeness of your thinking on the matter and to point out any deficiencies or fallacies that may not have occurred to you. At the same time, you will also be making your contribution in the most objective and rational manner possible.

Maintain Attitudes of Sincerity, Open-Mindedness, and Objectivity. Above all, remember that a serious discussion is not a showplace for prima donnas or an arena for verbal combatants. When you have something to say, say it modestly and sincerely, and always maintain an open, objective attitude. Accept criticism with dignity and treat disagreement with an open mind. Your primary purpose is not to get your own view accepted, but to work out with the other members of the group the best possible choice or decision that all of you together can devise and, as a team, to present a variety of viewpoints to the audience.

HUMOR IN PUBLIC SPEAKING

In Chapter 18, while discussing the speech to entertain, we briefly discussed humor and its general uses in society. We suggested that humor could be used to (1) deflect an audience's antip-

athy toward a speaker, (2) make people in the audience feel more like a group than they did before hearing the speech, and (3) offer in palatable or biting form a critique of one's society.

We noted that a speech to entertain generally had one of those uses of humor as its specific purpose.

More can and should be said, however, about particular uses of humor in other types of speeches. That is, in almost every speaking situation you may need to use humor in one or more parts of a speech. Following are some of the ways humor can be used in different portions of speeches.

Using Humor in Speech Introductions

Speakers ought to consider using humor in introductions to their speeches if (1) they themselves are tense and can tell relevant stories well enough to relax or (2) the audience is stiff, bored, or hostile, and, hence, in need of a jolt from the lectern. That is, a good story or joke is therapeutic, and, because beginning communication transactions often are traumatic for both speaker and listeners, such therapy often will significantly improve the rest of the communicative exchange. Make sure that the story or joke is *relevant, in good taste,* and *well-told.* That is, do not just tell a story for the sake of telling a story; an audience sees through that technique right away. Do not tell a dirty joke, because even if you offend only one listener, others in the audience likely will recognize the offense, feel embarrassed, and take their embarrassment out on you. Finally, do not tell jokes if your timing is bad, if you tend to forget the punch line, if you cannot handle the dialect, and so on. A badly told joke is worse than no joke at all.

Consider the following speech introduction: "I came home the other night to find my eight-year-old ready with a joke. 'Daddy,' he said, 'what's green and red and goes a hundred miles an hour?' 'I don't know,' I said wearily. 'What?' 'A frog in a blender!' he shouted triumphantly. That time of the evening, the story merely turned me green. Upon reflection, however, it has caused me to think about the ways in which modern technology—right down to the blender on the kitchen counter—has invaded our thinking, our values, yes, even our humor. And today, I want to . . . . "

In this introduction you will not find a rib-rattlingly funny story; as a matter of fact, most audience members probably would simply smile rather than laugh. That is all right, because the story can still do its job; it still can relax the speaker and the audience. As a matter of fact, if you expect audience members to react with full hilarity to a joke and then they do not, you are liable to be more tense than you were before you started the story. Remember that you are a public speaker *using humor for your purposes,* not a comic.

Using Humor in Midspeech

You also may want to use humor in the middle segments of speeches to (1) lighten a comparatively dense or heavy section, (2) serve as a memorable illustration of an important point, or (3) improve certain aspects of your credibility. More specifically, humor gives:

- *Contrast.* After an audience is hit with a lot of statistics or a pile of philosophical abstractions, a little humor not only provides some important psychological contrast, thereby improving listeners' abilities to attend to your speech (see Chapter 2); it also lifts their spirits and rallies their minds, making them more willing to stay with you for the rest of the speech.
- *Illustration.* Most people can remember a joke more easily than an abstract discussion of something. Even concrete details are more memorable, for many people, if they are offered humorously.
- *Credibility.* One important dimension of credibility is dynamism—the audience's perception of the speaker as an alive, vital human being. A speaker's dynamism ratings—and, hence, overall credibility—improve when humor is used.

Once again, you do not need to work long, involved comic monologues, or even full-blown funny stories into the middle of a speech. Simply the way you *phrase ideas* can add the contrast, make the illustration memorable, and give a little push to your credibility. Review the speech by Garry Trudeau in Chapter 18 for examples.

Using Humor in Speech Conclusions

Good speakers may also end a speech on a humorous note. Humor can be used in speech conclusions to (1) make the separation of speaker and audience a pleasant event, (2) drive home the main point one last time, or (3) leave the audience with a sense of finality as the speech concludes.

1. *Separation.* When you are listening to good speakers, you often want their speeches to continue; when listening to people you greatly admire, you want to stay in their presence. Even good speakers and admirable lecturers, however, must quit talking sooner or later. To make their separation from the audience as painless as possible, such speakers often use light humor to make the audience smile or laugh as they leave the rostrum.
2. *Emphasis.* A good story likewise can emphasize the main point of the whole speech; nearly every cleric who has been trained to preach has been taught this type of concluding strategy.
3. *Finality.* The speaker who says, "And so, everything I've been saying can be summed up in the story about the ten-year-old who . . . ." is overtly signalling an audience that the speech is about to end, that the audience should prepare to ask questions, applaud, or leave. Why should you offer such signals to listeners? All of us can think of occasions when we were not sure when a speech was to end, when there was an awkward moment when the speaker thought, "Can I go now?" and listeners thought, "Well, is it over or is she just thinking of the next words?" Signalling the end can reduce some of the awkwardness that otherwise might accompany the end of a good talk.

Overall, therefore, while humor certainly is very important to speeches to entertain, it likewise can be a part of any speech on almost any occasion. Make sure, however, that you use humor appropriately, that you use it to make a point rather than merely to get a cheap laugh, and that you train yourself to tell stories well—naturally, completely, and pointedly. Humor can bond speaker and listener together in a positive relationship and, hence, is a tool important to any speaker's collection of skills.

A MODEL FOR ORGANIZING AND EVALUATING ARGUMENTS

Writing in 1958, the British philosopher Stephen Toulmin proposed that arguments be diagrammed in a visually clear pattern that would help ensure that all elements—implicit and explicit—were recognized. The following elements, and the visual model that illustrates the relationships between and among them, will aid you in analyzing and critiquing your and others' arguments.

1. *Claim.* Put simply, what are you proposing for audience consideration? This can be, as we suggested in Chapter 17, a claim of fact, value, or policy.
2. *Data.* What materials, in the form of illustrative parallels, expert opinion, statistical information, research studies, and the like, can you advance to support the claim?
3. *Warrant.* What is the relationship between the parallel case, statistical data, or expert opinion and the claim? Upon what kind of assumption or inferential pattern does its acceptance as support for the claim depend? Materials do not function as evidence or support for no reason; facts do not speak for themselves. What makes an audience believe in the strength of the reasons as

support lies in the following kinds of assumptions that warrant acceptance of the link between data and claim:

a. An expert knows what he or she is talking about.

b. Past economic, social, or political practices are reliable predictors of future occurrences.

c. Inferential patterns (for example, cause, sign) suggest the linkage is rational.

We know, for instance, that the credibility of an expert is a major determinant in gaining acceptance of the opinions being offered. In the development of the argument, this factor operates as an implicit *warrant* connecting the opinion to the claim. In matters involving economics, we know that the regularity of certain marketplace functions, such as supply and demand, exert a powerful influence on events. Hence, when we claim that the prices of finished products will rise as a result of the increases in the cost of raw materials, we are tacitly assuming the normal operation of the marketplace. Likewise, the value of using parallel cases as support for your position rests on the regularity of an inferential pattern: when two cases are parallel, similar results can be expected.

4. *Backing.* Does the audience accept the relationship between the data and the claim as given? If not, what further data would be helpful in supporting the warrant? When the warrant linking a reason and claim is accepted by the audience, explicit development of this facet of the argument is unnecessary. Thus, if the audience accepts the opinion of a local university scientist, an extended development of her credentials would be a waste of time. If an audience already understands the logical pattern of an analogy and believes that the substance of the argument being presented is analogous, spending time to support the analogous nature of the relationship would be pointless.

When a relationship between the reason and the claim is not automatically accepted, you will have to provide additional support focused on the warrant rather than the original claim. Thus, in supporting an argument against continued economic aid to the "Contras" with testimony from a politician, you might need to establish her expertise to increase the likelihood of audience acceptance. Thus, part of your argument will have to develop backing for the warrant.

5. *Reservations.* Can significant counterarguments be raised? In most cases, arguments on the opposite side are not only readily available, but may even be as strong as your own reasons. Anticipating reservations in advance will help you strengthen your own argument. In general, these can be thought of as "unless" clauses in your argument.

6. *Qualifiers.* How certain is the claim? Note that we do not ask how certain *you* are; you may be absolutely sure of something for which you cannot offer verifiable support. How much can one bank on the claim that you are putting forward as an acceptable basis for belief or action? How certain are you that continued economic aid is a worthless idea? Are you *sure* that economic aid will be used for military purposes? Such qualifiers as *probably*, *presumably*, *virtually*, and *may* should be incorporated into the claim to reflect the strength of the argument.

These six elements operate as a general framework for the construction and analysis of an argument. The interrelationships between and among the elements can best be displayed through a visual diagram. The numbers in the diagram correspond to the elements discussed. (See the figure on page 491.)

The model has three principal uses in organizing your arguments. First, by setting forth the arguments' components in the manner indicated, you will be able to capture visually the relationships among the components. How, for example, are the data you present linked to the claim? What sort of warrants (assumptions, precedents, rules of inference) are you using to ensure that the audience sees the connection between the data and the claim?

Second, once you have written a brief description of the data and have identified the

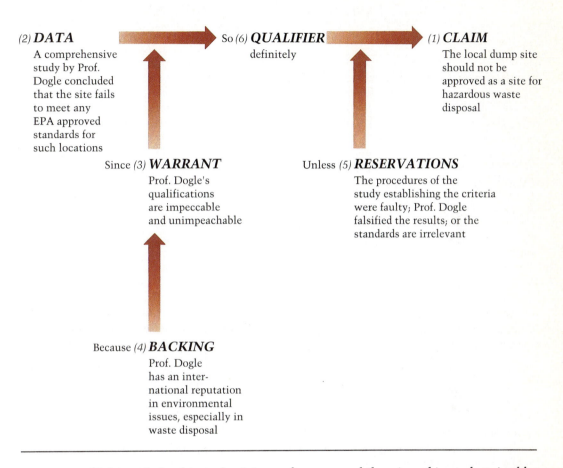

(2) **DATA**
A comprehensive study by Prof. Dogle concluded that the site fails to meet any EPA approved standards for such locations

So *(6)* **QUALIFIER**
definitely

(1) **CLAIM**
The local dump site should not be approved as a site for hazardous waste disposal

Since *(3)* **WARRANT**
Prof. Dogle's qualifications are impeccable and unimpeachable

Unless *(5)* **RESERVATIONS**
The procedures of the study establishing the criteria were faulty; Prof. Dogle falsified the results; or the standards are irrelevant

Because *(4)* **BACKING**
Prof. Dogle has an international reputation in environmental issues, especially in waste disposal

warrant on which its relationship to the claim rests, you can more clearly determine whether you wish to offer the claim as definite, or as only probable, likely, or possible. You also will be reminded to reflect on the audience's grasp of the warrant. Is it a generally accepted relationship—will it be in this case?

Finally, by thinking through the possible reservations that others will have to your argument, you will be in a better position to shore up weaknesses in advance and, where necessary, to build a stronger base from which to respond to issues that might undermine rather than directly refute your case. As you react to possible reservations, avoid the temptation to build into your case answers to every possible counterargument. Your case will become cum-bersome, and there is nothing to be gained by answering reservations that your opponents have not even thought of yet.

The model also is helpful to listeners in analyzing the strength of arguments. The elements help sharpen your ability to question an argument. The data may be misleading or in error; the relationship between the data and claim may be highly questionable (lacking a strong warrant); there may be so many reservations that the claim must be highly qualified; advocates may be pushing claims harder than the data will warrant. Using the model as a means of thinking about arguments can help you determine whether a claim goes beyond what can reasonably be supported by the evidence and available warrants.

PARLIAMENTARY PROCEDURE AND SPEECHMAKING

In groups, parliamentary procedure often is used to regulate discussion and decision making. The primary intent of procedural rules is to ensure that discussion is orderly and that minority voices have the opportunity to be heard. Although it can be used to frustrate members' wishes (as is sometimes the case in legislative assemblies), on the whole, parliamentary procedure is a useful aid to a group's decision-making processes. We cannot cover all of these procedural rules, but we will introduce the major devices and offer some practical advice regarding their use.

Major Procedural Rules

The table on pages 494–95 outlines the most often used procedural rules and indicates whether they require a second, whether they permit discussion, and what support they require for approval. First, however, we will define the major categories of motions.

The *main motion* is the proposal brought before the group. It may be introduced very simply: "I move that . . ." The content of the main motion depends upon what you want the group to act upon (for example, "I move that we hold the fund-raising event on October 5"; "I move that we authorize the president and the treasurer to review existing needs and purchase equipment as needed to get us ready for the new year"; "I move that this group go on record as opposing the nuclear freeze movement"). The motion may simply express the sentiment of the group and require very little discussion prior to a formal vote, or the motion may be highly controversial and engage group members in impassioned debate over the proposal's merits. When motions are controversial, the use of *subsidiary*, *incidental*, and *privileged motions* becomes important.

Subsidiary motions have a direct bearing on the main motion. They seek to alter the content of the motion, to change the time of discussion, or to place the motion before a subgroup for further study. The motion to postpone indefinitely has the effect of killing future discussion of the proposal. Perhaps the most confusing of the subsidiary motions is that which seeks "to amend." If an amendment is offered and seconded, the discussion must focus on the merits of the proposed change in the main motion. Once discussion has concluded, the *amendment* is passed or negated. In either case, the discussion now must revert to the main motion, either as originally presented (the amendment failed) or as altered (the amendment passed). Once discussion is concluded (assuming no new amendments are offered), the vote is taken on the main motion as presented or altered. As long as you work backward from any amendment to the main motion, voting at each step, you will avoid controversy and confusion. When discussion seems to lag or becomes highly repetitious, the *previous-question motion* ends discussion. Voting on the previous question also causes confusion, as some may think they are voting on the main motion. All the previous-question motion does is seek agreement to stop discussion. In some groups, moving the previous question can be handled informally. Once it has been moved, the chair can ask if there are any objections to ceasing discussion. Hearing none, the chair can move immediately to a vote on the main motion. This saves time by avoiding a separate vote to close debate when the result is clearly favorable. Amendment, previous-question, and the remainder of the subsidiary motions can be raised at any time—they take precedence over the main motion and over each other. The following sequence could occur:

1. The main motion is presented and seconded; discussion ensues.

2. The main motion is amended, seconded, and discussion continues.

3. A member seeks to limit discussion to ten minutes; this is seconded but is not open to discussion.

4. Another member moves to amend the limit-discussion motion by striking ten minutes

and inserting twenty minutes. This is seconded and discussion begins until someone reminds the group that the amendment is not debatable because the motion to which it is applied in this case is not open to discussion.

5. The chair reminds everyone that the motion before the group is the amendment to limit discussion to twenty minutes instead of ten. The group votes on the amendment; it fails.

6. The chair announces that the motion to limit discussion to ten minutes is now before the group and is not open to discussion. The chair calls for a vote; the motion passes.

7. Eight minutes of discussion ensue, during which the previous question is called. The chair asks if there is any objection; hearing none, she bypasses a formal vote on the previous question and reminds everyone that the vote is on the *amendment* to the main motion. The amendment passes.

8. The chair reminds everyone that discussion is now open on the main motion as amended. A member moves to refer the motion as amended to a committee. This is seconded and discussion ensues on the move to a committee. The chair reminds the group that the discussion limit has passed and asks if everyone is ready to vote on the referral-to-committee motion. Hearing no objection, the chair calls for a vote; the motion fails.

9. The chair restates the motion as amended and once again asks if the group is ready to vote. Hearing no comment, the chair asks if all are ready to vote. The chair restates the main motion as amended and the vote is taken. The motion passes.

Although ordinary discussion may not be so contorted, this sequence does suggest the confusion that group members can create for themselves if they do not have a clear sense of the rules of procedure (and a chair that seeks to make each step clear).

Incidental motions also affect the progress of a main motion. They are important in reserving rights for individuals who are attempting to influence the flow of events. The motion to *suspend the rules* allows a person to introduce a proposal out of its normal order;

the *point of order* motion can come at any time during a discussion and allows a member to remind a group that it is not following accepted rules of procedure (for example, in point 4 of the previous illustration, the discussion of an amendment to the limit-discussion motion could be questioned by rising to a point of order). If the chair did not know the rules and said, "It's OK, let's continue discussion," a member would have the right to appeal the decision of the chair. Check the accompanying table and note the problem that has been created. Is the appeal debatable? When in doubt, discuss. After all, the purpose is not to alienate members but to regulate the discussion. The motion to *divide a question* is useful when the main motion contains more than one main idea. It also can be used when you sense that one part of a motion may pass and a second portion may fail. By moving to divide, you may save part of the proposal.

Privileged motions also help regulate the process. There is little to be gained by a *call for the orders of the day* if everyone but you is satisfied with the events of the meeting. If, on the other hand, the group appears restless and is wandering around several topics, it may be good to issue this form of reminder. The *question of privilege* protects an individual's right to hear what is going on or to understand what action is being voted on. The motions to *recess* and to *adjourn* are not intended to frustrate a group's desire to resolve whatever problem is before it. If there is a great deal of tension, it may be wise to request a recess in order to allow tempers to cool; likewise, if tensions persist, it might be useful to suggest an adjournment to a specific time. The *unclassified motions* provide a means to bring a topic that has been tabled at a previous meeting before the group, or to alter action that has been taken (*to reconsider, to rescind*). Take special note of the restrictions on the use of these latter motions (see the table, notes 13 and 14).

Speaking in Parliamentary Groups

If you are in a meeting governed by parliamentary rules, there are several things you can do to increase your effectiveness:

PARLIAMENTARY PROCEDURE FOR HANDLING MOTIONS

Classification of Motions	Types of Motions and Their Purposes	Order of Handling	Must Be Seconded	Can Be Discussed	Can Be Amended	Vote Required (1)	Can Be Reconsidered
Main motion	(To present a proposal to the assembly)	Cannot be made while any other motion is pending	Yes	Yes	Yes	Majority	Yes
Subsidiary motions (2)	To postpone indefinitely (to kill a motion)	Has precedence over above motion	Yes	Yes	No	Majority	Affirmative vote only
	To amend (to modify a motion)	Has precedence over above motions	Yes	When motion is debatable	Yes	Majority	Yes
	To refer (a motion) to committee	Has precedence over above motions	Yes	Yes	Yes	Majority	Until committee takes up subject
	To postpone (discussion of a motion) to a certain time	Has precedence over above motions	Yes	Yes	Yes	Majority	Yes
	To limit discussion (of a motion)	Has precedence over above motions	Yes	No	Yes	Two thirds	Yes
	Previous question (to take a vote on the pending motion)	Has precedence over above motions	Yes	No	No	Two thirds	No
	To table (to lay a motion aside until later)	Has precedence over above motions	Yes	No	No	Majority	No
Incidental motions (3)	To suspend the rules (to change the order of business temporarily)	Has precedence over a pending motion when its purpose relates to the motion	Yes	No	Yes	Two thirds	No
	To close nominations [4]	[4]	Yes	No	Yes	Two thirds	No
	To request leave to withdraw or modify a motion [5]	Has precedence over motion to which it pertains and other motions applied to it	No	No	No	Majority [5]	Negative vote only
	To rise to a point of order (to enforce the rules) [6]	Has precedence over pending motion out of which it arises	No	No	No	Chair decides [7]	No
	To appeal from the decision of the chair (to reverse chair's ruling) [6]	Is in order only when made immediately after chair announces ruling	Yes	When ruling was on debatable motion	No	Majority [1]	Yes
	To divide the question (to consider a motion by parts)	Has precedence over motion to which it pertains and motion to postpone indefinitely	[8]	No	No	Majority [8]	No
	To object to consideration of a question	In order only when a main motion is first introduced	No	No	No	Two thirds	Negative vote only
	To divide the assembly (to take a standing vote)	Has precedence after question has been put	No	No	No	Chair decides	No

Privileged motions						
To call for the orders of the day (to keep meeting to order of business) [6, 9]	Has precedence over above motions	No	No	No	No vote required	No
To raise a question of privilege (to point out noise, etc.) [6]	Has precedence over above motions	No	No	No	Chair decides [7]	No
To recess [10]	Has precedence over above motions	Yes	No [10]	Yes	Majority	No
To adjourn [11]	Has precedence over above motions	Yes	No [11]	No [11]	Majority	No
To fix the time to which to adjourn (to set next meeting time) [12]	Has precedence over above motions	Yes	No [12]	Yes	Majority	Yes
Unclassified motions						
To take from the table (to bring up tabled motion for consideration)	Cannot be made while another motion is pending	Yes	No	No	Majority	No
To reconsider (to reverse vote on previously decided motion) [13]	Can be made while another motion is pending [13]	Yes	When motion to be reconsidered is debatable	No	Majority	No
To rescind (to repeal decision on a motion) [14]	Cannot be made while another motion is pending	Yes	Yes	Yes	Majority or two thirds [14]	Negative vote only

1. A tied vote is always lost except on an appeal from the decision of the chair. The vote is taken on the ruling, not the appeal, and a tie sustains the ruling.
2. Subsidiary motions are applied to a motion before the assembly for the purpose of disposing of it properly.
3. Incidental motions are incidental to the conduct of business. Most of them arise out of a pending motion and must be decided before the pending motion is decided.
4. The chair opens nominations with "Nominations are now in order." A member may move to close nominations, or the chair may declare nominations closed if there is no response to his/her inquiry, "Are there any further nominations?"
5. When the motion is before the assembly, the mover requests permission to withdraw or modify it, and if there is no objection from anyone, the chair announces that the motion is withdrawn or modified. If anyone objects, the chair puts the request to a vote.
6. A member may interrupt a speaker to rise to a point of order or of appeal, to call for orders of the day, or to raise a question of privilege.
7. Chair's ruling stands unless appealed and reversed.
8. If propositions or resolutions relate to independent subjects, they must be divided on the request of a single member. The request to divide the question may be made when another member has the floor. If they relate to the same subject but each part can stand alone, they may be divided only on a regular motion and vote.

9. The regular order of business may be changed by a motion to suspend the rules.
10. The motion to recess is not privileged if made at a time when no other motion is pending. When not privileged, it can be discussed. When privileged, it cannot be discussed, but can be amended as to length of recess.
11. The motion to adjourn is not privileged if qualified or if adoption would dissolve the assembly. When not privileged, it can be discussed and amended.
12. The motion to fix the time to which to adjourn is not privileged if no other motion is pending or if the assembly has scheduled another meeting on the same or following day. When not privileged, it can be discussed.
13. A motion to reconsider may be made only by one who voted on the prevailing side. It must be made during the meeting at which the vote to be reconsidered was taken, or on the succeeding day of the same session. If reconsideration is moved while another motion is pending, discussion on it is delayed until discussion is completed on the pending motion; then it has precedence over all new motions of equal rank.
14. It is impossible to rescind any action that has been taken as a result of a motion, but the unexecuted part may be rescinded. Adoption of the motion to rescind requires only a majority vote when notice is given at a previous meeting; it requires a two-thirds vote when no notice is given and the motion to rescind is voted on immediately.

1. *Know the appropriate rules yourself.* Do not depend upon a good chair to keep you informed regarding the process. The more knowledgeable you are, the less confused you will become as the process of using parliamentary rules unfolds. Also, you will be able to counteract efforts to use the rules to create an unfair advantage for one or more persons.

2. *Listen carefully.* Stay on top of what is going on. If the chair does not keep the group on track by constantly reminding members what is pending, you may need to take on that responsibility. Hopefully, you and others will be kept informed regarding what is on the floor by a conscientious leader.

3. *Ask questions.* If you are not sure about the procedures or become lost in the parliamentary thicket, do not hesitate to raise a question of personal privilege. Be specific in asking the chair or the parliamentarian (if there is one appointed) what is on the floor or what motions are appropriate under the circumstances.

4. *Speak to the motion.* Limit your remarks to the specific motion on the floor. Do not discuss the entire main motion if an amendment is pending; instead, comment directly on the merits of the amendment.

5. *Avoid unnecessary parliamentary gymnastics.* If group members yield to the temptation to play with the rules, parliamentary procedure becomes counterproductive. The rational process of decision making is undermined by such game playing. Refrain from piling one motion on top of another, cluttering the floor (and the minds of members) with amendments to amendments. Also guard against raising petty points of order. Parliamentary procedure is instituted to ensure equal, fair, controlled participation by all members. It provides a systematic means of the introduction and disposal of complex ideas. Unnecessary "gymnastics" will impede rather than foster group decision making.

A comprehensive guide to parliamentary procedure, adopted by many groups in their by-laws, is *Robert's Rules of Order.* Consult this or other guides to answer questions that go beyond the material presented in this review.

REDUCING COMMUNICATION APPREHENSION: SYSTEMATIC SOLUTIONS

Researchers have estimated that as much as 20 percent of the college population may experience *communication apprehension,* defined as "an individual's level of fear or anxiety associated with either real or anticipated communication with another person or persons."[1] The consequences of a high level of communication apprehension include lowered self-esteem, lowered academic achievement, and, in general, negative effects on a person's relationships with other people.[2] This personality trait affects all areas of a person's communicative efforts, from calling on the telephone to presenting a public speech.

Communication apprehension is distinguished from the experience of *stage fright,* which involves specific situations in which a person is orally presenting material in a public setting (for instance, a play, speech, or panel presentation). Stage fright is a normal experience; it may or may not be accompanied by high communication apprehension. Thus, a person who has no major problems interacting with others in most situations can feel nervous when called upon to present ideas in public.

Systematic solutions to reducing communication apprehension have focused on the phenomenon as a trait, rather than as a state. Thus, reducing the nervousness felt in presenting a public speech has been only one goal of treatment programs. Nevertheless, the treatments suggested for trait communication apprehension have relevance for the more specific situation speakers face. In this section, we will focus on three major treatment approaches and suggest ways in which they might be adapted to the reduction of your own stage fright.[3] As such, the advice will supplement that offered in Chapters 1 and 3.

Systematic Desensitization

Systematic desensitization is a treatment program that assumes that you *do* have the ability to accomplish a specific task. Your fear is so great, however, that it impedes your successful behavior. For example, assume that you are afraid of height, and, as an actor, must walk the catwalks of the theater. Walking, as a behavior, is not the problem. The fear of height causes you to become nauseated when on the catwalk and, thus, is potentially harmful. Persons trained in systematic desensitization would establish an ascending series of events that would provoke increasing amounts of your fear. They would ask you to imagine each aversive situation while in a relaxed state. Once you are able to accept a low-level fear-producing situation, you would be asked to imagine a slightly higher-level situation. This would continue until you were able to imagine yourself on the catwalk and remain relaxed.

Cognitive Restructuring

As in the case of systematic desensitization, a treatment approach via cognitive restructuring assumes that you have the necessary behaviors but are unable to enact them due to your anxiety. This approach further assumes that your fear is a result of a misperception of the event and that you lack sufficient reinforcement to overcome your misperception. In the program, a trained counselor would seek to correct your perception of the event. In particular, the consultant would seek to change your mostly negative "self-talk" regarding the situation. You probably are your own worst critic; your presentation is not as bad as you tell yourself it is. In cognitive restructuring, you would be counseled to see the event in more realistic, and less personally negating, terms.

Skills Training

Unlike the other programs, this approach assumes your anxiety is due primarily to a lack of skilled behavior. Thus, if you are taught specific skills, you will be able to react more competently and comfortably in a situation. A trained instructor would use a variety of teaching strategies (coaching, modeling, rehearsal, goal setting, actual performance) to help you acquire specific behaviors. Skills training can be used to instill more assertive behavior, to learn how to say "no," or to respond effectively in clearly defined interpersonal or public situations. Special programs have been created as part of college interpersonal and public communication courses (separate sections, workshops, or labs) to help students reduce their apprehension. Typically, these programs have focused on those experiencing a high level of trait apprehension.[4]

Reducing Stage Fright

Systematic desensitization is a program that requires expert assistance. Thus, the advice offered here will not include this approach as one you could undertake on your own or with the assistance of an untrained person. We might assume that both cognitive restructuring and skills training would be beneficial aids. That is, you can work on your perception of the event—is it as terrible as you think? Are you really as poor a speaker as you think? By talking with a public speaking instructor, or simply by asking friends who observe your performance, you may get a clearer picture of your strengths and weaknesses. Being willing to let go of your own perceptions and to accept the critique of others is essential to the restructuring of your perspective on the situation.

Second, we might assume that your skills can be refined and improved. By taking this route, your self-confidence may grow, and you will find it easier to control your anxiety. There are several things you can consider, either on your own or with an instructor's assistance.

1. *Audio- or videotape.* If the necessary equipment is available, you can practice your presentation and play it back on an audio or video recorder. A careful critique of your performance with or without assistance (if your own attitude is generally negative, self-appraisal may simply reinforce a negative image) will suggest areas for improvement.

2. *Role playing.* You or an instructor can create role-playing situations that simulate the behaviors that you need to refine. If these are realistic, they will help you feel more comfortable when you face an actual public-speaking situation.

3. *Rehearsal.* Practice your presentation before the live event, and ask friends or an instructor to critique your performance.

4. *Goal setting.* This can be a formal procedure worked out with an instructor, or your own informal assessment of what you want to work on.[5] Define a goal and then a set of specific behaviors that you want to accomplish in meeting that goal. For example, your goal might be expressed: "I want to be more articulate in the next presentation." A specific behavior would be: "I want to reduce the use of such words as *like* and *you know* to no more than two in the entire performance."

Reference Notes

1. James C. McCroskey, "Oral Communication Apprehension: A Summary of Recent Theory and Research," *Human Communication Research* 4 (1977): 78.

2. McCroskey, 78–96; Susan R. Glaser, "Oral Communication Apprehension and Avoidance: The Current Status of Treatment Research," *Communication Education* 30 (1981): 321–41.

3. Glaser's essay is used as the basis for this review.

4. For additional information on treatment programs, see Jan Hoffman and Jo Sprague, "A Survey of Reticence and Communication Apprehension Treatment Programs at U.S. Colleges and Universities," *Communication Education* 31 (1982): 185–93; Karen A. Foss, "Communication Apprehension: Resources for the Instructor," *Communication Education* 31 (1982): 195–203.

5. Gerald M. Phillips, "Rhetoritherapy vs. the Medical Model: Dealing with Reticence," *Communication Education* 26 (1977): 34–43.

RESPONDING TO QUESTIONS AND OBJECTIONS

In most meetings (and at other times as well), listeners are given a chance to ask questions of speakers. Panelists frequently direct questions to each other; professors ask students to clarify points made in classroom reports; clubs' treasurers often are asked to justify particular expenditures; political candidates normally must field objections to positions they have taken.

Sometimes, questions require only a short response—some factual material, a yes or no, a reference to an authoritative source. These sorts of questions need not concern us, but at other times, questions from listeners can require a good deal more. Specifically, some questions call for *elaboration and explanation.* For example, after an oral report, you might be asked to elaborate upon statistical information you presented or called upon to explain how a financial situation arose. Other questions call for *justification and defense.* In open hearings, school boards seeking to cut expenditures justify their selection of school buildings to be closed. At city council meetings, the city manager often has to defend ways council policies are being implemented. In these two situations, a "speech" is called for in response to questions and objections.

Techniques for Responding to Questions

Questions calling for elaboration and explanation are, in many ways, equivalent to requests for an informative speech. Think about them as you would any situation wherein you are offering listeners ideas and information in response to their needs and interests.

Give a "Whole" Speech.

Your response should include an introduction, body, and conclusion. Even though you may be offering an impromptu speech (see Chapter 3), you nonetheless are expected to structure ideas and information clearly and rationally. A typical pattern for an elaborative remark might look like this:

1. Introduction—a rephrasing of the question to clarify it for the other audience members, an indication of why the question is a good one, a forecast of the steps you will take in answering it.
2. Body—first point, often a brief historical review; second point, the information or explanation called for.
3. Conclusions—a very brief summary (unless the answer was extraordinarily long); a direct reference to the person asking the question, to see if further elaboration or explanation is needed.

Directly Address the Question As It Has Been Asked.
Nothing is more frustrating to a questioner than an answer that misses the point or drifts off into irrelevant territory. Suppose, after you have advocated a "pass-fail" grading system for all colleges, you are questioned about how graduate schools can evaluate potential candidates for advanced degrees. The questioner is calling for information and an explanation. If, in response, you launch a tirade against the unfairness of letter grades or the cowardice of professors who refuse to give failing grades, you probably will not satisfy the questioner. Better would be an explanation of all the other factors—letters of recommendation, standardized tests, number of advanced courses taken—in addition to grade point averages that graduate schools can use when evaluating candidates. If you are unsure what the point of the question is, do not hesitate to ask before you attempt an answer.

Be Succinct.
While you certainly do not want to give a terse yes or no in response to a question calling for detail, neither should you talk for eight minutes when two minutes will suffice. If you really think a long, complex answer is called for, you can say, "To understand why we should institute a summer orientation program at this school, you should know more about recruitment, student fears,

problems with placement testing, and so on. I can go into these topics if you would like, but for now, in response to the particular question I was asked, I would say that . . ." In this way, you are able to offer a short answer yet are leaving the door open for additional questions from listeners wishing more information.

Be Courteous.
During question periods, you may be amazed that one person asks a question you know you answered in your oral report, and another person asks for information so basic you realize your whole presentation probably went over his or her head. In such situations, it is easy to become flippant or overly patronizing. Avoid these temptations. Do not embarrass a questioner by pointing out you have already answered that query, and do not treat listeners like children. If you really think it would be a waste of the audience's time for you to review fundamental details, simply say that the group does not have time to discuss them but that you are willing to talk with individuals after the meeting to go over that ground.

Techniques for Responding to Objections

A full, potentially satisfying response to an objection is composed of two verbal-intellectual activities. *Rebuttal* is an answer to an objection or counterargument, and *reestablishment* is a process of rebuilding the ideas originally attacked.

Suppose, for example, that at an office meeting you propose your division institute a management-by-objectives system of employee evaluation. With this approach, the supervisor and employee together plan goals for a specified period of time; so, you argue, it tends to increase productivity, it makes employees feel they are in part determining their own future, and it makes company expectations more concrete. During a question period, another person might object to management-by-objectives, saying that such systems are mere busywork, that supervisors are not really interested in involving underlings in work decisions, and that job frustration rather than job satisfaction is the more likely result.

Radio and television appearances allow you and your message to reach a great number of people with minimal effort. Seek out these opportunities, and make the most of them.

These few tips will get you started; you will soon discover additional rules that apply to your own modes of talk in front of the mike and camera.

STRUCTURING ARGUMENTATIVE SPEECHES

Arguing with others usually involves more than a single presentation of your ideas. If you are going to be faced with an opponent's presentation, there is more pressure to orchestrate the materials that will be used to defend your position. When you have the opportunity to respond formally to an opponent—either in the same setting or at a later time—you need to think in terms of *multiple messages.* More specifically, you need to plan your argumentative approach with respect to (1) constructing your case, (2) anticipating counterarguments, and (3) rebuilding your case.

Constructing Your Case

Your first concern is finding suitable materials for the development of your argument. Assume, for example, that your community is considering the use of its present landfill dump as a site for the disposal of hazardous wastes. In presenting an argument against this proposal at a city council hearing called to review the merits of the plan, you know that in attacking this policy claim you must (1) gain attention, (2) develop the specific criteria for allowing hazardous waste disposal at the dump, (3) demonstrate the failure of the dump to meet the established criteria, (4) note the advantages to be gained by the acceptance of your analysis, and (5) appeal for a "no" vote on the proposal. As you think about this skeletal outline in terms of your argument, notice that you have several major problems to overcome in constructing your case:

1. You must demonstrate that the *criteria* for allowing hazardous waste disposal provide a relevant, comprehensive, and significant set of standards for judging any proposed

dump site. If you cannot do this, your opponents can argue that the criteria you propose are irrelevant or insignificant, and if your set of criteria is incomplete, your opponent can counter by arguing that you have unfairly "stacked the deck" by your selection of "convenient" standards.

2. Even if your criteria are acceptable, you must address the *relationship* between the criteria and the dump site in question. Does the site meet the standards considered acceptable? If this is not answered in direct, explicit fashion, you leave yourself open to the accusation of having failed to discharge your major burden; however, dealing with this issue does not mean your opponents will quit the fight; they can still object to the relationship you seek to establish.

3. The *advantages* that would flow from acceptance of your position may appear obvious and important to you, but they often must be weighed against other advantages to be gained by your opponent's position. You may be faced with issues that have a direct impact on the case you are building: for example, a chemical company employing 2000 workers has threatened to close its plant if it cannot use the existing site; the town stands to profit from dump fees charged for disposal and claims a reduction in property tax as a side benefit.

Thus, your carefully constructed case may meet the problems cited in 1 and 2, but will be challenged by counterarguments that shift the focus to the relative merits of safety versus economic health in the community: what level of risk is acceptable in order to sustain the economic life of the community? In so doing, your opponents will not directly refute your allegations but instead will seek to minimize their significance in relation to the economic benefits to be realized. This developmental outline is, of course, only one of several that might be applied; even a cursory inspection of the topic and of the demands of this type of speech will indicate those points you must argue especially well. Returning to problems associated with this hypothetical case—establishing *criteria*, developing a *relationship* between criteria and dump site, and noting *advantages*—think about how you might proceed to solve them.

- *Where can you find supporting materials to establish criteria for determining a dump site's safety?* Are there any governmental studies or agency standards that would be of value? Are there technical reports from scientists? Have respected persons within the community commented on the issue of criteria? What criteria have other communities used when faced with similar questions? In other words, the suitability of the criteria can be obtained by various kinds of testimony—from technical reports, government-approved standards, expert opinion—and from parallel cases (the experiences of other towns).

- *How can you demonstrate the reliability of your conclusion that the dump site fails to meet the standards?* Have other dumps with similar features been used for disposal, and have they been judged successful? Have studies been done to determine the characteristics of the landfill (for example, proximity to underground water sources)? Have scientists or others already commented on the suitability of the site? Once you have specific information on the characteristics of the dump site, the relationship to criteria can be accomplished in a fairly straightforward manner, by citing the relevant features of the dump and drawing conclusions that the site will not meet the necessary conditions adequately. You also can argue from parallel cases, using past experiences at similar dump sites as a basis for comparison to the potential experience with this dump site. You also could develop, in more dramatic

style, a *hypothetical illustration* of what would happen in a "worst-case" scenario if the dump site were utilized.

- *How do you deal with issues that challenge the advantages you cite?* To begin with, the advantages you might stress would center on the health of citizens in the area surrounding the dump site or those affected by its use. Although this general advantage may seem obvious, it may be useful to underline its significance with testimony from medical experts or from respected town leaders on the problems that dumping hazardous waste products would cause. Without anticipating, at this stage of the analysis, other issues that may be brought forward (for example, unemployment, increased revenue), the best approach is to build the strongest case you can for the health issue. When and if the argument shifts to a comparison of advantages, you will have made it more difficult for the opposition to undermine the significance of your advantage. Leaving it as "obvious" may only serve to quicken its dismissal by the opponents.

With the preceding analysis as a guide, it appears possible to construct a reasonable case for your position. The foregoing has, in a general fashion, identified the potential sources and kinds of information that may prove helpful and has revealed several possible points on which you can be attacked. Of course, you still have to assemble the actual materials—the technical data, expert opinion, relevant parallel cases—that will allow you to present your case. As you put this together, the next element of the process will assist you in carrying your argument forward.

Anticipating Counterarguments

As you construct your case and outline your argument, you will be sensitized to potential attacks. For instance, if you oppose the use of the local community dump as a hazardous waste disposal site, your opponents may counter your arguments by maintaining that your parallel instances are insufficient or irrelevant as evidence of the unsuitability of the present site. They also may attack your evidence concerning the composition of the soil, its likelihood of leaching substances into the local water supply, and so on. Other opponents will no doubt bring up the threatened closure of the town's major employer if the site application is not approved, or will concentrate their responses upon the projected revenue loss to the city. Thus, even before you actually present what might be called your "constructive case," you need to be aware of some potential objections and vulnerabilities.

Do not, however, build defensive reactions into your initial argument. If you are a speaker who attempts to anticipate and answer all possible objections before they are lodged, you are in double danger. (1) You may appear paranoid and thereby cause listeners to say, "Boy, if she is this unsure, then maybe the proposal isn't any good." (2) Worse, you may actually suggest negative aspects of your proposal others had not thought of. You may, in other words, actually fuel discontent by proposing counterarguments.

As a rule, therefore, you should set forth your initial case directly and simply, and then sit back and await the counterarguments presented by others. You may even want to work from a flowchart—a sheet of paper that enumerates your principal arguments down the left-hand side, with space along the right-hand side for recording objections. In that way, you can identify where you are being questioned, note carefully how the attacks affect your overall analysis, and think specifically in terms of answers.

In sum, reacting critically to attacks on your arguments involves (1) a careful recording of counterarguments so as to be fair and (2) a decision on how to answer germane objections. You have to be cool and dispassionate enough to do both.

Rebuilding Your Case

Having isolated and considered possible counterarguments, your next task is to answer those arguments to rebuild your initial case.

This rebuilding requires *rebuttal* and *reestablishment*.

Rebuttal.
Your first rebuilding task is to rebut counterarguments. In our example this would mean answering to the satisfaction of your audience objections based upon revenue loss to the city or potential unemployment if the plant closes because the application fails. To refute the revenue loss argument, you might indicate that the loss is projected rather than actual; you also may be able to demonstrate insignificance if the amount of revenue lost would not appreciably affect local tax rates. The objection regarding projected unemployment is much harder to meet, as there will be members in the audience who depend upon the plant for their own jobs. You might be able to argue that closure is likely on other grounds, hence negative action on the dump site is a moot point. This is, however, a weak counter, as your opponents may quickly point out that approving the application is precisely the gesture the company needs to be convinced that it should remain. You also may be able to rebut the argument by examining the potential impact of such unemployment and by noting the probability of new industry absorbing much of the loss without the same risk to the health and safety of the community. Finally, you may have no other choice but to rebut by facing the possibility straight on and arguing that the risk to health and safety outweighs any possible economic considerations. In this extended illustration, we see most of the principal communicative techniques used by successful respondents.

Be both constructive and destructive when responding to objections. Do not simply tear down the other person's counterarguments; constructively bolster your original statements as well. Reestablishment not only rationally shores up your position, but it psychologically demonstrates your control of the ideas and materials, thereby increasing your credibility.

Answer objections in an orderly fashion. If two or three objections are raised, sort them out carefully and answer them one at a time. Such a procedure helps guarantee that you respond to each objection, and aids listeners in sorting out the issues being raised.

Attack each objection systematically. A speech that rebuts the counterarguments of another ought to be shaped into a series of steps, to maximize its clarity and acceptability. A unit of rebuttal proceeds in four steps:

1. State the opponent's claim that you seek to rebut. ("Joe has said that a management-by-objectives system won't work because supervisors don't want input from their underlings.")
2. State your objection to it. ("I'm not sure what evidence Joe has for that statement, but I do know of three studies done at businesses much like ours, and these studies indicate that . . . ")
3. Offer evidence for your objection. ("The first study was done at the XYZ Insurance Company in 1986; the researchers discovered that . . . The second . . . And the third . . . ")
4. Indicate the significance of your rebuttal. ("If our company is pretty much like the three I've mentioned—and I think it is—then I believe our supervisors will likewise appreciate specific commitments from their subordinates, quarter by quarter. Until Joe can provide us with more hard data to support his objection, I think we will have to agree . . . ")

Keep the exchange on an impersonal (intellectual) level. All too often counterarguments and rebuttals degenerate into name-calling exchanges. We all are tempted to strike out at objectors. When you become overly sensitive to attacks upon your pet notions and other people feel similarly threatened, a communicative free-for-all can ensue. Little is settled in such verbal fights. Reasoned decision making can occur only when the integrity of ideas is paramount, and the calm voice of reasonableness is more likely to be listened to than is emotionally charged ranting.

In sum, answering questions and responding to objections can be a frightening experience. Many of us feel threatened when we are made accountable for what we say by questioners and counterarguers. Yet, we must overcome our natural reticence in such situations if we are to weed out illogic, insufficient evidence, prejudices, and infeasible plans of action from our group deliberations.

Reestablishment.

In most instances you cannot be content merely to answer opponents' objections. You also should take the extra step of reestablishing your case as a whole. That is, you should first point out what portions of your argument have *not* been attacked and indicate their importance. Then you should introduce more evidence in support of your reconstructed case—further testimony, additional parallel cases—to bolster your argument as a whole. To return to our earlier example, you might indicate that no one has questioned your evidence on the site's unsuitability or the parallel cases you have presented. Underscoring these points once again with new material (perhaps held in reserve for just this situation) that paints a more dramatic picture of the safety risks may cause the audience to heed the issue, in spite of the counterarguments.

In conclusion, argumentative speaking demands many talents. To argue well, you must be able to determine rationally the evidence and inferences needed to support your claim, to distinguish between solid and fallacious reasoning, and to build both constructive and refutative speeches to meet the demands of give-and-take in public decision making. These are not easy tasks, yet they are worth attempting to accomplish. In times when people do not or cannot argue well, despotism and chicanery tend to triumph, whether in the political arena of legislation or the business arena of marketing and sales policy. In learning to argue well, ultimately, you are learning to make yourself and your world more informed and enlightened.

WORKING BIBLIOGRAPHY: ADDITIONAL READINGS

The bibliography that follows is not meant to be comprehensive, but rather suggestive. Additional books and articles can be found in the reference notes that follow most units of this *Speaker's Resource Book.*

Other Public-Speaking Textbooks

Bryant, Donald C., Karl Wallace, and Michael C. McGee. *Oral Communication: A Short Course in Speaking.* 5th ed. Englewood Cliffs, NJ: Prentice-Hall, Inc., 1982.

Gronbeck, Bruce E. *The Articulate Person: A Guide to Everyday Public Speaking.* 2nd ed. Glenview, IL: Scott, Foresman and Company, 1983.

Gronbeck, Bruce E., Douglas Ehninger, and Alan H. Monroe. *Principles of Speech Communication.* 10th brief ed. Glenview, IL: Scott, Foresman and Company, 1988.

Hart, Roderick, Gustav Friedrich, and Barry Brummett. *Public Communication.* 2nd ed. New York: Harper & Row Pubs., Inc., 1984.

Jeffrey, Robert, and Owen Peterson. *Speech.* 3rd ed. New York: Harper & Row Pubs., Inc., 1988.

Logue, Cal M., et al. *Speaking: Back to Fundamentals.* 3rd ed. Boston: Allyn and Bacon, Inc., 1982.

Lucas, Stephen. *The Art of Public Speaking.* 3rd ed. Westminster, MD: Random House, Inc., 1989.

Osborn, Michael, and Suzanne Osborn. *Public Speaking.* Boston: Houghton Mifflin Co., 1988.

Patton, Bobby R., Kim Giffin, and Wil A. Linkugel. *Responsible Public Speaking.* Glenview, IL: Scott, Foresman and Company, 1983.

Thrash, Artie, and John I. Sisco. *The Basic Skills of Public Speaking.* Minneapolis, MN: Burgess Publishing Co., 1984.

Verderber, Rudolph F. *The Challenge of Effective Speaking.* 7th ed. Belmont, CA: Wadsworth Publishing Co., 1988.

Walter, Otis M., and Robert L. Scott. *Thinking and Speaking.* 5th ed. New York: The Macmillan Co., 1984.

Supplementary Reading for the Chapters

Andrews, James R. *The Practice of Rhetorical Criticism.* New York: The Macmillan Co., 1983.

Arnold, Carroll C., and John Waite Bowers, eds. *Handbook of Rhetorical and Communication Theory.* Boston: Allyn and Bacon, Inc., 1984.

Becker, Samuel L., and Leah V. Ekdom. "That Forgotten Basic Skill: Oral Communication." *Association for Communication Administration Bulletin #33* (August 1980).

Bem, Daryl. *Beliefs, Attitudes, and Human Affairs.* Belmont, CA: Brooks/Cole Publishing Co., 1980.

Bettinghaus, Erwin, and Michael Cody. *Persuasive Communication.* 4th ed. New York: Holt, Rinehart & Winston, Inc., 1987.

Bitzer, Lloyd. "The Rhetorical Situation." *Philosophy & Rhetoric* 1 (January 1968): 1–14.

Burgoon, Judee K., David B. Buller, and W. Gill Woodall. *Nonverbal Communication: The Unspoken Dialogue.* New York: Harper & Row Pubs., Inc., 1989.

Einhorn, Lois J., Patricia Hayes Bradley, and John E. Baird, Jr. *Effective Employment Interviewing: Unlocking Human Potential.* Glenview, IL: Scott, Foresman and Company, 1982.

Harte, Thomas. "The Effects of Evidence in Persuasive Communication." *Central States Speech Journal* 27 (Spring 1976): 42–46.

Larson, Charles U. *Persuasion: Reception and Responsibility.* 5th ed. Belmont, CA: Wadsworth Pub. Co., 1989.

Littlejohn, Stephen W. *Theories of Human Communication.* 3rd ed. Belmont, CA: Wadsworth Pub. Co., 1989.

Littlejohn, Stephen W., and David M. Jabusch. *Persuasive Transactions.* Glenview, IL: Scott, Foresman and Company, 1987.

Littlejohn, Stephen W. "A Bibliography of Studies Related to Variables of Source Credibility." *Bibliographical Annual in Speech Communication: 1971.*

Ed. Ned A. Shearer. New York: Speech Communication Association, 1972, 1–40.

Malandro, Loretta A., Larry Barker, and Deborah Barker. *Nonverbal Communication*. 2nd ed. Reading, MA: Addison-Wesley Publishing Co., Inc., 1989.

Ong, Walter J. *Orality and Literacy: The Technologizing of the Word*. New Accents Series. New York: Methuen, 1982.

Osborn, Michael. *Orientations to Rhetorical Style*. Procomm Series. Chicago: Science Research Associates, 1976.

Rieke, Richard D., and Malcolm O. Sillars. *Argumentation and Decision Making Processes*. 2nd ed. Glenview, IL: Scott, Foresman and Company, 1984.

Salomon, Gavriel. *Interaction of Media, Cognition, and Learning*. San Francisco: Jossey-Bass, Inc., Pubs., 1979.

Satterthwaite, Les. *Graphics: Skills, Media and Materials*. 4th ed. Dubuque: Kendall/Hunt, 1980.

Shimanoff, Susan B. *Communication Rules: Theory and Research*. Sage Library of Social Research, No. 97. Beverly Hills: Sage Publications, 1980.

Simons, Herbert W. *Persuasion: Understanding, Practice, and Analysis*. 2nd ed. New York: Random House, Inc., 1986.

Smith, Mary John. *Persuasion and Human Action: A Review and Critique of Social Influence Theories*. Belmont, CA: Wadsworth Pub. Co., 1982.

Steil, Lyman K., Larry L. Barker, and Kittie W. Watson. *Effective Listening*. New York: Random House, Inc., 1983.

Stewart, Charles S., and William B. Cash, Jr. *Interviewing: Principles and Practices*. 5th ed. Dubuque: Wm. C. Brown Publishers, 1988.

Toulmin, Stephen, Richard Rieke, and Allan Janik. *An Introduction to Reasoning*. 2nd ed. New York: The Macmillan Co., 1984.

Vernon, Magdalen D. "Perception, Attention, and Consciousness." *Foundations of Communication Theory*. Ed. Kenneth K. Sereno and C. David Mortensen. New York: Harper & Row Pubs., Inc., 1970, 137–51.

Weitzel, Al R. *Careers for Speech Communication Graduates*. Salem, WI: Sheffield Pub. Co., 1987.

Wells, Lynn K. *The Articulate Voice: An Introduction to Voice and Diction*. Scottsdale, AZ: Gorsuch Scarisbrick, Pub., 1989.

Wilcox, Roger P. "Characteristics and Organization of the Technical Report." *Communicating Through Behavior*. Ed. William E. Arnold and Robert O. Hirsch. St. Paul: West Publishing Co., 1977, 201–6.

Wolvin, Andrew D., and Carolyn G. Coakley. *Listening*. 3rd ed. Dubuque: Wm. C. Brown Publishers, Inc., 1988.

Woodward, Gary C., and Robert E. Denton, Jr. *Persuasion and Influence in American Life*. Prospect Heights, IL: Waveland Press, Inc., 1988.

Index

Literary Credits

page 54 From "Women in Leadership Can Make a Difference" by Geraldine Ferraro, *Representative American Speeches*, 1982–1983. Reprinted by permission of Geraldine Ferraro.

page 59 "Inventory of Shyness Reactions" from "The Silent Prison of Shyness" by P. G. Zimbardo, P. A. Pilkonis, and R. M. Norwood. The Office of Naval Research Technical Report Z-17, November 1974. Reprinted by permission of Philip G. Zimbardo.

page 62 "Plastic Pollution Threatens the Oceans' Wildlife" by Bret Ludwig from *Winning Orations* 1988. Copyright © 1988 by the Interstate Oratorical Association. Reprinted by permission.

page 149 From "Cost Containment of Health Care" by Richard J. Hanley in *Vital Speeches of the Day*, November 15, 1984. Reprinted by permission.

page 151 From "The Foreign Aid Cancer" by Richard T. Montoya in *Vital Speeches of the Day*, August 1, 1987. Reprinted by permission.

page 152 Excerpt from "Can You Trust God?" by Dr. Louis Hadley Evans. Reprinted by permission of the author.

page 153 From "Seapower" by James H. Webb in *Vital Speeches of the Day*, December 1, 1987. Reprinted by permission.

page 154 From "Don't Drink the Water," by Pam Williams. Reprinted from *Winning Orations*, 1980, by special arrangement with the Interstate Oratorical Association, Larry Schnoor, Executive Secretary, Mankato State University, Mankato, Minnesota.

page 156 From "A Look at the Fundamental School Concept" by James K. Wellington from *Vital Speeches of the Day*, 46, February 1980. Reprinted by permission of Vital Speeches of the Day.

page 156 From "Where Were You Twelve Years Ago?" by Joseph N. Hankin in *Vital Speeches of the Day*, March 1, 1988. Reprinted by permission.

page 156 From a speech given at the University of Maine, spring term, 1982. Reprinted with the permission of Ms. Theriault.

page 157 From "Dow and South Africa" by Richard K. Long in *Vital Speeches of the Day*, June 15, 1987. Reprinted by permission.

page 158 From "Working with the Federal Election Commission" by Joan D. Aiken, from *Vital Speeches of the Day*, 47, February 1981. Reprinted by permission of Vital Speeches of the Day.

page 158 From "A Crossroads in U.S. Trade Policy" by Ronald K. Shelp in *Vital Speeches of the Day*, August 1, 1987. Reprinted by permission.

page 160 From "Lung Cancer in Perspective" by Charles A. Le Maistre in *Vital Speeches of the Day*, July 1, 1987. Reprinted by permission.

Photo Credits

Aids to Choosing Speech Topics

The beginning speaker often has difficulty in selecting a suitable speech subject. If you find yourself in this situation, study the following list of subject categories. These categories are not speech subjects; rather, they are types, or classes, of material in which speech subjects can be found. To decide upon a suitable subject for a public speech, consider them in terms of your own interests and knowledge, the interests of your audience, and the nature of the occasion in which you are to speak.

Personal Experience

1. Jobs you have held
2. Places you have been
3. Military service
4. The region you come from
5. Schools you have attended
6. Friends and enemies
7. Relatives you like — and dislike
8. Hobbies and pastimes

Foreign Affairs

1. Foreign-policy aims:
   What they are
   What they should be
2. The implementation of policy aims
3. Ethics of foreign-policy decisions
4. History of the foreign policy of the United States (or another nation)
5. Responsibility for our foreign policy
6. How foreign policy affects domestic policy
7. War as an instrument of national policy
8. International peacekeeping machinery
9. The United States and the Middle East
10. Terrorism
11. Arms control
12. Peace

Domestic Affairs

1. Social problems:
   Crime
   The family (marriage, divorce, adjustments)
   AIDS
   The homeless
   Problems of rural areas
   Problems of races and ethnic groups
   Problems of juveniles or the aged
   Child abuse
   Abortion
   The drug culture
   Sexual mores
   Pollution
2. Economic problems:
   Federal fiscal policy
   Economically deprived persons and areas
   Fiscal problems of state and local governments
   Taxes and tax policies
   Inflation
   Unemployment
   International monetary policies
   Energy
   Foreign investment in the United States
3. Political problems:
   Powers and obligations of the federal government
   Relations between the federal government and the states
   Problems of state and local governments
   Parties, campaigns, and nominating procedures
   The courts: delays in justice, the jury system
   Congress vs. the president